Alfred the Great

The Man Who Made England

JUSTIN POLLARD

JOHN MURRAY

© Justin Pollard 2005

First published in Great Britain in 2005 by John Murray (Publishers)
A division of Hodder Headline

Paperback edition 2006

The right of Justin Pollard to be identified as the Author
of the Work has been asserted by him in accordance with
the Copyright, Designs and Patents Act 1988.

3

A CIP catalogue record for this title is available from the British Library

ISBN 978-0-7195-6666-0

Typeset in Bembo by Hewer Text UK Ltd, Edinburgh
Printed and bound by Clays Ltd, St Ives plc

Hodder Headline policy is to use papers that are natural, renewable
and recyclable products and made from wood grown in sustainable
forests. The logging and manufacturing processes are expected to conform
to the environmental regulations of the country of origin.

John Murray (Publishers)
338 Euston Road
London NW1 3BH

Justin Pollard

Justin Pollard read archaeology and anthropology at Cambridge. For the last ten years he has worked as a historical writer and consultant in film and television. His television credits include Channel Four's popular archaeology programme *Time Team*, *Geldof in Africa*, *Barbarians* and setting questions for the BBC quiz show *QI* starring Stephen Fry. He has written and produced documentaries on everything from cannibalism amongst the Kondh in India to the career of Vlad the Impaler, for presenters including Terry Jones, Bettany Hughes, Vic Reeves, Alexei Sayle, Tony Robinson, Stephen Fry and Bob Geldof. He was historical consultant on the films *The Four Feathers* and *Elizabeth* and is currently consulting on the sequel, *Golden Age*. He is also working with director Joe Wright on his adaptation of Ian McEwan's novel *Atonement*.

Also by Justin Pollard

Seven Ages of Britain

For Pudding and Baxter – my Athelney

Contents

List of illustrations

Picture acknowledgements: 1, 6, 8, 15, 16, 17, 18, 20, 22, 28, 30 and 31, Stephanie Farr; 2, 3, 4, 5 and 29, Author's collection; 7, 10, 14, 25 and 27, The Trustees of the British Museum; 9, 11, 12, 19 and 23, Professor Mick Aston; 13 and 24, The Ashmolean Museum, University of Oxford; 26, The Master and Fellows of Corpus Christi College Cambridge.

Acknowledgements

T HERE ARE SO many people to thank in the writing of any book
that I always live in fear of missing out a vital contributor so I
should really begin by offering my thanks to 'the unknown contributor'.

As always I have received a great deal of academic help and
encouragement during this project and everyone who has made a
suggestion, great or small, deserves my thanks. In particular, for
permission to quote from their translations of ninth-century and
other Anglo-Saxon sources, I should like to thank Simon Keynes,
Michael Lapidge, Kevin Crossley-Holland, Jinty Nelson, Philip
Tunstall, Sally Crawford and the CELT project of University College,
Cork. For helping me over particular dead ends in my research I
would like to thank Jesse Byock, Bernie Frischer and Jinty Nelson. I
should also like to thank Jane Rugg for her help searching out some of
the more obscure references.

A project like this, and in particular retracing Alfred's steps on the
ground, is not something to be lightly undertaken with a two-year-
old in tow. There are therefore many people I must thank simply for
their logistical help with this, including Barbara and David Farr, John
Lloyd and family, and any and everyone else who entertained Connie
en route. Not least I should perhaps thank Connie for allowing her
father to make such a ludicrous series of trips.

I must make special mention of my wife Steph, who somehow
found time to take many of the photographs for this book and who
has, as always, helped in every way possible at every stage of writing. I
would also like to thank Mick Aston for the loan of many photographs
from his collection, and John Hardacre and Carlton Bath at Winchester Cathedral for allowing me to clamber around on the roof of that
magnificent building.

My thanks too to all those who believed in this project enough to turn it from an idea into reality, namely Roland Philipps and Rowan Yapp at John Murray, my copy-editor Celia Levett and Julian Alexander at LAW.

Finally, but I think most importantly, my heartfelt thanks go to those who have taken the time to read, comment on and hence vastly improve the early drafts, including Mick Aston, Michael Hirst and Bettany Hughes. Foremost amongst these, however, is my great friend Stuart Hill, who has not only brought his incisive historical talents to bear on the text but who has made suggestions that have not only improved but transformed parts of this book. Alfred himself summed up such people best when he said: 'Then I say that true friends are the most precious of all this world's blessings.'

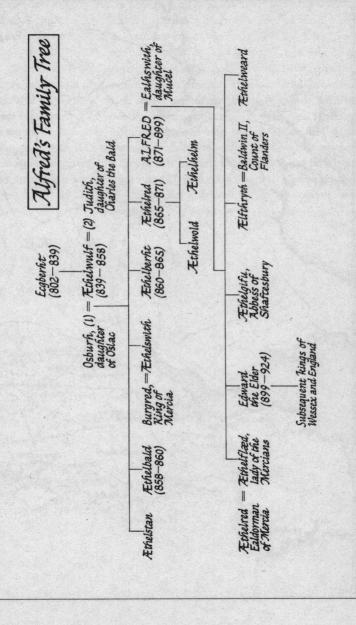

Alfred's Family Tree

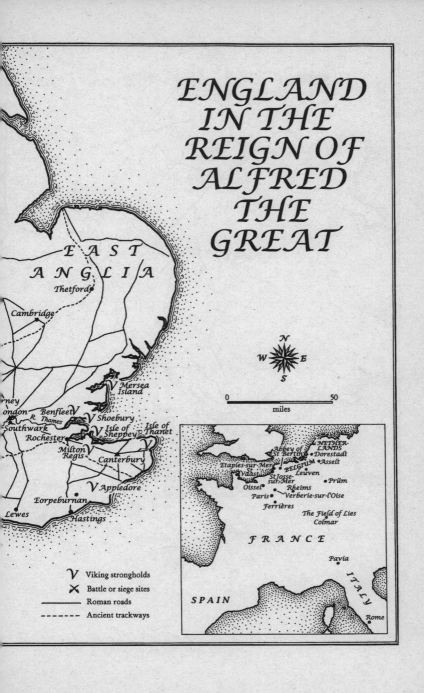

ENGLAND IN THE REIGN OF ALFRED THE GREAT

EAST ANGLIA

Thetford

Cambridge

Mersea Island

ney
ondon
Benfleet
R. Thames
Shoebury
Southwark
Isle of Sheppey
Isle of Thanet
Rochester
Milton Regis
Canterbury
Appledore
Eorpeburnan
Lewes
Hastings

N
W E
S

0   50
miles

NETHER-LANDS
Abbey of St Bertin
Dorestadt
Etaples-sur-Mer
BELGIUM
Assett
Wahsi
Leuven
St Josse-sur-Mer
Prüm
Oissel
Rheims
Paris
Verberie-sur-l'Oise
Ferrières
The Field of Lies
Colmar

FRANCE

Pavia
ITALY
SPAIN
Rome

V   Viking strongholds
X   Battle or siege sites
——   Roman roads
- - - -   Ancient trackways

Introduction

B URROW MUMP IS a peculiar, conical hill crowned with a ruined church that rises high above the relentless flatness of the Somerset Levels. From here you can see far to the north, across King's Sedge Moor towards the Polden Hills, and to the south you can just make out the coppice of trees that hides the little church at Aller. If your eye follows the road that skirts the Mump and heads south-west, however, you might also glimpse a stubby Victorian monument that stands on the summit of an otherwise almost unnoticeable knoll. What it marks is today a private farm called Athelney, merely a grassy hill only a few feet above the water meadows, but a little over a thousand years ago it marked the place where 'England' began.

In 878 the view from Burrow Mump was very different. Long before the church stood sentinel you might have been joined there by a solitary lookout, casting his gaze over what was then a virtually impenetrable labyrinth of marsh and reed beds, searching for signs of a Viking troop riding down from the hills or a longship threading its way through the sinuous channels of the river Parrett. To the south-east a clump of alder trees then indicated where Athelney lay and from above the trees you might have seen smoke rising. For hiding behind that screen of trees lay a temporary camp and at its centre was Alfred. Only weeks earlier, he had been king of Wessex, ruler of what was once the most powerful Anglo-Saxon kingdom in England. Now all those kingdoms were gone, destroyed by an enemy that no one in Christendom seemed able to either understand or answer in kind. All that was left was the Isle of Athelney, the last refuge of a small band of Anglo-Saxons who still held allegiance to Alfred and who had not, at least yet, bent their heads to new Viking overlords. It was a very damp, very cold and very small kingdom that Alfred now ruled but this one solid piece of ground in the swamp would provide the first footings for what would become the kingdom of England. It would also lay the foundations for a way of life that affects everyone in the Western world to this day.

It is therefore hardly surprising that legends gathered around the figure of the king as he stalked gloomily around the edges of his island home. It was said that long-dead saints visited him in visions by day and returned again in dreams at night. But here also was born a tale that has outlived all the others. About a century after Alfred's death an anonymous monk began writing a life of St Neot and in it he told a story that might even then have been old. He wrote of how Alfred, in his dejected wanderings in the Levels, came upon the house of a poor swineherd. Neither the herdsman nor his wife recognized the king but they invited him in and gave him refuge nonetheless. It was here that the king, absorbed in his own misery, failed to notice that the bread being baked by the swineherd's wife was burning. When she smelt the smoke she turned on the king and scolded him for his idle inattention. Despite his royal blood, Alfred humbly accepted this rebuke from one of his lowliest subjects and vowed to pay more attention in the future. But if the bread (or cakes in some versions of the tale) emerged from the smoke of that legendary fire, Alfred did not. From that moment he became more myth than man – England's greatest king, remembered solely for a fable that almost certainly never happened.

The unmistakable smell of smoke still hangs about the memory of Alfred the Great. It is partly the smoke that rises from battlefields and burning cakes, and partly the smoke that, with mirrors, conspires to distort our view of him. Somewhere in the midst of it all stands Alfred himself, a real man and a real king but wrapped in a fog of legend.

Alfred is the only English king ever to have been granted the title 'Great' and yet if he is remembered at all today as anything more than a name, it is for the legend of the burning of the cakes. It is as though Mahatma Gandhi was remembered simply for wearing spectacles or George Washington for being a reasonably good surveyor. That Alfred has come to be so remote a character has much to do with the yawning centuries that separate us from him but it also has something to do with the man himself. For at the centre of his story lies a mystery – that strange sojourn in the wilderness when the king, rejected by all around him, decided to fight back. In the process he set in train a revolution that would lead eventually to the foundation of England and colour much of what it would later become.

It was a time that Alfred wanted recorded in a very particular way; indeed, to ensure it he would go as far as ordering the rewriting of the whole history of his people. But part of this record was a lie, told with good reason, but it has, ironically, since masked the true nature of his achievement. In finding and unpicking that lie it might be possible to come not only to the real origins of the myth of the 'burnt cakes' but to an understanding of why Alfred became the only king that the English call 'Great'.

Alfred lived and died in the ninth century, a time when nearly every known individual is as much fable as fact. It was a mysterious age, before dragons were confined to the pages of bestiaries, when saints walked on earth and when God proved his presence through almost daily miracles. But the God of the ninth century was as much a scourge as a comfort and his miracles were often set against a background of despair. For this was an era in which the established kingdoms of Europe faced a new and devastating enemy, who appeared without warning and who spread terror and misery without mercy.

When the Vikings first emerged from their cold northern home they heralded for many no less than the arrival of the Apocalypse. These were pagan peoples, attracted south by the hope of land and plunder, who had no care for the sanctity of churches and no belief in the power of a Christian god to protect the people they attacked at will. Their raids in England and continental Europe were unpredictable and indiscriminate, spreading fear amongst populations who looked to their kings to protect them. On each occasion those kings failed until one, himself driven to the edge of destruction, found a way to fight back.

He was Alfred, king of Wessex, and the first man ever to have some right to call himself king of the English. His campaign was unique, waged not merely with weapons, but with a vision of a new type of kingdom, where protection and prosperity resulted not from physical force alone, but from education, public building, commerce and law. That a king in any age should prove so far-sighted is remarkable in itself, but history shows that Alfred was more extraordinary still, for we can piece together the story of how he achieved this from first-hand accounts. His is the earliest life of any Anglo-Saxon king to have been recorded by a contemporary biographer and it is one of only two to survive. That record enables us to stand at Alfred's shoulder in this darkest of all centuries. But more than that, we actually have Alfred's own words, preserved in the books he read in Latin and which he personally translated into his native language so that his people could understand them too. Hidden in those often rather free translations is a secret autobiography, revealing the private thoughts of a Saxon king – the only English king to have written anything before James I, some seven hundred years later, and the key to how a kingdom was saved.

The ninth century may be an era of legend, of Tolkeinesque armies and fabulous beasts, but in Alfred we can reach out and touch a real man from this seemingly mythical world, a man unsure of the future but bold enough, and sometimes resigned enough, to step into it anyway. Alfred fought the terror of his age with force but also with knowledge, education and great diplomacy. The result was the saving of Wessex and the making of England.

This book is a journey into Alfred's story, to peel away the confusion of myths and legends, which in many cases are virtually all that remain of him in the popular imagination, and to reveal the man underneath. He is to some 'the saviour of Wessex', to others 'the scourge of the Vikings'. To the Victorians he was the ideal king and hence, in a more cynical twentieth century, he has become often little more than an invented imperialist cipher. In ages when the history of Britain was considered to be the history of its rulers, he was a hero. In more recent times even the materials on which his life is based have been questioned, consigning him to the fringes of history.

This is not, however, an academic discussion of the nature of Anglo-Saxon kingship – there are many of those already – but simply an attempt to tell the story of Alfred's life, using wherever possible original sources from his time. Those sources are often hard to interpret, sometimes confused and confusing, and nearly always incomplete. What is more, as with all history, nothing was written without purpose – and that purpose, even when long forgotten, still holds a ghostly influence over what the reader is allowed to know, or even believe. Thus there is virtually nothing that an academic historian, with hand on heart, could say was 'absolutely known' about the ninth century. It is for this reason that most academic texts on Alfred are as much footnote as narrative. This book is intended to be different. It takes a very particular and personal view of Alfred and his times but, as a narrative intended for any interested reader and not simply an academic readership, it is not dense with notes; indeed, they occur only to give the source of quotations. That is not to say that this book does not rely on a vast academic corpus of books and papers but I hope that the authors to whose works I am indebted here will be content with a place in the bibliography and will forgive their every point not being noted individually in the text. Every book listed there has influenced this telling of Alfred's tale and every one deserves to be read.

The memory of Alfred is clearly still strong – his name continues to be familiar to us all – but the real man behind the myth seems fainter than ever. But by returning to the documents on which all our history of this time is ultimately based, it might just be possible to recover the more vivid, more dramatic story that lies beneath the legend. Through the paperchase of asides and veiled references in European chronicles, in the letters of popes and saints, in the apparently bald language of legal charters and in the florid heroics of the sagas, is preserved an echo of life in an era of unaccountable terror, which perhaps has some dim resonance with our own. It is a trail that is complicated by the fact that nothing that survives is quite as it seems. But between these lines can be read how one man found a solution to the apparently insoluble problems of his day and there can be recovered the extraordinary story of the real Alfred and his time.

PROLOGUE

Losing Alfred

> And it came to pass, that when Jehudi had read three or four
> leaves, he cut it with the penknife, and cast it into the fire that
> was on the hearth, until all the roll was consumed.
>
> Jeremiah 36: 23 (King James Version)

THERE WAS A definite smell of smoke in the air that day, but that
was hardly unusual in a room that was permeated with it. The
bressemer beam over the kitchen hearth was black from the fumes that
billowed into the room every time the wind caught in the badly
designed chimney stack. The wood in the baking ovens smouldered
and spat with each downdraught.

An hour later the smell was still there, but subtly different – a
stronger taint that caught in the back of the throat and had nothing to
do with the burning wood. The air too seemed thicker, warmer and
growing gently more opaque. There was no doubt about it: something else was alight.

An unchecked fire in the kitchen here at Ashburnham House in
Little Dean's Yard, Westminster, was certainly cause for alarm. The
house was old, built in the seventeenth century by a disciple of Inigo
Jones, but incorporating parts of the old prior's residence from a
mediaeval monastery dissolved on the orders of Henry VIII. It was,
from one perspective, a grand old mansion but from another it was
simply an ancient pile of tinder-dry wood, if a rather well-arranged
one.

On this day – Saturday, 23 October 1731 – as it had been for some
years previously, this decaying house was home to Dr Bentley and his
son. It was also their place of work, where they tended a thing of the
rarest beauty but something of an embarrassment to the government: a

library. In fact at that time there were two libraries at Ashburnham House. The first was a collection of printed books and manuscripts known as the Royal Library. The second was the greatest collection of mediaeval manuscripts in existence: Robert Cotton's library.

It was Cotton's library that was the chief source of embarrassment. Sir Robert Cotton, an antiquary, had been born at exactly the right time. The end of the sixteenth and the beginnings of the seventeenth century were a golden age for anyone interested in collecting manuscripts as, with the Dissolution of the Monasteries, hundreds, in fact thousands, of ancient documents had come on to the market, often at knock-down prices that no collector could resist. As islands of literacy in the Anglo-Saxon and mediaeval worlds, monasteries had treasured these pieces of flotsam from the wreckage of the centuries, preserving the letters, chronicles and charters that made up the early history of England. Now the monasteries were gone and their treasured manuscripts were for the taking. Surrounded by a new generation of propertied men whose interest lay more in the contents of former monasteries' rent books than in the contents of their libraries, Cotton saw this as the opportunity of a lifetime and he seized it with glee.

The collection that Cotton amassed was quite extraordinary, covering everything from a fifth-century copy of the Book of Genesis to the state papers of mediaeval kings. His library included the Lindisfarne Gospels, two of the four surviving copies of Magna Carta, the papal bull declaring Henry VIII 'Defender of the Faith', illuminated missals, breviaries and psalters, books of hours, royal charters and Anglo-Saxon poetry. A large proportion of all the great documents that had survived from a thousand years of British history, protected for centuries in the scriptoria of monasteries, was now in Cotton's great library.

It was a vast but confused collection. Some works were entire books in themselves, others no more than a single crumpled parchment. In some instances monasteries had copied out their charters and grants into cartularies, containing hundreds of documents, many of them forged. Others had survived loose in muniment boxes. To try to bring some order to this rambling assortment, Sir Robert had, in his later years, gone about organizing them in his own rather idiosyncratic way. Having bound his entire collection into 958 manuscript volumes, many of which contained several books and documents combined together, he had chosen to follow the example of antiquity by arranging his collection in fourteen great oak bookcases (known as 'presses'). Each was surmounted by a classical bust. Twelve of the busts were Roman emperors, whilst the last two represented what were to him the two greatest 'Roman' women of the classical era: the Empress Faustina and Queen Cleopatra. To find any particular volume in the catalogue, one had simply to note which bust stood on the press, what letter was painted on each shelf – starting with 'A' and working down – and what position on the shelf the volume was, counting from the left. Hence Otho A xii was the twelfth volume from the left on the top shelf of the press bearing the bust of the emperor Otho. This is also a volume to which we shall return later.

Sir Robert did not, however, content himself with simply cataloguing other people's writings. In the years leading up to the English Civil War he also began producing his own political works. These would place him as well as his library in grave peril. Having been caught distributing a paper that hinted that the rule of the monarch Charles I was 'arbitrary and unconstitutional', he was arrested in October 1629. In the king's mind the very existence of Sir Robert's library now presented a threat. He saw it as a dangerous collection of uncontrolled knowledge, which in the hands of radicals might be used to undermine the state. The king therefore hit Cotton where it most hurt and ordered the precious collection sealed. And so it remained two years later – unfinished and only partly catalogued – when Sir Robert died, still in the midst of his appeal to have his beloved library returned to him.

Following the execution of Charles I and the establishment of Cromwell's Commonwealth, the library was finally returned to the family in 1650. Although no longer a political pawn, it had become an expensive, cumbersome and now neglected burden. Sir Robert's son and grandson continued to make small additions, but it soon became clear that the size and complexity of the collection made it too unwieldy for any one individual. So, in 1700, Cotton's grandson generously gave the whole thing to the nation in the hope that it would form the foundations of a 'British Library'. Sir Robert would finally achieve the goal that he had first suggested to Queen Elizabeth, probably in 1602, for 'A proiect touching a petition to be exhibited vnto her maiesty for the erecting of her library and an Academy'.

It was perhaps the most valuable single bequest ever made to the nation, but it was also a strangely unwanted one. The problem that Parliament had with the Cotton library was that it was expensive – expensive to house, expensive to maintain and, if it were to be made available to all interested parties as Cotton had wished, expensive to use. Their response to this problem was to offer the usual political solution: ignore it and hope that it went away. And some of it was about to do just that.

The Cotton library had arrived at Ashburnham House by a circuitous route. It had originally been kept in Cotton's own house in Westminster, on a riverside plot that is today partly covered by the House of Lords, but Cotton House had itself become dilapidated. When a representative of the group of MPs appointed as the library's trustees visited the building in 1703 he found 'in ye Room above the Library . . . there are not only a good quantity of printed Books, but some Manuscripts; very many Originall Charters of different Ages, as high as ye Conqueror's time, and a very great Number of Originall Letters & Writings of value which have already suffered great hurt, & will be utterly spoiled if care be not taken of them.'

The librarian at the time, Mr John Elphinstone, was faring little better than the library he managed. Despite the promises of the late King William III he had not been paid for tending the library, nor had he been given any money to clean and conserve the books in his care. Instead he was forced to pay for all necessary work out of his own pocket. Furthermore the house seems to have been used mainly for preparing meals for neighbouring residences. The numbers of fires lit there for this purpose had so alarmed Elphinstone that he had taken to sleeping in the library so that he could keep a fire watch at all times. This was also, of course, unpaid.

Eventually the trustees were forced to act, but only when the house became so ruinous that it was in danger of collapse. The collection was moved to Essex House near the Strand but, following an inspection, that was considered to be an even greater fire risk. Finally, the collection and its keepers came to rest in Little Dean Yard, opposite Westminster School, where Sir Robert Cotton had been educated as a boy and, perhaps appropriately, where his love of ancient documents had first been kindled.

Sadly, on the night of 23 October 1731, it was not just an idea that was being kindled in the fires of Ashburnham House. One of the servants was the first to notice the smoke coming from the floor below the library. In a large open fireplace a spark had caught in the wooden mantel-tree that ran across its top. The spark had settled and smouldered. By the time the servant found it, both the mantel and the surrounding wooden frame were alight, although this was not of itself cause for great concern. Fires were an everyday hazard and the judicious application of a little water usually put paid to them. This is exactly what the untroubled servant began to do. There was no need to raise the alarm and certainly no thought of removing the books.

It was a little later, about 2 a.m., that Dr Bentley and his son were awoken by the smell of smoke. Not the damp smell of a fire doused, but the dry, acrid smell of a fire well established and aiming at greater things. The fire in the room below the library had spread to the wainscot and from there via the wooden wall studs to the floor of the library itself. It was only now, as smoke oozed through the floorboards around the great Cottonian book presses, that it became clear that the books would have to be evacuated. Whilst a boy was sent to fetch a fire engine, the deputy librarian, Mr Casely, began emptying the Augustus press, which contained the books he considered to be the most valuable. Rousing people from the other houses around, the Bentleys ensured that other cases were also soon being unburdened of their books, with both case and contents being carried down into the courtyard below.

But removing the 958 large leather-bound volumes – let alone the huge oak presses they were kept in – was taking too long, almost as long as the fire engines were taking to arrive. The delay caused by manhandling these admittedly fine but replaceable cases was soon to prove fatal to part of the collection when the fire broke through the floorboards and began to lick up the back of the two presses known as Vitellius and Otho. By the time the fire engines finally arrived, the fire had taken hold of the room and Dr Bentley knew there was little point in saving the wooden shelves themselves. The only hope now was that the books in them might be preserved. Braving the rising flames, Dr Bentley and his son fought their way into the smoke-filled library and began attacking the backs of the burning cases with hatchets.

As the water from the fire engines began to shower down around them, they prised open the backs and lifted out the smouldering manuscripts by the armful. There was no time to take them gently downstairs to safety, however, so instead the window was broken open and the books, still smoking, were hurled out into the courtyard below in a flurry of ash and sparks. Finally, as the storm of books abated, Dr Bentley himself emerged from the burning house, still in nightgown and wig, with one of the great treasures of the King's Library stuffed unceremoniously under his arm. That lucky volume was the Codex Alexandrinus – a fifth-century copy of the Old and New Testaments and one of the most important early Bibles extant. No one could return through that smoke and heat. Whatever remained in the burning presses was gone for ever.

In the courtyard Dr Bentley ran into a shocked group of onlookers watching in horror as blistered and burnt fragments of paper and parchment floated down around them like black snow. Running between them, the boys from Westminster School, roused from their dormitory opposite by the commotion, scoured the ground for illuminated fragments to take home as souvenirs.

The following morning brought the terrible realization of the true extent of the damage. In the grey half-light of that Sunday morning a more sombre group of schoolboys could be seen, now under the watchful eyes of their masters, carrying in procession the remains of the Cotton and King's libraries from the school captain's apartment and Little Cloisters, where they had initially been taken, to the new scholars' dormitory where a committee from Parliament was due to inspect the damage.

News of the disaster was quick to spread and the October edition of the *Gentleman's Magazine* chose to record the event in its 'Casualties' column:

23 [Oct.]. A Fire broke out in the House of Dr Bentley, adjoining to the King's School near Westminster Abbey, which burnt down that part of the House that contained the King's and Cottonian Libraries. Almost all the printed Books were consumed and part of the Manuscripts. Amongst the latter, those which Dr Bentley had been collecting for his Greek Testament for these last ten years, valued at 2000 l.

With the press about to break the story, Parliament now became far more interested in the fate of Cotton's collection. Even the most indolent of MPs were girded into action, as the official report of the committee sent to inspect the damage shows:

> The Right Honorable the Speaker of the House of Commons came down to Ashburnham-House, as soon as he heard of the Fire, to see that due Precaution was taken, that what had escaped the Flames should not be destroyed or purloined; and on Monday following the Right Honourable the Lord Chancellor, the Lord Raymond, Lord Chief Justice of the King's-Bench, and Mr. Speaker, being Trustees for the Cottonian Library, were all three at the Dormitory.

And what they found was a truly dreadful sight. Nearly all the printed books from the King's Library had been destroyed, either by the fire itself or by the 'engine-water' from the fire tenders. The manuscripts presented a similarly sorry picture. The heat from the flames had caused the animal fats in the vellum to seep out, leaving the pages curled and brittle. This ooze had then set around the singed page edges, turning once beautiful manuscripts into shapeless, molten lumps. Where words and illuminations were still visible on some pages, the engine-water had streaked and stained them, and the ancient inks had run.

Initial reports stated that, of the 958 volumes, 114 were completely spoilt through either the action of fire, water or both. A further 98 were severely damaged but retrievable, if only partly. In fact, over the following centuries improved conservation techniques, together with more detailed examination of the surviving fragments, have restored at least a few parts, and sometimes more, of all but 13 volumes.

Those thirteen lost books were nearly all from the Otho press, which Bentley had torn open in his desperate attempts to save them. The list of contents reads like a roll-call of the dead. The Bull confirming the title 'Defender of the Faith' on Henry VIII was a charred fragment and the great seal on Magna Carta had melted into an amorphous lump. As for Cotton's pride and joy, the fifth-century copy of the Book of Genesis, which he proudly holds in his only known portrait, that was reduced to a few blackened pieces.

But most of the lost books were from the Anglo-Saxon period. Gone was the 'G' manuscript of the *Anglo-Saxon Chronicle*, the year-by-year account of the history of the Anglo-Saxon kingdoms of Britain from the earliest times. Also destroyed was the only copy of

Æthelweard's chronicle, a Latin translation of a long-lost version of the *Anglo-Saxon Chronicle*, written in the tenth century by a great-great-grandson of King Alfred's brother. The oldest copy of the *Burghal Hidage*, a unique document listing the towns of Saxon England and the provision made for their defence, was also lost. So was an eighth-century illuminated gospel book from Northumbria, as well as the only copy of the Saxon epic poem recounting a clash between Viking and Saxon armies, known as *The Battle of Maldon*. Even the precious, sole-surviving manuscript of the great Anglo-Saxon epic *Beowulf* was burnt, in some places beyond recognition.

And one other now-useless block of burnt parchment lay somewhere amongst the ruins. It too had once merited a place on the Otho press on the top shelf A, twelfth from the left. It too was a work of the Anglo-Saxon period, also an only surviving copy, but this little book was different. It was perhaps the most important document from the whole Anglo-Saxon period, one over which more controversy has raged than any other: a unique record – a biography – written by a Welsh priest called Asser about the king he knew and loved. It told the story of the reign of the most extraordinary ruler ever to have lived in the British Isles. It was an eyewitness account of the life and times of King Alfred.

With Asser's *Life of King Alfred* lost in the flames of the great Cottonian fire, it began to look as if this most extraordinary of kings would be lost with it.

But there was hope and it came from the men who had helped Cotton to found his collection. The Elizabethan antiquarians who had met in Cotton's old house on the Thames were responsible for more than simply collecting antiques and curios. These men had an interest in recovering the past, not just in owning but also in reading and understanding the history contained in the ancient documents they collected. The founder of this group had been another great manuscript collector, Matthew Parker, archbishop of Canterbury. It is largely thanks to him that we can recover something of what was lost in the fire and hence begin to see Alfred again through the smoke.

For Parker, with great foresight, had produced a copy of Asser's biography, which he published in 1574. This was not a literal word-for-word transcription, however, but, in the fashion of the day, it included a number of Parker's own 'improvements', adding into the text other stories that he considered to have been authored by Asser and which he thought had somehow become 'detached' from the manuscript. This included various supernatural and folk tales from the *Annals of St Neot's*, including the incident with the cakes, which Parker wrongly believed Asser had written. When another great antiquary – William Camden – republished Parker's work in 1602, he also added a new story to help settle a debate raging at the time about the antiquity of Oxford University. Now Asser was additionally made to claim that his master had refounded that university. Needless to say, this addition too was less than accurate. Oxford University was in fact most probably founded (for the first time) in the late eleventh or early twelfth century, not the ninth.

This heavily altered version is the main text from which we now have to try to reconstruct what lay in Asser's original. That, and the frontispiece from a very poorly received book by Francis Wise.

Wise was not, even in his day, considered to be the greatest of academics or antiquarians, but his ambition kept him in work in Oxford University. The new edition of Asser that he produced in 1722 was hence not the best-received of volumes, the diarist Thomas Hearne describing it as 'a most wretched edition . . . full of foolish and wild fancies'. What set Wise's edition apart from the earlier transcription of Archbishop Matthew Parker was a single engraving used as its frontispiece. Although Wise could not be bothered to study Cotton's Asser manuscript (instead he merely copied out Parker's printed version), he did have the foresight to send another antiquary and artist, James Hill, to draw a facsimile of its first page for his new edition. That engraving is now all that survives of the lost copy of Asser. One final, parting glimpse of Otho A xii.

The origins of that manuscript, its fate in the fire and what we can learn of its original contents from Parker's and Wise's variable transcriptions make all the difference in trying to rescue the real Alfred from that smoke. The problem is that since Cotton's early manuscript of the book was destroyed, doubts have surfaced as to whether it may have been a forgery in the first place. If Asser's *Life* is indeed an original work, written by the king's friend and mentor, it is a unique insight into the life of an Anglo-Saxon king. If not, it is a dangerous mirage further obscuring our view of an already distant king.

To begin with, there is no doubt that there was a man called Asser at Alfred's court. He was with Alfred through good times and bad; he certainly had the chance to ask the king about his life, his wars, his family, his faith and what he believed his purpose in life to be. If the book bearing Asser's name is by that man, then it records intimate moments in the private life of a king, the sort of moment we simply do not have for most monarchs either before or since. As it discusses the life of Alfred, it also provides a chance for us to find out just what it was, if anything, that made him 'Great'.

But the Asser of *The Life* is a strangely elusive and intangible character. There are elements in the work that seem absolutely 'of their time' – references to versions of the Bible that were already going out of fashion in the ninth century, and obscure Welsh names used for English towns. These are details that would hardly be known to, or cared about by, a later forger, but which would fit in perfectly with what we know of the historical Asser. But then there are bizarre apparent flaws. The writer of this biography, whilst claiming to be a personal friend of Alfred, seems not to know the name of his wife – a problem that he sidesteps each time it looks as if he might have to name her. Furthermore, there are numerous chronological errors concerning the age at which Alfred could read and the relative ages of his brothers, which surely no close friend of the king's could make. So how can this Asser be both so knowing and so ignorant?

Anyone on first leafing through Asser's book would agree that this is a very odd biography indeed, even if we can identify and remove the more eccentric additions with which Parker and Wise 'improved' their versions. First it seems to be unfinished, the initial part running from Alfred's birth (for which, strangely, Asser consistently fails to get the date right) up to the year 887, and the second being written no later than 893 (which we can date accurately as Asser tells us how old Alfred was in the year he was writing). Then there is the strange bipartite nature of the work. The first half almost slavishly follows the *Anglo-Saxon Chronicle*, adding little extra information, repeating its mistakes and looking suspiciously like a simple 'crib'. After that the chronological narrative abruptly breaks off and is replaced with a collection of intimate recollections of events in the king's life, which themselves then suddenly cease. We know that the historical Asser outlived Alfred by ten years and that many of the king's greatest achievements occurred after he stopped writing. So why did he stop at all?

The full details of the problems with the text, as well as possible solutions to them, are technical and sometimes esoteric, and have been argued about for well over a hundred years. Whilst they may well be essential to any complete understanding of Asser's life, they should perhaps, in the words of the great Alfredian scholar Charles Plummer, be 'safely relegated to the relative obscurity of a footnote' – or in this case a bibliographical note.

What we can safely say at this point is that, first, the work that we call *The Life of Alfred* is certainly unfinished; indeed, it is probably little more than an initial collection of material for writing up into a book that was either never written or has not survived.

Second, if it is a fake, no one has successfully answered the old legal question: *cui bono?* – who benefits? Why might a later forger want to fake a biography of Alfred? Mediaeval monks were, of course, famed for forgery but their targets were usually ancient rights and privileges granted in dubious charters by shadowy patrons. Finding an old charter that showed that a long-dead king had granted your abbey a certain piece of land could be the decisive factor in often protracted legal disputes and so there was always a reason for 'creating' these documents. But forging a *Life of Alfred* was a huge undertaking, fraught with pitfalls and easily discovered, which offered no obvious benefit to the forger. If this Asser is in fact a later forger, he misses numerous opportunities to grant himself or his community unknown privileges. He appears instead to go to all this trouble for nothing.

Finally there is no single deadly flaw in the text itself, no lone point where a later forger betrays himself, and in a work of this complexity no lapse at all on the part of the forger would indeed be a miracle. At this point, therefore, even if it is only by faith, we can accept that Asser did write about a king he knew, that his work is in truth the only extant biography of a Saxon king and not just any king but the only one to be called 'Great'. Hence on this journey into the life of Alfred it will provide a unique and invaluable guide, taking us into the presence of the royal court and of the king himself. But in the process we will not take Asser at face value. Hidden within his pages there is also another story, of politics and intrigues, power and propaganda, not explicitly stated but woven into the words Asser uses, his careful combination of fact and legend and, perhaps most importantly of all, the episodes he hints at but chooses not to reveal.

And with that we can leave behind the academic debates of the twentieth and twenty-first centuries, the smouldering remains of Cotton's great library, Parker's transcript, and even the mediaeval chroniclers, to head back to a time before even Asser had written, when the story of Alfred really begins with a visit from abroad.

I

The Prophecy of Jeremiah

Behold, a people shall come from the north . . . They shall hold
the bow and the lance: they are cruel, and will not shew mercy:
their voice shall roar like the sea.

Jeremiah 50: 41 (King James Version)

T HE FIRST HINT that the ninth century would be one like no
other came some eleven years before that century even started,
before Alfred, his father or even his grandfather were king. It occurred
on the south coast of what is today the county of Dorset and what was
then the Anglo-Saxon kingdom of Wessex.

It may have been a lookout that first spotted it, or perhaps a trader
on the Portland beach staring out to sea for a sail that would signal the
approach of another trading ship from Carolingian Francia across the
Channel. It cannot have been an unusual sight. If you walk today
along the eastern side of the long gravel beach that runs out to the Bill,
in the area that is now Portland harbour, it is easy to see why
merchants would choose this place. As late as the nineteenth century,
before the harbour walls were built, it was easier still. It was quiet,
sheltered from storms by the limestone crag of the Isle of Portland and
the pebble bank connecting it to the mainland where ships could be
safely beached. Yet from the top of that bank there were clear views
for miles around – down the vast stretch of Chesil Bank to the west,
east to the Isle of Purbeck and far out across the Channel. It was a good
place for Frankish ships to seek out – secure but visible – a place for
trade. Indeed, the short strip of water separating the island of Britain
from continental Europe had long been more of an international
highway than a barrier, and the connections between the magnificent
Frankish kingdom of Charlemagne and the Wessex of King Beorhtric

were good. That is not to say that Beorhtric himself was a ruler on quite the same scale of Charlemagne, so his expectations of any trade brought by ships from Francia must have been relatively modest. Charlemagne had no need to send embassies or supplicants to the House of Wessex, which relied for its very existence on the goodwill of its far more powerful neighbour to the north, Mercia. Beorhtric himself was married to Eadburh, a daughter of that Mercian royal family – in fact a daughter of its king, Offa – so he was, in a manner of speaking, 'family', although he well knew that Offa was *primus inter pares*.

But if Wessex bowed to the overlordship of Mercia in matters of foreign policy, it remained independent in terms of its own internal affairs and in how it dealt with those who approached its shores. So when three sails did break the horizon off Portland that day in 789, the mechanisms of the Wessex state, such as they were, swung into action. Whoever first saw those ships reported to the small settlement of Dorchester where a royal official named Beaduheard received the news. He immediately called together his men and set out to learn more about them.

Beaduheard was a reeve (from which we derive the word 'sheriff' – a 'shire reeve'), an important administrator in the primitive government of Wessex. From Dorchester he exercised control over local royal estates, gathering in the rents – often then still paid in foodstuffs rather than money, as well as supervising many areas of the king's justice. He would have had a right to be arrogant. Everyone in the region would have known him and most would have feared him, whether or not he exploited his position. He was a man with the king's ear, a man on the king's business, a man who carried the majesty of the state of Wessex with him as he rode.

Beaduheard had three things in mind as he urged his horse out on to the slippery gravel of Chesil Bank that day and they all centred on knowing what type of men these ships carried. First, if they were traders, he would be expected to extract some form of duty from them and in that he was, in effect, one of England's earliest customs and excise officers. That customs existed across the Channel even at this time we know from an incident in Francia. When Offa of Mercia presumptuously asked for the hand in marriage of Charlemagne's daughter, the indignant emperor closed French ports to all English ships. This admirably demonstrated his considerable power over cross-Channel trade and the request was quickly withdrawn. King Beorhtric of Wessex was not especially powerful, but through Beaduheard he was at least trying to emulate his grander neighbours as well as turn a profit.

Second, there was always a need for news. Merchants brought not just goods but tales of foreign politics, letters from foreign potentates and information on foreign affairs. In the fluid politics of the eighth century this sort of knowledge was vital to a successful king and Beorhtric would want to know what news, if any, these traders brought.

Finally there was the matter of security. If the men turned out to be robbers or pirates, the reeve and his men would have to remind them that such miscreants were not welcome in civilized Wessex.

As Beaduheard approached the shore, the ships that only hours before had been mere specks on the horizon were now already being pulled up on the shingle beach. It was always an awkward moment. The new arrivals were cornered, unable to quickly return to sea, and until he had identified them they were potentially dangerous. Even language must have been an issue. If they were English there was of course no problem. Frisians (from modern-day Belgium and the Netherlands) also spoke a language similar enough to English for them to be understood. Beaduheard may even have had a smattering of Frankish to aid him in bringing French traders to court. But these men were alien. They certainly heard the reeve's command to accompany him to Dorchester into the presence of the king, but whether they understood or not, their reply was understandable in any language. They would not be ordered anywhere, even by someone as important as the royal reeve. Beaduheard had made a mistake, his last, in fact. The men disembarking from the ships were not Frankish traders but something else entirely, and they answered his order not with meek agreement but with the edge of a sword. Beaduheard and all his men were cut down where they stood. The Vikings had arrived and whilst this particular warband was never heard of again, the coming century – Alfred's century – would also very much be theirs.

The England in which the Vikings had landed for the first time that day was not altogether unknown to them. Even if those particular individuals had never set foot on her shores before, other Scandinavians had. Although the origin of the term 'Viking' is uncertain, one suggestion is that *Vik* refers to the trading centres of the European coast, which were known as *wics*. Hence Vikings are simply people who visited these places. If their interest had been limited to trade, the Vikings would have ushered in an age of a very different kind. The land they now stood on – Beorhtric's kingdom of Wessex – was one of a group of Anglo-Saxon kingdoms in England that had emerged in the late fifth and sixth centuries after the collapse of Roman rule. We call these kingdoms 'Anglo-Saxon' after two Germanic tribes, the Angles and the Saxons, some of whom seem to have migrated to Britain in this period. The exact number of Saxons, Angles and other Germanic peoples who came over to England then is still hotly disputed, but regardless of how many actually made the journey, those who did seem to have been in the ascendancy. The culture of the succeeding generations, at least in England, might reasonably be described as theirs.

Anglo-Saxon England was an overwhelmingly agricultural land, of scattered farmsteads and small villages in a landscape dominated by forests that had actually increased in size since the end of the Roman period. In the South three great forests, Andredeswald in the east, the central Ashdown Forest, and Selwood in Somerset and Wiltshire, covered much of the land and were still home to wolves, wild boar and beavers. Between these dangerous obstacles and around the scrub, wastelands and heaths, lay upland pastures on which sheep, goats and cattle grazed. The woods offered pannage for pigs and in the lowland fields the staples of Anglo-Saxon life – wheat, barley, oats and rye – were grown.

Those who lived in this place were, in the vast majority, poor farmers growing enough for their own families to eat and perhaps a little more besides for trade. At the bottom of a scale in which everyone was judged by their wergild – the fine payable for their murder or manslaughter – lay the slaves, who even at the time of the Norman Conquest still formed 10 per cent of the population (25 per cent in Cornwall). They were the workhorses of this agricultural world, the men often working in ploughteams and the women as dairymaids although some slaves might be trained in more delicate crafts, even goldsmithing. They had been reduced to this sorry life in a number of ways. Warfare was the great source of slaves, captured peoples often being sold abroad. In the ninth century the Vikings would run a very healthy trade in slaves they had captured through raiding in Europe. Christian monarchs, if outwardly disapproving, were often complicit in what they continued to view as a trade in a vital resource. Bad debt might also lead to enslavement and, amongst the very poorest, there was even the option of voluntarily selling yourself or your family into slavery. Finally, the other way to come to this life was simply by birth. The children of slaves belonged to their parents' master just as their parents did and, until Alfred's reign at least, could be sold, beaten or even killed at that master's whim.

Above the slaves were the freedmen, granted their freedom by their owners, often in their wills. Then came the largest category of all, the free peasants, or ceorls, who whilst not necessarily wealthy had their freedom and in return bore the duties of public service and taxation along with the right to participate in local courts. Although they were in the vast majority farmers, there was some job specialization amongst this class, as a tenth-century book known as *Ælfric's Colloquy* shows. The *Colloquy* consists of a series of discussions between a kindly and teasing monastic master and his young pupils (many of whom would have been given over by their parents to the monastery aged only seven), designed to improve their conversational Latin. In it he asks the children to pretend that they are each a member of ordinary Anglo-Saxon society and in this vein he asks them about their various occupations. It is a unique insight not only into a teaching method that had survived the centuries but also into the daily lives and perceived roles of the majority of Anglo-Saxon peasants as imagined by their schoolboy contemporaries. Here we meet the proud hunter, employed directly by the king to feed his household, who catches stags in nets and hunts boar with lances, and who tells us, 'a hunter can't afford to be timid, because all kinds of wild animals live in the woods.' In contrast the fisherman is much more circumspect, preferring to take easy prey from lakes and rivers, 'eels and pike, minnows, trout . . . and whatever small fish happen to be swimming in the water'. When the master asks him if he would like to go to sea and catch a whale, he replies, 'Not I! . . . catching whales is dangerous . . . I don't dare try it.' Here we also meet the fowler, who explains how he catches and trains hawks each year, the shoemaker who boasts that no man could get through a winter without his craft and the merchant who risks death at sea to bring luxuries to the king's court. There is also a salt-worker who, long before anyone worried about their blood pressure, asks, 'Is there a man amongst you who can truly enjoy his food without flavouring it with salt?' We also meet a baker who calls his bread 'the staff of life', a cook, an oxherd, a shepherd and, of course, a child at a monastic school. Towards the end of their long discussion, however, they all agree that for all the relative merits of their jobs they should all make peace with the farmer, 'because he provides us with food and drink . . . No matter who or what you are, whether a priest, or a monk, or a peasant, or a soldier, concern yourself with the task before you and perform it, and be what you are, for it is very harmful and disgraceful for a man not to know who and what he is and what he needs to be.'

Above this lively cast of ceorls in the social hierarchy we enter the ranks of nobility and the world of the landowning classes, the thegn, which literally means 'the one who serves', although in the thegn's case this service is to the king rather than the people. These were individuals with local power and influence who also had a place at court; as such they were the vital link between king and country. These men could be officers in the royal household, helping to run the administration; they might be friends or relatives of the king; they would certainly be expected to answer the royal call to battle. But they were also the most important people in each district, connected to the local social network and thus able to take the king's commands into the countryside, down from the court to the level of the ordinary man and woman. When the king called for money or fighting men, he relied on the thegns to ensure that his words were not simply heard but acted upon. Foremost amongst these men stood the ealdormen who by Alfred's reign had become leaders of individual shires – men capable of raising whole armies and hence of making or breaking a kingdom.

The glue that held this society together was a Germanic concept of kinship, where at every level an individual held allegiance to the head of his kin group – the child to the father, the father to the head of the extended family, thence to the local lord and so up through the ranks of the aristocracy to the king himself. Even amongst kings there was an order of precedence, the title of bretwalda (probably meaning 'ruler of

Britain') belonging to the king who claimed at least nominal over-lordship of the others. In the late eighth century, that king, as Beorhtric of Wessex well knew, was Offa.

Although this was a society that had largely adopted Christianity in the seventh century, it was still one that rarely 'turned the other cheek'. Warfare between kingdoms and between the dynasties within them was considered a perfectly normal part of political life, and the bloody feats of warriors were still lauded in the Anglo-Saxon poetry regularly recited in the lord's hall. Although written laws did exist, the blood feud was still an important part of the machinery of justice. Every man and woman of every rank had a price – alive, dead or variously maimed – and an attacker was required to pay the individual (or relatives, in the case of murder) that 'blood-price'. Failure to do so could result in a feud where cheated relatives might legally exact their own bloody revenge on the culprit.

Other elements of old pagan ways could also still be glimpsed through the veneer of Christianity. Kings might claim descent from the ancient pagan Germanic gods and the exploits of the old pagan warlords were still celebrated in works such as *Beowulf*. Such tales were often given a thin Christian gloss, of course, but their true origins frequently showed. When the hagiographer Felix talks about the early life of his hero St Guthlac (who was born a pagan aristocrat), he has the young warrior return a third of the plunder that his warband takes from innocent victims, as a sign of his future Christian goodness. He does not record what those victims made of this 'bandit with a conscience'.

With this often violent pagan heritage, perhaps the peoples of the Saxon kingdoms should have been less surprised by the arrival of Viking warbands who resembled what they themselves had been some centuries earlier. But if times were still violent and folk memories of pagan times lingered on in Saxon songs and stories, Christianity had changed the mindset of these people. In their Christian world view, God was everywhere, able to intercede on behalf of believers and to punish those who strayed from the true path. This was a time when saints were not just fables but real living men and women, when miracles really seemed to happen. God heard and saw all, and an oath made in his name was the highest law in the land. Now they were about to face an enemy who did not believe in their God or the terrible sanctity of his oath.

In uncovering the motives and policies of the Saxons who faced this threat, we have had some historical records to help us, thanks mainly to a tradition of literacy that had built up in monasteries both in England and Francia. To understand more of those men standing on Portland beach with blood on their swords, however, is much harder. Scandinavian cultures at this time were largely illiterate. No contemporary Viking account exists to tell us who they were and why they came. Many hundreds of years later, mainly in the eleventh and twelfth centuries, the oral folk traditions of these people, some of which may date back to their arrival in England, were finally written down in a series of stories and sagas. However, by that time events, even if they had a kernel of fact in them, had been embroidered with myth and studded with fantastical legend. Divining the truth beneath these splendid tales is hence fraught with difficulty.

The *Anglo-Saxon Chronicle* does give one hint about these early raiders. The 'F' version of the chronicle states that they were from Hörthaland in Norway. If correct, this distinguishes the Norwegians of this initial onslaught from the later Danish armies who, during ·Alfred's reign, would be driven by a desire not just for plunder but for conquest. But most Anglo-Saxon sources simply refer to all these Vikings as *Dene* – Danes, regardless of where they were from – and the chances are that they could have come from more than one country.

Whatever their origins, the aims of these first raiders are clear. They may have been illiterate, but the people they were attacking were not and they recorded in graphic detail the destruction wrought on them. This forms its own eloquent if macabre testimony to what drove them. The Northmen were in the business of harvesting booty – collecting as much portable wealth as possible at the least possible risk to themselves, with whatever degree of violence proved necessary. They were asset-strippers and what attracted them to the shores of Britain and Francia was a source of plunder that must have seemed almost too good to be true.

The early Christian communities of England and Francia offered those without a fear of the Christian God an apparently easy and endless source of wealth. Anglo-Saxon monasteries were often located in coastal areas far from other population centres as their communities strove to cut themselves off from the temptations and distractions of secular life. Inside these institutions there was also treasure. The relics of saints held a powerful fascination for Anglo-Saxon Christians and their remains were often kept in elaborate reliquaries crafted from precious metals. The devotion of wealthy benefactors also showed itself in the decoration of altars, the provision of elaborate vestments and the embellishment of religious books with jewelled bindings. Hence for Viking raiders there was a source of immense movable riches in a location that was easily reached by their shallow-draughted ships. But what made this into a real booty bonanza was the fact that all these valuables were protected not by warriors or kings, not by the legendary Viking dragon Fafnir — slain for his treasure hoard by the hero Sigurd — but by monks. It really could not be easier.

News of the rich pickings to be had in Christian Europe travelled fast around the Scandinavian world. In the years following the Portland landing, the word *pagani* — 'pagans' — begins to ripple through the chronicles. A charter from the autumn of 792 shows that Offa had decided to impose new duties on the churches of Kent to provide for the construction and repair of bridges and fortifications, and for expeditions 'contra paganos marinos' — against the pagan seafarers — but it was only in the following year that the true nature of the threat was brought home to all the rulers of the Christian North.

The *Anglo-Saxon Chronicle* for 793 states that in that year, 'dire portents appeared over Northumbria and sorely frightened the people. They consisted of immense whirlwinds and flashes of lightning, and fiery dragons were seen flying in the air.' These were, in the minds of any God-fearing Christian, a clear omen and this was an age when omens were taken very seriously. God must be displeased and he would have his vengeance. He was sending something to scourge his people, to return them to the true Christian path. His missive was the Vikings. The mediaeval chronicler Simeon of Durham concludes his chronicle entry for that year:

> In that same year the pagans from the northern regions came with a naval force to Britain like stinging hornets and spread on all sides like fearful wolves, robbed, tore and slaughtered not only beasts of burden, sheep and oxen, but even priests and deacons, and companies of monks and nuns. And they came to the church of Lindisfarne, laid everything waste with grievous plundering, trampled the holy places with polluted steps, dug up the altars and seized all the treasures of the holy church. They killed some of the brothers, took some away with them in fetters,

many they drove out, naked and loaded with insults, some they drowned in the sea.

At low tide Lindisfarne today can still be approached by the Pilgrim's Path, a safe route across the treacherous tidal flats marked out with tall posts to guide walkers to the island. Walking on this, one can imagine those beaten and wounded monks who were lucky enough to have survived that day in June, being driven across the sands, scattered by a new and to them incomprehensible force.

The site of the monastery from which they were fleeing is now buried beneath the modern village but the parish church of St Mary the Virgin contains some Anglo-Saxon stonework that may have been part of the church of this time. Church builders have always been conservative in their choice of location and once-hallowed places rarely shake off their religious associations. The remains of the church that the Vikings sacked that day most probably still lie beneath the foundations of the present church, and below them can probably be found the place where St Aiden first knelt to pray when he founded his monastery in 635.

Of the monks themselves who faced this slaughter, all that remains are gravestones, now gathered up in the Priory Museum. One of them offers a clue as to how the community of Lindisfarne viewed this terrible turn in their history. Where other round-headed stone slabs are carved with traditional crosses, this one depicts in high relief seven rampaging human figures waving swords and battleaxes above their heads.

The sacking of Lindisfarne was to be only the first of many attacks on monasteries. The response of the chroniclers, both contemporary and later, gives a vivid insight into the extraordinary effects that these raids had on Christians and pagans alike. Simeon of Durham's account shows graphically the difference in mindset between the two groups who clashed on Holy Island on 8 June 793. To Simeon and the other chroniclers – all of whom were in holy orders themselves – the attacks were the worst blasphemy imaginable. The loss of treasure was not the most galling aspect for them but the murder of holy men and women, the ransacking of the religious furniture and the desecration that the very presence of pagans brought to the holy places. However, in Simeon's description we can also glimpse the sense of amazing good fortune that those Vikings must have felt. Here they were in a group of undefended and (to them) meaningless buildings, which contained huge amounts of portable wealth, defended only by unarmed monks who were easy to kill or perhaps equally easy to enslave and sell at home for a healthy profit. The only sanction that protected these communities seemed to be the wrath of a God that the Vikings did not believe in and who, even if he existed, did not seem interested in protecting his believers.

The following year, the writer of the *Anglo-Saxon Chronicle* could at least comfort his readers with a small, if pyrrhic, victory. That year the Vikings returned and plundered Northumbria again, although this time some seem to have been shipwrecked in bad weather, the survivors being killed by the locals as they swam ashore. But it was only a minor setback. One year later the Irish annals record the first Viking raid on their country and the famous monastery of Iona was sacked for the first of three times. By 804, Abbess Selethryth of Lyminge could be found searching around Canterbury for a new home for her nuns, safe behind the city's ancient walls and far from the dangers of their old, exposed, coastal nunnery.

Pagan raids had also begun in continental Europe and it was a Northumbrian who had the dubious honour of recording the first of these, in Aquitaine. Alcuin had been a scholar at the monastic school at York when that city was still one of the greatest centres of learning in Europe. His work there had even come to the attention of Charlemagne who had tempted him away to run the Palace School at the Carolingian court. This school had since become famous as the home of the Carolingian renaissance, the most civilized, cultured and literate place in northern Europe. But it would prove a short-lived renaissance and soon Alcuin would have to record the beginnings of its destruction both on the continent and back home in his native Northumbria.

For Charlemagne these early attacks were really no more than a vague insult to his dignity. In 800, Pope Leo III crowned him emperor – a title that had been out of use in the West since the abdication of Romulus Augustulus in 476 – and he was now undoubtedly the most powerful man in Europe. However, the buzzing of pirates around his shores was a nuisance, both politically and economically, so he took practical steps against them, setting a coastguard along his sea frontiers to report on, and hopefully repel, any attacks.

But whilst Charlemagne instigated measures to try to reduce the risk, the response of the religious community who stood in the front line of these attacks was on a different plane. Thoughts of the Day of Judgment loomed large in the minds of clerics. In the terrifying Anglo-Saxon poem known as *Christ III*, we are presented with the scene that day as the stars are scattered, the moon falls from the sky, the sun dims and dies, and the world is illuminated only by the light from a blood-stained cross. To religious men like Alcuin the beginnings of these raids looked eerily like the opening scenes from that Judgment Day. These Vikings were not simply an annoyance, or an insult, they were a punishment from God, the fulfilment of an ancient prophecy and the herald of the end of time itself.

On hearing of the Lindisfarne attack, Alcuin immediately wrote to the king of Northumbria, Æthelred, warning that there was more to this than mere chance: 'Consider carefully, brothers, and examine diligently, lest perchance this unaccustomed and unheard-of evil was merited by some unheard-of evil practice.' For Alcuin the sudden arrival of the heathen Northmen was not directed against God but *by* God against what he considered only a nominally Christian people. They had strayed from the path of righteousness and were now worthy of punishment. He goes on to warn the king against corruption, fornication and 'luxurious habits' before announcing with grim satisfaction (and something of a flourish) that in his opinion the end of the world was indeed nigh: 'Behold, judgement has begun . . .'

Alcuin was just as forthright in his next letter to the bishop of Lindisfarne. He offers his sympathy but, just as importantly, warns him that the attack was not random but 'was well merited by someone'. Intriguingly, however, he also shows that there seems to be some contact between the pagan raiders and the court of his master Charlemagne. He promises, when he next sees the emperor, to bring up the issue of the 'youths taken into captivity', by which he seems to mean the young monks taken into slavery during the Lindisfarne raid. Clearly he thinks that Charlemagne may be able to exert some sort of influence on either the raiders or the rulers of their homelands to get them returned.

We do not know whether the monks taken away by those Vikings ever saw their home again, but the exhortations of Alcuin do not appear to have produced a revival in morals amongst either the political or the religious leaders of the region. For King Æthelred of Northumbria at least, judgment was indeed at hand. Three years after the letter from Alcuin he was assassinated by members of his own court. As coastal raids intensified, few religious authorities could now doubt that the prophecy of Jeremiah was coming true at last: 'Out of the north an evil shall break forth upon all the inhabitants of the land.'

To the south the political situation had also changed by the turn of the century. Offa and his son had both gone to meet their vengeful God in the same year and the last of the line of Mercian bretwaldas, Coenwulf, now ruled. In Wessex, King Beorhtric continued to defer to his Mercian overlords until 802 when his death brought to the throne an old enemy of both his and Mercia's. He was Ecgberht, grandfather of Alfred the Great.

Ecgberht had attempted to seize the throne of Wessex back in 786 but had been defeated by Beorhtric with the help of Offa. He had spent the intervening years well, however, having taken refuge on the continent at the most glittering and sophisticated court of all, Charlemagne's. Here he heard of the coming of the Vikings, perhaps even talked to Alcuin of the divine vengeance being wrought on the ungodly kings of Britain, and no doubt he also watched with interest the steps taken by Charlemagne to prevent incursions into his own kingdom.

In 802 the death of Beorhtric provided Ecgberht with a second try at the throne of Wessex and this time, with his old enemies dead, he succeeded. But Wessex alone was not enough for a man who had witnessed the might of Charlemagne. Ecgberht's ambitions lay beyond his own kingdom, he wanted that most coveted of Saxon royal titles, bretwalda. His success would prove short-lived, but in establishing himself as one of the major players in the complex and dangerous politics of the early ninth century, he laid firm foundations for the House of Ecgberht. That strength and stability in an age of internecine warfare would itself provide the base for the rule of his grandson Alfred.

In 815, Ecgberht began to hone his campaigning skills beyond Wessex's borders with an invasion of Cornwall, which he is reported as ravaging 'from east to west'. His chance for greatness, however, came in 821 with the death of the last true Mercian overlord, Coenwulf. Far more importantly, no one was in a position to take control unopposed and the Mercian royal house was in turmoil. The heir apparent, his son Cynehelm (later known as St Kenelm), was murdered shortly after, legend has it on the orders of his jealous sister Cwoenthryth. Mercia now descended into aristocratic anarchy with several dynasties competing for the throne whilst the real power of the now rudderless kingdom slowly slipped from their grasp.

It is almost impossible to identify these competing dynasties from the bald records of their accessions, depositions and deaths in the *Anglo-Saxon Chronicle* as family links between them are rarely recorded. All we have to go on is the regular occurrence of rulers whose names all begin with either the letters 'B', 'C', 'W' or 'L'. This suggests that these might each represent one dynasty whose names all began with the same letter – just as Alfred's father's, brothers' and sister's names all began with 'A' or 'Æ'. In this case, Coenwulf was replaced by another 'C' dynast who was himself deposed only two years later by Beornwulf of the 'B' family. He would now become Ecgberht's target.

In 825, Ecgberht drew the Mercian king into battle at Ellendun (now Wroughton in Wiltshire) and avenged the insult of his years of exile. A subsequent incursion by his son and heir Æthelwulf into the smaller kingdoms of Kent, Surrey, Sussex and Essex quickly brought about their submission. This was shortly followed by that of the larger kingdom of East Anglia. To complete the victory the East Anglians even arranged for the murder of King Beornwulf. They too were keen to escape the Mercian yoke.

The Mercian collapse was not yet over, however. The murders and depositions continued until, in 829, Ecgberht administered the *coup de grâce* to this fundamentally compromised kingdom, conquering Mercia itself and then leading an expedition north to Dore in South Yorkshire where the presence of such a successful (and seasoned) army ensured the submission of the last English kingdom of substance, Northumbria. According to the later chronicler Roger of Wendover, King Eanred of Northumbria was even forced to pay tribute.

That Northumbria had fallen into line with little if any fighting also says a great deal about the political situation in the aftermath of the murder of King Æthelred and in the face of continuing Viking raids. Here too the line of succession had been broken and numerous contenders alternately manoeuvred or resorted to outright warfare in their pursuit of the crown. The details of this infighting remain sketchy as the northern annals, probably begun in the eighth century, do not survive past 801. The chronicler Roger of Wendover later recorded, along with the payment by Eanred, that Ecgberht pillaged Northumbria, information that he may have obtained from a northern annal that was still extant at the time of his writing in the thirteenth century. If he did have such an invaluable source it has since been lost and its contents have their only echo in Roger's own work. We also know from Frankish sources that around 806 a King Eardwulf lost the throne of Northumbria and that he, like Ecgberht before him, fled to Charlemagne's court, then at Nymegen, and thence to Rome. He later returned triumphantly to Northumbria with envoys from both powers who ensured his reinstatement. At least in the short term they clearly made the right impression as Eardwulf later became the first Northumbrian king in a hundred years to peacefully hand on the succession to his son.

The dynastic squabblings of the Anglo-Saxon kingdoms had provided Ecgberht with a unique opportunity to assert his lordship over them and it was with great pride that the Wessex-based *Anglo-Saxon Chronicle* for the year 829 recorded that 'He was the eighth king who was Bretwalda.' To celebrate he issued his own Mercian coinage in London and even had himself written into the Mercian royal genealogy. Yet just a year later a certain Wiglaf seems to have retaken control of Mercia. However, at the same date the *Anglo-Saxon Chronicle* records further submissions to Ecgberht, this time by the Welsh, who would surely not have been keen to submit to him if he had just lost the kingdom bordering their lands. This may therefore indicate that Wiglaf was reinstalled as under-king with Ecgberht's consent.

The fate of Mercia was an object lesson for Ecgberht and his son Æthelwulf, Alfred's father. They had witnessed the ease with which an already politically divided kingdom could be conquered. This was a lesson they would need to remember in the coming decades when a new enemy from beyond England's shores would exploit just such fault lines in search of their own land to settle.

The fate of the Carolingian Empire of Charlemagne also gave reason for Ecgberht to reflect on the value of a strong and united dynasty. The only heir of Charlemagne to outlive his father was Louis I, who took control of the whole empire in 814. Louis was considered and thoughtful, as one might expect of a child brought up during the Carolingian renaissance. His fondness for doing public penance for his sins made him hugely popular with the monastic chroniclers of the day, who dubbed him 'Louis the Pious'. His careful plans for the division of the empire between the three grown sons of his first marriage – Lothar, Pippin and Louis – were thrown into doubt, however, in 823 by the birth of a fourth son, Charles, to his second wife, Judith. Palace revolts had followed and in 830 Louis was deposed, only to be restored by two of his sons, fearful of the power now wielded by their older sibling Lothar. Nevertheless, three years later all three eldest sons were reunited in their desire to prevent Louis from carving out a kingdom for little Charles from their patrimony. They called Louis to a council just outside Colmar on 30 June 833 to settle their differences. But when he arrived he found his sons and their allies arrayed against him in full battle order. Moments later the imperial troops defected in what was probably a pre-planned manoeuvre. The shocked and humiliated king was forced to abdicate on the spot and the site from that day gained the name of Lügenfeld – the Field of Lies.

Even this extraordinary coup did not settle the succession, however. Within a year Louis' second and third sons had again restored their father in order to protect themselves from the growing power of Lothar. On his deathbed in 840 the old king was still attempting to organize a fair partition of the empire between his warring sons.

Amongst the courts of Saxon England such dynastic wrangling might have been the object of little more than idle gossip but it certainly drew the attention of the Vikings who lived behind the great defensive dyke – the Danevirke – that they had thrown up between the Carolingian Empire and their own Scandinavian world. Dynastic trouble spelt political weakness, and political weakness opened up cracks into which they would soon flood.

Up until the year of Louis the Pious' death, Viking raids on Britain and the continent were only sporadic, probably the work of small independent groups of pirates with no overall plan or ambition beyond returning home at the end of the summer with a hold full of bullion. Some small land grants had been made to individuals, the earliest record being a grant in Frisia in 826 to one 'Harald' (probably Harald Klak). But mostly these were summer raiders less interested in land than in treasure. In addition to the splendidly profitable mon-asteries, these pirates were now also turning their attention to the coastal trading posts or settlements, particularly those that serviced cross-Channel trade.

Beginning in 835 the trading settlement of Dorestadt in Frisia was raided four times in as many years, which can hardly have allowed time for the place to recover. Raids on Frisia became so frequent that the writer of the *Annals of Xanten* had later to admit that the over-whelming number of Vikings in Frisia – apparently under the command of Rorik, a son (or possibly a nephew) of Harald Klak – had forced the Carolingians to simply cede Dorestadt to them to prevent further predations. The year that the Vikings first came to Dorestadt was also the year that they first attacked Sheppey, an island just off the north coast of Kent, which may also have possessed some form of trading station and which was home to an ancient royal nunnery founded by the daughter of an East Anglian king. What the Vikings discovered here, however, would prove far more valuable than plunder. Sheppey was exactly the sort of easily defensible, offshore base that they, ever keen to protect their ships and hence their means of escape, preferred. They would remember this place and one day would return, with very different and far-reaching conse-quences for both Alfred and England.

The following year the Irish chronicles record sixty Viking ships on the Boyne and another sixty on the Liffey, whilst a further fleet of anywhere between twenty-five and thirty-five ships (depending on which version of the *Anglo-Saxon Chronicle* you read) landed at Carhampton in Somerset. It was a typically bold Viking move. Carhampton was not on the remote outskirts of Europe but in the heart of Wessex. A Viking presence here would have to draw a response from King Ecgberht and indeed it did. Ecgberht was bretwalda, the man who had defeated the armies of Mercia and brought about the submission of all the Anglo-Saxon kingdoms. He wasted no time in drawing up his armies and marching to face this bold new foe. The army that he assembled was led by at least two bishops and two ealdormen, and it probably contained levies from at least two shires. Sadly for Wessex we know of these leaders only because their names are on the roll-call of the dead. This was not to be another great victory for Ecgberht; indeed, even the Anglo-Saxon chronicler is forced to grudgingly admit there was a 'great slaughter'. Ecgberht lost.

The size and effect of the defeat are glossed over in the *Anglo-Saxon Chronicle*, which was first compiled in Alfred's reign, perhaps even on the king's orders, to explain and promote the rise of Wessex, the House of Ecgberht and, of course, the rule of Alfred himself. As such we cannot really be sure what sort or order of magnitude this battle was. Chroniclers across Europe quite naturally take a very anti-Viking stance in their records. After all, these people were preying on them and, worse still, they were heathens. Writers tended to exaggerate the size of the threat and equally to minimize the impact of defeat on the Christians.

To gauge numbers we are forced to guess at what chroniclers mean by terms like 'ship' and 'army' – terms that in their minds might have been associated with specific numbers of men. We know that in the laws of the early eighth-century West Saxon king Ine, for instance, a *here* – an army – was considered to be anything over thirty-five men. Likewise, a 'ship' may have implied a specific number of fighters. The surprising agreement between chroniclers on the numbers of ships that formed various Viking fleets suggests that this may well be the case. We do not know, however, what that magic number 'per ship' was. Modern estimates put it at between thirty and sixty fighting men per vessel, indicating that attacks like that on Carhampton may have involved between 750 and 2,100 Vikings in total. Not perhaps an invasion force but still enough to defeat the most powerful king in England, which in itself says something about the reality behind Ecgberht's claims to the bretwaldaship.

News of the defeat of the apparently invulnerable Ecgberht raced around the kingdoms of the British Isles. In 838, we find one of his old enemies, the native British rulers of the Cornish – or 'West Welsh' as the *Anglo-Saxon Chronicle* refers to them – allying themselves with a Viking force. Cornwall was at this time an independent kingdom and a British rather than a Germanic one, where the native language was Celtic Cornish, not Anglo-Saxon. As it also bordered directly on to a part of the kingdom of Wessex, the acquisitive Ecgberht had already made attempts at its conquest. However, his ravaging of Cornwall in 815 clearly had not dislodged the shadowy native rulers who, on the arrival of a Viking 'great naval force' in the summer of 838, chose not to fight it, but to join it in a challenge to Ecgberht's authority. Ecgberht may have learnt lessons from the previous year or he may simply have been fortunate to have the right force in the right place at the right time, for when the two armies met on Cornish ground at Hingston Down, the outcome was very different from the previous year's encounter. The *Anglo-Saxon Chronicle* joyfully records that 'both Cornish and Danes were put to flight'.

Ecgberht, now about sixty-eight, was a very old man by the standards of his day and he had held the throne of Wessex for thirty-seven years. This was an extraordinary achievement in itself, in an era when his contemporaries in other kingdoms rarely survived in power for more than a handful of years. Since he had come to the throne, neighbouring Mercia had lost six kings whilst four Northumbrian rulers had found to their mortal cost that their greatest enemies lay not across the sea in Scandinavia or even to the south in Wessex, but in their own courts.

In his advancing years, and having achieved so much, Ecgberht's thoughts must have turned to the succession. He had seen how competing dynasts had torn apart Mercia on Coenwulf's death, he knew of the political assassination in Northumbria and he had in fact benefited greatly from both. Now he was determined that the fate of Louis, son of his old protector Charlemagne, at the Field of Lies would not await him and his heirs.

Succession was not a simple matter, however. There was no Anglo-Saxon law to determine who should be king on the death of one incumbent. No hard and fast rules seem to have governed the order in which family members might inherit or, indeed, whether one particular family had the right to claim that inheritance in the first place. Even if rival families and the individual members of the ascendant family could be reconciled, there was still the matter of the king's council – the witan (literally 'wise men'). This group of councillors consisted of some of the most important people in the kingdom: the relatives of the current king, the ealdormen who effectively ran the civil and military administration of each county, archbishops, bishops and abbots, as well as the landed aristocracy or thegns.

The kings of Wessex had to consult their witans over many great issues of state, not because they formed some sort of representative protodemocracy but because they were members of powerful families whose agreement was essential to maintain order in the kingdom. Whilst later kings such as James I of England claimed to rule by 'divine right', the kings of Wessex were elected by their witan from amongst their own members. This meant not only that the witan did not necessarily have to approve that king's heir, it also meant they could 'unelect' any king who did not continue to enjoy their approval during his reign. This would be an aspect of Wessex law that Alfred, Ecgberht's grandson, would one day have reason to fear, and had he looked to the past there was good evidence to see why. The Wessex witan had unelected a king before, back in 757, when they had deposed King Sigeberht for his 'unjust acts'. His fate had been something of a salutary lesson to any Saxon king. Robbed of his royal office, he was outlawed to the Weald of Kent where a local swineherd stabbed him to death in a blood feud.

So the situation facing the ageing Ecgberht was delicate. In order to secure the acceptance of his son Æthelwulf as the next king of Wessex by the witan, he could adopt one of two tactics: force or bribery. An example of the unwanted effects of the first course was still fresh in everyone's minds. When the last great Mercian bretwalda Offa had died, his son had inherited his throne thanks largely to the violent intimidation that Offa employed in his own lifetime to gain acceptance for him. That son Ecgfrith had indeed inherited Mercia but died in the same year as his father, sparking dynastic disputes that brought the nation to the brink of collapse. Alcuin, again observing from the relative safety of the continent, and always able to see the hand of God at work in the affairs of men, wrote to the Mercian ealdorman Osberht shortly after this, giving his opinion of events: 'For truly, as I think, that most noble young man [Ecgfrith] has not died for his own sins; but the vengeance for the blood shed by the father had reached the son. For you know very well how much blood his father shed to secure the kingdom on his son. This was not a strengthening of his kingdom but its ruin.' Whether or not God was visiting the sins of Offa on his son, Alcuin was quite right that the bretwalda's heavy-handed attempts at controlling the witan had contributed to the dynastic struggle that had overtaken the kingdom. It was perhaps with this in mind that Ecgberht took the second route to ensure his son's success: bribery.

How he went about this can be seen in a charter in favour of the monastic community at Canterbury, which, as a Kentish institution, had only recently come under the nominal authority of Wessex. Drawn up at Kingston in Surrey on Wednesday, 20 November 838, this document restores some land that he had previously seized from the monks, but in return Ecgberht expects that 'we ourselves and our heirs shall always hereafter have firm and unshakable friendships from Archbishop Ceolnoth and his congregation.' Having the support of the most senior clergyman in England and his (now Wessex-controlled) community was essential to achieving a smooth transition of power. A very similarly worded grant to the community in the old Wessex heartland of Winchester ensured their support at the witan as well.

When Ecgberht died the following year, the efforts he had put into ensuring the succession bore fruit. Æthelwulf succeeded in 840 to the kingdom of Wessex without incident, the first time a king of Wessex had inherited the throne directly from his father for almost two centuries.

Æthelwulf began his reign with two dreams. The first was a simple ambition to make the pilgrimage to Rome to meet the pope and see the relics of the Holy Fathers. The second was quite literally a dream, reported to him by a priest, and both found expression in a letter he wrote in that first year as king to his Carolingian counterpart, Louis the Pious, who was at the time entering his last year on earth. The letter itself to Louis does not survive, nor is there any mention of it in the surviving English chronicles of the period, but the haunting contents did have a clear impact on the writer of the Frankish *Annals of St Bertin*, Prudentius of Troyes.

Perhaps Prudentius was not so much impressed as mortified. In the letter Æthelwulf asked permission for safe transit through the kingdom of the Franks on his way to Rome. He goes on to recount his other dream – not so much a dream as a nightmare. Æthelwulf tells Louis that he has been visited in the dream by a priest, who was himself visited in his sleep by a man who took him to an unknown kingdom filled with wonderful buildings. There they entered a beautiful church full of boys, all diligently reading books, and when they approached to examine the books the priest found they were written in alternate lines of black ink and blood. When he asked his guide what this meant he was told:

The lines of blood you can see in those books are all the various sins of Christian people, because they are so utterly unwilling to obey the orders and fulfil the precepts in those divine books. These boys now, moving about here and looking as if they are reading, are the souls of the saints who grieve every day over the sins and crimes of Christians and intercede for them so that they may finally be turned to repentance some day.

But now, warned the prophecy, the sins overwhelmed even these saintly intercessors and that terrible Day of Judgment was at hand. Æthelwulf then reminds Louis of how recent crops had failed due to the 'sins of men' and warns that if some restitution were not quickly made, 'for three days and nights a very dense fog will spread over their land, and then all of a sudden pagan men will lay waste with fire and sword most of the people and land of the Christians along with all they possess.'

It was certainly a story that Prudentius could relate to. He had come to the Carolingian court as a young lawyer from his native Spain, which itself was feeling the effects of pagan invasion from the Saracens. Of course such warnings of imminent doom were meat and drink to many of the ecclesiastical writers of the day, obsessed as they were with the end of days and the endemic moral decline that they believed they saw all around them. But for a king, even a devout one, sending such a letter might have been considered a little over-zealous. Æthelwulf, however, was not making a moral point, but a prediction. The prophecy of Jeremiah was about to come true.

2

Invitation from the Wolf

Dear men, understand that this is true: the world is in haste and it
approaches the end, and because it is ever worldly, the longer it
lasts, the worse it becomes.
> The Sermon of the Wolf (Wulfstan) to the English,
> in K. Crossley-Holland, *The Anglo-Saxon World*, p. 265

I F ÆTHELWULF'S ACCESSION was peaceful, the years that followed
it were certainly not. The nature of the Viking menace was
changing and the occasional day-raiding of the previous decades
was giving way to something more disturbing. Precisely what that
change would mean for the English can be first glimpsed in the same
year that Æthelwulf took the throne, across the sea in Ireland.

In 839 a Viking force arrived for the summer – a now regular, if
unwanted, occurrence – and went about its usual business of plunder.
But come the autumn it became clear to the Irish that something was
different. Viking raiding had been a seasonal activity; indeed, warfare
in general was something to be undertaken only at times when it did
not interfere with annual agricultural imperatives. The coastal peoples
of Europe could therefore look forward to the end of summer when
the Viking warbands would return to their ships and set sail for their
icy homelands far to the north. They would not, as everyone knew,
return until the spring.

But the Viking band on the banks of Lough Neagh that autumn
presented something of a puzzle. They had finished a season's raiding
in the north of Ireland but they showed no sign of preparing to leave.
No sailors caulked planks and mended sails, no crews swarmed about
their ships careening barnacles from the hull in preparation for the
long voyage home. In fact they were not going home, they were here

to stay, and a new era of Viking activity was about to begin. The following spring they emerged from their winter camp and attacked Louth, carrying 'bishops, priests and scholars' into captivity, according to the writer of the *Annals of Ulster*, before returning to their new home on the lough. From now on there would be no winter respite.

With no contemporary Scandinavian records to help us it is hard to be sure what turned these occasional raiders into permanent predatory warbands and, later, into European settlers. It may be that the Norse and Danish 'kings' who sailed to Europe from the 840s onwards could no longer find a place for themselves in their homelands, which were coming increasingly under the control of a few powerful families. We know from a later Norwegian traveller who came to Alfred's court that his country possessed very limited agricultural land, confined to a narrow coastal strip, so any growth in population must have forced out the weak or the adventurous to seek their fortunes elsewhere. With the escalating dynastic crises in European royal families, these dis-affected groups perhaps saw an opportunity not simply for financial gain but for carving out new and more manageable kingdoms for themselves.

Whatever the reasons, 840 ushered in a fresh era of attacks and another phase in European history. On the continent, news that Louis the Pious was near death must have drifted across the Danevirke. His death would, as they knew, inevitably lead to civil war amongst his heirs. The Vikings wasted no time in exploiting this. Sailing up the Seine, a warband sacked Rouen, the capital of the province of Neustria. For the first time the Northmen walked through the streets of the city that would in less than a century become the capital of their own province of Normandy and see them transformed from 'North-men' to Normans.

With the death of Louis the Pious the title of emperor fell on the shoulders of his eldest and most rebellious son, Lothar. It was now up to him to find a way to check the Viking advance but his response was calculated to cause consternation amongst both his own people and the religious chroniclers. Unsure of his hold on the throne in the face of potential rebellions from his brothers, Lothar took the Danish king Harald Klak as an ally, granting him the island of Walcheren near the mouth of the Rhine in return for Viking support. No one who had followed the pattern of early raiding in Europe can have been in any doubt as to the dangers of such a move. Viking armies favoured small, easily defensible sites such as islands as bases for their ships. Giving away such a location at the mouth of one of the greatest rivers in Europe was letting the wolf into the fold. Prudentius of Troyes, who was more concerned for the Christians who lived on the island than for the tactical blunder, certainly made his feelings clear in the *Annals of St Bertin*, when he wrote: 'This was surely an utterly detestable crime, that those who had brought evil on Christians should be given power over the lands and the people of Christians . . .; that the persecutors of the Christian faith should be set up as lords over Christians, and Christian folk have to serve men who worshipped demons.'

Æthelwulf of Wessex was not so keen to invite the enemy into his lands, but they were arriving with increasing frequency all the same. The Wessex settlement of Hamwic (modern Southampton), then one of the major trading ports of Wessex and entirely undefended, naturally proved an irresistible lure to a Viking force. On this first occasion at least the people of Wessex managed to repel the attack. Further west along the coast at Portland, the ealdorman Æthelhelm with the men of Devon were less fortunate in their encounter and the king's commander lost both the battle and his life. Not long after, another ealdorman, Hereberht, was killed by the 'heathen men' in the Romney Marsh in Kent. There is also mention in the annals of other attacks in the English kingdoms of East Anglia and Lindsey. Perhaps more sinister still, just beyond Æthelwulf's horizons, in Ireland, the Vikings at Dublin were building their first *longphort* – a permanent fortress and the seed of what would become the Viking kingdom of Dublin. In Ireland at least, the seasonal raiding was over and the *landnám* – the time of settlement – had begun.

Closer to home, the English kingdoms had other problems. In Mercia the new king Berhtwulf was coming to terms with an enemy just as dangerous as foreign attacks: poverty. The few documents surviving from the period show that he was running out of money, which for any Anglo-Saxon king, like running out of land, was like running out of blood. Kings stood at the centre of a web of obligation and expectation in which they were required to reward service with gifts of land, money or precious objects. The gifts that a ruler gave to his senior lords in turn provided the store from which those lords rewarded their dependents and so on down the chain of kinship. The giving of these gifts tied the receiver to his lord, and the bonds of giving and receiving, begun in the royal court, reached out to the meanest country hall. Indeed, kingship and lordship are often referred to in Anglo-Saxon poetry in terms of gift-giving. In the poem *The Wanderer*, an exile speaks of his former lord as his 'gold-friend' sitting on a 'gift-throne'. In the epic poem *Beowulf*, the eponymous hero of the Geats comes to Heorot – the royal hall of the Scyldings – after hearing that it is being terrorized by the monster Grendel. Beowulf duly kills the monster and returns the hall to its king Hrothgar. At the subsequent feast the old king's wife hands round the celebratory mead cup and takes the opportunity to remind her husband the king of his duty to reward Beowulf:

> Accept this cup, my loved lord,
> treasure-giver; O gold-friend of men,
> learn the meaning of joy again, and speak words
> of gratitude to the Geats, for so one ought to do.
> And be generous to them too, mindful of gifts
> which you have now amassed from far and wide.

The problem for the kings of Mercia, who were no doubt well aware of the legendary generosity of Hrothgar, was that they seem to have exhausted their store of gifts to give, with potentially disastrous results for the fabric of Mercian society. The desperation with which Berhtwulf was shoring up his finances can be seen in a charter from him in favour of the church of Worcester in which he returns lands that he had apparently stolen and then given away to his retainers. The charter is, of course, phrased in such as way as to make the theft seem like the unfortunate consequence of some poor advice to the king – more a misunderstanding than a theft – but one clause makes it quite clear that restitution from the king came only at a price. Whilst the land is returned apparently freely, the charter goes on to state that 'at the same time also the bishop made a gift [to the king] . . . i.e. four very choice horses and a ring of 30 mancuses and a skillfully wrought dish of three pounds and two silver horns of four pounds; and he gave to the queen two good horses and two goblets of two pounds and one gilded cup of two pounds.' The mention of these 'gifts' in a charter returning land was not simply a case of happy coincidence; in fact it demonstrates the ransoming of land back to its owners by the king. One effect of this new poverty, beyond making Berhtwulf shift uncomfortably on his throne, was to drive Mercia to look for closer contact with her old enemy Wessex. Certainly from the date of the accession of Berhtwulf, Mercia and Wessex use similar coinage and often employ the same moneyers to strike them, implying perhaps at least a desire to standardize trade between the two nations.

Berhtwulf was also looking for personal protection, as his dwindling finances could no longer be guaranteed to paper over the cracks that had opened at his turbulent accession. Berhtwulf had only come to the throne of Mercia following the suspicious death – almost certainly murder – of Wigstan, the son and heir of King Wiglaf of Mercia. Wiglaf and the House of Ecgberht, however, had been on good terms and if Berhtwulf wanted to survive longer than most Mercian dynasts, he would have to make his peace with Wessex. Without their support his tenure could prove as brief as his predecessors'. From Æthelwulf's point of view reconciliation also made sense. No one was safe on the Mercian throne, even the resurgent 'B' dynasty, and that made them pliable.

As such it was an unpleasant but practical alliance, although neither Æthelwulf nor Berhtwulf could have known at that time to what degree. For the time being, the surviving members of the 'W' dynasty, who were already revering Wigstan as a saint at their cult centre of Repton, were merely a minor irritant. Soon enough they would become Mercia's nemesis.

If Mercia had its own problems, they were as nothing compared to Northumbria's. This kingdom, which for so long had been at the academic and philosophical heart of Anglo-Saxon England, now stood on the brink of destruction. The nation that had been home to Bede and Alcuin was now racked with dynastic infighting, and a series of rulers who appear in the records as little more than names were making the nation fit only for conquest. All that survives from these fraught years are the echoes of that long-lost northern chronicle, preserved in the writings of Roger of Wendover and in a handful of letters from Lupus – then abbot of the Frankish monastery at Ferrières – addressed to two Northumbrians, Archbishop Wigmund and Abbot Ealdsige of York.

Lupus was one of the most cultured and refined men of ninth-century Francia, not only a friend of Charlemagne's biographer Einhard and a former pupil of Alcuin's but also a prodigious correspondent. In addition he was something of a man of action, fighting for the Frankish king Charles the Bald in his wars with his brothers, even once being captured in battle and ransomed. But his letters to Wigmund and Ealdsige in 852 have a particular and poignant resonance. To the archbishop, Lupus writes that he is glad of the respite from recent troubles in Francia, both during the fighting amongst the sons of Louis the Pious (who had thankfully finally agreed a peace at Meersen in the previous year) and at the hands of Viking raiders. He was clearly hoping to have time for some reading, and in writing to the abbot Lupus adds a particular request. He asks Ealdsige for books in the knowledge, or at least the belief, that York was still a great centre of Christian learning. His requests, which are not unusual for their time, include a number of commentaries on various religious works and an ancient secular work by Quintilian, *Concerning the Training of an Orator* (Lupus was a well-known lover of the classics). But one volume that he requests betrays his fears of a different and darker future. It was an essay on a book that was now haunting academic minds across Europe – Jerome's commentary on the Book of Jeremiah. He ends his letter: 'Farewell, and as soon as opportunity offers, gladden us with the reply we hope for.'

But there was to be no reply. It seems that Lupus never received his copy of the commentary on Jeremiah, as several years later he can be found asking Pope Benedict for one. In fact, there were to be no more letters out of Northumbria at all. Lupus' last line marks the end of learned correspondence between that realm and the continent. Soon the Christian Anglo-Saxon kingdom would be dead. Lupus had said farewell to a whole nation.

At the time that Lupus was writing those last words to the clerics of York, he also took time to write two further letters. The first was addressed to Æthelwulf, king of Wessex, asking whether so generous and pious a king would consider donating some lead for covering the roof at Ferrières. Not prepared to rely entirely on flattery to further his project, however, Lupus also wrote to Felix, an old friend he had known from their days at the monastery at Faremoûtiers who was now King Æthelwulf's secretary. This shorter letter urged his fellow Frank to encourage Æthelwulf to provide the lead and gave directions for its delivery: 'I pray that my petition to your laudable lord, Æthelwulf, may have effect through your diligence . . . If I obtain this by the abundant clemency of God and your zealous co-operation, it will again be your care to see that his generous benefaction is conveyed to the village of Étaples.'

Both of these letters were written from the 'cell of St Judoc' – a small hostel for English pilgrims (in what is now the town of Saint-Josse-sur-Mer) who were setting out on the perilous journey across Europe to either Rome or, for the very daring, Jerusalem. The abbot of this hostel had at one time been none other that Alcuin himself and it had sheltered a number of important dignitaries making the weary journey either for personal reasons or on state business. As the first stop on any English pilgrimage, this little French village near Étaples held a unique place in English affections. The remains of the saint venerated there – a Breton hermit – were eventually transported to Winchester where they became one of the major attractions of the Minster. The saint's hair and fingernails held a particular fascination as these were said to keep on growing. Although centuries have now passed since English pilgrims came this way, even today the village retains a peculiarly English feel, consisting as it does of small cottages surrounded by colourful cottage gardens that seem to belong more in a Victorian watercolour than in the French countryside.

Lupus' mention of this place may have brought to Æthelwulf's mind his own thoughts of a pilgrimage to Rome as he perused the abbot's request. Indeed, perhaps that had been Lupus' very intention all along.

Whatever Æthelwulf's hopes for visiting Rome, he knew that in 852 the time was not right. The previous few years had seen the political skies darken further with more Viking attacks in Europe, including the sacking of Paris. The Northmen were also at work farther afield and their first raids into Moorish Spain had even prompted an Arab delegation to journey north in an attempt to come to terms with the men they called *Majus* – the fire worshippers. One, no doubt highly exaggerated report even claims that 600 Viking ships were on the Elbe. The air positively rang with Alcuin's proclamation that 'judgment had begun'.

But it was not simply the dangers of travelling through Europe that kept Æthelwulf at home; it was the very real fear that if he left his kingdom it might not survive to see his return. Since the mid 840s his ealdormen in Somerset, Dorset, Kent and Wessex had all faced Viking incursions with varying degrees of success. Only two years before, in 850, the situation had worsened when a Viking army stayed the winter in England for the first time, on the Isle of Thanet in Kent. Thanet was home to one of the most important royal nunneries in England and it had extensive trading links with Francia. As such, it was a wealthy trading centre with suitable facilities for large numbers of ships, yet it was under the control of defenceless nuns – an irresistible temptation for any Viking.

Closer to home, just the previous year Æthelwulf himself had faced their army at Aclea (possibly Ockley) in Surrey. Although he and his son Æthelbald had won a famous victory there – famous enough for it to have come to the attention of Lupus who makes flattering mention of it in his letter to the king – this was only after the Viking horde had stormed Canterbury and seized the important Mercian trading port of London. The increase in the intensity of these attacks was also marked by new types of action, including a naval battle between the ealdorman Ealhhere of Kent and a Viking fleet off Sandwich in which nine Viking ships were captured and the rest put to flight.

No, in the face of ever-increasing attacks and despite these victories, this was certainly not the time for the king to leave his realm. But as Æthelwulf sat at his court in 852 reading the letter from Lupus, his thoughts focused on someone who could make the trip for him, a representative from the House of Ecgberht, whose presence in the Apostolic See could only help both the cause of Wessex and his family. That person perhaps sat near by that day; indeed, his biographer says he was, unusually, kept at court by his parents throughout his childhood. At the time he was just a toddler, a little boy only three years of age, and entirely unaware of the storm building around him. His name was Alfred.

Alfred had been born, in or around 849, into the most important Anglo-Saxon family in England. His father Æthelwulf was king of Wessex and some of his older brothers were already important men in their own right in matters of state. Alfred was the youngest of five children, most of whose ages at the time of his birth can only be gauged through inference. It is likely that his elder siblings were only half-brothers, being born to a previous and unknown wife of Æthelwulf's. The eldest, Æthelstan, had been made sub-king of Kent by his father at the time that the latter took the throne of Wessex in 839, so he must have been at least twenty and possibly thirty years older than Alfred. The next brother down, Æthelbald, also came from a different generation as he too is witnessing charters by the year 841. It is not known how old the children of the king needed to be to witness charters but later Saxon laws give the age at which a man comes into his majority as twelve. In Alfred's day it was very probably at least ten, which would make Æthelbald not less than twenty years older than Alfred. The third brother, Æthelberht, was certainly old enough to take the reins of power temporarily in 855, when Alfred was just six. So again he too seems to come from another generation, as perhaps was Alfred's only sister, Æthelswith, who was married just a year after the letters from Lupus arrived. That left Alfred and one older brother, Æthelred, who were closer in age.

Alfred and Æthelred, according to Asser, were the children of Æthelwulf by his wife Osburh. Osburh is a shadowy character whose only mention in history is her appearance in Asser's biography and even that is only fleeting. The fact she does not appear to be a major player in the events of the day is nevertheless not particularly surprising. Women in royal West Saxon society did not share equal rights with their husbands. Even Alfred, who would become famed for his wisdom and justice, states specifically in his will that he wished his land to pass 'on the spear side and not on the spindle side' – that is, to the male, not the female, line.

This does not mean, however, that women in Anglo-Saxon society as a whole were considered second-class citizens – far from it. Women, especially wealthy women, seem to have had much more power and influence in the Anglo-Saxon period than under later Norman rule, when they were viewed as little more than the possessions of their fathers or husbands. Evidence from wills and charters, as well as the presence of female names in place names, suggests that women took a full role in this society. They were certainly able to acquire their own property and to dispose of it as they saw fit (not as their husband saw fit). As such they had a legal presence in society, which meant that they could bring (and defend) their own legal cases and were considered 'oath-worthy', being able to prove their legal claims by taking an oath supported by their friends and family. This legal existence, very different from the legal invisibility of Norman women, also provided strict penalties for sexual assaults and rape, whether committed against free or enslaved women. These crimes were punished severely and the compensation payable for such an assault was, from Alfred's time at least, paid directly to the woman herself (unless she was a slave), not to her father or husband. Likewise the 'bride-price' – the fee paid by a husband for his wife – went not to her family but directly to the bride herself as did the 'morning-gift', which was paid to her the morning after the consummation of the marriage. Nor was marriage itself an inescapable institution. In the case of fraud, impotence or enslavement on her spouse's part, a woman could have her marriage annulled and whatever its outcome she remained a legally separate entity, bore no responsibility for her husband's actions (unless she was complicit in them) and kept sole control of her own property.

In the monastic world women had also taken a lead and the 'double monasteries' of the seventh and eighth centuries (which contained separate houses for both men and women) were ruled over by abbesses who were not, as in later times, under the spiritual control of men. Judging from their learned correspondence with some of the great academic clerics of the day, they were certainly considered to be some of the best-educated and most literate people in the Anglo-Saxon kingdoms. This acceptance of women as equals in many areas of life even spread into the theology of the day. In the Anglo-Saxon poem known as *Genesis B*, Eve is not portrayed in the usual mediaeval manner as the knowing cause of man's fall from grace but as having been fooled by a heavenly vision that is actually created by the devil. She therefore acts in good faith throughout and hence the stain of 'original sin' is not, for once, laid solely at the door of women.

But if women had power and freedom in much of Anglo-Saxon society, the role of the royal wives of Wessex was particularly limited. Whilst they were recognized as wives, they were certainly not queens. The House of Wessex seemed intent on keeping its women as little more than ciphers and preventing them from wielding any power. Asser attributes this to the ancient custom of the Germanic people, which the Anglo-Saxons had perverted in recent years to their cost. Even he feels the need at this point in his narrative to stop and explain why the wives of kings should not be queens in their own right, and to do this he recounts in some detail an extraordinary story from the not too distant past.

This relates to King Beorhtric of Wessex, the man who had successfully expelled Alfred's grandfather from the kingdom with the aid of the Mercian bretwalda Offa. Offa had sealed their alliance, and the effective submission of Wessex, by marrying his daughter Eadburh to Beorhtric. It also appears that she had used her position not only as wife but as queen to effectively hobble her husband the king – much, no doubt, as Offa wanted. Asser claims that as soon as she gained her royal powers, she set about denouncing those closest to the king and, where such public condemnations failed to produce a result, she resorted to poison. In the end he claims that her attempts to poison one of the king's favourites backfired when the king himself took the poison and promptly died. Unable to stay in Wessex, Eadburh fled across the sea to Charlemagne's court, taking a great deal of the treasure of Wessex with her, of course. Here Asser introduces us to the Solomon-like wisdom of the great Charlemagne, who, he says, asked Eadburh to choose between him and his son, Louis the Pious, for her husband. Eadburh, greedy as ever for power, said that she would take his son because he was younger and Charlemagne replied that, had she asked for Charlemagne himself, she would have married his son, but as she had asked for the son she would have neither of them. Instead she was sent off to become abbess of a nunnery but, true to form, she was caught in flagrante with a Mercian and was expelled by her horrified nuns. She died, so Asser tells us, in poverty and misery on the streets of Pavia, accompanied by only a single slave boy.

Like so much in Asser's biography there is as much allegory here as there is historical truth. Eadburh's husband had been the arch-rival of Ecgberht, Alfred's grandfather, and in explaining the rise of the House of Ecgberht, Asser did no harm to portray this former king as little more than a creature of the great Offa, controlled by the whim of that great king's daughter. In truth the story says little more than that Beorhtric's wife was more powerful than her husband and, as she was the daughter of the bretwalda, this was probably so. The humiliation did not stain Ecgberht's family, however, as they had taken the throne from Beorhtric and hence restored it to its former dignity. In Asser's eyes the kings of Wessex need only beware one thing: giving their wives too much power!

This salutary lesson perhaps goes some way to explaining why Osburh remains so distant a character, a wife and mother but never anything more. Nor, sadly, do we have even a hint of the nature of the relationship between Æthelwulf and his wife. Royal marriages in the ninth and many subsequent centuries were political affairs, not affairs of the heart, and it is hard to recover any intimate moments between kings and their consorts. That is not to say that love did not exist and some marriages proved very long-lasting but there was little room in the sparse accounts of the time to record such things. This was long before the Age of Chivalry and the creation of the Court of Love by kings and nobles with much more time and far fewer problems on their hands. Romance, such as it was, was confined to the poetry of the day, and men in particular were required by this martial society to conceal their feelings. As it says in *The Wife's Lament*:

> Young men must always be serious in mind
> and stout-hearted; they must hide
> their heartache, that host of constant sorrows,
> behind a smiling face.

What we do know of Osburh is what mattered most to writers like Asser. We are told that she came from a noble family, as we might expect, which claimed descent from the line of Stuf and Wihtgar, the legendary Germanic conquerors of the Isle of Wight, who had seized that island from its native British inhabitants many centuries earlier. Her father Oslac is referred to as Æthelwulf's 'famous butler', in fact a very high position at court rather than an apparently subservient one. In the Frankish court the 'Mayor of the Palace', which was perhaps an equivalent position, had been held by Charles Martel, Charlemagne's grandfather, and he had been able to use the position as a launching pad for his dynasty's claim on the throne itself.

Asser says that Osburh had given birth to Alfred at the royal estate of Wantage in Berkshire but quite what the king's wife was doing there remains something of a mystery. We might expect a heavily pregnant Osburh to have retreated to one of the more secure estates in central Wessex for the birth of her child where she, and the baby, could be protected from opportunistic raiders and neighbours. A king's wife and a baby prince would have been worth a king's ransom to a passing Viking warband, and even relations with Mercia were not necessarily always so cordial that risks could be taken with the royal family. But despite this we find her on an exposed estate that stood on the very borders of Wessex and Mercia. Indeed, we know from a charter that Berkshire was still in Mercian hands only five years before Alfred's birth and we have no record of how or why it was transferred to the control of Wessex in the intervening years.

This strange state of affairs has of course been used as evidence that Asser's work is a forgery and that the real writer was unaware that Wantage was, at the time, not in fact under the control of Wessex. However, there is no evidence that the estate had *not* come into the hands of Wessex by this date, and as the child that Osburh carried was not the eldest nor necessarily the heir, perhaps concerns over its safety were not as high as they might otherwise have been. Also, as many mothers can testify, babies are not always born where and when planned, and wherever Osburh found herself at the onset of labour she would undoubtedly have been grateful for the shelter, regardless of its strategic location. Childbirth was a dangerous business in the ninth century, as the low life expectancy of women – around thirty-two years – starkly testifies. Many years later Alfred's own daughter, Æthelflæd, would find the experience so unpleasant that she absolutely refused to sleep with her husband after the birth of their first child, as William of Malmesbury recorded: 'Because of the difficulty experienced in her first, or rather her only labour, she ever afterwards refused the embraces of her husband, protesting that it was unreasonable for the daughter of a king to give way to a pleasure which after a time produced such painful consequences.'

We also perhaps have a hint from Alfred himself that Wantage was his birthplace. In his will he leaves a number of iconic estates – places that had been central to his life and reign – to his wife and amongst them is Wantage. There thus seems no reason not to say that Alfred began his life in Wantage in 849 in the district known as Berkshire, which, so Asser tells us, takes its name from Berroc Wood where the box tree grows abundantly.

Today Wantage is a pretty market town that is still unsure of its precise location, no longer being a part of Berkshire but officially lying in Oxfordshire. As with nearly everything from Alfred's time, nothing remains of the place Alfred knew beyond the changeless hills, rivers and ancient paths that surround the town. But the ghost of Alfred is still here, in the names of a handful of shops and streets and, most visibly, in the statue built to commemorate the thousandth anniversary of his birth but which, due to financial difficulties, was not unveiled until 1877. It shows Alfred through Victorian eyes, in the rough Saxon clothing that they imagined for such people, but marked out from the ordinary by a simple crown. In one hand he holds the battleaxe of a savage age but it is balanced in the other hand by a scroll representing his enlightenment. He stands boldly on a stone plinth on which is carved the legend:

> Alfred found learning dead and he restored it
> Education neglected and he revived it
> The laws powerless and he gave them force
> The church debased and he raised it
> The land ravaged by a fearful enemy from which he delivered it
> Alfred's name will live as long as mankind shall respect the past.

Its sculptor was Count Gleichen, a cousin of Queen Victoria and hence someone who, through some creative genealogy, could himself claim descent from Alfred. But if the count's genealogy was tenuous, at least the people present at Alfred's birth would have understood its value. At that moment all we are told, other than the place, is the genealogy, both real and legendary, of the new addition to the royal House of Wessex. It is an extraordinary list, designed to tie the new arrival into the bloodlines not just of immediate ancestors but of the important characters from both Christian and pagan history and myth. We are told that Alfred is descended from Woden and Geat, from Noah, Methuselah and, inescapably, Adam. Osburh, by contrast, who had just brought him into the world, is not even mentioned by name.

It is just a few years later when Asser allows us briefly to meet Osburh in one single incident from Alfred's childhood – the dimmest of ghosts in a peculiarly faint tale – but it is the closest we can approach to her. We read that the young Alfred was one day in the company of his mother and brothers at court when she produced a small volume of English poetry, which she showed to them. Alfred was transfixed by the illuminated capital letter on the first page and was delighted when she told them that she would give the little book to the first of them to learn it. Alfred, although the youngest, took it and ran off to his tutor with whose help he then learnt the contents. When he was word-perfect he ran back to his mother and recited the poems. She, in fulfillment of her promise, duly gave the volume to him. It is the shortest of anecdotes, yet even in this we can almost see the smile on her face as she hands over the book to the excited child.

But then she is gone. That is the last time we meet Alfred's mother, at the moment of her handing over that book, Alfred's first. Not only do we hear no more of her life, but we are not even told when she died. Indeed, the only evidence of her death is that Æthelwulf remarries. But the ghost of Osburh is not so easily put to rest. Even her presence in this short tale has caused years of heated debate amongst historians. The problem is that, in writing about Osburh and Alfred's childhood, Asser seems to make many mistakes, recording events whose chronology seems unlikely at best and impossible at worst. This incident in particular has often been cited as proof by those who claim Asser's work to be a later forgery.

We know that Osburh must have been dead by the time Alfred was seven as his father remarried that year, but Asser tells us in the previous paragraph that that Alfred 'remained ignorant of letters until his twelfth year, or even longer'. This begs the question: how could an illiterate Alfred read this book and hence win the competition? It also seems unlikely that a competition for a book that would fire the imagination of an infant Alfred would have had much interest for some of his brothers, who were already in their twenties or thirties and one of whom was a king in his own right.

A clue, however, to what really happened that day lies in the lines that follow Asser's strange assertion that Alfred could not read until he was twelve. Immediately below, he says: 'However, he was a careful listener, by day and night, to English poems, most frequently hearing them recited by others, and he readily retained them in his memory.'

There had been a great tradition of oral poetry in Anglo-Saxon England since the earliest times, and poets committed tales to memory long before they were ever written down. Indeed, a number of those poems that survive in written form begin with the word *Hwæt!* – 'listen' – a memory of the shout of the Anglo-Saxon poet or *scop* for quiet across the mead hall before he started his tale. These tales, told in English by professional poets, were at the very centre of an evening's entertainment in Saxon England, and nowhere was that more true than at court. From his earliest years Alfred would have listened to the stories of Beowulf and his fight with Grendel, to the confusing and often bawdy riddles later collected in the *Exeter Book*, to the laments of lost souls caught in the words of *The Seafarer* and *The Wanderer*, and the tales of the days of giants preserved in *The Ruin*. It was stories like these that were written in the book Osburh offered, and in running off to his tutor Alfred was probably simply looking for a reader who could repeat the poems to him again and again until he could recite them from memory. To learn the contents of this book he had no need to be able to read himself.

As for his older brothers and sister, it certainly seems unlikely that many of them would have taken part in such a contest, but there is no reason that Alfred's nearest brother Æthelred, only a few years older than himself and perhaps Osburh's only other son, could not have been there.

Of course there is no way of proving that this little cameo moment from the middle of the ninth century ever really took place beyond taking Asser at his word. The readership that Asser had in mind for his work may well have been the Welsh rather than Alfred and his court, and in showing the king to be precociously bright the story serves its author perfectly, regardless of truth. But it does in fact sit surprisingly well with what the life of a small boy at the Wessex court must have been like at that time. It also explains the origins of Alfred's life-long love affair with books, an affair that would one day shape the future of England. So even if it is only the faintest shadow of the mother that Alfred must, after all, have had, then it is still a shadow worth savouring.

The little else we know of Alfred's childhood also comes largely from Asser. He tells us that Alfred was the best-loved of Æthelwulf's children, as indeed we would expect any royal biographer to say. He also goes on to insist that the young Alfred was brought up entirely in the royal court and suggests that this was unusual in itself. Normally the children of kings and nobles, as well as some from the lower orders of society, do not seem to have spent all their childhood with their parents but were fostered out for long periods to other households. In an age when death might well overtake parents long before their children reached adulthood and where the more kin one had, the better one fared, this made a lot of sense. For the son of a king it also provided a safer and more protected environment in which to grow up. Alfred was different, however, and he stayed at the side of his father.

The court of King Æthelwulf must have been a very strange world for any young boy to inhabit, representing Anglo-Saxon society at its most sophisticated and luxurious. Every entertainment and diversion available to a ninth-century boy would have been found here. Personally Alfred would have owned a few toys such as leather balls, hoops and whipping tops – centuries-old favourites, examples of which have all survived from the Anglo-Saxon period. But there was also a full complement of adult pursuits available to him. We know from written sources that, besides the aristocratic pastimes of hunting and falconry, the wealthy enjoyed dog and horse racing, ice-skating in winter and swimming in summer. In poor weather indoor activities were also available, including board games such as *tafl* – a forerunner of chess with two 'armies' of pieces but only one king – and various dice games. As evening approached the whole household might settle down to enjoy the poems and epic tales of professional *scops*, accompanied by music played on fruitwood harps and pipes carved from the hollow wingbones of swans.

But the court was also a place of relentless work. Whilst Winchester may nominally have been the 'capital' of Wessex, the royal court at this date had no permanent base but travelled around the country from royal estate to royal estate. This wandering existence was not so much due to the restlessness of kings as a necessary part of managing royal property, ensuring that law and order, such as they were, were maintained throughout the realm, as well as keeping a reasonably firm control on those magnates whom the king relied upon to administer his kingdom. It was a gruelling and uncomfortable slog, travelling the old Roman roads and prehistoric trackways of the kingdom. There were no royal carriages in Alfred's day so these journeys would have been undertaken either on the back of the small, stocky horses of the period – more akin to ponies than the horses of today, in wooden carts, or on foot. It was a world permanently either being packed up, unpacked again or on the move. But if the court was a hectic place, it was also a stimulating one, forever filled with petitioners seeking the king's justice and messengers either catching up with the court or rushing on ahead to prepare for the next stop in this never-ending royal progress. Here Alfred could have witnessed the everyday business of kingship – the granting by charter of lands or privileges in return for loyalty, and the delicate negotiations between the kingdoms both in England and beyond with which Wessex dealt.

The major business of state, however, remained war and the main responsibility of any Saxon king and court was the defence of the land and people. Even those in religious orders were not necessarily as meek as the monks of Lindisfarne who so passively met their deaths at Viking hands. The bishop of Sherborne, Ealhstan, was a renowned warrior who had been present at the battle at the mouth of the river Parrett in 845 when the people of Dorset and Somerset defeated a Viking force and 'made a great slaughter'. It was larger-than-life characters such as these who came and went from Æthelwulf's court as it attempted to stem the Viking tide and it was in this very serious and very adult world that the young Alfred found himself at the time the letters from Lupus arrived.

As Æthelwulf sat with Lupus' letter, turning over in his mind the idea of pilgrimage, he must have scanned his court for candidates to undertake the trip on his behalf. Nobles, warriors, even saints were all around him but his eye swept past them all. If he was to send an emissary to the threshold of St Peter's, if he could not travel himself, he would send one of his own. His pilgrim would be his infant son Alfred.

3

The Decimation of Æthelwulf

Faith, Hope and Charity – these are the three anchors which
hold fast the ship of the mind amidst the dangers of the waves.
Alfred the Great, *Angustine's Soliloquies*, in S. Keynes
and M. Lapidge (trans.) *Alfred the Great: Asser's Life of
King Alfred and Other Contemporary Sources* p. 142

THAT ALFRED'S FATHER would even consider sending his son to
Rome seems extraordinary today. The boy was only three,
possibly four years old and the journey was a long one – first over
pirate-infested waters and then across a continent that was plagued by
Vikings to the north and by Saracens to the south, as well as being
regularly rocked by civil wars. But despite all those dangers people did
regularly make the pilgrimage to Rome and had done so for centuries.
To aid the weary pilgrims on this road a number of religious hostels
had been founded by monastic orders, including the cell of St Judoc,
near the trading port of Quentovic, from which Lupus had written.
The monks of Brescia also kept a lodge for pilgrims at Pavia, which
perhaps explains the death of the disgraced Queen Eadburh in the city,
as she may well have been en route to Rome at the time.

For a royal pilgrimage Æthelwulf also expected help from his fellow
rulers, particularly the Carolingian Charles the Bald who, since
agreeing the Treaty of Verdun with his brothers in 843, had been
king of the West Franks. Charles would now be expected to ensure his
son Alfred's safety in Francia and to arrange suitable hospitality there.
Æthelwulf had written to Charles's father asking for safe passage when
he had first taken the throne; now it was time to ask the Carolingians
to make good that promise and protect his son on this most important
of journeys.

And the journey was worth making. For all the warlike array of the Wessex court, the king and his council were devout Christians and in their eyes the very centre of their religion resided in the person of the pope in the Apostolic See in Rome. To them the increasing Viking menace was also viewed in terms of divine retribution, as Alcuin had so eloquently put it. So the presence of penitent royalty on the threshold of St Peter was actually a practical step that constituted a form of spiritual resistance. There were also good political reasons for the journey. Æthelwulf hoped for news from the Carolingian court en route; indeed, he may already have been in negotiation with the Franks about a surprise announcement he was planning. And of course Rome itself was always buzzing with news. The presence of one of his family at the papal court would confirm his dynasty's legitimacy and place them where he wanted them to be, at the centre of European politics, not on its margins.

But why send a little boy? For Alfred's biographer the answer was simple – because Alfred was his father's favourite, a male child already marked out for greatness, and hence the son whom Æthelwulf would want blessed by the pope. The truth, however, may have been harsher and more calculated. Æthelwulf's eldest sons were heavily engaged in matters of state as it was. Æthelstan, the eldest brother, seems to have died sometime between late 851 and 855. Æthelbald was already fighting at his father's side against the Vikings, as he had done at Aclea. His sister Æthelswith was about to marry. Æthelberht, also a grown man, was needed at home, which left only Æthelred and Alfred. The journey was dangerous, the risk high and, as Alfred was the youngest, he was the most expendable. It was a daunting prospect for a four-year-old.

Alfred set out on his journey to Rome in 853 accompanied by a suitable entourage of court officials and a bodyguard. No doubt Æthelwulf's Frankish secretary arranged for an early stop to be made at the cell of St Judoc, where the young prince might have met the famous Lupus and brought word of a gift of lead for the roof at Ferrières. But from the moment they left the shores of Wessex, the pilgrims seem to have escaped the attentions of the few chroniclers recording such trips, at least until they came to Pavia in Lombardy (in what is now northern Italy) and the hostel of St Mary of the Britons, run by the monastery of Brescia. Their success in getting this far also shows, of course, that they had escaped the attentions of the numerous bandits operating on the pilgrimage routes in Francia and Italy.

St Mary of the Britons was one of the major stopovers on the pilgrimage route from England known as the *via francigena*, whose hostels are recorded in a surviving itinerary produced by Archbishop Sigeric, who made the journey to Rome to collect the pallium (the woollen stole that was the archbishop's mark of office) a century after Alfred. From that alone we might infer that the Wessex royal party must have stayed at the hostel but another ancient document kept by the community of Brescia actually brings us closer to the young Alfred. The mediaeval monks there kept an account of travellers who gave their monastery gifts after staying in the Pavia hostel; recorded on this list as an early visitor is the name 'Elfreth' – Alfred. Accompanying him was one 'Ederath', which may be translated as Æthelred, although the lack of mention in other sources of Alfred's brother during this trip suggests that this Æthelred – a common name – was an aristocrat and not Alfred's brother. Equally, since Alfred would one day have good reason to wish to distance himself from his brother and his supporters, writing him out of such an early adventure would ensure that the light of fame shone solely on Alfred himself.

Some of the ancient cities of Europe that the pilgrims passed through must have dazzled the young Alfred, but little could have prepared him for the strange combination of magnificence and decay that was Rome itself. Eight hundred and fifty years had passed since the first emperor Augustus had 'found Rome built of brick and left her clothed in marble', and her face bore the scars of the many misfortunes she had borne since then. After the collapse of Roman power in the West she had been repeatedly sacked by barbarians and just seven years previously the papal suburb itself had been devastated by a Saracen fleet. Yet even amongst the ruins of the old Roman city Alfred must have been in awe. The wreck of the Coliseum still rose many storeys higher than most buildings of the time, and this continues to be true even today. How much more breathtaking must these monuments have appeared to a four-year-old whose life had been lived in single-storey wooden halls. His home was a place where stone buildings were still almost unheard of outside of a few minster churches. Yet here were buildings like the vast concrete dome of the Pantheon, now converted from pagan temple to Christian church and, in Alfred's eyes, surely no less than a work of God.

The pope who welcomed the travellers from England was Leo IV, a man of extraordinary energy who had himself come to power at a time when his city was oppressed by foreign raiders – in this case the Saracens. Leo had begun his pontificate by repairing the defences of the papal suburb, which still lay in ruins after the last Saracen attack, rebuilding eighteen of the city gates and ordering a new wall to enclose the Vatican Hill itself. This last work, paid for with the aid of money from the Emperor Lothar, had only been finished the previous year and the pope was no doubt eager to show the young Alfred the gleaming walls around what would from that time onwards be known as 'The Leonine City'. He was also hard at work in the city itself, restoring churches damaged during the last raid, including St Peter's, although despite his efforts the latter would never recover all its former magnificence.

Then there was the Schola Saxonum – the Saxon School, which was in fact a small quarter of the papal suburb with its own church, St Mary's in Saxia, given over to English visitors and residents in the Holy See. Here Alfred and his entourage must have stayed. This too was in some disrepair following a disastrous fire in 817. Leo must have hoped that the king of Wessex had sent money for its long-overdue restoration and improvement, something Alfred himself would later take very seriously.

Having rested in the Schola Saxonum, the pilgrims had an opportunity to take in some of the sights of the city, which, most importantly for any devout pilgrim, meant the chance to marvel at the thousands of saintly relics, including those of the apostles themselves, gathered in the hundreds of churches. There was even a rudimentary English guidebook written in the eighth century, known as the *Malmesbury Itinerary*, which listed forty of the best churches to visit for their reliquaries. This rather ghoulish devotion to body parts was central to Anglo-Saxon Christian belief. Alfred's trip to Rome may have first kindled his lifelong passion for relics. For him they were a piece of religious history, a direct contact with the stories from the hagiographies and the Bible itself. They were also magical, imbued by God with the power to heal and to bind those who swore oaths over them with a power greater than that of any legal system. And in Rome there were relics very different from the types he had known at home. Most of those brought over to England with the early Christian missionaries were secondary relics – items that had often done nothing more than touch the remains of a saint. Since then, of course, England had produced its own saints and hence provided its own supply of first-class relics, but these home-grown saints were still absent from the Bible stories that Alfred knew. In Rome, the scriptures of the New Testament were made flesh for the young Alfred. Here was the cross on which Christ died, here were the bones of the men and women who knew him, and the hundreds and thousands of saints who followed later and died for him. Nowhere on earth was the connection to God stronger and nowhere else could one meet the direct successor to an apostle: the pope.

Alfred was still little more than a toddler when he was ushered through the cavernous Basilica of St Peter's and into the magnificent presence of Leo IV, successor to St Peter, attired no doubt in his full papal vestments. It was time for the main purpose of the visit, the real reason for all those months of travel and hardship. Asser, and probably Alfred himself in later life, were very clear about what happened next in the Vatican precincts, although perhaps we should not take it at face value. Asser states boldly that 'At this time the lord Pope Leo was ruling the apostolic see; he anointed the child Alfred as king, ordaining him properly, received him as an adoptive son and confirmed him.' That the pope would have anointed this little boy as king of Wessex seems highly unlikely at a time when his father and several elder sons were firmly holding the reins of power with no apparent intention of simply disappearing into the background. The later writer, Ælred of Rievaulx, claimed that Leo IV could see into the future, so he would have known that Alfred was destined for greatness.

However, the real reason for Asser's claim has more do with hindsight than foresight. It would become necessary for Alfred in later life to claim that he had been anointed king, giving him an aura of preordained greatness. To be fair, such coronations were certainly not unheard of. Charlemagne himself had been anointed emperor in Rome on Christmas Day 800 by Pope Leo III; just three years earlier, this same pope had anointed Louis, the current emperor Lothar's son, as co-emperor with him. Perhaps Æthelwulf was hoping to make a similar connection for his son, well aware as he was of the need to gain as much legitimacy as possible for his children if Wessex was to avoid the civil wars that had racked Francia.

Wessex was hardly on a footing with the Carolingian Empire, however, and whilst Leo III's crowning of Charlemagne effectively split temporal and spiritual control of Europe between pope and emperor, there was little for Leo IV in such an alliance with Wessex. Perhaps, mindful of the small boy who undoubtedly stood quaking in his shoes amid the magnificence of St Peter's, a simpler explanation could be put forward: that a four-year-old being confirmed by the pope could be forgiven for thinking that he had been made a king, particularly when years later as a true king he looked back fondly on those long-distant and only half-remembered days.

If Asser and Alfred were confused about what happened that day, the pope certainly was not and in case there might be any doubt he wrote a letter to Æthelwulf in which he explained: 'We have now graciously received your son Alfred, whom you were anxious to send at this time to the threshold of the Holy Apostles, and we have decorated him, as a spiritual son, with the dignity of the belt and vestments of the consulate, as is customary with Roman consuls, because he gave himself into our hands.' The title of Roman consul was archaic and purely ceremonial by this time, being no more than a name, but in presenting his son to the pope, Æthelwulf had received more than a useless title for his son. With the pope as godfather to Alfred, Æthelwulf had made a link of kinship – so important in Saxon society – between Rome and Wessex, between the papacy and the House of Ecgberht. It was a bond that Alfred would feel deeply for the rest of his life.

The Wessex pilgrims did not spend long in Rome, considering the difficulties they had overcome and the distance they had covered to get there. Alfred was back in England by the spring of 854 but despite his relatively short absence much had changed since he had left. Viking attacks had continued to increase. A sortie by the ealdormen Ealhhere of Kent and Huda of Surrey, with their respective local levies, had fought a disastrous engagement against the pagans on Thanet in which both ealdormen had lost their lives. Many of their men were said to have been drowned in the waters of the Swale.

Better news had come from Mercia where the 'B' dynast Burgred had been king since 852. Relations between that kingdom and Wessex were clearly good as, while Alfred had been away, Burgred had appealed to Æthelwulf for help in subjugating the Welsh. Tied into this negotiation was a marriage request and, just after Easter of 853, Alfred's sister Æthelswith was married to Burgred at the royal Wessex estate of Chippenham with all the formal pomp one would expect from a marriage not simply between individuals but between royal houses and, indeed, kingdoms. Burgred reaped the first rewards of this alliance when Æthelwulf and Wessex did answer his call for help and together they subjugated the Welsh, at least for the time being. Of course only time would tell whether Burgred would return the favour and respond in Wessex's hour of need.

Since then nearly a year had passed and the recently returned Alfred, with his parents and three surviving brothers, were spending Easter at Wilton, the settlement on the river Wylye from which Wiltshire gets its name. Beyond its obvious religious significance, the gathering together of a large number of family members and magnates in one place at Easter also made it a time for business. And it was an eclectic and varied group that gathered to quiz the young Alfred about his journey across the sea to Rome.

Prominent amongst them was the clergy, one of the most powerful groups in Anglo-Saxon society, with an obvious interest in news from Rome. The term clergy would have meant a range of things to a West Saxon and in itself implied nothing more than 'not laity'. The religious life in Wessex was highly hierarchical, consisting of two orders. The lower or 'minor' orders consisted of vergers (known as doorkeepers), lectors (who read Biblical lessons), acolytes (who helped at the altar with the Eucharist) and exorcists, who recited prayers to expel malevolent spirits. These roles were given by appointment and the simple act of officially handing a layman the symbols of each office – keys for a verger, a book for a lector, a candlestick and ewer for an acolyte and a pamphlet of exorcisms for the exorcist – granted him that title.

In the upper echelon were the professional clergy of the 'major' orders, divided into deacons, priests and, at the very top, bishops and archbishops. These bishops often controlled extensive Church estates, which made them major magnates in their own right and hence political players at court. But even in their ranks there were stark differences in outlook.

Both ends of the ecclesiastical spectrum were present at Wilton. At the one end stood Ealhstan, the indomitable bishop of Sherborne. As a close family ally, he had been at Æthelwulf's side when he annexed Kent during Ecgberht's conquest of southern England back in 825. He had also come to blows with the Vikings since then and would continue to exchange his pastoral crosier for a sword at every opportunity. Indeed, this formidable character would spend fifty years as bishop, never afraid to back up the word of God with the actions, violent if necessary, of man. With talk of future royal pilgrimages in the air, Ealhstan also had another reason for his interest in Alfred's travellers' tales although he had no intention of showing his hand just yet.

At the other end stood Swithun, the quietly devout bishop of Winchester. He was said by later tradition to travel on foot rather than horseback so as not to appear vainglorious, but equally he was said to always travel at night so that passers-by might not see him and think his walking a sign of false modesty. What is actually known of the life of this obscure prelate is limited to his appearance in a handful of charters and a later, perhaps tenth-century poem, which records that he built a new bridge for the city of Winchester at the east gate. He was of course to gain considerable fame after his death (around 860) as Saint Swithun, rain on whose feast day was said to mark the beginning of forty days of bad weather.

Although the story is simply superstition it bears some relation to the character of the man. The fable grew up when on Saturday, 15 July 971, his body was moved by Bishop Æthelwold from his original and rather unassuming tomb, outside the west door of the Old Minster at Winchester, to a more sumptuous shrine inside. The former bishop was by that time already renowned for his humility and Wulfstan, who wrote a life of Swithun and who was present at the translation of his body, states that a terrible tempest blew up that day, which frightened the monks and rather dampened Æthelwold's plans for the ceremony. Later this storm was taken to be a sign of the humble Swithun's unhappiness at being translated out of his modest tomb and into its new lavish setting in the minster. Eventually the cult of Swithun developed in Winchester until it was said that rain on St Swithun's day would presage another forty days of rain; yet should it remain dry, it would stay so for the forty days that followed.

That of course was legend, but that Easter at Wilton, the living Swithun was very much present, with the talk all of Rome and the news that Alfred had brought back. Clearly what the little boy and others in the entourage told the assembly impressed the king for he soon made the decision, perhaps even that Easter, that the time was finally ripe for his own visit to the Eternal City. But even though Æthelwulf was the undisputed king of Wessex, leaving his kingdom was no casual matter, certainly not when he would have to be away for a year or so.

Even a king as apparently secure as Æthelwulf had to make detailed preparations for such a journey, not so much to guarantee his own safety abroad but to ensure that there would be a kingdom for him to return to afterwards. Although his eldest surviving son was already ruling the eastern provinces of his kingdom, it was by no means a certainty that the witan would accept him, or any other of Æthelwulf's children, as their next king. The ruler's absence abroad could provide an ideal opportunity for other powerful families to make bids for the throne, even assuming that the king's own children did not attempt to usurp him themselves.

Æthelwulf was, of course, aware of how his own father had secured the throne for him – through bribery – and so he lit upon the old Saxon habit of gift-giving with an eye to ensuring the peace whilst he was away. And he went about it in the most extraordinary way.

Tracking the political manoeuvrings of an Anglo-Saxon king is a precarious business, not least because the documentary records that survive from such a distant era are themselves not always what they seem. Much of the domestic policy of kings from this and many later periods is gleaned through studying the charters drawn up by them – documents that record grants of land and privileges agreed between individuals and organizations. Traditionally, particularly in the case of land grants, two copies of such documents would be made, one for the records of the grantor – such as the king – and one for the records of the receiver of the grant. In the case of mediaeval monasteries, which were perhaps the largest receivers of land, these charters were in effect title deeds, recording as they did the gifts of kings and magnates, which might often later be disputed were it not for the presence of such clear and legally binding documents. But these valuable pieces of vellum or parchment were fragile; damp, mice, insects and neglect could all take their toll in the end. It was therefore usual for monasteries to copy out charters into large books known as cartularies for safe keeping, but it was during this process that documents could become something other than what was first intended.

For all their profession of piety such a practice posed a terrible temptation for any scriptorium monk. As they copied out often ancient charters that granted land to their monasteries, it would be so easy for them to add clauses, increase the size of the gift, reduce the obligations attached, or even just create whole new grants. In short, there was the opportunity for forgery and the monks often took it. Very few charters from the Anglo-Saxon period exist in their original form, but instead are later copies (and copies of copies, often many times over), each, any and all of which might have forged parts. As a result all have to be treated with a high degree of scepticism. Such is the case with a group of documents that were probably originally produced that Easter at Wilton by Æthelwulf, but which have since suffered many subtle, and not so subtle, changes.

What Æthelwulf began that spring and continued into the following year was, if the charters are to be believed, the most extraordinary act of largesse, or perhaps bribery, ever performed by an Anglo-Saxon king. According to a charter in the Abingdon cartulary, the king issued a general privilege in which he granted a tenth of all his lands to the Church. The scribe duly noted the granting of this tithe with the word *decimationem* – a late Latin term for the removal or destruction of a tenth. Henceforth the grant would be known as 'The Decimation of Æthelwulf'. He also extended this gift to include some of his secular lords, as his charter to his thegn Dunn suggests: 'I, Æthelwulf, king of the West Saxons and also of the people of Kent, on account of the tithing of land which, by the gift of God, I have decided to do for some of my thegns, I will give you, Dunn, my thegn, one dwelling . . .' Æthelwulf was attempting to buy off the entire country, both religious and secular, with grants of land prior to his going, as it says in the same charter, 'beyond the sea to Rome'.

The problem with this 'decimation' is that it simply provided an opportunity too good to miss for any monk employed in copying out, and perhaps embroidering, his monastery's cartulary. The decimation was recorded in the *Anglo-Saxon Chronicle*, so knowledge of it was freely available to monks years, and sometimes centuries, later. If unable to find a charter relating to the decimation in their own records, the monks could always invent one to ensure that they got their share. The Abingdon and many other charters are almost certainly later forgeries. What is less clear is the degree to which they were based on genuine originals and precisely what those originals gave away.

But regardless of the original size of the gift, the mention of it in the *Anglo-Saxon Chronicle*, and the survival of some reasonably genuine charters such as the one in favour of Dunn, do suggest that Æthelwulf was indeed buying time for his trip to Rome. The question would be: had he bought enough?

Æthelwulf had to settle one other important matter before he could undertake his pilgrimage. Who was to rule in his place? The decision he came to was based, not surprisingly, on the division of power that his father Ecgberht had made with him, where the elder had governed Wessex proper and the younger had ruled the eastern provinces. So it was decided that Æthelbald, now his eldest surviving son, would rule Wessex, whilst the younger Æthelberht would take control of the eastern provinces of Kent, Surrey, Essex and Sussex. Æthelwulf was now free to set out across the sea to Rome, taking with him another, now seasoned traveller, his little son Alfred.

Being accompanied by his father the king would make this a somewhat different experience from Alfred's previous journey. Travelling with a reigning monarch, however minor, required a certain level of pomp, on the part of the pilgrims as well as the royal courts they visited en route. But there was also to be considerably more to this journey than just a sightseeing trip. They began the journey as before, enjoying the hospitality of Lupus at the cell of St Judoc before heading to the court of Charles the Bald. Here final preparations were made for an extraordinary announcement to be made on Æthelwulf's return. Then Charles himself escorted the king to the edge of his territory where he handed over his safe keeping, no doubt with some trepidation, to his quarrelsome brother, the Emperor Lothar. The party was now joined by a veteran of the pilgrimage route, Markward, the former abbot of Prüm who had also previously been a monk at Lupus' monastery of Ferrières. He was appointed by Charles as a guide for the royal party, particularly for the dangerous journey into northern Italy, where even the protection of the sons of Louis the Pious could not guarantee their safety.

Markward certainly seems to have done his job well and the pilgrims are next found safely in St Mary of the Britons in Pavia where, once again, the monks who ran the hostel recorded a generous benefaction from Æthelwulf and his son Alfred. From there the pilgrimage route wound through Piacenza to Lucca, San Gimignano and Siena, Bolsena, Montefiascone, Viterbo, Sutri and finally to Rome. Passing through the gates of the Leonine City the party no doubt made their way with a suitable papal guard of honour to the Schola Saxonum and the church of St Mary's in Saxia to give thanks for their safe arrival. The sight of the new pilgrimage hostels and church in the Anglo-Saxon quarter would have been pleasing to Æthelwulf, who had probably sent money to help finance its rebuilding two years before. For Alfred it was perhaps a stranger prospect. Since his previous visit the pope had issued a bull entirely reorganizing the quarter as a pseudo-monastic community, which must have transformed it from its previous state of devastation evident on Alfred's earlier visit, following the terrible fire of 817 and the Saracen attack of 846. Leo IV had had prior warning that Æthelwulf was coming and had put his Saxon house in order.

But Leo, Alfred's godfather and a man who must have made an extraordinary impression on Alfred on his first visit to Rome, was not there to welcome his godson. When the West Saxon royal party reached the precincts of the Vatican, the first news they received was that the pope had died on 17 June that year. This was a blow for Æthelwulf, as through his son he had hoped to foster a link with the papacy. It was also undoubtedly another bereavement for the young Alfred who, as we can surmise from subsequent events, had only recently lost his mother Osburh.

The death of Leo had repercussions for another royal family – that of the Emperor Lothar. Even since the coronation of his grandfather Charlemagne, the Carolingians and the papacy had maintained a tacit agreement to divide the temporal and spiritual overlordship of Christian Europe between them. A major part of making this work was the unwritten arrangement that the emperor would have a major, in fact a deciding, say in the election of new popes. On the death of Leo, however, the people and clergy of Rome had selected one Benedict as their new pontiff without reference to Lothar. In furious retribution, Lothar had appointed an antipope, Anastasius. The two sides appeared set for conflict.

Papal legates were formally dispatched to Lothar with the news of the election of Benedict but when they returned it was with Lothar's own choice, Anastasius, in tow. Immediately taking control of the Lateran Palace, the antipope ordered Benedict arrested and stripped of his papal vestments. As tensions in the city rose to breaking point, Anastasius was declared excommunicated by Benedict's supporters and fights began to break out between the two factions. With mobs rioting in the streets the legates finally agreed a compromise and arrangements were made for new elections in which both candidates would stand. If Lothar hoped that the presence of his nominee in the Lateran Palace would sway the opinions of the Romans, however, he was sorely mistaken. When the election results came in, there was another overwhelming vote for Benedict. Aware of the hopelessness of the situation, the Frankish envoys of Lothar finally gave way. Benedict was returned as the elected pope and crowned in September of 855. It is said that Lothar died on the very day of the coronation, his impending demise presaged by two shooting stars.

Watching the all too bloody power politics of Carolingian Europe must have been instructive to both Æthelwulf and his son. It was clear now that the spiritual and secular overlordship of Europe would not fall under the control of the sons of Louis the Pious and that cultivating the friendship of the pope might prove more fruitful. It was perhaps with this in mind that the Wessex pilgrims eagerly handed over the treasures that they had intended for Leo to his successor, now Benedict III. The *Liber Pontificalis* records the pope receiving a golden crown weighing four pounds, a golden goblet, a gilded candlestick, an inlaid sword and a number of costly religious robes, including one dyed imperial purple and embossed with golden keys. Having witnessed at first hand the power of the Roman mob, Æthelwulf wisely took his munificence beyond the environs of the papal court, scattering gold and silver coins to the crowd outside.

In all, Æthelwulf and Alfred spent a year in Rome. In part this was because the devout king wished to visit the hundreds of religious shrines in the city, but it was also partly due to the bloody ructions of the papal succession, during which they must have waited with bated breath in the Schola Saxonum for news of the outcome of the power struggle between emperor and pope.

It is during this strange year for the young Alfred that a singular tale has been placed. Mediaeval traditions held that after the death of Leo IV another pope had been quickly elected, who took the title John Anglicus. His reign was to be short, however. During an Easter procession between St Peter's and the Lateran Palace, an excitable crowd accidentally pushed the pontiff from his horse. The shock of the fall brought on premature labour and 'John' promptly gave birth to a baby. John was in fact Joan – a woman – and an English woman at that, who had usurped the papacy by dressing as a man. Her undoing had been her failure to remain chaste. With her shameless secret revealed, the crowd expressed their horror. They dragged her through the streets of Rome tied to a horse and then stoned her to death, thus making their opinion of female popes abundantly clear.

The story is, of course, entirely fictional and probably dates from a later mediaeval conflict between the Holy Roman Empire and the papacy where it probably served as an imperial satire on the popes. But within the story there might be just a hint of a memory of the damaging events of 855 when empire and papacy first clashed. Possibly – in the insistence that Joan was herself English – there is even a confused memory of the presence in the city that year of an important party of pilgrims from England, a party that included Alfred.

It was 856 by the time Æthelwulf and Alfred finally bade their farewells to the now safely ensconced Benedict III and headed north across the Alps towards Francia. Although the most difficult and dangerous part of the journey lay behind them, the king's greatest gamble has yet to come. On their arrival back at the court of Charles the Bald, then at his palace at Verberie-sur-Oise, the other great purpose for Æthelwulf's pilgrimage could now be brought to fruition.

Charles had a daughter, Judith, then just a girl of twelve or thirteen years, but old enough to play her part in the politics of Europe. After what must have been protracted negotiations, dating back to Alfred's first visit or earlier, she was to be married, and her husband was to be none other than the fifty-year-old widower Æthelwulf himself.

Since the death of Alfred's mother Osburh sometime in the preceding few years, the king of Wessex had been free to marry again and, as any king knew, this was an occasion where love came a poor second to politics. The opportunity to marry into the Carolingian royal house still held enormous kudos, despite the fragmentation of that empire. Æthelwulf must have been aware that the great Offa himself had once petitioned Charlemagne for his daughter's hand in marriage but had received for his troubles not a bride but a trade embargo from the affronted emperor. Now the House of Ecgberht was to succeed where even the Mercian bretwalda had failed. This would prove to be only the second time that an Anglo-Saxon king married into continental royalty. It would also prove to be the last.

If this was a political triumph, it also came at a considerable cost and with no small element of risk. Choosing a Carolingian bride was a far more serious business than marrying the daughter of a member of your own aristocracy. Charles the Bald had bargaining power and he intended to use it on Judith's behalf, both to further his own political aims and to preserve the dignity of his family name. Æthelwulf would no doubt gain trading benefits for Wessex and might perhaps forge an alliance against the Vikings in the process, but in return he would be asked for something that only recently had been unthinkable.

The full impact of this implication would only hit the Wessex pilgrims as they watched the marriage ceremony at Verberie on Thursday, 1 October 856. The scale and grandeur of their surroundings alone were beyond the comprehension of most West Saxons. The palace that Charlemagne had built, where the forest of Compiègne runs down to the banks of the river Oise, was simply magnificent. It was approached through acres of terraced gardens, criss-crossed with canals and studded with lakes. The building itself stretched some 1,386 feet, protected on all sides by round stone towers, its walls carved with bas-reliefs and its pediments topped with huge statues. Inside, Charles the Bald's guests walked on marble mosaics and rested on gilded furniture.

In this setting Charles now unleashed the full, formal pomp and majesty of the Carolingian court, presided over by the imposing archbishop of Rheims, Hincmar, who intoned the service of marriage that joined the royal houses. But the service did not end with the marriage vows and the Mass. Many amongst the party from Wessex must have looked on uneasily as Hincmar then proceeded to begin a formal *ordo* of coronation. As he called on God to purify and strengthen the young girl who sat before him, he told his audience that God had chosen Judith not just to be Æthelwulf's consort but to rule with him. Then with the words, 'May the Lord crown you,' he anointed her head with the holy chrism, an unction made of balsam and olive oil. As the chrism touched her, so, in ninth-century minds, did Judith's status change for ever. She was now ordained by God and a queen but of a country where no such role was recognized.

Charles, of course, would have nothing less in rank for a daughter of the Carolingians, but Æthelwulf was taking a serious risk. As Asser was at great pains to point out, kings of Wessex did not make their wives into queens ever since the terrible episode with Eadburh. Similarly the guests from Wessex knew that, whilst their people would welcome the return of their king with a wife, they would not take so kindly to his returning with a queen. But as the words, 'May the Lord crown you,' rose again in the church and Hincmar placed a crown on Judith's head, all they could do was hope that the West Saxons would learn to live with it.

It was mid-October by the time the king, his new queen and her stepson Alfred reached the Channel. Alfred's concerns were childishly simple. His mother was dead but the relentless politics of royal life had moved on and he now found himself with a second and foreign mother who was only five or six years older than himself. For Judith, the prospect of a journey over the sea to an unknown and certainly more primitive home must have been an equally daunting prospect. She would have to adapt to rougher ways and learn a new language, hardships that were only tempered by the thought that she would at least have some Frankish friends amongst her immediate entourage including her husband's secretary Felix. He would no doubt report her progress back to her father. For Æthelwulf, the problems were starker still.

Word must have reached Wessex of the marriage and the coronation not long after they took place. Despite the difficulty of communications throughout Francia, trade continued and news travelled fast. Similarly, Æthelwulf may well have had tidings from Wessex as he stood on the Channel coast, awaiting fair weather for the crossing home. Indeed, to even attempt to cross the Channel that late in the year implies that he knew he had to return whatever the risk, and quickly.

For once the Channel proved calm, despite the season, and Æthelwulf and his entourage crossed safely. In fact, the waters of the Channel would prove calmer than the land of Wessex to which they had returned. As he stepped ashore on the south coast, what awaited him was as potentially damaging, both to his house and his country, as the years of infighting that had plagued the European family into which he had just married. Æthelwulf was walking on to his own Field of Lies, a bitter wedding gift from the turbulent Carolingians.

In his absence, Asser tells us, the son whom Æthelwulf had left in charge of his kingdom had rebelled, aided by the ealdorman of Somerset and the redoubtable Bishop Ealhstan of Sherborne. Æthelbald now held the throne of Wessex and he had no intention of returning it to his father. Since he was supported by some of the most powerful figures in both Church and State, it seemed that there was little the old king could do. The Decimation of Æthelwulf had failed.

The reasons for the rebellion were many. Certainly the arrival of a queen amongst the people of Wessex provided a catalyst for the coup as this was expressly against the customs of Wessex. But this was purely an excuse and the real reasons were far more prosaic and practical, if painful. Æthelwulf had been seventeen years on the throne and at fifty was an old man by the standards of his day, in an era that valued the ability of a ruler to physically protect the kingdom he ruled. Thanks to the Vikings these were dangerous times in Wessex, as both the ealdorman of Somerset and Bishop Ealhstan had seen at first hand, and there must have been growing doubts as to an old king's ability to defend his nation from them. In the minds of his people, it was perhaps time for him to step aside in favour of a younger and more vigorous son who had proved his mettle in battle at Aclea and who had now, during Æthelwulf's absence abroad, clearly been capable of ruling his kingdom as well.

Æthelbald himself must also have seen that his time had come. He was well aware of the fact that he had not been entrusted with the whole of his father's kingdom (his brother Æthelberht had been given the rule of Kent, Surrey, Essex and Sussex) and he must have wondered whether he would ever enjoy the complete rule that his father and grandfather had enjoyed before him. Now at least he had greater Wessex in his grasp and he could hardly be blamed for wanting to retain his hold on it. Then there was a more pressing matter arising from his father's marriage. Æthelwulf may have been old but he was still capable of fathering children and his bride still had her whole reproductive life ahead of her. Æthelbald was aware of the dangers presented by any further children born to Æthelwulf, as an example of what might happen was still bitterly evident across the Channel in Francia. It was, after all, because of the late arrival of Louis the Pious's last son Charles – the man whose daughter had now married his father – that the Carolingian Empire had fragmented and descended into civil war. He could not allow that to happen to Wessex as well.

That Wessex did not at this point collapse into the sort of chaos that bedevilled the continent was put down by Asser to the 'indescribable forbearance' of Æthelwulf but between the lines of his protestations the realpolitik of the situation can still be glimpsed. Asser tells us that on the king's return: 'the entire nation was so delighted (as was fitting) at the arrival of their lord that, had he allowed it, they would have been willing to eject his grasping son Æthelbald from his share of the whole kingdom, along with all his councillors.' This was clearly not the case, however, for we then hear that Æthelwulf agreed to leave Wessex proper in the hands of Æthelbald, whilst his younger brother Æthelberht dutifully handed back to his father the eastern provinces that had been in his care. Æthelwulf was still in overall charge, according to Asser, but clearly he had, in fact, been deposed from the main seat of power and given a subsidiary kingdom as a sop. War had been avoided, Wessex was not subject to a foreign queen, and a younger and more vigorous son of the House of Ecgberht held the main reins of power. Æthelwulf would have to content himself in the role in which he had begun his regal career under his father, as ruler of the eastern and less important provinces. It was also a snub for Judith, so recently fêted as queen in the marble halls of Verberie-sur-Oise, but queen of a country whose greater part she would never rule.

The events that he had seen on the continent and now in England had a lasting effect on the young Alfred. The apparently immovable solidity of personal power seemed everywhere to have been shown up as little more than a mirage. He had witnessed the sordid human reality of the selection of the man he was told was the heir of St Peter; he had seen the machinations of the sons of Louis the Pious; and he had surveyed the remnants of the once great and unified empire that their grandfather had forged. Back at home he sat in the court of his father, the law-giver, seeing him swept aside by the ambitions of his sons with the connivance of his subjects. It was a realization of the fragility of power that would affect the rest of Alfred's life. Many years later as he sat down to translate Boethius' *The Consolation of Philosophy*, memories of this and later betrayals must have come back as he translated the Lady Philosophy's thoughts on the nature of kingship:

> Yea, kings may rule over many peoples, yet they do not rule all those that they would wish to rule, but are miserable in their mind because they cannot come by all they would have . . . it was for this that a king who in old times unjustly seized the kingdom said, 'Oh, how happy the man over whose head no naked sword hangs by a fine thread, as it has ever been hanging over mine!'

Whilst Alfred was learning the lessons of kingship young, his father was still in danger of giving that inheritance away. Sometime after his return from Rome, during the last two years of his life, Æthelwulf began to draw up his will. The original document no longer exists but Asser mentions it, saying: 'In this document he took care to have properly committed to writing a division of the kingdom between his sons (namely the two eldest).' In this will, Æthelwulf was apparently making plans for the entire kingdom of Wessex, perhaps indicating that in this, at least, his sons still deferred to him. Equally it might simply indicate how Alfred in later years wanted his betrayed father remembered – as a king of Wessex in its entirety.

Clearly, however, the old king perceived the division of Wessex into eastern and western halves as permanent. He very conspicuously did not bequeath his remaining kingdom in the east to Æthelbald, his rebellious son. Perhaps this was out of respect for Æthelberht, who had stood aside for him on his return; perhaps it was to prevent the ungrateful Æthelbald from ever claiming rule over the whole nation that he and his father had once ruled. Instead he intended that the loyal Æthelberht should found his own dynasty in the eastern provinces with his children as heirs, whilst Æthelwulf's other sons would have to contend for control of Wessex proper, each in their turn. Had this division survived, the process of fragmentation that had led to wars in the Carolingian Empire might have torn Wessex apart too. Alfred, by the time he was old enough to rule, might have only ever become king of a county or two if, indeed, he had ever become even that. The whole process of consolidation and growth amongst the kingdoms of Saxon England would have been put into reverse and their future, in the face of an organized and concerted Viking attack, might have been very different.

Fortunately, Æthelwulf's will was not done, at least in this respect — assuming that any of his sons took such a document seriously in the first place. A better testimony for Æthelwulf lies in the description of a more modest bequest he made, a bequest that he could actually fulfil. Asser tells us that 'he enjoined on his successors after him, right up to the final Day of Judgment, that for every ten hides [one "hide" being a tax assessment equivalent to a notional 120 acres of land] throughout all his hereditary land one poor man (whether native or foreigner) should be sustained with food, drink and clothing.' It was a considerably smaller 'decimation' than the one with which he had begun his Roman odyssey, but it speaks of the old king's concern for his people, which had not deserted him despite his ill fortunes. It is an attitude that seems to have deeply affected his little son Alfred, who on a cold January day in 858, still only nine years old, watched the stone grave-slab being hauled over his father's tomb at his small estate of Steyning in Sussex. Alfred was now in his brother's hands.

4

Legends of the North

DURING THE YEARS of feuding amongst the royal families of
Europe, the Viking threat had not gone away. Indeed, it had
grown and, thanks to the efforts of the Frankish and Irish chroniclers,
it had even gained a name. The threat from the Northmen had
condensed into a person, part man and part legend, and that person
was Ragnar Lothbrok.

He is the first real Viking personality to emerge from the hazy
accounts of the period but in many ways he still belongs more in the
fable-filled pages of the sagas than amongst the sober entries in the
chronicles. That there even was an individual called Ragnar is still a
matter of some debate, due not least to the eagerness of contemporary
writers to kill him off – something that is dutifully recorded a number
of times, on a number of dates and accompanied by a number of
different reasons.

He first sails out of the realm of Norse mythology and into
something like history in 845, the year that Bishop Ealhstan was
fighting Vikings on the river Parrett. At that time a leader of this name,
or perhaps the similar-sounding 'Ragnall', is recorded as leading a fleet
of 120 ships up the Seine to besiege Paris. Here, in one account, his
men were beset with a plague of heaven-sent dysentery and, so the
annalists would have it, Ragnar himself succumbed, thus marking the
beginning and ending of his career in a single event.

The problem is that Ragnar then crops up again and again over the next decade, prowling the seas off the coast of Scotland and the Western Isles, before apparently settling in Viking Dublin. Here he once more met his death, around 852, at the hands of other Scandinavians, either in battle or tortured to death depending on which traditional tale you read. He is recorded dying again at Carlingford Lough at the hands of rivals, then again during a raid on Anglesey, and finally in Northumbria where he was said to have been thrown into a pit of venomous snakes.

Clearly no one man, not even a Viking hero, could die that many times and doubts must be raised as to which, if any, of these Ragnars were the same person and which of those were real. To put any flesh on the oft-buried bones of the Ragnar of the annalists, we are forced to turn to what later Scandinavian poets recorded in the *Saga of Ragnar* and *The Tale of the Sons of Ragnar*. These are not history in a modern sense, of course, but the dramatic, fictionalized stories of long-dead heroes whose connection to reality might be little more than a name, that essential hook that allowed poets not only to tell a wonderful tale, but also to claim in hushed tones that it was true too. Theirs is a Ragnar who killed a ferocious dragon and hence won the hand of a beautiful maiden; he is a hero not a villain; and his sons are, as the runic graffiti claim in the chamber tomb of Maes Howe on Orkney, 'what you would really call men'.

That these early pirates should become folk heroes is not as surprising as it might at first seem. The currency of the emerging Viking leaders was not bullion but fame. To command a great army, a Viking leader needed fame: fame to bring men to his side, fame to persuade them to follow him to danger and perhaps death, and fame to put fear in the hearts of his enemies and his rivals. Reputation could make or break Scandinavian warlords, and tales of their achievements were vital to their success. No doubt these were often greatly exaggerated even at the time and then further embroidered with each retelling, so that by the time we reach the era of the saga writers such leaders had often become impossibly heroic. And of all these heroes the archetype was Ragnar. It is only to be expected that many who followed would be called 'Sons of Ragnar', a title that was often as much of a mark of honour or aspiration as a statement of genetic fact.

The appearance of these early Viking heroes across the seaboards of northern Europe also betrays something of the nature of the threat they presented. These bands were highly mobile mariners, using the seas and rivers to launch lightning raids. Targeting coastal settlements was effective as it made predicting their landfall extremely difficult thus forcing defenders to spread their forces more thinly than they would have liked. But it was really Viking riverine expeditions that showed this new enemy at their best. With Europe and England still split into many competing kingdoms and principalities, the great rivers often formed boundaries between states – and were formidable barriers between peoples. To Vikings, however, they were quite the reverse: highways, up which their shallow-draughted vessels could sail, taking their threat into political heartlands and, with different kingdoms often on each bank, splitting the defenders' forces and loyalties. Many a petty kingdom gloated when a Viking force rowed up their river to disembark on the opposite, 'foreign' bank. Their joy was usually short-lived, however. Viking fleets were also highly responsive to the changing situation that their presence brought about. When one area looked ripe for raiding, Ragnar and his like could make up a fleet of whichever mercenaries and pirates came to hand, and quickly head for the new prey. Equally, when an area became impoverished through raiding or was made dangerous by more organized defences, they could melt away back to sea, only to appear again later in richer and more vulnerable places.

If Ragnar represents the first semi-mythical generation of pirate kings, those of the second generation who emerge around the time of Æthelwulf's death are somewhat clearer and more real. In the outlines of two in particular we can at last in part disentangle from later legends the careers of real Viking warlords. These are the first Vikings to step clear of the initial hysteria of the monastic chronicles, obsessed as they were with the arrival of divine vengeance and the terrible desecrations of the pagans. And what is interesting is that they are not simply black-hearted pirates, not just personifications of the Final Judgment, but ruthless and practical players in a game of power politics in which Christian kings were also happy, or at least willing, to indulge.

A career that perhaps best displays the culpability of the Christian West in the nurturing of the Viking menace is that of Weland. According to Prudentius of Troyes, Weland had first appeared around

859 on the banks of the river Somme where he made camp with his warband. It is not known where he had come from nor how he had risen to lead this particular army. But arrive he had. The appearance of this sizeable Viking force in Charles the Bald's empire came at a very bad time for the emperor, who was even then considering what to do about another pagan force encamped on the island of Oissel in the Seine, a base from where the Northmen threatened Paris itself.

Charles did not look like a man in control of the situation. Not only was he threatened by Vikings on two fronts but he was increasingly afraid of his own people. When a group of peasants between the Seine and the Loire formed their own confederation to attack the Vikings (having despaired of his help), the Carolingian seems to have taken fright at this co-operative army and sent his own troops against it. Prudentius of Troyes notes coldly: 'But because their association had been made without due consideration, they were easily slain by our more powerful people.' Bizarrely, Charles was not only attacking his own subjects, but those who were having the most success against his real enemy. Clearly as frightened of his own ranks as of the Vikings, and perhaps thinking he could set a thief to catch a thief, he decided to engage in a very dangerous game. He would play the two forces off against each other, offering to employ Weland's men to besiege and dislodge the Oissel Vikings. Like any good mercenary band, Weland and his men agreed to this, in return for 3000 pounds of pure silver (around 880,000 silver pennies, worth), to be weighed out, as Vikings always insisted, using their own scales and under their own supervision. Vikings were always good businessmen.

Charles, however, did not have this sum of money to hand; indeed, it would take him some considerable time to raise it via taxation, levies on Church treasures and tolls on merchants. In response Weland, not a man to be kept waiting, headed not for Oissel but for the Channel coast where he took hostages from the Franks (to ensure that Charles continued with his revenue raising) before setting off for further plunder in England. The removal of Weland's force to England may have provided some respite for Charles, but it also set the pattern for Viking raiding whereby England's loss was Francia's gain and vice versa. Weland, however, would be back.

In fact the Somme Vikings found England somewhat better prepared to repel their attacks than their Frankish neighbours. Landing in Hampshire, Weland attacked and sacked Winchester before any large-scale resistance could be mounted, no doubt to the dismay of the ageing Bishop Swithun. A wiser Viking might then have returned to sea, ready to strike again along the coast, but Weland, no doubt spurred on by such an easy success, headed farther inland, giving the ealdormen of Hampshire and Berkshire time to raise the county levies. Vikings were rarely successful when separated by too much distance from their ships. As they headed back to the Hampshire coast, laden with booty from what had apparently been an easy raid, they were intercepted by the combined armies of Hampshire and Berkshire and were routed. Asser noted with barely concealed glee that 'the Vikings were cut down everywhere and when they could resist no longer, they took to flight like women, and the Christians were masters of the battlefield.'

But this particular warband was not finished yet. Weland and his men managed to reach their ships and sail back to Francia, although without much of their loot. Here they finally received Charles's payment, which went a long way to making good the loss and, true to their word, they laid siege to the Oissel Vikings. Of course in the intervening period the Oissel Vikings had also been busy. Indeed, much as Charles had feared, they had sacked Paris, but with his own mercenary Viking force in England, he had proved powerless to stop them. Now, to the howls of the monastic chroniclers, he had to watch his 'ally' Weland's fleet of perhaps two hundred ships, reinforced by another newly arrived warband of some sixty more, sail up the Seine to besiege another group of Vikings – and just hope that the victor would then persuade the loser to leave his kingdom in peace. To make matters worse, while the siege continued Charles was also forced to provide Weland and his men with food and money to prevent them from simply looting the surrounding countryside. Prudentius of Troyes was not impressed with Charles's strategy, moodily noting in his annal the total cost – another 4,850 pounds of silver, which was considerably more than Weland's initial fee. With friends like these Charles hardly needed enemies.

Weland, for his part, continued to do well from the deal. The siege soon left the Oissel Vikings starving and disease ridden, forcing them to come to terms. He now managed to extract a further 6,000 pounds of gold and silver out of *them* in return for their release. This bullion had, of course, probably been taken from the Franks in the first place when they had sacked Paris, so Weland was profiting from Charles on both sides. Nor was Charles's luck about to improve as, to his utter consternation, the first thing that the Oissel Vikings then did on their release was to join up with Weland. With winter approaching fast, there was no chance that this enlarged army would sail back to Scandinavia so Charles was forced to allow it to split up into small bands and hope that these would not inflict too much damage on the region around the Seine basin. Perhaps the only comfort for Charles was that one of these Viking bands chose that winter to sack Meaux where his truculent but weak son Louis the Stammerer was staying. Louis, for his part, may even have believed that the attack on his stronghold was orchestrated by his father as a shot across his bows. Charles certainly needed to keep his rebellious family in check, but if he was doing this using Viking armies, he was playing with a weapon he could barely hope to control and which was just as likely to blow up in his face.

In fact by the following year Charles does seem to have changed tack, finally tiring of attempting to deal with his slippery allies. That spring he raised armies to take positions on the Oise, Seine and Marne, threatening the Viking escape routes to the sea. At the same time he also began work at Pont de-l'Arch, downstream from Pîtres, creating a fortified bridge crossing. As it controlled the river, it effectively gave him the power to open and close it as he saw fit. In response the Somme and Oissel Vikings, who were no fools and wanted money much more than they wanted a fight, finally agreed to leave his territory and seek out other places to harass. They did not, of course, have to look far.

Now Weland's luck ran out and we find him in 863 at the court of Charles, for reasons that will become clear. In the face of this unusual turn of events Weland remained unflustered, returning the hostages he had taken before the Winchester expedition and doing fealty to the king as his overlord. He then promised to quit the kingdom and, to seal the deal, offered himself, his wife and his children for baptism.

It was this that was his undoing, not at the hands of the apparently triumphant Charles, but, like a true pirate, at those of his crew. It seems that by the time he had offered himself up as a supplicant to Charles, he had already been replaced as the leader of his warband and thus may have found himself politically cornered. His life as a pirate king may seem romantic from the outside but his restless Channel crossing and desperate desire for loot during his tenure as their chief hints at the true nature of the life of a Viking leader. What kept his men together and maintained his position as their leader was his ability to bring home the loot month after month, year after year. Within a limited field of operations he had to weigh up the relative benefits of taking pay from different European dynasts in their wars with other Vikings as well as with each other, or looting their territories as Vikings themselves. With each raid, of course, the situation changed; old enemies became allies, allies became enemies. Weland had to balance this against the relative risks to his men from attacks against increasingly prepared defenders and the risk to his own position from not delivering the booty.

He had played a dangerous game and when the money dried up his mercenary force was more than happy to dispense with his services. This is how Weland found himself kneeling at the feet of his only remaining 'ally' Charles. It was a practical move by a practical man, playing the Christian game of fealty to win protection and support. It naturally required that he accept baptism as a Christian himself, but this was not something that usually bothered Viking leaders; indeed, some converted (and then apostatized) many times, depending on the direction that the political wind was blowing.

But Weland had converted for the last time. Strangely, perhaps aptly, it was not the cynical Carolingian court that branded Weland a hypocrite, nor his new Christian godfathers who marked him out as a liar and his conversion as a sham, but one of his own. Several of his crew had gone with their old leader to the royal court and they too had received baptism. Just a year later, two of these new converts took the opportunity to accuse Weland of taking his vows in vain and of converting simply for convenience. It was a slur that could not go unanswered and it required a legal response. The legal recourse available at that time in the Carolingian court was not a matter of lawyers and witnesses, however, but a call to trial by battle. In front of Charles, his wife and entourage, Weland and one of his accusers fell to mortal combat and hence, in the minds of the Christians of the day, put the matter into the hands of God, who would of course protect his own. And it seems he did. Weland was cut down and died on the floor of the royal court, marking the end of one of the first great Viking careers, but eliciting few tears beyond the huddle of his own family. Their fate must have instantly become precarious but they disappear from the pages of history along with their protector at the moment of his death.

The other historical Viking sailing through the waters of the mid-ninth century had grander ambitions than Weland and these would bring him one day to England. Hæsten, in a long and bloody life, saw the world the Viking way, in raids from the North Sea to the Mediterranean, and his extraordinary exploits allowed him to make the miraculous transition from scourge of Christian Europe to the first great hero of the Normans. His audacious Viking expedition would mark him out as the boldest and most daring raider before Ingvar the Far-Travelled, whose eleventh-century voyage took him as far as the Caspian Sea. In 859, Hæsten and his new ally, Bjorn Ironsides (who was called a 'Son of Ragnar Lothbrok'), were planning the ultimate raid: the sacking of Rome itself.

Setting out from their bases on the Loire, the two Viking captains sailed sixty-two ships down the coast of Francia, raiding as they went, travelling on into Moorish Spain, then under the control of the Umayyad Caliphate of Damascus. Turning east through the Straits of Gibraltar, the fleet continued ravaging the coastlines that it passed, sacking the mosque at Algeciras before crossing to North Africa to sack Mezemma on the Moroccan coast. From here one party may have turned back, eventually arriving in Ireland where the annals report the strange arrival of 'blue men'. This in itself may be a misinterpretation of the Old Norse *blámenn*, which can mean blue but also black and so may indicate the appearance of black African captives amongst the Viking raiders. The main force, however, continued on its mission, sailing up the Mediterranean seaboard of Spain and across to the Balearic Islands. By now the autumn weather was deteriorating and the fleets needed to find safe moorings for the winter. Having plundered Roussillon in France, they made for the Camargue in the Rhône delta. Having found there the combination of defensible islands and fast escape routes that Vikings everywhere preferred, they settled down to a closed season of localized raiding on the Côte d'Azur.

The following spring, now groaning under the weight of booty, they set off once more for their final target, tracking along the coast of southern France before heading south down the Italian peninsula to Pisa. By now the journey must have been inspired more by glory than by booty as plundering Spain, France and northern Italy must have left virtually no room aboard the fleet for the treasures of Rome. Perhaps Hæsten and Bjorn saw themselves as latter-day Alarics, moulding themselves on the exploits of the fourth-century king of the Visigoths; certainly they were aware that the greatest reward for a Viking chief was not money but fame. So they continued south.

For all their bravura and the brilliance of their plan, Rome was not to be theirs, however. Today we often think of Vikings as great navigators – the discoverers of Iceland, Greenland and, indeed, America – but even Vikings could lose their bearings. Approaching the town of Luna some 300 kilometres to the north of Rome, Hæsten and Bjorn seem to have become convinced that they were approaching the Eternal City itself, despite the huge discrepancy in size and geography. Of course, compared to the settlements of Scandinavia, where there were still very few groupings of houses that could be considered more than villages, any Italian town was a veritable Rome, but this was very definitely Luna.

Whilst this was not their intended target, it was still a highly defended city and unlikely to fall to a straightforward assault, so, the chroniclers tell us, Hæsten resorted to a famous and ancient stratagem. Having made a treaty of 'eternal peace' with the inhabitants, he agreed to be baptized by the local bishop who would also become his godfather. This, of course, sealed the deal in Christian eyes but it meant absolutely nothing to the Vikings. He then left the city and returned to his men who were camped on the beach. The early eleventh-century writer of *The Lives of the Normans*, Dudo of St Quentin, tells us he called to his men and told them:

'Now, make a bier for me, and place me upon it as though I were dead. Place my arms in it with me and, with lamentations, station yourselves in a ring around them. Go howling through the streets, and compel your followers bewail me. Let your cry raise a tumult throughout our tents. Let the cry of those who preside over the ships sound along with that of the rest of the troops. Have armbands and belts borne before the bier. Display axes and swords adorned with gold and gems.' What that calamity-causing one had commanded is no sooner said than done.

The bawling of howlings and the roar of mourners is heard. The
mountains resound, ringing with the cries of deceitful moaners.

On hearing of the death of Hæsten, the elders of Luna dutifully
allowed the 'body' and all the armed Viking mourners into the city for
his Christian funeral. The wolf had entered the fold. Once inside the
walls, Hæsten jumped from his bier; his men instantly turned on the
people of the city and slaughtered them.

This very Viking approach to the old Greek stratagem from the
Trojan Wars no doubt seemed appropriate to a mediaeval historian
telling tales of Northmen in the Mediterranean world, but it probably
has more to do with fiction than fact. One indisputable fact that must
have come to the attention of the plunderers during the sacking of the
city, however, was the fact that this was not Rome. Daunted perhaps
by the prospect of what Rome must itself be like, or simply weighed
down by too much treasure already, the Vikings decided that they
would set sail for home.

It was not to be an easy voyage, crossing a Mediterranean bulging
with other pirates and then having to make the dangerous passage
through the Arab-controlled Straits of Gibraltar. It was here that an Arab
fleet attacked them with the sticky, burning, petroleum-based mixture
known as Greek Fire, a technological marvel that must have shaken
even Viking resolution. By the time the survivors limped back home to
their bases in the Loire, only a third of the original fleet was left. Hæsten
and Bjorn were amongst them, however, loaded with both riches and
fame. News of their exploits must have raced around the European
courts and may even have come to the ears of those at the Wessex court,
then ruled by Æthelbald. On the lips of messengers or later perhaps in
the poems of *scops*, it was here that the ten-year-old Alfred might have
heard of this superhero amongst Vikings. If so, he would have done well
to listen carefully. He would one day face Hæsten himself.

That Hæsten did not turn his attentions to England at this time was
fortunate. A man of his wealth and reputation gathered pirates and
mercenaries like a magnet and Wessex, which was still poorly
defended, would certainly have fared worse against him than it
had against Weland. Hæsten had other plans, however, and many
years of continental raiding lay ahead before he would look acquisi-
tively across the sea to English shores.

If the Wessex court feared Viking attack, as they surely did, the place they should have looked to was not Francia but Ireland. There another Viking who claimed to be a son of Ragnar Lothbrok had emerged into the Irish chronicles with a name and a legend that came to haunt the kingdoms of Anglo-Saxon England: Ivarr the Boneless.

The Saga of Ragnar Lothbrok tells a strange tale of the birth of Ivarr to explain how he attained his unusual sobriquet. It was said that Ragnar's second wife, Aslaug, was a sorceress blessed, or perhaps cursed, with the power of foresight. On the night of her wedding when Ragnar came to her, she warned him that she had had a dark vision of the future and that they should not consummate the marriage for three nights, saying:

> Three nights together, but yet apart,
> Shall we bide, nor worship the gods as yet;
> From my son this would save a lasting harm,
> For boneless is he thou wouldst now beget.

Ragnar – ever the Viking – would not wait, however, and that night Aslaug became pregnant with their child Ivarr. When that child was delivered, he was born with gristle in the place of his bones, as his mother had predicted, and hence was known from then on as Ivarr the Boneless.

It has recently been suggested that this curious tale represents an attempt to explain the birth of a child with a serious genetic disorder, perhaps the brittle bone disease *Osteogenesis imperfecta*, which left Ivarr unable to walk. Stories of Ivarr's handicap only occur in the much later sagas, however. It is not mentioned by contemporary chroniclers who might be expected to have commented on the sight of a paraplegic Viking warlord being carried into battle on his shield, had they seen it. In the brutally practical world of ninth-century Scandinavia, it must also be doubted that so handicapped a child would have survived or, amongst a warrior elite, even have been allowed to survive, let alone grow up to lead Viking armies into battle and carve out a kingdom for himself.

Indeed, the saga story may simply be a later attempt to explain a name that at the time of its creation several hundred years earlier was itself a misunderstanding. The Old Norse *inn beinlaussi* – 'boneless', or 'legless' – may have been a misreading (or mishearing) of *inn barnlausi* –

'the childless one'. Alternatively perhaps even the Latin *exosus* – 'hateful' – was misheard as *exos* – 'boneless'. Ivarr certainly gained a reputation that would have made him hateful in the eyes of many of those he crossed, both Christian and Viking alike. Even *The Tale of the Sons of Ragnar* says Ivarr was childless, not due to any genetic problem but 'because of the way he was, with no lust or love, but not short on cunning or cruelty'.

Whatever the reason for his strange name, and regardless of the tales of sorcery and magic behind it, north Europeans of the mid-ninth century had reason to take note of the name Ivarr the Boneless and to fear it. If extraordinary legends grew up around the real historical character, it was because the real Ivarr was extraordinary enough to be worthy of them. Ivarr first appears in the Christian annals of Ireland in 857 when an 'Imhar' is recorded as beginning a campaign of violence and looting there that would occupy five of the next seven years. Then in 863, the same year that his compatriot Weland was fighting for his life at the court of Charles the Bald, Imhar weighs anchor and slips out of the Irish annals altogether. Two year later he would sail back into view, this time in the pages of the *Anglo-Saxon Chronicle*.

During the years of the early adventures of Weland, Ivarr and Hæsten, Viking attacks on Wessex and England had, in general, been more of an annoyance than a serious threat to the House of Ecgberht. From Asser's point of view a far greater threat to the security of the realm had come shortly after Æthelwulf's death when Æthelbald, the treacherous son who had rebelled against his father, took the old king's wife as his own. Asser put it bluntly: 'Æthelbald . . . against God's prohibition and Christian dignity, and also contrary to the practice of all pagans, took over his father's marriage bed and married Judith, daughter of Charles the Bald, king of the Franks, incurring great disgrace from all who heard of it.'

As usual, Asser is a partisan witness and is not always correct in his absolute assertions. In fact, it was not unknown amongst pagans for a son to marry his widowed stepmother – the seventh-century pagan king of Kent, Eadbald, had done just that – but clearly in Asser's mind such a move was worse even than the terrible and damnable crimes of the pagans. He was right, however, that this was an unusual act amongst Christians; in fact, even the pagan Eadbald had renounced his wife/stepmother on his conversion. Bede tells the story in his *History of the English Church and People* of how the first archbishop of Canterbury, St Augustine, wrote to Pope Gregory for firm guidance on this, amongst other matters, and received the reply: 'But to wed one's stepmother is a grave sin, for the Law says: "Thou shalt not uncover the nakedness of thy father". Now the son cannot uncover the nakedness of his father; but since it says, "they shall be one flesh", whosoever presumes to marry his stepmother, who was one flesh with his father, thereby commits this offence.' It is a convoluted interpretation worthy of any lawyer but it made it clear to Asser, Bede and St Augustine that such a marriage was abhorrent and uncanonical in the eyes of the Church. Strangely it does not seem to have particularly bothered the writer of the Frankish *Annals of St Bertin*, who, despite the role of a member of the Carolingian House in the apparent 'scandal', simply records the marriage without further comment. Perhaps Charles the Bald finally had what he wanted: his daughter, an anointed queen, on the throne of Wessex. Nor for that matter does there seem to have been any complaint from the leading men, religious or secular, in greater Wessex, who were perhaps more concerned to find themselves now ruled over by a queen, rather than just a king's wife.

If the arrival of a queen and wife/stepmother created any ripples in Wessex, they had little time to develop into anything more damaging. Just two years later, in 860, Æthelbald was himself dead and Judith suddenly found herself short of allies. It was unclear who would inherit what parts of which kingdoms and whether the succession would continue as Æthelwulf had desired, with a permanent split between Wessex proper and the eastern counties. In fact it was Æthelberht – who had meekly stood aside for his father during his brother's coup – who acted decisively. Unwilling to rule just half of the kingdom, he moved quickly to regain control of Wessex as well. Whilst Æthelbald's ageing ally Bishop Ealhstan was still intoning the Mass over the dead king's grave at Sherborne, Æthelberht was seizing control of the whole kingdom, reuniting the patrimony of Ecgberht.

For Judith, still only sixteen years old, this marked the end of her English adventure. It was just one incident in what was already and would continue to be an adventurous life. As there was no suitable new husband for a Carolingian princess in England, she sold up the possessions she had in Wessex and crossed the Channel once more to return to her father's court. She was now forced to bide her time and wait for Charles to procure for her a new husband who was worthy of an anointed queen and a descendant of Charlemagne.

That at least was how such matters were usually conducted. Judith took her place beside her father (then at Senlis) as a dutiful daughter should but her years as queen had made her less willing to bend to the will of others. With the active help of her brother Louis the Stammerer, who was at that time in revolt against his father, she began conducting an affair with the Count of Flanders, Baldwin I, known as 'Iron Arm', and shortly after she eloped with him, infuriating and humiliating Charles in the process. Indeed, so angry was he that he managed to persuade the pope to excommunicate Baldwin, who in his turn travelled to Rome to personally petition the pontiff to effect a reconciliation. Eventually Charles seems to have relented and accepted Baldwin as his son-in-law, making him Count of Ghent so that he might hold a title worthy of his wife. Charles could not, however, on any account be persuaded to attend the formal marriage ceremony.

Back in England this was a tense time for Alfred, then around eleven years of age, and more particularly for his brother Æthelred who might, under the terms of their father's will, now have expected to rule part of Wessex in his own right. He had undoubtedly been usurped by Æthelberht, but it shortly became clear that the new king did not intend to disown or destroy his little brother. Indeed, Æthelred's time on the throne of Wessex would come sooner than he thought, and perhaps sooner than he would have wished.

Æthelberht's motives for the annexation of Wessex may have been no more complex than his wish to reunite the whole of the Wessex kingdom, his lust for power or perhaps his desire to undo what he may have considered the incestuous 'evil' of his brother's reign. Whatever the reason, in defying his father's deathbed wishes he (perhaps unwittingly) did much to save the kingdom, which, had it stayed divided, would have provided much easier pickings for the Vikings.

We can gain an idea of how Æthelberht's coup was brought about by reading between the lines of one of the many remarkable documents left to us by Alfred: his will. It was written twenty or thirty years after this time but, in explaining how he intended to distribute his own estate and his power, Alfred was eager to make clear to his readers why the will of his father Æthelwulf had been ignored, and how he and his brothers had hence come to the throne. It seems that, far from being a *coup d'état*, the decision to let Æthelberht rule the entire kingdom was made in council and out of practical considerations for the safety of the country. We can imagine the scene at court with a teenage Æthelred and his younger brother Alfred nervously handing over their birthright. In his own words Alfred recounts the scene: 'Æthelred and I, with the witness of all the councillors of the West Saxons, entrusted our share to our kinsman King Æthelberht, on condition that he would restore it to us as much under our control as it was when we entrusted it to him.'

It was a gamble for the young princes but there was really no other option. It was shortly after Æthelberht's coronation that Weland's fleet sacked Winchester, his nominal capital; and it was that same year that the last of the 'saints' at court, Bishop Swithun, had died and been buried in his first, simplest and, if legend is to be believed, preferred tomb. Difficult times were coming to Wessex and a country with a single strong king was infinitely preferable to the divisive warring of the Carolingians. Æthelred would have to bide his time, as would Alfred, but their patience would not be tested for long.

The ever-faithful Æthelberht was true to his word and the charters of his reign not only provided for his security but also for his brothers Æthelred and Alfred as he had promised. It was not the sort of work that marked out kings as 'great' but it put Wessex back on a footing for which Alfred would one day be grateful.

King Æthelberht only enjoyed mastery over Wessex for five years. We cannot be sure which year he was born but he was probably in his early to mid-thirties at the time of his death in 865. The *Anglo-Saxon Chronicle* sees nothing noteworthy in his passing. It fails to record a reason or, indeed, to provide any information beyond saying that Æthelred now inherited the kingdom. The lack of comment may be taken to imply that Æthelberht avoided some terrible end, either at the hands of God or the Northmen – if the two were separable in Anglo-Saxon minds. The sad truth is that Æthelberht was a fairly old man for his day, and the death of fairly old men often passes without surprise or comment. And so the kingdom of Wessex changed hands once more, passing to Æthelwulf's fourth son, Æthelred, only one step away from the young Alfred himself.

5

The Arrival of the Sons of Ragnar

Now when Ragnar's sons were fully grown, they went raiding
far and wide.

The Tale of the Sons of Ragnar, trans. P. Tunstall

WITH THE ACCESSION of Æthelred, the kingship of Wessex
seemed to step down a generation, falling to a man in his early
twenties who could be ably assisted by the young Alfred, now about
seventeen and in his prime. Alfred, as the next in line to the throne,
might now have expected some share in power himself, particularly if
we can trust the *Liber de Hyda* (the chronicle of the abbey that Alfred
later founded as king) in its assertion that Alfred was Æthelred's
favourite brother. He and Æthelred were, after all, closer in age than
the other brothers, perhaps because they were the only two children
of Osburh. But the new situation allowed little room for filial affection
and Æthelred would not share power with anyone – at least not yet.
He had stood aside whilst his elder brother took control of the whole
kingdom and he expected his little brother to do the same for him. If
anything, he was actually less likely to hand over control of the eastern
provinces where traditionally the younger son got his first taste of
power, as those eastern provinces had themselves just received another
taste of a more unyielding and unwelcome force.

In the last year of Æthelberht's life the Vikings had again plundered
Kent and there was the distinct possibility on their return to the
continent they would tell other warbands of the rich pickings to be
had. Indeed, they may even have been reconnoitring the terrain with
a grander plan in mind. Æthelred therefore felt the need to take total
control of his country and when Alfred asked for his share in the
kingdom, the answer was a resolute 'no'.

That Alfred did ask, we again know from his own will. With a startling honesty he tells us: 'I asked him [Æthelred] in the presence of all the councillors that we might divide that inheritance and he should give me my share. Then he told me that he could not divide it easily.' Æthelred was learning from the mistakes of his father and from the five years he had spent watching Æthelberht. Clearly he was unwilling to see the resources available to the king diluted by any premature settlement. He did, however, make an undertaking to Alfred: 'and he said that he would leave after his death to no person sooner than to me whatever he held of our joint property and whatever he acquired. And I gave ready assent to that.' Alfred was wise to agree; indeed, had he been successful in separating his inheritance he would have left both himself and Æthelred dangerously vulnerable to being picked off one at a time by Viking war-fleets. And the timing could not have been more fortunate, for just such an armada was already massing on the Frankish coast.

The Viking fleet that hove into view over the Kent horizon in the autumn of 865 was different from every warband and brigand who had come before; different from the pirate kings with their 'smash and grab' raids; different in kind and different in size. Even the Anglo-Saxon chronicler was forced to take note and find some way to record this sea change. Where he had written so many times of handfuls of 'pagans' coming here and going there, of ten or twenty ships prowling along the coast, this time he wrote of the arrival of a single, terrible entity: the 'Great Heathen Army'.

If the people of Kent had been alarmed by the previous year's raid, they had every right to be simply terrified by the huge force that now made landfall on Thanet. What was particularly unnerving was that it must have been clear from the start that this Viking army intended to stay. Chroniclers' estimates of numbers are notoriously unreliable but the type of language used by them suggests that perhaps three to four hundred *drakkars* – slim, swift and shallow-draughted warships – were now being drawn up on Thanet's beaches. From their hulls some five thousand armed men emerged, along with innumerable camp followers. By modern standards this might not seem an overwhelming force but the population of Britain at the time was well under a million (and that of greater Wessex was probably under half a million), spread thinly across a rural landscape, making it difficult to muster men in any numbers. And even if they could be mustered, they would comprise a force largely made up of farmers, whilst ranged against them was a professional mercenary army, who abided by no Christian rules of war, with no fields to tend, no lands to protect – no reason not to do simply whatever they wanted.

We can get an idea of the wide-ranging experience of these professional Viking warriors from a hoard of 250 coins buried probably by one of their number in Croydon five or six years after their first arrival on Thanet. This personal booty included Frankish coins of Louis the Pious and Charles the Bald, suggesting that their owner was actively campaigning in Francia throughout the early 860s, as well as Arabic dirhams, indicating either raids farther afield or certainly contact – probably deadly – with merchants who were trading with the Arab world. Also found were three ingots of silver, the owner's share of the melted-down booty from other raids, as well as an extensive collection of English silver pennies, which speak ominously of what, in the mid 860s, still lay ahead for the people of England.

Not surprisingly, this exceptional army was led by exceptional men. Halfdan was referred to by the chroniclers as a 'king'. He may have been at least a princeling from a Scandinavian royal family and hence able to muster considerable forces and resources. Another, according to the chronicler Abbo of Fleury, was Ubbe and he, Abbo tells us, was 'united through the devil' with the army's third and greatest leader, Ivarr the Boneless. The man who had disappeared from the Irish annals just two years before was back.

Whilst terror must have spread through the eastern provinces of Æthelred's kingdom at the arrival of Ivarr and his army, the apparently imminent Day of Judgment did not follow quickly on. The Great Heathen Army that landed that autumn on Thanet was not yet ready for a fight; it moved off into the neighbouring kingdom of East Anglia, then ruled by the Christian King Edmund, and waited. King Edmund for his part could do little to stop these invaders and was simply grateful that they came easily to terms so that he could make peace with them. The terms for that peace do not survive but they were most probably dictated solely by the Vikings. They included Edmund paying a substantial sum of protection money (a fee known later as Danegeld), as well as providing food, shelter and horses for the

Viking army. Edmund would also be required to look on passively as the ranks of that fearsome army continued to swell.

Throughout that winter as well as the next spring and summer, continental warbands flocked to Ivarr's side and the Viking wasps' nest steadily grew. In the spring of 866, Charles the Bald paid a huge tribute, including large quantities of wine and some 4000 lbs of silver, to persuade another Viking fleet to leave his kingdom. For once these Vikings were content to take the money and run. Since the death of Weland three years earlier, they had had thinner pickings in Francia as the Carolingians developed more effective strategies to counter them, so for many Northmen it may have seemed like a good time to look elsewhere for plunder. The Vikings still infesting the Seine (Weland had not got rid of them for long) had also suffered their fair share of illness, cooped up on an easily defensible but unhealthy island near St Denis. An outbreak of disease amongst them in the previous year was recorded with graphic delight by Prudentius of Troyes, who clearly saw the hand of God at work punishing the desecrators of the Frankish royal church: 'The Northmen who had sacked St. Denis became ill with various ailments. Some went mad. Some were covered in sores, some discharged their guts with a watery flow through their arses: and so they died.'

Francia's gain was to be England's loss. Throughout the summer of 866, Viking bands drifted towards the Channel coast and busied themselves repairing their ships. Not all of them were bound for England but many must have heard of the great mustering by the legendary sons of Ragnar Lothbrok. Accordingly they set course for East Anglia.

By that autumn, Ivarr and his fellow 'kings' had finished their preparations and were ready to move out. A year had passed, a year in which the kings of every Anglo-Saxon realm desperately sought clues as to the Great Army's next move. The foolish must have hoped that the army would return to the continent; the naive might have hoped to broker a deal similar to East Anglia's; the realists knew they could do little but pray. But with this huge force mustered, rested, fed and horsed, the whole country, not least King Edmund, must have held their breath.

Only one kingdom perhaps had failed to register the threat. Far to the north in the ancient realm of Northumbria, the internecine feuding was continuing. In 858, King Osberht of Northumbria had been ousted by one Aelle. Whatever Aelle's claim to the throne, and the Anglo-Saxon chronicler pointedly records him as 'with no hereditary right', the civil war that followed resulted in a political and financial crisis. The struggle was bleeding Northumbria dry and the anonymous writer of *The History of St Cuthbert* remained deeply unimpressed with both claimants who, he says, were each robbing the lands of Lindisfarne to support their claim.

It was just the sort of situation that suited Vikings. With an unclear power structure, popular disaffection with both parties and insufficient capital to mount an organized defence, Northumbria, once the jewel amongst Anglo-Saxon kingdoms, had never been weaker. Here was an opportunity to divide and rule, so when Ivarr came to lead his army out of East Anglia, he headed north.

Of course the later saga writers could never have so prosaic a reason for their hero's choice of victim, so they wove a more elaborate tale of murder and revenge. The legend has it that Ragnar Lothbrok, Ivarr's oft-killed and semi-legendary father, had met his death at the hands of Aelle who had had him thrown into a snake pit. Initially the snakes had refused to touch him owing to a magical silk shirt he was wearing. But when Aelle noticed this and had it removed, the snakes bit Ragnar and in his dying breath he prophesied: 'The little pigs would grunt if they knew how it fares with the old boar.' The sagas say that when those little pigs – the sons of Ragnar – heard the news, the first, Hvitserk, who was playing chess at the time, seized a piece so hard that blood oozed from his fingernails; Bjorn Ironsides grabbed a spear with such force that he left an indentation in the wooden shaft; whilst Sigurd Snake-in-Eye, who was trimming his nails, cut clear to the bone. But it was another of the little pigs who would prove the avenger of the tale for, legend or not, Ivarr the Boneless was now on his way to Aelle's kingdom.

The Northmen arrived late in the autumn, long after the campaigning season was over, when weapons had been oiled and put away until the following spring, and friends and foes traditionally settled down to peacefully sit out the dark winter months. It was a long, cold and gloomy winter in Northumbria, and after so much civil war no one was in a mood to fight. No one, that is, except Ivarr – and that was precisely his plan. Not only would the Northumbrians be unprepared for war at this season, but Ivarr had chosen a specific day to catch them at their most unawares. That day was Friday, 1 November – All Saint's Day, one of the major religious festivals in the Northumbrian calendar. It was a trick that Ragnar himself had used in an attack on Paris, which had occurred over Easter.

The city that Ivarr chose to attack had become one of the most important royal and ecclesiastical centres in the North of England in the seventh and eighth centuries and in the process had also become a flourishing trading centre. Excavations in the Fishergate area of the modern city of York have shown that Eorforwic, as it was then known, was one of the most sophisticated English cities of its day. Traders here imported exotic items such as lava quern stones from Germany, combs from Frisia (traded by Frisian merchants living in the city) and Frankish drinking vessels. Closer to home, stone was brought in from the surrounding hills and domestic pottery arrived from East Anglia, whilst a thriving local jewellery industry served clients who had become wealthy enough to afford such exotic gems as emeralds and garnets. The recent political upheavals had undoubtedly taken their toll on the city but the potential for Ivarr must still have been very apparent.

The initial All Saint's Day attack was a stunning success; indeed, the shock appearance of the Great Heathen Army seems to have led to a complete rout of whatever Anglian forces were defending the city, followed by its rapid capitulation. This was not to be the end of the war, however. Both claimants for the Northumbrian throne, Aelle and Osberht, escaped the initial battle; this alien onslaught drove them to bury their differences, at least for a time, and join forces in attempting to recapture the city. Whilst the Northumbrians desperately mustered what men they could, the Vikings dug in.

The city was exactly the type of settlement that Norsemen knew and understood. It is even possible that they may have been trading with the Anglian settlement here for many years before invading. York stood on a piece of land between two rivers, which offered plenty of room to draw up ships on the beach as well as excellent access, both to the network of rivers into the interior that ran to north and south, and to an escape route, if needed, into the North Sea. The city was also a major node in the old Roman road system, something that appears still to have been in use at this time and of which Viking forces apparently had a working knowledge. Added to these advantages, it also possessed an old Roman wall, possibly not in the best state of repair but nevertheless a practical defence against attack. This, like Dublin, which Ivarr also knew, was an ideal Viking city, a place for trade, a base from which to make lightning strikes anywhere in the country and a refuge from enemies.

Vikings are often portrayed as either ruthless bandits or, in more recent years, as successful and misunderstood traders, when in fact their society could easily produce both. Whilst Ivarr's initial interest in York may well have been due to the quantity of plunder that it could produce, his campaign was aimed at taking control of resources rather than simply consuming them. Short-term plundering was necessary to pay his army but in the longer term he did not intend to destroy York, but rather turn its wealth-creating potential to his own use. What raiding started, trading would sustain. This was why he had been drawn to the city. There was no question that he now intended to stay.

It was the following spring before Osberht and Aelle finally found themselves in a position to mount a campaign to retake York. The date they chose was 23 April, Palm Sunday, an unusual choice for Christians attacking pagans but perhaps designed to throw Ivarr off guard; after all, surely Christians would not give battle on a major feast day? If Ivarr was meant to be surprised, however, the tactic does not seem to have worked. The attack began well for the Northumbrians, or so the chroniclers tell us; the Danes who were caught outside the city's defences broke ranks and were forced back.

The Northumbrians now approached the old Roman city walls. These had once been York's greatest advertisement and its greatest defence. Even today one of its old towers, built in the early years of the third century, and patched and repaired for centuries since, still rises over the Museum Gardens in the city centre. Walking up to the face of this vast bulwark you can thus stand as the Northumbrians must have done that day and place a hand on the twenty or more feet of cold stone – as they believed, all that stood between them and their city. But the wall was not the insuperable obstacle that it appeared. Whilst the *elrondyng* (or multi-angular tower as it is now called) presented a formidable face to attackers, elsewhere the walls had been allowed to fall into ruins. The Northumbrians are reported to have torn down whole sections and flooded into the narrow streets of York itself.

It looked like victory but was, in reality, a deadly mistake. Vikings have often been portrayed as immensely brave and fearless fighters, always happiest seeking death or glory in open battle, but this view owes more to the legends and sagas woven around their leaders than to the truth. Vikings, in fact, did not like risking their lives unnecessarily. Whilst they may certainly have believed that a death in battle was a good death, they were plunderers, not holy warriors. On the continent they had shown that, given the choice, when threatened they preferred to cut a deal and then, if possible, renege on it, and escape rather than fight. If they had to fight, they liked the odds stacked in their favour and their escape vessels close at hand. This is exactly what they had prepared in York.

As the exultant Northumbrian levies poured through the breaches in the city walls, they found themselves in narrow and congested streets where a traditional massed battle was impossible. They had forsaken any advantage of numbers that they might have had in an open field, instead taking on professional and well-armed mercenaries in street fighting. In short they had been tricked and the result was a bloodbath.

There are no figures for casualties from the battle – Christian chroniclers were notoriously shy of recording the full toll from amongst their own people – but there was room to list the more important fatalities. Eight ealdormen died that day and with them fell both claimants to the throne, Osberht and Aelle. The streets of York ran not just with the blood of Northumbrians but with the lifeblood of the whole nation. An independent kingdom, which traced its direct line of kings back to 664, was dead.

Ivarr's victory was the very stuff of sagas and *The Tale of the Sons of Ragnar* dutifully recorded the vengeance of this particular 'little pig'. Indeed, Norse sources go much further than contemporary Anglo-Saxon chroniclers in recording the aftermath of the Northumbrian defeat, telling a story of brutal and personal revenge that still divides academics into two camps: those who consider it may hold a ghostly memory of a forgotten pagan rite and those who think it the fanciful invention of a poet. The legend states that Aelle did not die in the fighting but was captured and brought before Ivarr as he revelled in his victory. Seeing the humbled Northumbrian king before him, Ivarr ordered revenge for his father's death but Aelle's sentence was not to be death by snake, but by eagle. He had to be sacrificed to Odin in thanks for the victory in the ceremony of the blood eagle. The early eleventh-century skaldic poet Sigvatr is the first to mention this, stating, in a poem in praise of the later Scandinavian king of England Cnut, that 'Ivarr, who dwelt in York, carved the eagle on Aelle's back'. But the thirteenth-century *Tale of the Sons of Ragnar*, in referring to Sigvatr's poem, goes further, describing how the ceremony involved hacking open the victim's chest and throwing the lungs over the shoulders so that they resembled the folded wings of a bloody eagle.

Had Aelle in fact been blood-eagled we might perhaps have expected some of the contemporary English sources to mention it; they were after all very ready to attribute terrible acts to their pagan enemies. Similarly, Wulfhere, the archbishop of York, who survived the fighting and kept both his life and his post, might have been expected to recoil from working with such barbaric new masters. However, clearly he did work with them and may even have brokered the peace. But equally Wulfhere knew that he had little choice in what he did and the very presence of the term 'blood eagle' in the contemporary Norse language may imply that some terrible fate not unlike that described by Sigvatr befell the unfortunate Aelle.

What was important for the Vikings listening to stories of Ivarr's exploits – and to Saxon kings hearing the reports from the messengers who now hurried south – was that Aelle was dead. This was not a raid, it was a conquest, and it would not be the last.

Ivarr had conquered Northumbria but he was not yet ready to settle down and rule peacefully. There were still more lands to conquer and there was more treasure to be had. Whilst he was gathering it, a puppet ruler would serve Viking interests in Northumbria as well, if not better. A Christian nominee might retain at least a vestige of acceptability amongst the conquered Northumbrians and would certainly be more tolerable to them than a pagan lord. There would be plenty of time later, when the wounds were less raw, for Ivarr to replace that puppet in person if he so desired.

So having installed an English 'king' called Ecgberht (who was no relation to the Royal House of Wessex) to rule in York on his behalf, Ivarr was soon back at the head of his Great Heathen Army and, by the autumn of 868, was marching towards new conquests. Northumbria, riven as it was with political dissension, had perhaps been a relatively easy target but, thanks to the earlier exactions of Osberht and Aelle, it may not have been financially a very rewarding one. Mercia, however, was a different matter. This vast Midlands kingdom had remained quiescent during the Viking march north, allowing the army to move freely across its territory and apparently unwilling to get involved in what its king, Burgred, must have hoped was very much someone else's problem. Sadly for him it was not to remain that way and, instead of their returning peacefully through his country, Burgred now found the great army marching towards his own city of Snotengaham – Nottingham. By the time he had mustered an army himself, the Vikings were already encamped in the city and were well enough defended to prevent any outright assault on them. Burgred's response was to prepare for a siege, to see whether the enemy could not be cut off and starved out as the Oissel Vikings on the Seine had been by Weland. He also thought that now was the time for more concerted action by the Anglo-Saxons to remove this threat once and for all in a unified campaign that would prevent kingdoms being picked off piecemeal. He therefore called on his wealthy and relatively stable ally to the south, Wessex.

This was not, of course, the first time that Burgred had appealed to Wessex for help. Æthelwulf had come to Mercia's aid in her subjugation of the Welsh and clearly the alliance had been successful. So Burgred was keen to try the tactic again, although well aware, no doubt, that military aid from Wessex would come at a price. That price seems to have been a marriage alliance to strengthen the friendship between the kingdoms – an attempt by Wessex to gain a further say in Mercian affairs. Æthelred could not make the alliance himself, however; he had by then been married to his wife Wulfthryth for at least three years, and Burgred too was married – to Alfred's sister Æthelswith. The most available and valuable commodity in the marriage stakes was in fact the nineteen-year-old Alfred. Hence it was with the prospect of his forthcoming Mercian marriage in mind that Alfred, his brother the king and their army set out for Nottingham.

Surrounded by the combined forces of Mercia and Wessex the Vikings should have been in a precarious position but this was not in fact the case. Prolonged sieges drained the resources of both besieger and besieged, and the Anglo-Saxon forces were less well equipped to cope with the practicalities than their counterparts behind the walls. The Viking army was used to moving quickly and living off the land, and the Saxon siege does not seem to have been tight enough to prevent Viking foraging parties operating out of the city. For their part, the men of Mercia and Wessex could not simply stay put around Nottingham indefinitely.

The armies of Æthelred and Burgred were made up of several groups. At their core were the households of the royal families, the people who lived off the largesse of their 'ring-giver' and in return offered their services in war. These were effectively professional soldiers and each lord at court may have been called upon to provide a number of these men from his own household. This was, however, only a very small fighting force and the majority of the men standing waiting around Nottingham in 868 were from the fyrd – the levies of ordinary men summoned by the ealdormen of each shire. Because of their background, they were handicapped in ways that the Vikings were not. They were not professional soldiers, nor were they well equipped; they too were having to live off the same land that was forage for their more professional Viking enemies. But their greatest handicap was that they needed to get home quickly. Like the over-whelming majority of Anglo-Saxons, these fyrdmen were farmers and time away from their farms meant trouble in the coming year as crops remained unplanted or unharvested. Keep a Saxon army in the field for long enough and you did not need to defeat it: it would starve next winter anyway. So the situation at Nottingham rapidly drew towards a humiliating climax for Burgred and the young Æthelred. After failing to starve Ivarr out, they were forced to come to terms. They had flexed their Anglo-Saxon muscle and received no more than a shrug of Ivarr's Viking shoulders in reply.

It is certainly to Burgred's and Æthelred's benefit that the terms of this peace settlement do not survive; indeed, had they survived and fallen into Alfred's hand in later years, one could hardly have blamed him for destroying them together with the memory they bore of this first abortive contact with his great enemy. Asser, circumspect as ever in describing events, says: 'Since the pagans, defended by the protection of the fortress, refused to give battle, and the Christians could not break the wall, peace was made between the Mercians and the pagans, and the two brothers Æthelred and Alfred returned home with their forces.' As usual with Asser there is as much written here between the lines as on them. Vikings did not make peace for nothing and Asser enjoys telling us in detail when the terms were unfavourable to them. The baldness of his description of this truce implies that Burgred was forced to make a substantial payment for it, probably in line with the thousands of pounds of bullion now regularly being demanded of Frankish rulers on the continent. For a king who was probably already in some financial difficulty, this was a bitter price. Asser also very neatly uncouples Æthelred and his brother Alfred from the negotiations, saying it was a peace made purely between the Mercians and the Vikings, and that once a deal had been struck between the two parties, the Wessex army simply went home. Asser wants no part for his hero in this military humiliation. It was enough to make the recently departed Bishop Ealhstan turn in his grave.

The abortive siege of Nottingham had certainly not been the glorious success that the House of Ecgberht was hoping for but there was something to be salvaged from the wreckage. Back inside Wessex in the formerly Mercian county of Berkshire, the Wessex royal family celebrated a wedding: Alfred's.

Alfred's marriage at the royal vill of Sutton Courtenay was a momentous occasion, marking the emergence from boyhood of the man who, in the coming decades, would change the political and cultural map of England for ever. His wife-to-be was Ealhswith, the daughter of Mercian nobleman Mucel, who was said by Asser to be an ealdorman of the Gaini – a mysterious group only ever mentioned here but perhaps the name of one of the ancient tribes of Mercia. It was not the most 'royal' of matches for Alfred, compared to a father and brother who had both married (the same) Carolingian princess, but then Alfred was not likely to inherit Wessex soon, as long as a young and apparently vigorous Æthelred remained on the throne. In any case he could hardly marry any of the children of Burgred as that king's wife was his own sister. Ealhswith did have royal blood in her veins, however, as chroniclers are at pains to tell us, through her mother – ominously called Eadburh – who was, no doubt much to

Alfred's relief, a very different proposition from the last Mercian of that name to marry into Wessex royalty.

The celebration of this further alliance between Mercia and Wessex was held over several days and was accompanied by the usual feasting and gift-giving beloved of Anglo-Saxon kings. From this point onwards, Alfred would be a full member of the court and of adult society, in charge of his own household of noble retainers, soldiers and servants. He was now very much the second man in the kingdom, the heir apparent, and he may even have been given some of the responsibilities of state. But this marriage feast also marked the beginning of another less welcome episode in Alfred's life, which would dog him until his death.

An Anglo-Saxon marriage feast should have been one of the highlights of the calendar. Although there are no surviving English recipes from before the fourteenth century, from archaeological finds and asides in some contemporary texts we can reconstruct the sort of meal that Alfred enjoyed that day. This was an occasion on which no expense was to be spared so the most plentiful and appreciated food was the meat. Farmers in Wessex and Mercia kept pigs, sheep, goats and cattle for meat, although cattle were more valuable for milk and as beasts of burden. Wild animals, particularly harts, red and roe deer, boar and hares, were also hunted with dogs, nets and spears to provide for the table. Many birds were also eaten, including some wild species, as well as ducks, geese and hens. Fish, including sea- and fresh-water species as well as lobster and crabs, were also available. This heading included sea mammals such as porpoises – conveniently allowing for them to be eaten during Lent. The folk tale that barnacle geese were born out of barnacles rather than eggs likewise helped to widen the Lent diet.

Meat would be boiled, griddled, fried, baked or spit-roasted and, at court at least, its flavour could be improved with exotic imported herbs and spices, such as ginger, cloves, mace and cinnamon, as well as locally grown coriander, dill and thyme. Accompanying this expensive fare were the cereals and seasonal vegetables that made up the majority of a more ordinary Anglo-Saxon's diet. These included peas, beans, parsnips and small purple carrots, more akin to their wild Afghan cousins than the orange vegetable of today. A boiled mix of barley, rye or oats with a few of these vegetables formed *briw*, the

Anglo-Saxon staple pottage, although this was hardly suitable fare for a wedding feast. Instead the diners might have enjoyed their cereals in the form of bread made with wheat, which gained in popularity throughout the Anglo-Saxon period. Finally eggs and dairy produce rounded off the range of savoury dishes.

Desserts were also available, often sweetened with honey in a culture where sugar was very rare and was usually reserved for medical use. Many of these were based on fruit, again largely local, and consisting of apples, sloes, plums and cherries in season. A royal marriage feast might also encompass more expensive imports such as figs and grapes. All of the above might be served in as many as ten courses with huge quantities of the most important ingredient of all – alcohol – in the form of imported wine for the wealthy, mead for those less well off and beer for everyone else.

But at some point during these expansive celebrations, Alfred was taken ill with a mysterious disease that continued to afflict him for the next twenty-five years. So bad was it that some said that he must have been placed under a spell by one of those around him. In the ninth century such magical causes for physical complaints were considered an all too real danger, as demonstrated by a case from the following century in which a woman was executed for making an effigy of someone she wished to harm and driving pins into it. The exact nature of Alfred's disease remained a mystery, both to the doctors at court and to modern doctors today. All we know is that Alfred was suddenly seized with terrible pain, to the point of distraction, which might come on without warning and which was so violent that the fear of its return was nearly as debilitating as the pain itself. Some modern commentators have suggested that he may have been suffering from Crohn's disease, an ulcerative condition of the bowel causing abdominal cramps, fevers and diarrhoea. Several days of feasting and heavy drinking might have provided the ideal first foothold for the complaint.

Whatever its real cause, Alfred's collapse must have been a blow for the assembled Mercian and West Saxon royalty. This generation of Ecgbert's family had no great reputation for longevity – three of Alfred's brothers were already dead – and now it appeared that the health of the youngest was badly compromised. The recurring pain of the disease would also profoundly affect the devout young Alfred who, like many in his age, saw the hand of God in many physical afflictions, be they Viking attacks or stomach cramps. As Alcuin had been so fond of saying, 'God chastiseth every son whom he receiveth.'

The appearance of this disease also inspired the young prince's interest in medicine and his relentless search for relief. Prayer was undoubtedly the foremost cure in his mind; it had after all cured him of a previous illness, possibly a rather unromantic case of piles, which disappeared after a visit to the shrine of the obscure Cornish saint Gueriir, but clearly he also believed in taking more practical action. Medicine in Alfred's day was nowhere near as primitive as might be believed. During his reign a book was compiled; in fact it was three books, which are known today collectively as *Bald's Leechbook* and *Leechbook III*. They demonstrate the full range of treatments available and also contain a clue to Alfred's own problem.

The term 'leechbook' simply means 'Doctor's book' and has nothing to do with leeches. Bald seems to have been the owner of this particular volume, not its author according to the colophon at the end of Book Two. These books display a wide-ranging and practical knowledge of medicine (for the period) and include the best material gleaned from ancient sources such as the prolific Roman author Galen. A knowledge of such classical authors was essential to an understanding of the body, as the human form was considered sacred in Anglo-Saxon England so dissection was forbidden. The same had been true for Galen but he had systematically sidestepped this by dissecting animals and working with the corpses of gladiators (who repeatedly dissected each other). To complement this knowledge of anatomy, the leechbooks prescribe numerous potions and poultices for a range of complaints, created from an extensive pharmacopoeia that included not just locally available herbs but exotic ingredients from as far afield as China, India and South-east Asia. Even surgery was sometimes suggested for particular conditions, and instructions survive for bloodletting, trepanation, amputation and sewing up wounds with silk sutures.

Not everything had such a modern resonance, however, and Anglo-Saxon medicine also contained many echoes of an earlier time. This was a world where amulets were still worn for protection against disease and to ward off evil magic. Here, in books such as the *Lacnanga*, we find charms and spells invoked, particularly in the case of difficult problems that available medicine or surgery seemed unable to cure or for problems that today would not be considered medical at all. So we find cures for a nagging wife, spells to improve the fertility of the soil and to settle swarms of bees, chants to remedy 'water-elf disease' and archaic spells to shrink cancerous tumours or 'wens'.

But in *Bald's Leechbook* is a specific reference to Alfred and his mysterious problem in a series of entries entitled: 'All this Elias, Patriarch of Jerusalem, commanded thus to be told to King Alfred.' These deal mainly with medicines for abdominal complaints and prescribe, amongst other things, taking petroleum for 'inward tenderness'. The fact that suggestions for remedies came all the way from Jerusalem shows the degree of energy with which Alfred searched for a cure and hints that his disease must have been highly debilitating.

These entries also reflect the wide and cosmopolitan network of correspondents maintained by the king. We know that, in 881, Elias had sent a round-robin letter to the rulers of Europe, asking for money to help him restore his churches, as there is a record of its arrival at the court of Charles the Fat that year. It may well have been the arrival of a similar letter at Alfred's court that prompted the idea that Elias might be able to help with his own nagging problem in return for some funding. If so, it shows that, in all his dealings, the illness that had begun to affect the young Alfred at his wedding feast was never far from his mind.

Whatever the cause of the illness that first manifested itself that day in 868, it was clearly a bad omen, as all those present knew. The health of a king reflected the health of his realm and any sickness in a prince might lead those ealdormen who elected kings to question his fitness to rule. So Alfred had much to gain from remaining fit (or appearing fit) and there was equally much capital to be made by his enemies from any perceived illness. Perhaps his strange and violent cramps showed that those enemies were already using darker forces to attack him. Certainly there were plenty of other claimants to the throne should Æthelred and Alfred both die. Æthelred and their elder brothers had children who would certainly make a bid and a little poison applied in the right quarter might help matters along. Then again, in Saxon minds, Alfred's illness could have been a curse. England was beset with pagan invaders, who had for the moment retired back to York, but few can have believed that they would stay there for long. Either God or the devil might be marking out the House of Ecgberht as the next lamb to the slaughter. No doubt suspicious glances also flew between Mercians and West Saxons. Despite their new alliance and shared coinage, Burgred had dealt with the Vikings and whatever bargain he had now struck to get them out of Mercia would undoubtedly be at someone else's expense. The question was, whose?

6

The Wild Boar of Ashdown

And the cuckoo, too, harbinger of summer,
Sings in a mournful voice, boding bitter sorrow.
The Seafarer, quoted in K. Crossley-Holland,
The Anglo-Saxon World, p. 51

WHEN THE SIEGE of Nottingham was over, Ivarr retired to York for most of the following year to marshal his forces and prepare for the second stage of his plan. The army's long stay in East Anglia and his probing raid into Mercia must have given him a good idea of the relative prosperity and military preparedness of the kingdoms he might face next. Both campaigns had also allowed his scouts to gain a firmer understanding of the inland waterways and road system that he would have to use to move his forces. It was undoubtedly a good time too to gather intelligence, both from the conquered people of Northumbria, who seem to have adapted quickly to life under Viking rule, and from any rebellious elements in the aristocracies of other kingdoms who might look to him for support. Indeed, it was just such disaffected Anglo-Saxon elements that would prove to be Ivarr's greatest weapon. He drew disgruntled nobles to his side, and to their kingdom's doom, like a Viking siren.

In fact such 'unholy' alliances between pagan Vikings and Christian nobles were nowhere near as rare as chroniclers might like to have us believe. In kingdoms without a formal structure for inheritance there were plenty of would-be kings who were quite happy to conspire with the devil for a chance of greatness. In Francia the hard-pressed Charles the Bald had a similar problem with his nephew Pippin II, the disinherited heir of the kingdom of Aquitaine. Having led several rebellions and then been reconciled (only to rebel again, as was the

Carolingian way), Pippin had finally agreed to take monastic vows but had renounced these at the first opportunity and was casting around once more for allies against his uncle. In 864 he had found what he was looking for in the form of a Viking warband on the Loire and he seems to have had no ideological problem in allying himself to them. *The Annals of St Bertin*, now under the authorship of Hincmar of Rheims, take a typically outraged Christian view, saying: 'Pippin, son of Pippin, who had changed back from being a monk to become a layman and an apostate, joined company with the Northmen and lived like one of them.' Clearly Hincmar wants us to believe that Pippin has gone so far as to become a pagan, thus placing himself beyond contempt, but the 'apostasy' probably only refers to the renouncing of his monastic vows. If simply living amongst Vikings was what damned him in Hincmar's eyes, then Wulfhere, who was still the incumbent archbishop in York (despite the presence in the city of Ivarr), would have a lot of explaining to do. In fact Vikings did not demand religious uniformity from any of their subjects or allies, as Wulfhere could testify. What made Hincmar so furious, and what led Charles later that year to indict Pippin at Pîtres as a 'traitor to his fatherland and to Christianity', was the realization that an alliance with the Vikings could change the balance of power and with it the very rules of Christian warfare.

There were many notables amongst the surviving Anglo-Saxon kingdoms of England who had everything to gain by making contact with Ivarr in the summer of 869 and the political manoeuvrings must have been intense. Every kingdom had would-be ruling families willing to run the risk of attempting a deal with the Northmen in return for power, even if that power was held on strictly Viking terms. Certainly there were plenty of Mercian dynasts who might have something to gain from the humiliation and defeat of Burgred and the 'B' dynasty, while Burgred himself must have been aware that it could prove fatal to alienate either his opponents or the Vikings themselves. Nor was it inconceivable for West Saxon elements to express to the Viking invaders their dissatisfaction with the House of Ecgberht. In this deadly game of diplomacy, the outcome would only be known when the Viking host was again on the march.

Then in the autumn of 869, with the puppet ruler Ecgberht apparently in firm control of Northumbria, news drifted south that the Great Heathen Army was in fact on the move. Travelling down the old Roman road of Ermine Street, Ivarr and his men headed into Mercia where no attempt was made either to check their advance or to meet them in battle. Indeed, apparently either unwilling or unable to do anything, Burgred simply stood by as the pagans marched into his kingdom. But whether he was paralysed by fear or simply biding his time, it was fair to say that he had no need to make a pre-emptive strike. Soon it would become clear, both in the field and at court, whether he was the next Viking target; all he had to do was wait. But those were uneasy days for Burgred as his scouts brought him regular bulletins on the whereabouts in his kingdom of the Great Heathen Army, and he scanned the eyes of his court to see whether any betrayed a glimmering of disloyalty.

The news each day seemed good, however. The Vikings showed no intention of stopping or turning from their route. Skirting around the fen, they continued south, making for the monastery at Peterborough, which in true Viking style they sacked, killing the monks and abbot in the process. Now was the real moment of decision. The scouts of three Saxon kingdoms must have watched with bated breath, knowing that one would ride hence with the dreaded news that his kingdom was the target. But when Ivarr did move out, the rider scrambling away from Peterborough with his heart in his mouth was not riding for Mercia, nor for Wessex, but back to East Anglia. Ivarr's next victim would be the nation he had first made peace with, the country that had nurtured and fed his army for that first fateful year he had spent on British soil. The cuckoo had returned to the nest.

The details of Ivarr's campaign against King Edmund and the East Anglians now form the backdrop to the creation one of England's most enduring folk tales for, in the following days and weeks, Edmund would lose his country but gain a martyr's crown.

Other than a rather matter-of-fact entry in the *Anglo-Saxon Chronicle*, our main source for the events of the last days of the life of both Edmund and the independent kingdom of East Anglia that died with him is Abbo of Fleury. A continental monk, he travelled to England to garner information for his hagiography of the king about a hundred years after the events he describes. The translator of Abbo's work into English gives us some additional information about this trip. It appears that whilst Abbo was staying at Ramsey Abbey, he took the opportunity to talk to an ageing archbishop who told him how in his youth he had heard St Edmund's armour-bearer speak of those fateful days at first hand.

The words of this old soldier were clearly still fresh in the archbishop's memory and Abbo passes on his excitement at first hearing the tale. He tells us that Ivarr invaded East Anglia suddenly – 'just like a wolf'. Edmund for his part was either completely taken by surprise or was for some reason unable to quickly muster a force. Having lived with the Vikings on his land for a whole year, he clearly expected that whatever peace he had formerly made would still hold. He may therefore have expected friendship from the Sons of Ragnar. Equally there is a hint in the sources that the arrival of the Great Heathen Army was accompanied by a sea-borne invasion, launched from Northumbria and possibly led by another of the Sons of Ragnar – Ubba. This would have divided Edmund's resources too thinly to fight off a two-pronged attack.

Whatever the circumstances, Abbo tells us that Ivarr scented blood and dispatched a runner with a peremptory message to the king:

Ivarr, our king, bold and victorious on sea and on land, has dominion over many peoples, and has now come to this country with his army to take up winter-quarters with his men. He commands that you share your hidden gold-hordes and your ancestral possessions with him straightaway, and that you become his vassal-king, if you want to stay alive, since you now don't have the forces that you can resist him.

Whether or not Ivarr ever spoke such words, the sentiment was certainly true, and it would have been in character for him to attempt to make Edmund his puppet rather than try for all-out conquest. Although this meant smaller short-term gains for his men, it avoided the problems of having to administer a kingdom. It also rendered the vassal weak enough in manpower, prestige and money to be easily removed at will, should that later prove desirable. But to his surprise Edmund refused, saying he would only submit if Ivarr became a Christian. It was a bold move, and a desperate one, on the part of a king still trying to appear to be in control. Knowing that this was not the case, Ivarr was in no mood to listen. If Edmund wanted to keep his kingdom, he would have to fight for it. He did. And he lost.

The final fate of Edmund is so bound up in legend as to be almost irretrievable. Some chroniclers say simply that he died in battle against the Great Heathen Army, as is most likely, whilst others claim that he was captured and executed. For his part Abbo tells us that Edmund was imprisoned by Ivarr and cruelly tortured, being beaten with sticks and whipped. When his assailants finally tired of this, the martyr was tied to a tree and used for archery practice until 'He was entirely covered with their arrows, like the bristles of a hedgehog.' Then and only then did Ivarr release him from his torment by beheading him. In a final cruel trick, the pagans were said to have hidden his head in a bramble thicket in the forest so that his people would not have an entire body to bury. By this point the story has drifted not only into England's wild places but deep into legend, for now the people of East Anglia begin searching through the woods for the head, calling, 'Where are you now, friend?' Rather surprisingly the head answers back, 'Here, here, here.' Eventually the talking head guides them to the thicket where they find it resting between the paws of a grey wolf that has guard over it. The legend of St Edmund had begun and the future prosperity of his cult centre, Bury St Edmunds, was assured.

Another legend, or rather saga, was also in the making. In just four years, Ivarr's Viking army had defeated two Anglo-Saxon kingdoms, executed their kings and wiped them from the map for ever. But before the Vikings could strike again, this figure also disappears from the scene. With Northumbria and East Anglia in his grasp, Ivarr now vanishes from the *Anglo-Saxon Chronicle* as well as from many other sources. According to Æthelweard, writing a century after events, Ivarr died shortly after St Edmund – divine justice finally catching up with the double regicide. But there is tantalizing evidence to suggest that he simply slipped out of one set of chronicles and into another, as he had done once before.

In 870, the year after Edmund's death, 'Imhar' returns to the Irish annals, where he is recorded as campaigning against the Picts at Dunbarton on the Clyde with his old ally, Olaf the White, king of Dublin. Ivarr, it seems, felt that his future lay in the North, in the great Viking cities of York and Dublin, and in prospective victories against the Picts of Scotland. If so, it was a perfectly logical move. Ivarr was a Scandinavian, and Scotland and her islands were closer to his central sphere of influence than southern England. If he could conquer Scotland to add to the Viking kingdoms in Dublin and

Northumbria he could create a whole new Scandinavian country with its feet in both North and Irish Seas. It might make him as powerful as any Viking had ever been.

The removal of Ivarr from southern England did not mark an end to the Viking threat there, however. If Burgred and Æthelred allowed themselves a sigh of relief at the Norseman's return north, they were allowing themselves too much. Ivarr may have gone, but the warlord Bagsecg and Ivarr's own brother Halfdan were still in East Anglia, along with a large portion of the Great Heathen Army. The Sons of Ragnar had not finished with the Anglo-Saxons and their subsequent port of call would be Wessex itself.

It remains a mystery as to why the Vikings chose Wessex next instead of consolidating their victories in Northumbria and East Anglia by the conquest of the huge nation that lay between them: Mercia. If Burgred had managed to broker some form of deal with the Sons of Ragnar after they moved out of Northumbria, we know nothing of it. Equally, having marched through Mercia and weighed her up, perhaps the Vikings considered that nation still a step too far. Wessex had a young and relatively untried king whose only real experience of Vikings had been the stalemate at Nottingham. They knew that his country was rich and that alone made it a target. Now it was time to see what the sons of Æthelwulf were really made of.

By the late autumn of 870, news reached Æthelred that the Great Heathen Army had crossed into Wessex, marching south across the Thames and into Berkshire, the county of his brother Alfred's birth. Their target was Reading, a royal centre from where they would have excellent access to the Roman road system that extended across Wessex. Reading also offered the ancient trackways across the Berkshire downs and, of course, the waterways of the Thames and the Kennet. It was a classic Viking winter base, at the confluence of two rivers, easily defendable but with excellent escape routes should that prove necessary. Such a base was an essential target for an army travelling in winter as, whilst winter fighting brought an element of surprise and made life considerably harder for the West Saxons, it also made living off the land – something the Viking army simply had to do – much harder too. This was perhaps the main reason for choosing Reading, for as a royal centre not only would it have laid in its own winter supplies but it would also have in store the local royal *feorm*.

Royal taxation in Alfred's day did not simply consist of collecting money; indeed, of what the king was owed, relatively little was paid in cash. As the king and his court were always on the move – and hence unable to tend land themselves – they were most in need of provisions. The *feorm* was the requirement of the people of Wessex to deliver to their local royal centre or vill sufficient supplies of both food and fodder to provide for the court when it arrived in their area, whenever that might be. What this involved is set out in the laws of Ine, the seventh-century king of Wessex, who required that each unit of ten hides deliver to its local vill '10 vats of honey, 300 loaves, 12 "ambers" of Welsh ale, 30 of clear ale, 2 full-grown cows, or 10 wethers, 10 geese, 20 hens, 10 cheeses, an "amber" full of butter, 5 salmon, 20 pounds of fodder and 100 eels'. This list not only demonstrates the large quantity of provisioning required by the court (which was probably larger still by the ninth century) but also gives an insight into the high-quality diet enjoyed by royalty. This is what awaited the successful captor of Reading. Gaining control of the place would also serve a double purpose, not only in providing the Vikings with ready supplies but in preventing Æthelred from getting hold of his food rents and hence making it harder for him to feed his own army.

Taking Reading itself would not prove difficult for a large and professional army. Although a royal centre, it was not a town in any modern sense, lacking both the manpower and the defences to put up much resistance. By the end of the year the Vikings were in place. Within a matter of hours, they set about fortifying a part of the site against attack and attempting to secure any resources in the neighbourhood before a hastily raised fyrd could cut or burn the local crops and attempt to starve them out. But the elements of surprise and speed, which had served the Vikings so well in their previous campaigns, failed them now. The local ealdorman Æthelwulf mustered his local levies more quickly than the Northmen had expected, perhaps guessing that Reading would be their target. A detachment of the Wessex fyrd and the Great Heathen Army met just three days after the Vikings took Reading, with unexpected results. It was Sunday, 31 December 870.

Halfdan and Bagsecg must have believed that they were relatively immune to attack during the twelve-day holiday of Christmas, which appeared to provide an ideal opportunity for them to reconnoitre the area and seize whatever they could before West Saxon troops arrived. But the large foraging party that they sent out that day under the command of two senior commanders or jarls was walking into an ambush. Having skirted the vast and largely impenetrable Windsor Forest to their south, they had followed the banks of the river Kennet towards Englefield. Here, on the old Roman road between Silchester and Dorchester-on-Thames, the Berkshire ealdorman's men took them completely by surprise. Not only were they routed but both their leaders – very senior men in the Viking army – were killed. Perhaps there was now a chance for the Saxons to capitalize on this sudden reverse and drive the heathens out of Reading into a hostile countryside in the middle of winter. If there was, it would go wanting for, having chased his enemy back behind their fortifications, Ealdorman Æthelwulf brought his army to a halt.

Whether he felt unable to press home his advantage due to the small size of his force, or whether he was under orders to wait for Æthelred and Alfred (who were even now marching hard for Reading), the delay proved fateful. The Vikings who had straggled back into camp that day were dismayed. They had simply not faced defeat on their recent campaigns and even the stalemate at Nottingham had been masterfully turned to their advantage. Now two jarls were dead along with unnumbered men and, without Ivarr, their army suddenly seemed vulnerable. But it was only a temporary weakness and time seems to have swiftly healed whatever wounds, real or imagined, the Englefield survivors brought back to camp with them. By the time that the king and Alfred finally arrived outside the town just four days later, the attitude inside had already changed.

After hearing of the surprise victory at Englefield, King Æthelred and his brother had raced to Reading, keen to drive home their advantage and make the victory their own. As soon as their force was mustered they immediately set about besieging the town. The chronicles report that a 'great slaughter' was made on both sides. But the Saxons faced not Vikings caught unawares in the field but a well dug in and regrouped force who were prepared for the attack and quite able to defend their position. The Vikings had used their time in Reading to dig a dyke between the Thames and the Kennet, thereby creating a fortified island defended with an earth rampart and probably a wooden palisade. Having 'retreated' to lure the West Saxon forces into the difficult terrain around this island, they burst out suddenly. The shock left the Saxons in utter disarray. Æthelred and Alfred were defeated. The *Anglo-Saxon Chronicle* flatly records that 'the Danes had possession of the battlefield'. The twelfth-century chronicler Geoffrey Gaimar adds further information, which may well be based on a now-lost source. He says that not only was the Wessex fyrd defeated but it was completely routed, and also that Æthelred and Alfred escaped solely due to their superior knowledge of the local terrain. Being pursued as far as Wistley Green, they were able to cross the Thames via a ford that was unknown to the Vikings. Even then, their army did not stop to regroup until it reached Windsor.

And there was worse news – a setback at least as great as the Viking loss of two jarls – when it became clear that the ealdorman of Berkshire, Æthelwulf, perhaps overeager to repeat his feat of four days before, had been killed. Recovering his body from the battlefield now became a priority. Another chronicler reports that, at great risk, his corpse was stealthily removed so that it could be buried in what was probably his home town of Derby. That the ealdorman of Berkshire should have wished for burial in a distant part of Mercia reveals how recently the former had been a part of the latter. As Æthelred organized the dispatch of his funerary cortège north, it raised a new question in his mind. While this Mercian-cum-West Saxon had been fighting for him, where was Burgred and the Mercian army? When this same Viking force had threatened Nottingham, he and Alfred had gone to provide support. Now it was Æthelred who was in need of help. But if he did call to Mercia, he received no reply. In this fight Wessex was on its own.

With their decisive victory at Reading, the Vikings lost no time in venturing forth from their base and prosecuting a winter war in the heart of Wessex. With their enemy in some disarray, it was in the Viking interest to try to bring the Saxons to battle again soon. A decisive victory would give them the freedom to move and forage across a larger area of the kingdom, avoiding the dangers of a long siege back in their Reading fort. Thus it was that Halfdan and Bagsecg set out along the old section of Roman road that ran from the abandoned Roman city of Silchester to Dorchester-on-Thames, in the direction of the settlement and the Thames crossing at

Wallingford, with the lands of the wealthy monastery of Abingdon beyond. It was a provocative move that would certainly require a response from the Wessex fyrd if it was to protect one of its most valuable fords and wealthiest monasteries.

So on the morning of Monday, 8 January 871, just four days after their defeat at Reading, Æthelred, Alfred and their army found themselves drawing up ranks at Ashdown, most probably on Kingstanding Hill on the Icknield Way, directly across the path of the advancing Great Heathen Army. Even today it is possible to see why Æthelred should have pitched his camp here. In the days before woods crowned the top of the hill, it held a commanding position over the local area. To the east the king looked down on the old Roman road known as the Icknield Way, whilst just beyond he could see the ford across the river Thames at Moulsford. To the west a still more ancient trackway, known as the 'Fair Mile', led south to Lowbury Hill. There it met up with the prehistoric Ridgeway path, which tracked across the chalk spine of the North Wessex downs and the Chilterns. If there was any place from which to observe the Vikings' approach and make sure you stood directly in their path, forcing battle, it was at Ashdown.

It was a suitable place for a last stand. The king must have known that the victorious Vikings would not stay in Reading long and that they would want quickly to inflict another, more crushing, defeat on him. Equally, he could not afford to allow them to take key strategic centres and pillage Wessex at will. The protection of Wessex was, after all, his first duty as king. If he was to retain the respect of the fyrd and his witan – and hence his crown – he needed a victory, and soon.

If the Viking army left Reading at dawn that day, they would first have come into sight of Æthelred's troops at about eleven that morning. Seeing the massed Saxon army before them, Halfdan and Bagsecg split their army into two forces, one led by the two kings and the other by the jarls. In response the Saxons also split their force, with one half under the command of King Æthelred and the other under Alfred. The Viking army now took up the standard military formation of the day – the shield wall – in which each division presented a front line of closely locked shields to defend the mass of troops behind. Then, shouting taunts at their opponents facing them, they slowly began to move forward.

As the enemy came closer, Alfred formed up his own shield wall and tracked the movements of the jarls' army to ensure that he was not outflanked. While he was concentrating on this, his brother's division should have blocked the forward path of Halfdan and Bagsecg's men but, no doubt to the dismay of many in Alfred's contingent, they were not yet ready to fight. Alfred and his men were alone in the field. The jarls' force was skirting around the sides of his defences, whilst Halfdan's army advanced relentlessly towards him from the front. The situation for the young prince could hardly have been more dangerous.

Whether this was a tactic or a mistake is obscured by later legend. Asser tells the story that Æthelred, always the devout Christian, was delayed because he had to finish hearing Mass before the battle: 'declaring firmly that he would not leave that place alive before the priest had finished Mass, and that he would not forsake divine service for that of men.' If this was bravura, it was reckless to say the least, although Asser is kind enough to credit this devotion with ensuring God's support in the battle, something that of course any Anglo-Saxon would have considered vital. As the Vikings took up position on the battlefield, Alfred's troops found themselves in an increasingly precarious position. They could not retreat, which would have allowed the enemy to take the better ground and, in the process, risk their withdrawal turning into full-scale flight, but could they stand alone against the entire enemy force? As the two Viking divisions began to close in on Alfred, he had to make a decision and he chose a bold one. Even if the whole situation was deliberate on the part of Æthelred, it put his brother and his whole army in mortal danger, for Alfred, unable to turn back, had only one choice. Without waiting for the king's support, he ordered the shield wall to close up and attacked, as Asser proudly puts it, 'like a wild boar'.

Battle in the ninth century was joined when the opposing shield walls met and it often proved a slow and bloody game of attrition. These battles were not characterized by heroic single combat or daring cavalry charges. As each side was protected from the other by round shields that reached from shoulder to knee, the two armies could only push against each other, looking for gaps in the opposite shield wall into which they might jab their long ash spears and steel-edged swords. The wealthy might enjoy further protection from a simple helmet and a leather jacket, or perhaps even a little chainmail, but most of the levy had to fight in their ordinary working clothes. With each jab and thrust, wounds would be inflicted until one individual in the shield wall gave way. Then another from the next rank would have to step up and fill the breach, and another, until either there were no more men to fill the void or the dead so clogged the front line that their courage failed them and the wall broke, forcing the survivors to flee.

But now, as the Viking divisions pressed down on Alfred from both sides, Æthelred suddenly entered the fray. According to Florence of Worcester, he hurried on to the field straight from his devotions, more of a white rabbit than a warlord, but whether accidental or deliberate his late appearance proved decisive. The arrival of his force seems to have come as a surprise to the Vikings. They had treated Alfred's small division as though it were the whole army, moving to simply outflank and engulf it. With the appearance of the rest of the fyrd, in trying to outflank Alfred they themselves became outflanked and were driven back. The battle was not a foregone conclusion, however, and it raged for many hours yet around a small thorn tree, which Asser informs us he has seen for himself, making him the earliest battlefield tourist in English history. At some point in this struggle, Bagsecg, one of the two Viking leaders, was killed and this turned the tide. The Great Heathen Army, bound together by the fame of its leaders, began to fragment and retreat, which turned rapidly to a rout. A delighted Asser records that 'the entire Viking army was put to flight, right on till nightfall and into the following day, until such time as they reached the stronghold from which they had come. The Christians followed them till nightfall, cutting them down on all sides.'

It was a bad reverse for Halfdan. The chronicles tell us that he had lost his co-commander as well as five jarls, in addition to the two he had lost against Ealdorman Æthelwulf. With so many important leaders having been killed, it is likely that the toll amongst the ordinary warriors was also very high, perhaps even into the 'thousands' mentioned by Asser.

Certainly the force that staggered back to the Reading fortress must have been severely diminished and greatly demoralized. It was one thing to be ambushed and routed when in a foraging party, but defeat in a set-piece battle did not bring the sort of fame that Halfdan needed if he was to retain control of his men. Æthelred, however, had avenged the defeat at Reading and might for the first time reasonably have allowed himself the thought that he would be the one to free England from this terrible Viking scourge. Alfred too had proved his mettle. If Æthelred's delay in entering the battle had been a mistake, Alfred had courageously stood alone. If, however, it had been a deliberate stratagem, Alfred had taken the dangerous lead that had sprung the trap. Either way Alfred was a hero. It was his first taste of victory in open battle, instead of stalemate and defeat in sieges. He had looked into the eyes of the Sons of Ragnar and lived. He also might have permitted himself a moment to reflect on a brighter future. But if either brother dreamt that night of having turned the Viking tide, they were to awaken into a very stark dawn.

For the next two weeks Halfdan stayed behind his Reading defences, licking his wounds and unable, or unwilling, to forage outside for food. It was around this time that he at last received the good news that reinforcements were in the Thames estuary and heading his way. Whether this was the catalyst, or the rapidly depleting food supplies in his camp, he was spurred to new action. After two weeks the Vikings, or a least a large party of them, moved out again into the Berkshire countryside. This time they thrust south towards the royal vill at Basing, prompting an immediate response from Æthelred. A move in this direction represented a direct threat to Æthelred's capital at Winchester, which might be read as an attempt to seize the city and deal a pre-emptive, knock-out blow to his regime. With this in mind the West Saxons did not so much march as scramble into the field.

The force that Æthelred, Alfred and their army found arrayed against them at Basing was clearly neither demoralized nor puny; it may even have already been reinforced with fresh Viking blood. For all its recent success, however, the Wessex fyrd presented a fairly sorry sight by now. This was their fourth battle in a month, in the coldest part of winter. The victory at Ashdown had boosted confidence but it had taken a bloody toll on Saxon as well as Viking forces. Numbers were depleted and those who had survived so far were anxious to return home.

Æthelred's problem was that he had no mechanism for rotating service in the fyrd, no way of resting troops and little hope of recruiting more. Apart from the soldiers who formed part of his own household, the vast majority of his county levies were called up to service by the ealdorman of each shire, primarily to fight in that county for its protection. Outside the areas immediately under threat, it was hard to persuade men to come to arms as they quite naturally wanted to protect their homes, should the menace suddenly head their way. In some respects the king also needed these other county levies to stay at home lest by his summoning the nation's entire fighting force to one place, the Vikings simply outflanked them and attacked the parts of the kingdom left unprotected.

So the men of the royal household and the Berkshire fyrd who now looked over their shield wall at Basing might have had the best of the recent fighting but they did not look like victors-in-waiting. And if they had defeat written in their eyes that day it was with good reason, for a few hours later they were fleeing, leaving Halfdan and his men as masters of the battlefield.

Although Asser and the Anglo-Saxon chronicler admit that Basing was a Viking victory, it does not seem to have been on the scale of Ashdown. Both Vikings and Saxons withdrew, exhausted, to relative safety in order to rest and regroup. February was not a month in which even Vikings chose to fight. Having failed to deliver a quick mortal blow on the House of Ecgberht as they had done to the royal lines of Northumbria and East Anglia, they probably needed time to rethink their strategy.

A rest also suited Æthelred and Alfred, who could be proud of the fact that they had not folded under the initial attack. Equally, however, they must have been acutely aware that they were still far from decisively expelling this enemy from their land. They too had plans to make. As the war diminished in scale to Viking foraging parties being harried by small Saxon militias, the House of Ecgberht gathered the witan at the unidentified site of Swinbeorg to discuss the dangerous days ahead.

The purpose of the meeting was brutal in its simplicity. In the coming months no one knew whether either Æthelred or Alfred would survive and some provision had to be made for the succession – a will for Wessex. The instigator of the meeting may well have been Alfred himself. He had been happy to leave his inheritance in Æthelred's hands when he acceded to the throne, but he now needed to be sure that, if Æthelred died in the coming war, as he very well might, then he, Alfred, would inherit both the kingdom and the resources to rule it. There was also the question of what would happen to their children. Æthelred had two sons – Æthelhelm and Æthelwold – and Alfred's daughter Æthelflæd may also have been born by this date. There was of course every chance that Alfred too would one day have sons.

The needs of these children, and their future prospects as heirs to Wessex, had to be protected but that protection had to be balanced against the importance of keeping them out of the equation until such time as was necessary. Alfred could not tolerate the possibility of a faction based around the children of his older brother trying to seize the throne if and when Æthelred died. A civil war could destroy Wessex as fast as a Viking army and the Vikings would no doubt be delighted to help. Alfred needed to know he had a free hand. The deal that he and Æthelred struck at Swinbeorg, which Alfred later dutifully recorded in his own will, was quite simple: 'and each of us gave to the other his pledge, that whichever of us lived longer should succeed both to lands and treasures and to all the other's possessions except the part which each of us had bequeathed to his children.'

But the bulk of the inheritance, as well as the role of kingship itself, was to pass as before from brother to brother. Hence the youngest brother would find himself not only king but with the right to dispose of his estate to whomsoever he wished. Whether the king or his young sons at court that day realized it yet, this meant that a child of Alfred's, not one of his older brothers', would one day be king. It was the right decision for Wessex in its hour of need but it would come back to haunt Alfred, bringing him betrayal and treachery. Although a terrible price to pay, it would eventually ensure that it was his descendants who inherited the throne of Wessex and transformed it into the throne of England.

It seems unlikely that there was any calculation on Alfred's part in this regarding his children. He needed to ensure that he would rule should his brother die and the witan must have been equally eager to ensure that Æthelred made the 'wild boar' of Ashdown his clear heir. That apart, it was probably the case that, should both brothers die and die soon, as was very likely, then the succession would fall to Æthelred's children, if the witan believed them old enough and strong enough to take on the mantle. There was no time to think about Alfred's infant daughter or his as yet unborn sons.

With the succession agreed there was barely a moment to breathe before news came that the Viking army was back in the field en masse. Æthelred and Alfred once again summoned the fyrd and marched towards 'Meretun' (possibly Marten, twenty miles north of Wilton) to meet them. The battle that took place there, probably on Thursday, 22 March 871, is not even mentioned in Asser's work but that should not be taken to mean that it was irrelevant. The *Anglo-Saxon Chronicle* is less shy. It tells us that Halfdan again split his troops into two units and that battle was initially joined on both these fronts with some success. At first the Vikings were driven back and for a while it looked as if they would flee the field, but late in the day something rallied them and they fought back strongly to seize victory.

Of course their initial withdrawal may have been tactical in itself, drawing forward the Saxon fyrd in the belief that it was winning, only to turn and suddenly throw it back. But either by luck, bloody labour or design, the Vikings held the field at the battle's end. The *Anglo-Saxon Chronicle* goes on to admit that this was more than just a minor reverse and that many important Wessex men died that day, including Heahmund, another fighting bishop who had succeeded Ealhstan in the see of Sherborne. As he had so recently recounted the names of all the important Vikings killed at Ashdown, perhaps it was this similar but more painful tally of Saxon names that caught in Asser's throat and made him reluctant to record the battle at all.

Another greater wound may also have been inflicted on Wessex at Meretun, one on the body of Æthelred himself. The king was only around twenty-five years old but after the battle the next time we hear of him is in his funeral obsequies. His death, shortly after Easter, which that year fell on 15 April, just twenty-eight days after the battle, may indicate that a wound received there, or at an earlier engagement, had finally taken its toll. Such a festering injury may have been the reason for calling the council at Swinbeorg in the first place, if Æthelred's life was already visibly ebbing away. Such a cause of death would certainly not be unexpected. From the roll-call of senior figures killed on both sides in the battles of early 871, it is clear that these engagements were not simply fought by foot soldiers while the rich and powerful looked on from a safe distance. Both in the Viking army and the Wessex fyrd, commanders were expected to lead from the front, which was what both Æthelred and Alfred had done. Now Æthelred, either through injury or illness, had paid the price with his life and the last of the children of Æthelwulf was called to the throne.

With a victorious Viking army celebrating in their Reading fortress and his brother's cortège already on its way to the family mausoleum at Wimborne, Alfred had no need of more bad news. But just at this moment scouts from Reading brought him one final devastating dispatch. Another whole Viking host – a 'Great Summer Army' – had sailed up the Thames and joined Halfdan. On board were thousands of fresh troops and three new Viking warlords. Amongst them was a sea king called Guthrum who would soon bring Alfred and Wessex to the verge of despair. Alfred finally had what he wanted – he was king – but king of what and for how long?

The peculiar hill of Burrow Mump rises over the landscape in which the legend of Alfred was born, the Somerset Levels

This facsimile of the opening page of Otho A. xii, drawn by James Hill in 1722, is as close as we can now get to the manuscript of Asser's biography of Alfred, destroyed in the great Cotton Library fire

Alfred in the swineherd's cottage, a typically romantic nineteenth-century engraving. A sullen and distracted Alfred sits reading while the swineherd's wife makes the legendary cakes

Domino meo venerabili piissimoque. Omnium Brittannie insulae xpiano rum rectori. ælfred. Anglorum saxo num. regi. Asser. omnium. servo rum dei ultimus. mille modam advota desideriorum. utriusque vitae. prosperitatem.

Anno domineæ incarnationis. dccc.xlix. natus est ælfred angul saxonum rex mulla regia quedicitur wanating mill apaga quenommat berroc scire quepagatauter uo catur aberroc silua ubibuxus babundan eissime nascit cuiusgenelogia talis talserie

The Hero King, Alfred meeting Guthrum in the Somerset
Levels. To the Victorians, Alfred was always a hero, never a failure,
and his time in the wilderness provided greater opportunity for
derring-do

right: Imperial Alfred. This engraving, first published in 1732, shows Alfred as the prototype English king: warrior, scholar, founder of the British Navy and hence originator of the British Empire

below: The bones of Alfred's grandfather Ecgberht were moved from the Old Saxon Minster at Winchester into the later Norman cathedral. Together with those of many other Anglo-Saxon kings, they were placed in their current Renaissance chests above the choir by Bishop Fox in 1525. As the remains were jumbled during the Civil War, it is now uncertain who lies in which chest

Above: These rings, bearing the names of Alfred's sister Æthelswith and father Æthelwulf, were probably not worn by them but were given as gifts to friends or retainers. Because of this traditional practice, lords were often referred to in contemporary literature as 'ring-givers'

ANCIENT COFFIN LID
OBSERVE THE TWO INCISED CROSSES INDICATING THE BURIAL OF AN IMPORTANT PERSON. THIS LID POSSIBLY COVERED THE BODY OF KING ETHELWULF WHO WAS BURIED HERE IN 858. HE WAS SUBSEQUENTLY EXHUMED AND LATER RE-INTERRED AT WINCHESTER. NEAR HIS SON KING ALFRED.

Left: An Anglo-Saxon coffin lid from Steyning in eastern Wessex. According to the *Annals of St Neot's*, King Æthelwulf was originally buried here, so this may once have covered his body

he monastic community on the island of Lindisfarne was the first in England to come
to contact with Viking raiders in 793. For many Anglo-Saxons this attack was an omen,
prelude to the end of the world

Left: The Cuerdale hoard the largest known Viking Age silver hoard from northern Europe, containing some 8,500 objects – was buried in a lead-lined chest on the banks of the river Ribble in Lancashire around 905 Despite its apparent quality, to its Viking owner it was simply scrap silver, nearly forty kilos of it

Below: Patched, mended and rebuilt many times since, parts of the old Roman walls of York still encircle the city, as they did in 866 on the arrival of Ivarr the Boneless

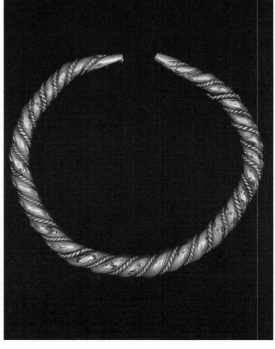

Above: In Alfred's day the Somerset Levels were an impassable wilderness of marsh, stream and reed bed, hiding low-lying islets of fir ground. It was the ideal refu for bandits and outlaws – an even a deposed king

Left: A stubby monument marks the location of the monastery that Alfred built a Athelney. The site was chose because this small hillock ha once been his home and his hiding place – the last part of Wessex he could claim to ru

7

The Lonely King

. . . a maiden of the Geats,
with her tresses swept up, intoned
a dirge for Beowulf time after time,
declared she lived in dread of days to come
dark with carnage and keening, terror of the enemy,
humiliation and captivity.

Beowulf, quoted in K. Crossley-Holland,
The Anglo-Saxon World, p. 141

ALFRED'S FIRST FEW weeks on the throne were days of sadness and memory. As he travelled west with his brother's cortège towards Wimborne, the young king had time to reflect on the fleeting nature of power and fame in the ninth century. All his brothers were now dead, from the eldest, Æthelstan, who had died before Alfred could even remember, to the boy he had grown up with at court, Æthelred, who at twenty-five now lay cold and still in the cart that he followed. Gone too were the great characters from his childhood; the turbulent and warlike Bishop Ealhstan; the quiet and considered Swithun; his godfather Pope Leo; his betrayed father and, of course, his mother Osburh, who by now can have been little more to him than a vague idea. All these ghosts walked and rode with Alfred towards Wimborne in May 871.

The site of Æthelred's burial had been carefully chosen, not for convenience, but to help maintain the dwindling prestige of the House of Ecgberht. Where a royal body rested mattered to the peoples of the Anglo-Saxon kingdoms, and various factions of power-ful families favoured different sites − usually religious foundations established by each dynasty and often ruled by its female members. These wealthy monasteries could grow into cult centres where long-dead members of the family, particularly those who had died violent deaths at the hands of other dynasts, became revered as saints and whose blessed memory made them powerful allies in seizing or retaining any throne.

Just such a site awaited Alfred and his ghosts at Wimborne. A double monastery had been founded there by St Cuthburg, a sister of King Ine of Wessex and hence someone from whom Alfred claimed descent. Cuthburg seems to have been a particularly devout princess who had founded the house after separating from her husband, King Aldfrith of Northumbria, so that she could take the veil. Indeed, the strict observance required by her and the royal abbesses who followed seems to have surprised and horrified some of the young women, many of noble birth themselves, who entered the house in succeeding years. Rudolf of Fulda, in his *Life of Leofgyth*, written in 836, describes an occasion on which another younger sister of Ine, Tette, by then abbess herself, had to intervene in an extraordinary scene more akin to life at St Trinian's than at St Cuthburg's. He describes how, following the death of a particularly severe and unyielding nun who had often been in charge of discipline, the young women of the nunnery gathered round the woman's freshly dug grave and 'as soon as they saw the place where she was buried, they cursed her cruelty, nay more, they mounted the mound and, trampling it as if it were the dead corpse, they reproached the dead woman with most bitter insults to relieve their mortification.' When Tette finally arrived at the scene, the nuns had spent so long dancing on the woman's grave that the earth over it had sunk down half a foot below the ground surface. Terrified that they would be punished by God for this desecration, she arranged for three days of fasting (the usual penance for a confessed sin) in the nunnery, after which the sunken grave was found to have been miraculously restored.

Such tales were part and parcel of the life of these royal institutions, which represented far more than mere outward signs of piety on the part of the important families who founded them. In fact, they were a popular focal point for a family's power and wealth, often being sited at the centre of extensive landholdings and surrounded by the estates and homes of their followers. They also provided a place where those awkward 'extra' family members who might otherwise get in the way of a smooth inheritance could be dedicated to God, taking on a useful and influential role in the other great power base of the state, the Church. Thus if the itinerant kings of Anglo–Saxon England could ever be said to have had homes, it was in places like these, where royal and religious authority came together to present to the world an idealized view of a family who could claim both the bretwaldas and the blessed amongst their number.

Our only glimpse of what this particular institution actually looked like, our only description of the sight that must have greeted Alfred as he approached it, is also from Rudolf of Fulda, who was himself describing things second-hand with a degree of literary licence. The site was, however, clearly imposing:

> In the island of Britain which is inhabited by the nation of the English, is a place called amongst that people by the ancient name Wimborne, which, interpreted, can be rendered 'fountain of wine'; it received this name because of the great clarity and excellent flavour, in which it surpassed the other waters of that land. Here two monasteries were of old founded by kings of that race, surrounded with high and stout walls, and supplied with a sufficiency of income by a reasonable provision; one a monastery of clerics, and the other of women.

Within those 'stout walls' and between the monastic churches would have huddled numerous smaller wooden buildings where the members of the community slept and worked, surrounded by kitchen gardens and animal pens. At a site as important as Wimborne there may even have been a stone hall to which the monastery's 'Book of Life' could be ceremonially brought so that Æthelred's name might be inscribed amongst the lists of dead benefactors who had been buried there. Of that impressive institution no hint remains today save for a fifteenth-century memorial brass in the minster, commemorating the burial of Æthelred somewhere near by. His grave, as well as the monastery itself, are long since gone, destroyed in a later era of Viking attacks.

For Alfred, his family and the monastic community at Wimborne, however, it was not, in the first instance, the corporeal remains of Æthelred that mattered. Their primary concern was to honour the *moneth's mynde* – the 'month's mind' – that marked a month of continual prayer for the soul of the departed, beginning on the day of his death. In between the special commemorations required on the third, seventh and thirtieth day after death, there was time for the Wessex witan to meet to confirm Alfred's election as king. In truth they had little other choice as no one else of the House of Ecgberht was of an age to take on such a dangerous task. If other families were now eyeing the throne, at least at Wimborne they kept their ambitions to themselves.

It is probable, however, that few could have wanted the throne at this moment. Whilst Alfred may have celebrated his coronation there, such as it was, the overwhelming mood must have been funereal. In fact, no mention is made of any official coronation, Asser simply telling us that Alfred now 'took over the government', but a West Saxon order of service for the anointing of kings exists from the early ninth century, implying that he was formally crowned. The anointing of the king's head with holy oil during a religious service marked a profound change in his nature in the minds of Anglo-Saxons. As the oil touched him, he became different from all the other ealdormen and thegns, all the other members of royal and noble families who might just as easily become king. But this otherness did not simply give him new rights; it also added new and heavy responsibilities.

Alfred himself in later life recalled his feelings on becoming king in his translation of Boethius' *The Consolation of Philosophy*, where his own memories of this time flood into his rather free translation: 'Look . . . you know that desire for and possession of earthly power never pleased me overmuch, and that I did not unduly desire this earthly rule.' And his reluctance was well founded. In heading west for Æthelred's funeral, Alfred had not left the Vikings cowering in their Reading lair. They were newly reinforced, buoyed up by recent victories and, by all accounts, hot on Alfred's heels. As Æthelred's *moneth's mynde* ended, in the last days of May, Alfred received news that drew him away from his brother's graveside. The combined Great Heathen Army and Great Summer Army were in the field, no longer simply skirmishing around Reading but deep in Wiltshire. They were said to be approaching the royal vill at Wilton, the very heart of Wessex. With the great magnates who had elected him still close at hand, at least Alfred could quickly order the summoning of the fyrd. What he did not know was how quickly the order, once it had been received by these shire ealdormen, would be carried out or what sort of numbers were left to answer it. Apart from these levies, Alfred would have to rely on the bloodied and weary households of his family and his nobles to step once more into the breach.

Somehow Alfred managed to put some form of army in the field and, just outside Wilton, came face to face for the first time with the new Viking kings who had joined Halfdan. Amongst them was the man who would very nearly prove to be his nemesis – Guthrum. The battle soon turned into the standard bloody labour that everyone must have expected, with much of the day spent pushing back and forth as parts of the shield walls weakened and yielded, only to be reinforced and reset. That Alfred's men could fight these (at least partly) fresh Viking forces to a stalemate speaks volumes as to the desperate nature of their struggle. It might take only the death or capture, or even the ignominious flight, of Alfred for the whole House of Ecgberht to fall, just as had Northumbria and East Anglia already.

But Alfred, the last of the sons of Æthelwulf, stood his ground. In the end the battle was brought to a conclusion, not by strength but by either a Saxon mistake or a Viking ruse. After hours of fighting, the Viking shield wall appeared to begin to collapse and they fell back. Such a sight must have seemed heaven-sent to the Wild Boar of Ashdown, who had seen his enemy turn their tails and run only once before, despite Asser's insistence that he was 'victorious in virtually all battles'. Sadly for Alfred, however, this was not to be a second Ashdown, but another false dawn. According to Asser, the fleeing Vikings turned and, seeing the paltry number of Saxons who chased them, their spirits revived. They counterattacked, forcing the Saxons from the field and claiming victory. This description of Asser's has all the hallmarks of a Viking ruse: using a feigned withdrawal to break the enemy's shield wall. Of course, it is possible that events unfolded exactly as he describes and that, seeing how close to exhaustion the Saxon army was – to the point where it could not organize a coherent pursuit, the Vikings decided that all was not lost and therefore made one final, successful attack. Either way, and no matter how Asser tries to explain the situation, it was a humiliation for the young king and one he could ill afford. The new Viking forces in Wessex had tasted blood, although at a high cost to themselves. Also, as they certainly knew, the defeat of a king in his first battle placed a question mark over his whole reign in the minds of his followers. Kings of Wessex ruled by consent forged from force, wealth and prestige. Alfred's hard-pressed ealdormen would not consent to many more defeats.

With most of the summer still ahead and the knowledge that Halfdan and Guthrum could well push the fighting season late into the year, Alfred needed a stopgap solution if he was to spend more than a few weeks on the throne. The answer was a dangerous gamble: to pay the Vikings to leave and buy at least a temporary peace. Such a strategy had had a decidedly mixed history. On the one hand it had arguably been the bedrock of Charles the Bald's policy in Francia for several years and he was still on the throne, but it risked causing resentment amongst a king's own nobles and bishops, who would of course be required to raise the huge sums of money asked for by the Vikings. Even when paid, the Northmen did not always keep their word by withdrawing and, even when they did, Vikings who had been paid once always came back for more in the end. There was also a very real risk of sliding into a dangerous game of tit-for-tat with other kingdoms. When the Vikings left one kingdom, they simply moved their sphere of operations elsewhere. When Charles the Bald paid them off, they often turned on England. If Alfred pursued the same policy they might return to Francia but eventually one or other king would run out of money and then the enemy would be there to stay.

But two other thoughts strengthened Alfred in his resolve. First, Charles the Bald had discovered that although payments did not buy lasting peace, they did buy time, which he had used well to build fortified bridges on his kingdom's major rivers to help prevent his enemy's return. Second, of course, Alfred had no other choice.

The ever-loyal Asser does not tarnish the memory of his king by going into details of the deal that was reached that summer with Halfdan, Guthrum, Anwend and Oscetel. He suggests, in fact, that Alfred had the upper hand, saying, 'the Saxons made peace with the Vikings on condition that they would leave them.'

It is not recorded what offer Alfred's emissaries took to the Viking fortress at Reading that summer, as it would not have sat well with the later, heroic image of the king. Whatever the offer was, it clearly appealed to the Vikings. Certainly a sizeable monetary payment must have been included. Some later charters suggest that Alfred required sums of money from his leading nobles and bishops that not all could readily raise. Instead they were forced to cede land back to the king in return for his paying their share. For Alfred this had the added benefit of increasing his landholding, which was essential if he was not to have a shortfall of land (and hence friends). To some religious houses, however, it appeared that they were preyed upon by enemy and friend alike, being robbed both by Vikings and by their own king. This might explain why a later mediaeval tradition at the monastery of Abingdon (which may have also been sacked around this time) compared Alfred to Judas. The comparison was nevertheless unfair as Alfred took only what was needed to preserve the kingdom, whilst his enemy was happy to take everything until all was destroyed. The monks of Abingdon had only to consider the smouldering ruins and freshly dug graves at the monastery at Peterborough to understand what would have happened to them if Alfred had not fought when he could and paid when he could not.

There must also have been another element to the peace negotiations that summer that may go some way to explaining the most extraordinary part of the whole affair: the fact that the Vikings kept to the bargain. After Alfred's recent poor showing at Wilton, it seems incredible that they should now agree to retreat, even in return for a large payment, but retreat they did, back to the Mercian port of London. And there may lie the key. A Viking king, when withdrawing from one area, always needed another to go to if he was to maintain the flow of plunder and payments that ensured his men's loyalty and prevent him suffering the fate of Weland.

One other kingdom fitted this bill, one that was large and vulnerable: Burgred's Mercia. When the Vikings had taken Nottingham, the Mercian king had asked for and received help from Wessex. When Wessex had faced invasion, however, Mercia had not come to her aid, and yet she had still fought the enemy to a standstill. That could only suggest to Viking minds that the Wessex fyrd was stronger than its Mercian counterpart. There were also other benefits to moving Viking operations to Mercia. First, the Mercian royal dynasty was nowhere near as securely installed as the House of Ecgberht in Wessex. As a result there were other dynasts to side with, which might enable the Vikings to simply divide and rule. Then there was the growing financial crisis in Mercia, in which the ruling dynasty had run short of land to lease or to grant to its supporters. Without land to give, support weakened, and where kings lost support, the Vikings knew they could benefit, just as they had done in Northumbria in the civil war between Aelle and Osberht.

If the Vikings wanted proof of this, they had only to look at the coins in Londoners' pockets. King Burgred's mint was producing pennies that now had a silver content of less than 20 per cent. The Vikings might be invaders but they offered an alternative (if an imposed one) to the current regime, one that might not be wholly unwelcome. After all, the Viking occupation of York had begun with a bloodbath but the city would eventually settle down to a period of unparalleled prosperity, keyed into the extensive trading networks of the Scandinavian world.

Halfdan and Guthrum's attention had been diverted from Wessex at a critical moment. It would have been in Alfred's interests in his negotiations with the Viking army to suggest they look to Mercia for further gains, perhaps even with an agreement from Wessex not to interfere. Alfred owed Burgred very little, after all, having received no Mercian help in recent battles, but such a move would have involved betraying his last close living relative, his sister Æthelswith. It is more likely that, while the Vikings withdrew to recover from a campaign that had been equally hard on them, word came through the Vikings' Mercian contacts in London that there were Mercians who would welcome the Vikings as no West Saxon currently would.

So Alfred bought at least a temporary peace and his enemy retired unmolested to London to share out the spoils. That it had been another profitable season is evidenced by the silver hoard discovered in Croydon, some nine miles to the south of London, which appears to be one Viking's treasure store from this date and which, for reasons now unknowable, he buried and never recovered. That collection of silver ingots, plus foreign as well as English coins, shows, as we have already seen, the wide range of these professional fighters. However, the location of this deposit also speaks of the smaller-scale effects of this first attempted Conquest of Wessex. The estate of Croydon at the time of the Great Heathen Army's withdrawal was owned by the archbishop and monks of Canterbury who had leased it to a man called Alfred, probably an ealdorman of Surrey. We know a surprising amount about him, thanks to the survival of both his will and an inscription in a contemporary book. Ealdorman Alfred held extensive estates in Surrey and Kent, both of which had felt the force of recent

Viking incursions. As a devout man with a special fondness for the monastery of Christchurch at Canterbury, he must have watched with horror not just the financial ruin of his county but in particular the destruction and desecration of her churches. At some point during these raids, perhaps even now as the Vikings peacefully retired to London for the winter, he managed to negotiate with them for the return of one particular religious book that they had plundered, and that meeting he dutifully recorded in the pages of the book he saved.

It is fair to say that the manuscript that this Alfred recovered from the Vikings was no ordinary book. The Codex Aureus is a masterpiece of eighth-century English illumination, lavishly decorated with gold and silver leaf and inscribed on pages alternately dyed purple and left white. What probably impressed the Vikings who had seized this book, however, was not the quality of the calligraphy or the contents of the gospels, but the valuable and probably bejewelled binding that enclosed it. Ealdorman Alfred must have been appalled that such a beautiful (and, in his eyes, sacred) work should be bundled up by its new Viking owners as just so much booty. He therefore agreed to buy it back. Inside his rescued treasure he wrote: 'I, Ealdorman Alfred and Wœrburh my wife obtained these books from the heathen army with our pure money, that was with pure gold, and this we did for the love of God and for the benefit of our souls and because we did not wish these holy books to remain longer in heathen possession.' He goes on to say that he has purchased the gospels to give to Christchurch, Canterbury, on the condition that they were read each month in memory of himself, his wife and daughter. He finishes by imploring 'that no man be so presumptuous as to give away or remove these holy books from Christ Church, as long as the Christian faith may endure'.

In this instance the Vikings at least kept to the first part of the bargain and exchanged the book in return for cash. Ealdorman Alfred's last wish, however, was not fulfilled by the monks at Canterbury. Today the book is not known as the Codex Aureus of Canterbury, but as the Golden Gospels of Stockholm, because at some point it was again spirited away from the cathedral library, reappearing only in the sixteenth century in the hands of Jerónimo Zurita, the governor of Aragon, before finally being purchased for the Swedish royal library in 1690. So in the end the Vikings got both the book and the ransom.

Alfred's peace in the winter of 871 may have allowed the West

Saxons to retrieve some items precious to them, but it also presented a direct threat to Mercia. London was a Mercian trading port at the time although the evidence that Alfred minted coins there might suggest that it was in reality something of a 'free port'. For protection, however, it looked to Mercia. Since a large Viking army was now lodged in the city Burgred would have to act. Like Alfred, he, too chose the payment route as an immediate solution, further swelling the Viking coffers and hence diminishing what little remained in his own. A document from the following year gives us a hint of how bad the situation had become. In it the Mercian bishop of Worcester, Wærferth, grants some land to one of Burgred's thegns in return for twenty mancuses of gold (one mancus was worth 150 silver pennies). Wærferth's reason for turning his estates into cash is then made abundantly clear: 'This, however, the above-mentioned bishop agreed to chiefly because of the very pressing affliction and immense tribute of the barbarians, in that same year when the pagans sat in London.' The bishop was clearly not happy about pawning his church's lands to pay off pagans, nor, judging from the hoard of Burgred's pennies found buried during the building of Waterloo bridge in 1895, were the Mercian merchants in London.

It was at this point that events outside the control of the Great Heathen Army overtook all the participants in this dangerous truce. News reached Halfdan and his fellow sea kings in the autumn of 872 that their puppet ruler in Northumbria, Ecgberht, and his archbishop Wulfhere had been deposed and that the people had resolved to throw off the Viking yoke. Angrily the Great Heathen Army gathered its forces and surged north. But rather than heading straight for York, they set up a base for their operations at Torksey in the ancient kingdom of Lindsey. This former kingdom to the north-east of Lincoln had retained a tenuous independence right up to 800 when its royal family had been absorbed into the Mercian nobility. Hence Lindsey was now a part of Mercia.

It was, as usual, an extremely well-chosen base, lying at the junction of the river Trent and the then navigable Roman canal known today as the Foss Dyke, which linked the Trent with the river Witham in Lincoln and hence the sea. Lindsey gave Halfdan easy access to Northumbria to put down the rebellion, as well as an escape route to the sea that also provided rapid access to his lands in East Anglia, should that kingdom's inhabitants be foolish enough to join in the revolt.

Most importantly of all, the Vikings' presence in Lindsey was of course an explicit threat to Mercia itself, but it was one that Burgred clearly felt he could not counter. No call came south to Alfred asking for support and, indeed, it is unlikely that Alfred could have offered any, even if he were so inclined. Instead, Burgred chose appeasement, demonstrating his pro-Viking credentials by welcoming the exiled Ecgberht and his archbishop Wulfhere under his protective wing.

The Northumbrian revolt does not seem to have caused the Vikings too many difficulties, however, and it was quickly and unceremoniously suppressed. Shortly afterwards Archbishop Wulfhere – a great survivor, who was still receiving friendly letters addressed to him from the papacy despite his extensive dealings with the pagans – was returned to his see, and the puppet king Ecgberht, who had died at some point during the proceedings, was quickly replaced with another Viking nominee called Ricsige.

With the Northumbrian revolt crushed, Burgred knew that time was running out. He began yet more desperate negotiations to try to ensure the heathens' exit from his kingdom. In truth, buying peace was simply not working for him. He had paid a high price to get the Great Heathen Army out of London, and yet all they had done was to move to a new camp in his heartlands, at a time when he might at least have expected that they would overwinter in York while the situation there stabilized.

Although the terms of the treaty that Burgred made at Torksey do not survive, they must have included another huge payment of the kind he was finding it ever harder to make. All that remains today to hint at this final financial humiliation is a carefully buried Viking hoard of ingots and hack silver from Torksey itself, plus another small hoard of nine neatly stacked coins of Alfred's first issue as king, together with coinage that would prove to be Burgred's last.

What Burgred could never know as he negotiated at Torksey was that no amount of money would now be enough. The peace treaty was of course duly agreed, the money, such as Burgred could raise, was paid, and Halfdan's men did indeed strike camp and move off. But they did not head north into their own lands, nor south again to Wessex or East Anglia, but south-west to Repton.

The arrival of the Viking army at Repton towards the end of 873 was a stunning personal blow to Burgred and it effectively marked the end of a free Mercia. Repton was to the Mercian nobility (or at least to a part of them) what Wimborne was to Æthelred and Alfred. Over the past centuries it had grown to become perhaps the major cult centre in the kingdom. Buried there were a number of important members of royal Mercian dynasties, particularly those associated with what might be called the 'good times', before Mercia had descended into dynastic infighting and before it had, at least temporarily, fallen under the sway of Wessex. Now the familial strife that had finally made the 'B' dynasty triumphant was about to come back to haunt Burgred.

Most notable amongst the tombs in the magnificent stone church at Repton was that of Ælfflæd, a daughter of the last great Mercian bretwalda, Coenwulf. After the death of her father and the murder of his son and heir, she had married into the 'W' dynasty and had given birth to Wigstan, another potential contender for the throne. Wigstan proved far more useful to this old branch of Mercian royalty when dead than he ever had when alive; indeed, his life had been short and violent, brought to a premature end by another contender for the throne, Berhtwulf, on whose orders the young prince was probably murdered. Wigstan too was buried in the Church at Repton. His tragic death had already made him revered as a saint. As a cult centre, Repton must hence have attracted many of the old Mercian families who saw Burgred and the 'B' dynasty as not just unsuccessful rulers, but usurpers and regicides.

Astonishingly, amid the decay and destruction of a century that left virtually no standing remains, the crypt where these saints and sovereigns were interred survives. Above ground the slender chancel of the Church of St Wystan in Repton is, of itself, one of the most important surviving examples of Anglo-Saxon architecture, decorated externally with graceful arcades of vertical stone strips. But inside, until 1779 at least, there was no indication of what lay below. At that time a workman digging a grave in the chancel floor broke through a hidden vault and fell headlong into a forgotten corner of the ninth century.

What he had stumbled upon was the mausoleum of the kings of Mercia, built around 750. Today, following extensive restoration, this crypt can be seen much as it was in that winter of 873, as the Viking army approached and as Burgred's enemies gathered here. Coming down the short flight of stairs, you enter one of those rare spaces where, as Howard Carter commented on opening the tomb of Tutankhamun, 'time is annihilated' and we step into a vanished world. The crypt is a small stone chamber, just sixteen feet square, consisting of nine square bays around four central columns. Each of these columns is carved with a spiral decoration in crude but doubtless devout imitation of the columns erected by the Emperor Constantine in front of the tomb of St Peter in Rome. Within four recesses in the walls, and now long since lost, once lay the remains of Ælfflæd, Wigstan and other kings of Mercia. What was preserved here was not whole bodies – none of the recesses was large enough to accommodate a whole tomb – but bones, removed from their grave after the flesh had rotted and set up in caskets or, in Wigstan's case, a reliquary. This object would have taken pride of place, his bones becoming items of popular veneration supported by the ghostly presence of his royal Mercian ancestors. Indeed, so popular had his cult become that two passages, in the north-west and south-west corners of the mausoleum, had to be cut through the massive extant stonework to facilitate the free flow of pilgrims past his shrine.

In 873 it was inquisitive Viking warriors who shuffled through the reverent silence of the tomb. But the pagan army that had set up winter camp here by the river was not about to loot this church. Notably the *Anglo-Saxon Chronicle* fails to mention the usual pillage and desecration that we might expect from a Viking army arriving in a wealthy royal cult centre, and that is because there was none. Halfdan did not need to sack Repton, nor did he need to fight Burgred; this was a coup, and he and his army were merely silent supporters. What must have terrified Burgred on hearing the news that Halfdan was at Repton was not the thought that the Vikings now held a valuable royal centre but that they were lodging in a place where he and his dynasty were unwelcome and where another dynasty had its power base. As if to emphasize this new alliance, the bank and ditch of the Viking camp, which was excavated in the 1970s and 1980s, actually encompasses the royal church within its length. The Vikings were not attacking St Wigstan's last resting place; they were taking it, and his family's cause, under their wing. Burgred had been quickly and brilliantly outmanoeuvred. As his friends fell away, and in fear of his life, his response was swift and simple. He quit the kingdom and, in the words of the day, exchanged his royal sceptre for a pilgrim's staff to set out, together with his wife Æthelswith, on the *via francigena* for Rome.

The true nature of the coup now became apparent. The Vikings immediately nominated a new king of Mercia, Ceolwulf II, whom the Anglo-Saxon chronicler, writing with hindsight, rather disparagingly refers to as 'a foolish king's thegn', but who in fact may have had a rather more prestigious background. Whilst it is notoriously difficult to reconstruct Anglo-Saxon family trees from the tiny scraps of evidence that survive, there is a reasonable chance that this Ceolwulf was himself another son of Ælfflæd and hence a rightful heir to the kingly name of Ceolwulf. He was also, usefully, a half-brother to the revered St Wigstan.

That Ceolwulf was not just a foolish thegn can also be seen from the reaction to his accession. The Mercian witan and bishops seem to have accepted him without dispute and carried on their business accordingly, although the presence of the Vikings at his shoulder must have influenced their decision. More tellingly, Alfred also continues in his dealings with the new king as though he was an acceptable ruler to negotiate with, despite the fact that Ceolwulf's accession resulted in his own sister being exiled to Rome. In fact, Alfred and Ceolwulf went so far as to undertake parallel reforms of their very debased coinage, both issuing pennies of the same type and fineness at the same mint in London, indicating, if anything, that the arrival of the new Mercian marked what Alfred saw as an opportunity for a fresh start. From the Repton perspective then, the golden days before the dynastic squabbles might be said to have returned. However, in reality they were more distant than ever.

Ceolwulf II was king but only while he retained the support of the Great Heathen Army that now prowled around Repton. After its throwaway insult, the *Anglo-Saxon Chronicle* goes on to record that Ceolwulf 'swore oaths to them and gave hostages, that it [Mercia] should be ready for them on whatever day they wished to have it, and he would be ready, himself and all who would follow him, at the enemy's service'. This, judging from previous experience, has a certain ring of truth about it. The 'C' dynasty was back, but only under sufferance. The real victors, once again, were Halfdan and his men.

Just as in Northumbria, they had discovered and exploited the political fault lines in a society and, in prising them apart, had fitted themselves into the gap. This time they had been even more successful, having achieved their goal – overlordship of Mercia – without so much as a skirmish.

Despite this, the Vikings did not have everything their own way at Repton. Just outside their winter camp was an old Saxon mortuary chapel that underwent reuse at this time. Recent excavations revealed that the contents of the chapel had been emptied out and the ground levelled. This was to make space for hundreds of bodies, at least 249 of which have been counted, to be stacked around the walls, leaving in the centre enough room for a very high-status male burial. The whole chapel had finally been covered with a low earth mound. Examination of these skeletons has determined that they were nearly all males of a non-local type with no signs of battle wounds. This suggests that they might well have been the victims of a plague that passed through the Viking camp that winter at Repton – the only enemy in 873 still able to beat the Vikings.

Repton might not have been a healthy place for a Viking army to rest but it was news from outside that finally girded it to action. The Irish annals for that year recorded that 'Imhar, king of the Northmen of all Ireland and Britain', was dead. The arrival of the obituary notice of Ivarr the Boneless quickly changed Halfdan's priorities. His presence was now required back in the North, in the lands that his brother had won for the Sons of Ragnar and which he now wanted to claim as his own. But not every Viking was prepared to join him, so in 874 when the army decided to move out it divided into two separate forces.

The survivors of the first Great Heathen Army had by then been in the field for nine years, gathering a huge quantity of booty and the prospect of large landholdings, as well as nine years of battle scars and ailments. For Halfdan at least, this marked the end of the great English expedition of the Sons of Ragnar. He and a portion of the Viking army moved back north into Northumbria to take up position on the Tyne, conquering the surrounding territory and finally parcelling it out amongst the victorious troops. Having helped to destroy the independent kingdoms of Northumbria, East Anglia and Mercia for ever, Halfdan would content himself with harrying the Picts and the Britons of Strathclyde, just as his brother Ivarr had before him.

What concerned the Saxon scouts, hiding in the countryside around Repton, was the intentions of the other portion of the army. This force was not so battle-weary, being largely made up of the adventurers who had come to England with the Great Summer Army that had reinforced Halfdan at Reading, so they were at once fresher and had also gained less for themselves. Having only been in the field for three years, their leaders, Guthrum, Anwend and Oscetel, proposed a new plan to the troops. They would finish what Halfdan had begun. They would march south – to Cambridge.

Burgred's long journey was then also coming to an end. The monks of Brescia dutifully recorded his and his wife Æthelswith's names in the list of donors who stayed in their pilgrim hostel at Pavia, where Alfred and Æthelwulf had once lodged. Even at that point Burgred must have wondered what sort of reception he could expect at the Holy See. His most recent contact with the papacy during the very last days of his reign had been a tirade from Pope John VIII, accusing him of allowing his subjects to marry nuns and 'women of their own kindred'. Now at least he could do penance in person for these perceived wrongs. In fact Burgred did find a welcome in Rome as well as a home in the Saxon quarter where he spent the rest of his life. He no longer held power and hence was no longer of interest to the pope, who allowed him a graceful if impotent retirement in his city. He was buried in the Church of St Mary's in Saxia where the infant Alfred had once knelt in thanks for his own safe arrival in the Holy See. After his death Æthelswith left the city, perhaps on her way to England and the court of her brother. But wherever she was heading, she would never see England or Alfred again, dying in 888 in the pilgrims' hostel at Pavia. However, in 874 this still lay many years in the future. As far as Alfred was concerned, he was the last of the children of Æthelwulf in England and the last Anglo-Saxon king who did not hold his position under sufferance from a Viking.

Those Vikings were now biding their time in Cambridge, where, indeed, they would spend a whole year. It was an opportunity to regroup and rearm, as well as providing a rallying point for any other Viking warbands who might take up the call to battle. But other political pressures were also at work and by the time the army prepared to move out early in 875, Guthrum's other previously named co-leaders were nowhere to be seen. For Anwend and Oscetel there were options other than fighting. To the North there was land and wealth to be had with Halfdan; alternatively just a few miles to the east Viking East Anglia offered similar opportunities without the overt dangers of battle. Even if these two men had decided to stay with the army, their mysterious disappearance from the chronicles proves that that, in the minds of the people they were about to fight, there was only one Viking leader now worth worrying about and he was Guthrum.

It had been a meteoric rise to power. Guthrum had probably come to England with the Great Summer Army in support of Halfdan. Where he had come from, other than somewhere in the distant North, is unknown and there are no reliable records of his career anywhere else in Europe before his appearance in England. The gaze of the Anglo-Saxon chronicler is first drawn to him at Repton, when the decision was made to split the Viking force, and he is named as one of the three kings who decided to fight on. A year later, however, as he mustered the 'great force' that the chronicle says he summoned at Cambridge, he was in sole command. He also had a plan.

8

Providence

Hunger will devour one, storm dismast another,
One will be spear-slain, one hacked down in battle.
The Fortunes of Men, quoted in K. Crossley-
Holland, *The Anglo-Saxon World*, p. 273

IN WESSEX MEANWHILE, as the Christmas of 875 approached,
Alfred could look back on more than four years of peace. But if that
thought gave him any satisfaction then he was fooling himself. Peace
alone was not enough, be it won, earned or, in his case, bought. What
mattered was what he had done with that precious time and it gave
him pause for thought. Recent events in Mercia were certainly an
object lesson in how not to deal with the Viking menace, and the
humiliation and flight of his brother-in-law, whatever their relationship, must have left the young king wondering what, if anything,
would prevent him from following in his footsteps. The fate of
Burgred was not inevitable, however, and apart from merely training
for battle, Alfred might do much to help secure his kingdom.

Had he looked to the continent he would have seen how Charles
the Bald had used the time that the Danegeld bought him to build
physical defences against the Vikings. By fortifying points on the rivers
that gave access to Francia, he hoped to choke off the free movement
of Viking fleets along their favoured attack routes and make them
think twice about running the gauntlet into his kingdom. More
ambitious physical defences were also a possibility. The Scandinavians
themselves had already built huge defensive earthworks such as the
Danevirke, which separated Denmark from the Carolingian Empire.
The idea was certainly not unique to those countries. A century earlier
Offa had employed a similarly impressive method to mark his

boundary with the Welsh. If Alfred was aware of these techniques, however, he does not seem in the preceding four years to have adopted any of them. He had neither the time nor the money for huge defensive gestures, nor had he yet developed the ideas that would one day lead every Viking to think twice before invading his kingdom. For the present he contented himself with some small-scale improvements to defences in extant towns and gave some thought to organizing a coastal fleet to warn of attack.

If Alfred took a lesson from the defeat of Burgred, it was that a king's most important defences were his own. He cannot fail to have seen how the Vikings turned what was in effect a Mercian coup into a conquest. With his own recent record of defeats at Viking hands, Alfred knew that he could not afford to take the loyalty of his ealdormen, or his people, for granted. Whatever the chroniclers said about rape and pillage, under Viking rule Northumbria, East Anglia and now Mercia were client kingdoms, whose numerous Saxon subjects appeared to be successfully carrying on their daily lives; indeed, in towns like York they seemed to be thriving. The Vikings may have remained monsters in the imaginations of monastic chroniclers but there was a real danger that Viking rule was becoming an option – perhaps even a desirable one – for some.

Little evidence survives of how Alfred went about shoring up his own support, which in itself indicates that – at least until Burgred's ousting – he failed to realize the seriousness of the situation. In his mind the Vikings were a heathen enemy, warring against his people as a whole. The possibility that some of those people might choose to side with pagans must have been profoundly shocking. Yet as an elected king he had always been surrounded by other potential contenders for the throne and he must have known that one of his main responsibilities was to prevent any one of those groups ever becoming discontented and powerful enough to represent a threat to the House of Ecgberht. Until Burgred's unceremonious flight from his kingdom, however, Alfred does not seem to have grasped how far those discontented elements might go.

Evidence for Alfred's positive actions in the previous four quiet years can be found in just a handful of charters in favour of loyal thegns, and in his reform of the currency, which now increases to a fineness of around 90 per cent silver. Shortly after his defeat at Wilton,

Alfred had debased his coinage, no doubt to help pay whatever Danegeld had been demanded of him. Debasing a currency is not a recipe for contentment at home, however, as the monarch effectively takes in good money, multiplies it and puts it out as bad in the hope that it will retain its face value in the community. Vikings were not stupid enough to fall for this trick; they always checked the fineness of the payments they received. It seems unlikely that Alfred's own people were that stupid either. Alfred recognized that he had a problem with his coinage shortly after Burgred's dismissal. His new 'cross and lozenge' penny required the same silver content as four of his old 'lunette' pennies and was, interestingly enough, issued in tandem with the coinage of the Viking puppet Ceolwulf. It was a bold move as it quartered the money supply at a stroke – at least in the time it would take to gather in and remint the coinage – but it sent out a message that here was a strong king confident in the value of his kingdom. He was about to find out what that kingdom was actually worth.

While Alfred had spent his years of peace in relative inaction, Guthrum certainly had not. As the Anglo-Saxon weighed up the value of his crown, the Viking was seizing the opportunity to do what he did best: attack.

Leaving Cambridge suddenly, in midwinter, the Viking army now walked into the Wessex heartland with apparent ease. Although the movement of this sizeable force cannot have gone unnoticed by Alfred, there was precious little he could do about it. In fact, Guthrum did not even trouble to skirt around the edges of Wessex, harrying the eastern provinces or making probing raids from the safety of Viking Mercia. Instead, as the chronicler said, he simply 'slipped past' Alfred and marched his army right across the centre of Wessex to a fortified position in the Dorset settlement of Wareham. It was a stunning move. Alfred could do nothing but hurry after the raiders, following the locust-like swathe that they had cut across his kingdom.

Arriving at Wareham, he found the surrounding countryside already devastated, and his enemy dug safely in behind the town defences. With little other choice he set about investing the town, hoping at least to force a stalemate, in which Guthrum would be no more able to break out than he was to break in.

In fact, Alfred and the Wessex fyrd were in far more danger than they could possibly know. It must have struck many of the West Saxons besieging Wareham that Guthrum had placed himself in a peculiar position. He had taken an important Dorset settlement with skill and daring but in the process he had outrun his overland supply lines from East Anglia or Mercia and then allowed the Wessex fyrd to effectively cut them altogether. The situation looked as senseless as it had done in Nottingham, as Guthrum was surely aware. Why then was he here? Guthrum was no fool; the Saxons knew that he must have a reason, but for the moment it eluded them.

Guthrum's 'reason' was even then sailing round the south coast. The Viking fleet was at sea. Guthrum was, after all, a sea king, and his overland march to Wareham was no more than a preliminary dash to secure a prestigious and useful town from which he could be resupplied as well as oversee the assembly of his main fleet. Alfred and his men could sit and starve in the scorched fields around the town for as long as they liked. Whilst they grew weaker, Guthrum would grow stronger and, despite being besieged, could dictate the coming campaign at his own pace.

The thought of those ships must also have nagged at the back of Alfred's mind. He was mindful that his enemy rarely strayed far from their vessels; wherever he had found them camped they had chosen their sites with an eye to the security of their ships first and foremost. Knowing Vikings to be brilliant sailors and skilled navigators, he scanned the horizon, fully expecting some form of reinforcement to come from the sea. What he could not have been prepared for was its size. The fleet approaching Wareham was not seven or even seventy strong: 120 Viking warships – a whole army – now darkened the horizon.

Guthrum's plan was as simple as it was brilliant. Alfred and the hastily gathered fyrd, languishing in the desolate fields around Wareham, had been drawn out to fight an apparently weak and cornered land force. Instead, they would be overwhelmed by naval power while Guthrum was encamped in the heart of Wessex, unopposed and hence its de facto ruler. If the story of Ubba using a fleet to help Ivarr conquer East Anglia was true, it was a tactic that had worked before. And if it had worked for the Sons of Ragnar, there was no reason why it should not work for Guthrum.

The fact that the remaining Sons of Ragnar were not involved in the attack was fortunate for Alfred. A parallel attack on the north coast of Devon or Somerset would have split and broken Alfred's forces even sooner but the Vikings of the Irish Sea were busy elsewhere. Halfdan was even now fighting a more deadly enemy, his former Norse allies in Ireland. After Olaf the White quit Ireland for Norway in 871, he had left his kingdom in the hands of his old friend Ivarr and his own son, Eysteinn Olafson. On Ivarr's death, however, Eysteinn had seized sole control, provoking a furious Halfdan to march north to reclaim the lands for the Sons of Ragnar. By 875, with his British territory secured, he had crossed to Ireland to confront Eysteinn in person. At the same time that Guthrum was forcing his way into Wessex, Halfdan was arranging the death of his brother's former friend. From now on Irish politics would keep Halfdan away from English adventures for good. Nor could Guthrum look to those other old confederates of the Vikings, the Cornish, whose king Dumgarth is recorded as drowning this year, marking the last mention in any record of a king of Cornwall. But such allies were surely unnecessary, increasing the numbers of the victors with whom Guthrum would have to share the spoils. With 120 ships on their way, he could defeat Alfred and Wessex at one time and in one place. He needed no help.

Scouts must have brought news to Alfred of the Viking fleet as it headed round from the Wash, passed the Isle of Wight and took shelter just beyond Wareham in Poole Bay. Perhaps even then he held out hope that the two sides were still at something of an impasse. Wareham, situated between the rivers Frome and Tarrant about a mile from where they spill into Poole Bay, was not the ideal place to land large numbers of troops. With Guthrum hemmed in inside the town, the surrounding areas were thus under Alfred's control and hence any landing might be resisted. Alfred's strategy was to make this possibility appear to be fact. He would be bold and, as at Nottingham, claim that there was a stalemate, then suggest mutual terms for a withdrawal. In the circumstances even this was a brave move.

Of course Alfred knew the dangers of negotiating with Vikings. He had only recently witnessed how Burgred of Mercia had received oaths from Halfdan, promising to leave his kingdom in return for money, only to find that he had no intention of doing so. What Alfred also knew, however, was that whilst Vikings had no respect for the threats of an unseen God, they did respect the threat of violence. Alfred's treaty with them after Wilton, which they had only won after a hard fight and at the end of a long campaign, proved to be one of the few that the Vikings had ever kept.

What Alfred needed now, most of all, was another treaty that he could believe would be observed, but it was a dangerous gamble. He might displace Guthrum from the unsuitable Wareham, merely to watch him make camp somewhere better where he could disembark his fleet – a fleet that Alfred had no means to defeat.

In the light of these problems, the deal that he managed to strike was innovative. Whilst the chroniclers, with the exception of the later Æthelweard, remain absolutely silent on the subject of payment, just as loyal Wessex chroniclers should, Alfred was not in a position to negotiate without paying a substantial Danegeld. This too was a gamble, buying him respite from Viking assault at the cost of further disaffecting his own nobles, who were the ones who would have to pay. Even assuming that a deal could be reached, however dangerous, it still remained for Alfred to attempt to impose some sort of sanction to ensure that his enemy, at least temporarily, stuck to their side of the bargain and left Wessex. To do this Alfred hit on a highly unusual tactic, which showed both his growing understanding of his enemy and his willingness to think outside the traditional boundaries of Saxon kingship. Instead of asking Guthrum to swear on Christian terms, he asked the Vikings to swear their oath to their own gods. As the *Anglo-Saxon Chronicle* excitedly reports, they took oaths 'on the Holy ring – a thing which they would not do before for any nation'.

The ring in question was probably a sacred gold arm-ring of a type that was associated with the thunder god Thor and which was usually kept in pagan temples. What we know of these mysterious objects comes from later sources, particularly from Iceland, where the thirteenth-century *Eyrbyggja Saga* describes an ancient pagan temple where 'off the inmost house was there another house, of that fashion whereof now is the choir of a church, and there stood a stall in the midst of the floor in the fashion of an altar, and thereon lay a ring without a join that weighed twenty ounces, and on that must men swear all oaths; and that ring must the chief have on his arm at all assemblies.'

Whilst there are hints in the *Annals of St Bertin* that at least one

Viking in Francia took a pagan oath 'after his own fashion', it was an extraordinary departure for such a formal ceremony to be used to conclude a peace, not least because it must have involved Alfred swearing on the Thor ring too. Indeed, so embarrassed was Asser when he came to précis this part of the *Anglo-Saxon Chronicle* in his own biography of Alfred that he removed the reference to the ring and replaced it with the less overtly pagan-sounding 'relics', although this might also imply that both parties had to swear on Christian relics as well. It must have made for a remarkable scene: an altar piled up with the remains of Christian saints in their jewelled reliquaries alongside the heavy gold arm-rings of the Vikings, and before them two supplicants – the pagan warlord and the Christian king. With the deal made, all that remained was for hostages to be exchanged to ensure each side's good behaviour.

It had seemed like a brilliant idea to a king desperately trying to probe the darker recesses of the Viking mindset for a solution to his country's predicament, but sadly it did not work. No matter how many relics, jewels and amulets had been heaped on the oath table that day, Guthrum simply did not believe that he was in a position where he needed to keep an oath, and clearly whatever vow he had made to his own gods mattered no more to him than the one he had made to Alfred's. What happened next is angrily recorded by the chroniclers: 'And then, under cover of that [treaty], they – the mounted army – stole by night away from the English army to Exeter.' It must have seemed to Alfred as though Burgred's last days were being played out again. That king had struck a deal and had paid his money only to find that his enemy laughed in his face and refused to leave. Now Guthrum was doing the same to him. But if Wareham was Alfred's Torksey, what must really have concerned him was that Exeter should not become his Repton.

Asser adds that, as an inevitable prelude to this escape, all the Anglo-Saxon hostages being held by Guthrum had their throats cut. We must imagine that, on finding those remains, the fate of the Viking hostages in Alfred's care was equally bleak.

But neither his oath nor the death of Viking hostages mattered to the ruthlessly brilliant Guthrum. He was now ensconced in Exeter, another well-defended site with easy access to the south coast where, before Alfred could raise the siege on Wareham and march down to him, he would be able to disembark the fleet that was already weighing anchor in Poole Bay and overwhelm Wessex. Guthrum had only ever been playing for time, manoeuvring to find a better way of using his fleet, and now he had it. Alfred, for all his cunning, was left empty-handed, holding only a broken promise and with another line of graves to dig.

From his position in Exeter, it looked to Guthrum as if the game was almost won. Within days Wessex would become the last major kingdom to fall and England would, in effect, become a Scandinavian nation.

It was at this point that nature intervened, as it has often done at moments of incipient national disaster. Just as the Viking fleet sailed past the headland at Swanage, off the Dorset coast, a terrible storm blew up (in some versions of the chronicle it is a strange 'mist'), as fortuitous for Alfred as the one that destroyed the armada sent against Queen Elizabeth I some seven hundred years later. The great Viking fleet was caught by surprise and foundered, their vessels being lost or, as the twelfth-century chronicler Geoffrey Gaimar gleefully put it, 'one hundred and forty of their ships went to the devil.'

No remains of this vast fleet have ever been found on the seabed off Swanage. From a vantage point on the promenade of this popular family holiday destination, it is hard to image scenes of such terror occurring just offshore. But the coastline here is deceptive and the gentle sandy bays with their safe swimming only exist because they are protected by exposed headlands where bad weather and furious tidal races can combine to defeat any sailor, even a Viking. Such tales of death and destruction are not perhaps what the holidaymakers on Swanage's beaches wish to imagine happening in their sunny bay, so this 'first armada' is only commemorated by a discreet and largely overlooked stone column, set up in the nineteenth century.

Alfred by contrast had it foremost in his mind. To say that he had been lucky would be something of an understatement. The loss of his whole main fleet was a catastrophe for Guthrum and a major naval disaster by any Viking standards. Working again on the conservative estimate of thirty warriors per ship, the Swanage disaster removed 3,600 men from Guthrum's force and left him without an escape route, should he be cornered again. And not far behind the news of the fleet's wreck came the intelligence that that was exactly what was about to happen. Alfred was marching on Exeter.

In Alfred's eyes, at least at one level, the pagan oath-taking had worked. He had persuaded an enemy to invoke the sanction of their own god in upholding a treaty and, when it had been broken, his enemy had suffered the worst natural disaster imaginable. It was far worse than anything he could have inflicted on them and therefore could reasonably be considered 'divine'. Whilst Alfred certainly did not believe that this showed the hand of Thor at work, he could raise a prayer to his own God and the Christian relics that he had placed on the table that fateful day alongside the Viking oath-ring. As he disposed his troops around Exeter he knew that he could now adopt a much more aggressive stance. With Guthrum's plan uncovered, Alfred had every reason to believe that the Viking's next treaty would be kept. Not because of gods or rings or relics, but because Alfred was now simply in the stronger bargaining position.

This time Guthrum offered as many hostages as the king of Wessex wanted, and no doubt Alfred ensured that they were not as 'expendable' as the last group at Wareham. With this the Vikings took many 'great oaths' and promised to quit the kingdom. In fact, without support Guthrum had no other choice and it was this alone that ensured the terms were kept. At the beginning of the harvest of 877, which in that period traditionally started on 7 August, the Vikings left Exeter and marched north to Gloucester in Mercia.

Because Alfred was apparently on good terms with the puppet king Ceolwulf II, news of Viking intentions in Mercia must have quickly reached the king and his witan. And the news was good. Just as under the terms of the Viking agreement with the Northumbrian puppet Ricsige, Halfdan had called on him to hand over his lands for settlement, Guthrum had taken the same approach in Mercia. Ricsige had afterwards died, according to Roger of Wendover from a broken heart, but the terms with Ceolwulf were to be more generous. The Mercian king was to hold on to his lands in the West, excluding Gloucester where the Viking army was now encamped. However, the eastern part of Mercia, including the area later known as the 'Five Boroughs' (Lincoln, Nottingham, Leicester, Derby and Stamford), plus Northamptonshire, Bedfordshire and probably London, were all to be divided amongst the new Scandinavian settlers. The Vikings, it seemed, had decided to settle down and, best of all, they had decided to do it somewhere else.

Even better news also came that year from the North. Halfdan was dead, killed during a skirmish at Strangford Lough in County Down in his bid to regain Ivarr's Irish kingdom. His treacherous murder of Eysteinn had angered the Dublin Vikings and a group of them had taken their revenge.

So, as 877 drew towards an end and Alfred prepared to retire to one of his estates for the twelve-day festival of Christmas, it might have seemed as though the era of Viking invasion was coming to an end. But one final piece of news arriving from Francia that year must have filled him with foreboding. Charles the Bald, who himself had enjoyed something of a respite from Norse attacks whilst the Great Heathen Armies were in England, had fallen in a palace intrigue, suffering a miserable end. Hincmar tells how Charles, racked by fever, was persuaded by his doctor to drink a powder that was poisoned and which some eleven days later led to his death 'in a wretched little hut'. This was not an end to the emperor's ignominy, however. His deathbed lay in a mountain refuge in the Alps, a very long way from the royal church of St Denis. Therefore, 'His attendants opened him up, took out his intestines, poured in such wine and aromatics as they had, put the body on a bier and set off to carry him to St Denis.' Because his sudden death had taken them all by surprise, their preparations for the body proved insufficient, as Hincmar explains:

> But because of the stench they could carry him no further, so they put him in a barrel which they smeared with pitch inside and outside and encased in hides, but even this did nothing to get rid of the smell. Only with difficulty did they manage to reach Nantua, a little monastery in the archdiocese of Lyons, and there they committed the body, with its barrel, to the earth.

It was a most insalubrious end for the emperor of the Franks, buried in a tarred barrel in a little-known monastery. It would be some years before anyone had the courage to dig up this hideous package and transfer his remains to Paris.

Worries crowded in on Alfred that winter as he made his way to the royal vill at Chippenham. He had once again fought the Vikings to a standstill and had secured their withdrawal from his kingdom, but at a price, and one that clearly gave the Church, and probably the nobility too, cause to complain. He also knew that he had been very lucky and that without a freak storm he might already be on his way to join King Edmund on a martyr's throne. Could he hope to be so lucky again if the Vikings returned? Could he find enough support from his already hard-pressed subjects to either fight them off or pay them off once more? Everything depended on whether the newly settled Vikings of Mercia kept the peace, and as the twelve days of Christmas began at Chippenham, with the traditional Mass, that fervent prayer must have hung on Alfred's lips.

9

Betrayal

Firstly we enjoin, what is most necessary, that each man keep
carefully his oath and pledge.
>The laws of Alfred the Great [1]2, in D. Whitelock,
>*English Historical Documents*, vol. I, no. 33, p. 373

WEDNESDAY, 25 DECEMBER found Alfred at his devotions.
Celebrating Christmas on that day was then still a relatively
recent phenomenon, the specific date of the 25th only having been
decided on at the Synod of Chelsea in 816. As such it had not yet
become the focus of feasting and gift-giving but was a solemn time for
prayer and thanksgiving. Its choice was not arbitrary, however. This
day also marked the beginning of both the new Anglo-Saxon year and
a twelve-day festival prescribed in Alfred's own laws for all free men
and women – a festival whose origins stretched deep into England's
past.

Many years before, Bede had recalled how, in the earliest days of
Anglo-Saxon rule, this had been 'Mother's Night', a time dedicated to
a pagan and now long-forgotten mother goddess who was believed to
give birth to the new sun after the longest and darkest nights of the
year. The names and gods had since changed but the festival, which
the pagan Vikings (like the earlier Saxons) still called Yol and which
the Christians knew as Yule, remained much the same. Beginning on
25 December, the festivities, many with roots still tangled in that
pagan past, would climb to a crescendo, culminating in the main
celebration on Twelfth Night.

The place where Alfred heard Mass that day was his royal vill at
Chippenham. He probably found himself there thanks to Guthrum as,
following his peace agreement, Alfred would have shadowed the

Viking army north out of his kingdom to ensure they did not cut too much of a swathe through the Wessex heartlands on their way back to Mercia. Chippenham would then have been a nearby place to which he could retire, to enjoy the holiday season whilst keeping a close eye on the border.

After such a difficult year this was a time for Alfred to gather together family and retainers, to display as best he could something of the majesty of kingship. It was finally a time for the music and plays he loved and for relaxation. A surviving music book from Winchester from the following century, *The Winchester Troper*, hints at the ebullient elaborations of the Mass that Alfred might have enjoyed that Yuletide. These were also beginning to be complemented by new explanatory plays or 'tropes', which filled out and commented on the religious messages of the text itself and which would later develop into the mediaeval plays of the mummers. Perhaps there was even wassailing, the term *Waes Hael* being an Anglo-Saxon cry of 'good health'. Here then Christmas really was in the making.

Across in Gloucester this was also a time of celebration for Guthrum and his men, although little is known about how pagan Vikings celebrated the midwinter and the return of the sun. That these peoples from the far North, where midwinter brought days of permanent darkness, did celebrate is not in doubt, however, and we have a glimpse of a pagan Viking celebration preserved in the court records of the early tenth-century Byzantine emperor, Constantine VII. These show how one Christmas the emperor, who had extensive trading links with Scandinavia, invited a party of these pagans to entertain him during the holiday. It describes how 'two companies danced in a ring, striking their shields with sticks and shouting "Yol, Yol, Yol!", and in each company two men were dressed in furs and masks'. But if the celebrations of Yule in Chippenham and Yol in Gloucester showed superficial similarities, the conclusions that they were racing towards would prove very different for Alfred and Guthrum.

Guthrum had not given himself over entirely to dancing, even if Alfred had lost himself in the intricate Christmas chants of his Mass priests. As the king of Wessex gathered his household for the great Twelfth Night feast at which presents would be given in memory of the arrival of the Wise Men in Bethlehem, and in recognition of

Alfred's role as 'ring-giver', so Guthrum was breaking camp and slipping out into the winter darkness.

What happened next was one of the most pivotal moments in all English history, a point at which the whole future of the nation hung in the balance, equally able to tip one of two ways. In a lightning strike, Guthrum attacked Chippenham, forcing Alfred to run for his life and leaving the Viking in sole control of Wessex. With a single blow he had decapitated the state.

This is all the chronicler chooses to tell us of the momentous events of Twelfth Night 878 and that in itself should be enough to raise suspicions. Few of the incidents of Alfred's reign are exactly as they seem, thanks largely to the fact that, through the *Anglo-Saxon Chronicle*, he gained the opportunity to write his own history as he saw it and in the way that he believed would best ensure the survival of his descendants. Yet this episode has for centuries been taken at face value: that Guthrum surprised Alfred, and that Alfred ran away to begin the most famous episode of his life amongst the reeds and rushes of the Somerset Levels. But between the sparse lines of the chronicle's account, it is in the omissions and lacunae in Asser, hidden within letters from the pope, in later charters and in Alfred's own musings that we might recover a very different story. This is the tale of a man betrayed, of a Christmas never to be forgotten, not because of Guthrum but because of his own people. It is a story that might go some way to explain how a king found himself almost alone in the wilderness and how the only English monarch ever awarded the title 'Great' could be remembered solely for a legendary incident with some cakes.

To understand what actually happened that Christmas, we must return to Monday, 6 January 878 – Twelfth Night – at Chippenham. Alfred's celebrations that day were more than just a Christian feast; they were a key part of his duty as king. The twelve days of Christmas had not been simply a holiday from the troubles of kingship; they were an opportunity for work. Alfred would therefore have been surrounded by the most important men in his kingdom: his immediate kin, his personal household, and the most senior ealdormen, ecclesiastics and thegns of his realm. With his witan assembled, Alfred could conduct the business of state, making gifts to ensure his nobles' loyalty, arranging political and ecclesiastical appointments, hearing legal cases and planning for the year ahead. With all the recent troubles with Guthrum, there can have been little time in the previous year for such gatherings, leaving his government in a state of suspended animation. There was much to talk about now. More, indeed, than Alfred knew.

That evening, as the king settled to distributing gifts amongst his followers, Guthrum and his men were already moving quietly across the frozen fields of Wiltshire towards him. But they were not acting alone. If we are to believe the *Anglo-Saxon Chronicle*, when Guthrum arrived at Chippenham he found that the king and his court had simply disappeared; tipped off and spirited away into the undergrowth. This in itself seems highly unlikely, as how could the entire court simply slip away from an advancing Viking army without it knowing – and where could it go?

Then there is the problem of what happened next. According to the chroniclers once again, Alfred spent months in hiding, a fugitive in his own land, unseen and unloved. Yet if he had escaped with at least some of his household, why did he not quickly summon the fyrd and counter-attack? That, after all, had been what he had done on every previous occasion.

And there perhaps lies the answer. The reason that Alfred is described as being alone, the reason why the fyrd was not immediately summoned to answer the insult of Chippenham, was that on Twelfth Night 878 the real surprise for Alfred lay not in the advancing Viking army but in the heart of his own court.

That night all was not well with the Wessex witan. The Church, and particularly the archbishop of Canterbury, had grown resentful of Alfred's ever-increasing financial exactions on them. Ever since Ecgberht had negotiated 'protection and lordship' over Canterbury's lands at the Council of Kingston back in 838, the House of Ecgberht had freely used the Church's land and money when they believed the state needed them. Alfred now had more need than ever and was hence demanding more than ever but this had prompted Archbishop Æthelred to wonder whether *he* needed Alfred. Nor were all of the secular lords happy. Alfred was still a sickly king with regular bouts of his old illness, which hardly inspired his witan with confidence. The finances needed to pay off the Vikings did not come solely from the Church either, and the ealdormen and thegns were all expected to pay their fair share. And for what? They had watched Guthrum take the money and simply come back for more; there was little doubt that he would continue this strategy if he could. The alternative, of course, was fighting but Alfred, for all Asser's protestations, had not had a very good record in this. This king, whom he claims was 'victorious in virtually all battles', had acted decisively in the victory at Ashdown, certainly, but the attacks at Reading, Basing and Meretun had all been defeats. The last battle in that campaign, and his first as king, had perhaps been the worst of all. He had clearly lost at Wilton and had been lucky to be allowed to buy four expensive years of peace.

But what had he done with those four years? The country seemed no better equipped to deal with the Viking army that had returned in 875 and had fared little better against it. Wareham had been a humiliation where Guthrum had openly laughed at Alfred's attempts at binding diplomacy. Exeter had been a success but only because the weather had intervened and destroyed the Viking fleet off Swanage. A king was meant to act in person to protect his country – not buy peace and hope for bad weather. In fact, the only really great successes against the Vikings had been at Ashdown and Englefield. Whilst Alfred had taken part in one of those battles, it was his brother Æthelred who had then been king.

Arrayed against this – at best – moderately successful and expensive king was Guthrum. He had proved himself a formidable enemy and, if not a good, then at least a less damaging, friend. Ceolwulf and his court had survived and thrived; Northumbria seemed stable. There seemed little reason therefore to think that, in accepting a settlement under his overlordship (and backed by his army), West Saxons might not also do well. Defeat at Viking hands must have seemed inevitable to many and it was surely better to strike a deal that left Guthrum pulling their strings rather than have those strings cut altogether.

So a solution to these problems, at least as some of the witan saw it, was presented to Alfred that night. The witan elected kings, and it could unelect them. And that is exactly what it did. The party of ealdormen and clerics who approached their ring-giver that evening were not there to symbolically reaffirm the old ties of kinship; they were there to sever them. The men who stood before Alfred informed him that he was no longer fit to be their king; in fact he no longer was their king. If any of his household reached for their swords at the news, the reports that Guthrum's men were already marching on the vill must have stayed their hands.

Twelfth Night 878 was not a Viking invasion but a coup, backed up by Viking muscle invited along for the occasion. Chippenham was to be Alfred's Repton. Deposed by his own witan and without the hope of raising an army, he, like Burgred, would have no other choice but to flee abroad. In his place would come a Viking nominee – a practical arrangement, similar to those currently working in Northumbria and Mercia. With a new king who had Viking support, there was no need for further financial exactions; indeed, the Viking army was now there to protect the witan, not destroy it. Nor did a heathen power behind the throne present the Church with any major problems. Wulfhere of York had cheerfully survived the installation of a Viking puppet and had even retained his position as archbishop of York following the recent revolt in the city. There was no reason why Canterbury could not do the same. Of course, there would be conditions, as everyone could see. The Vikings did not offer their support for free and everyone who witnessed the deal must have known that they were not accessories but the main players in the game. The Northmen's conditions must have sounded little different from the words that Abbo of Fleury put into Ivarr's mouth when he cornered St Edmund: 'He commands that you share your hidden gold-hordes and your ancestral possessions with him straightaway, and that you become his vassal-king, if you want to stay alive.' The Vikings would get their money just the same – and more – but crucially without disturbing the status quo and without wrecking the nation. They might be devils, but they were old and familiar ones, and this was a case of 'better the devil you know'.

Plans for the coup must have begun during those four peaceful years, the four years of inattention when Alfred failed to recognize the growing resentment amongst some of his leaders. In 876 there are signs of trouble in the archbishop's own county of Kent. A charter from this year shows Alfred trying to buy support amongst the nobles of the county in a document unusual for the extensive list of witnesses. Its length suggests that it was an attempt to get the most important families of the shire on his side. Amongst the names is that of Archbishop Æthelred of Canterbury. If this was Alfred's plan, it failed. In 877, Æthelred made his next move.

By this date the archbishop was already in correspondence with Pope John VIII, one of whose letters, addressed to him jointly with the archbishop of York, survives from 873–5. That John could address a letter to both Canterbury and York suggests that Æthelred had managed to sustain a dialogue with Northumbria and hence was monitoring how the Church there thrived even under Viking rule. In 877 he takes this further, writing to the pope to complain of Alfred's behaviour. Although we do not have this letter, we do have a copy of the pope's reply, in which he mentions a letter that he has sent to Alfred, scolding him for impinging on the dignity of Canterbury. What is telling about this rather foreboding document is that no copy survives in England, perhaps because neither Æthelred at the time nor Alfred later would want to be reminded of it. Instead our only copy come from the register of John VIII from Monte Cassino.

This letter has peculiar, if not frightening, echoes of another from the same pope to Burgred, sent very shortly (perhaps only weeks) before he was deposed. Both these missives are apparently concerned with moral issues such as 'fornication' but a heavy helping of politics lies hidden between the supposedly devout lines, hinting at a deeper meaning to the correspondence. If the letter is not actually 'coded', it is at the very least 'veiled'. In fact, in places the threat is quite explicit: 'For we have been at pains to admonish and exhort your king with a letter from the apostolic see, not to neglect to be obedient to you . . . – if he wish to keep safe the kingdom committed to him in this world.' This extra-ordinary warning follows on from a passage where the pope makes it quite clear to the archbishop what he expects of him in any forthcoming struggle with the House of Ecgberht:

> We, however, exhort and warn you, my brother, on account of the necessity of the present time, that you station yourself as a wall for the house of the Lord, laying aside every worldly fear, as a proper servant of God, and, kindled by zeal for him, do not cease to resist strenuously not only the King, but all who wish to do any wrong against it.

The letter ends with what seems to amount to the pope's blessing for any move to depose the king and replace him:

> We have admonished your king to show due honour to you for the love of Jesus Christ the Lord, and be anxious to preserve all the rights of your privilege in everlasting security and to keep them undiminished, if he wishes to have the grace and benediction of the apostolic see as his predecessors deserved to have by their well-doing.

Æthelred was effectively arranging a 'divorce' between the English Church and its Christian king, allowing it to support (or at least not hinder) a coup and the installation of a puppet – even a Viking puppet. For some elements of the Church at least, this was the solution to the prophecy of Jeremiah.

Other compelling evidence for what happened that evening at Chippenham can also be found in the *Anglo-Saxon Chronicle* and in Asser. The former is as passionless as ever in its description of events, saying: 'In this year in midwinter after Twelfth Night the enemy came stealthily to Chippenham, and occupied the land of the West Saxons and settled there, and drove a great part of the people across the sea, and conquered most of the others; and the people submitted to them, except King Alfred.' Yet even here there are peculiarities. In the first instance it should be said that the entry nowhere states that Alfred had been deposed, but that is hardly surprising. The *Anglo-Saxon Chronicle* was first compiled later in Alfred's reign and hence is a retrospective, pro–Alfredian history. It was written in better times when the question of Alfred's right to rule had been decisively proved in his favour. There was no place for betrayal and humiliation in his version of events.

What is notable about the *Chronicle*'s account is that it makes no mention of a battle, no fight at the gates, no escape of the ealdormen or their households. Only Alfred is mentioned, escaping with a 'small force' apparently after not so much as a skirmish. Guthrum's 'stealthy' approach might explain how the Wessexmen were so completely overwhelmed but it still begs the question as to how the Vikings could surprise the West Saxon court so completely in the first place. It would have been impossibly foolhardy for the Wessex court to meet on the edge of the kingdom, near to the enemy, without posting pickets and lookouts across the countryside around them. And if the attack was so swift, so complete, where are the hostages and captives? And how did Alfred escape? The *Chronicle* makes no mention of even one person being taken captive in this sudden raid, nor of any attempt by Guthrum to catch any fleeing ealdormen. The entire episode would read more convincingly if the Vikings' approach were only really a surprise to one man at court: Alfred.

Asser's account of events is even more peculiar. The first part of his *Life of Alfred* follows the year-on-year entries of the *Anglo-Saxon*

Chronicle almost slavishly. It is in this vein that it reaches the events before Chippenham in Chapter 50, in which he describes how Halfdan shared out the lands of Northumbria with his men. Chapter 51 is strangely missing, being the only lost chapter in the entire work. As we no longer have Otho A xii, we cannot directly check the contents of the original (or at least our oldest) manuscript but the best surviving transcription, made for Matthew Parker when he owned the manuscript in the late sixteenth century, passes from Chapter 50 straight to Chapter 52. As this transcript was made before many of the other interpolations were added to the text (by Parker and others), it would appear that the original *Life* of Asser lacked this chapter as well.

One missing chapter might seem insignificant, were it not the only one and a vital one. Had Asser filled in Chapter 51 as he did for the other *Chronicle*-based entries, he would have recorded how the Vikings left Wareham and went to Exeter, how their fleet was destroyed off Swanage, and how Alfred extracted oaths from them at Exeter, which ensured that they retired to Mercia later in the year. This might seem to anyone following Alfred's story to be a reasonably important part of Asser's narrative, something that neither he nor his king would want left out, marking as it does a victory (at least of sorts). Yet Asser chooses to go directly from the Viking arrival in Exeter to their attack on Chippenham. In the process he is forced to ignore a whole year of events leading up to the most important moment in Alfred's reign, and he fudges the geography and chronology of the campaign, making the enemy move straight from Exeter in 876 to Chippenham in 878 with nothing happening in between. There is no mention of Mercia, no mention of Swanage and hence no mention of anything leading up to the pivotal moment.

It may be countered that Asser simply had a faulty copy of the *Anglo-Saxon Chronicle* to work from and the entry for 877 was hence missing. But bearing in mind the completeness of the other entries and the presence of Asser at Alfred's court where the *Chronicle* was probably being compiled, this seems unlikely. And even if the material was missing it still begs the question: why did Asser not look for another source for the information on that year? The wrecking of 120 ships off Swanage must have been a celebrated story in itself and he was surrounded by people who would remember it.

If Alfred was deposed at Chippenham, however, that might well alter Asser's approach. One explanation for the peculiarly ad hoc nature of the book that we call Asser's *Life of King Alfred* is that it is not actually a book at all but simply a collection of material that Asser was gathering for a biography of his king. While the work of gathering stories and chronicles was still only partly complete, the propaganda need for it, generated by a later war, passed. Hence Asser never wrote up his final work, leaving us with his collections of annals, notes and homely vignettes from which to attempt to construct a biography of our own. If this is the case, the missing chapter begins to make more sense. The events leading up to Chippenham presented Asser with a problem. He was compiling his material after the event, at a time of national emergency, in which it would be extremely dangerous to recall how his king was once deposed in a coup. This was no time to suggest that there was ever any dissension at home, any other possible contender for the throne or any interruption to Alfred's rule. The purpose of Asser's narrative was to prove the right of the king to be on the throne and the overwhelming likelihood that he would, with God's help, win in this crisis as he had ultimately done in those in the past. The events leading up to that coup would therefore have to be carefully rewritten. In preparation for this he removed the annal for 877 (that is, if the compiler of the *Anglo-Saxon Chronicle* had not himself removed it for exactly the same reason). As the work was never finished, however, the need never arose to return to this awkward entry and so the missing year was simply forgotten.

If Alfred was usurped, it does of course beg the questions: who was in the conspiracy, and who was going to replace him? Æthelred of Canterbury seems a likely supporter of the move, having perhaps already secured his position with both the pope and the Vikings, as his counterpart in York had done. Then there is a curious charter from the early years of Alfred's son Edward's reign which also hints at another culprit.

In a grant of 901, King Edward the Elder disposed of lands that formerly belonged to Wulfhere, the ealdorman of Wiltshire, which he forfeited when 'he deserted without permission both his lord King Alfred and his country in spite of the oath which he had sworn to the king and all his leading men. Then also by the judgment of all the councillors of the West Saxons and of the Mercians he lost the control and inheritance of his lands.' Although this charter does not explicitly mention when Wulfhere deserted Alfred, it is notable that the ealdorman is a regular witness on charters up to 878, but conspicuous by his absence afterwards, suggesting that his fall from favour occurred around this time. It is also worth mentioning that as Chippenham was in Wiltshire, the ealdorman would have been on home territory, surrounded by people he could rely on to back him. That might also have made him responsible for arranging the king's security there, giving Guthrum's men free rein to approach the hall unchallenged. Finally the degree of his disloyalty was sufficient for him to be entirely disinherited of all his lands, which, as he was an ealdorman, must have been extensive. Few things other than a challenge to the throne could have warranted this.

Further changes in the names appearing in official documents after Alfred's flight from Chippenham also suggest other possible candidates. They include Ælfstan of Dorset, Cuthred of Hampshire, Mucel and Eadwulf, all of whom had been been key members of Æthelred's witan, as well as Milred, who had been a king's thegn since the 840s. Amongst the clerics the see of Winchester also changed hands around this date, suggesting that the former incumbent, Tunberht, was now *persona non grata*.

The Vikings, together with Wulfhere and the other conspirators, must already have agreed on a suitable nominee to replace Alfred but it is hard to say who. Certainly there were plenty of other contenders for an elected kingship, including the children of Alfred's older brothers. Wulfhere and many other ealdormen had been associated with Æthelred and may therefore have favoured one of his sons. Although they were still children, from a Viking point of view that might have been an advantage, offering a suitably malleable minority.

There are two reasons why we do not know for sure who was nominally on the throne of Wessex after 877. First, in later years Alfred would never allow evidence of such a memory to persist. Second, Alfred had not done like Burgred and fled to Rome. He was still in Wessex; he was not about to renounce his throne; he was going to fight.

Letting Alfred escape from Chippenham looks like a fatal error on the part of both the coup plotters and the Vikings, but in terms of their overall plan it made sense at the time. Their template for this coup had been Mercia, where a feasible alternative ruler, acceptable to both

Church and nobles, had been raised up, backed with the threat of Viking force to discourage any adherents to the old king. Realizing the hopelessness of his situation, the former ruler had fled abroad. Ceolwulf had gained immediate legitimacy, as his forerunner had not been actually forced to abdicate (nor, worse still, had he been murdered) but had deserted his kingdom of his own free will. He had abandoned his people. It could easily be argued, therefore, that they no longer owed him their allegiance. There was now every reason to think Alfred would follow suit.

For Guthrum it was the logical last step in his plan to control England without having to take on the mantle of an alien and imposed ruler. It had become abundantly clear, during the campaigns in Northumbria, East Anglia and Mercia, that gaining control of these hierarchical and kin-based Saxon societies was just a matter of targeting their leaders and replacing them with nominees. In Northumbria the Vikings had interfered in a royal dispute that had already weakened the kingdom. Then they had won it by killing both claimants and installing their own puppet. In East Anglia events had not run as smoothly, as the Northmen had rather precipitously eliminated the rightful king, leaving no clear heir and in the process creating an unwanted and potentially troublesome martyr. Mercia, however, had been a much greater success, where the Vikings had simply exploited dynastic feuds to drive one king abroad and replace him with another who was under their thrall. It was clear which system worked best.

Had Guthrum been right in his prediction of Alfred's next step, the whole history of Anglo-Saxon England, and perhaps even modern England, would have been very different. If Alfred had abandoned his throne, the last independent Anglo-Saxon kingdom would have fallen. The statement in the *Anglo-Saxon Chronicle*, that Guthrum 'occupied the land of the West Saxons', would have been as final as the death notices that the same scribe had already recorded for the three other great Anglo-Saxon kingdoms. From the borders of Cornwall to the Northumbrian hills, England would have been a Scandinavian state. Guthrum and the Sons of Ragnar would have been free to turn their attentions to the complete conquest of Scotland and Wales, and thus the incorporation of the whole of the British Isles into the Scandinavian world.

But Guthrum was wrong. Alfred's decision turned the situation in Wessex on its head. Guthrum and his puppet were now 'officially' in charge of the kingdom, whilst Alfred was the bandit, skulking secretly in the hidden parts of his country. This had never been a part of Guthrum's plan and it presented certain problems.

In the final analysis, Guthrum and his 'king' would always have to rule by consent as, without standing armies or police forces, there was simply no other way for such a primitive administration to be run. If Alfred had fled overseas, there would have been no difficulty, as he could have been portrayed as having abandoned his throne while Guthrum's nominee could be cast as Wessex's saviour. Now, however, he had the worst of both worlds with a puppet ruler who looked like the placeman he was and a potential Saxon hero stalking his every move. Suddenly what had begun as a swift coup was going to turn into a campaign of either canvassing for – or extorting – support from the ealdormen and people of Wessex. There were two contenders but it would be the people of Wessex who would decide.

Theoretically, Guthrum had the upper hand, as he was not the one in hiding. It must have seemed to him that all he had to do was persuade the great men of the Wessex shires to submit to his puppet as their new lord. The general population were offered no such choice and farmers on the land had simply to submit to whichever authority imposed itself most forcefully on them. For those in Wiltshire at least, that was clearly the Vikings.

But whilst Alfred lurked in the shadows, there was always another course open to the West Saxons. He was the quiet voice whispering at the back of the minds of vacillating ealdormen, the ghost at the mead bench, the rumour flying from village to village. For as long as this continued, he had a chance, although such thoughts must have provided cold comfort for the straggling band of West Saxons now picking their way through the Wiltshire forests. This, for the moment, was all that was left of Alfred's kingdom – just a former king and a few followers who 'journeyed in difficulties through the woods and fen-fastnesses'.

He was a hunted man in his own land.

10

The Once and Future King

Nothing is ever easy in the kingdom of earth,
The world beneath the heavens is in the hands of fate.
Here possessions are fleeting, here friends are fleeting,
Here man is fleeting, here kinsmen are fleeting,
The whole world becomes a wilderness.

The Wanderer, quoted in K. Crossley-
Holland, *The Anglo-Saxon World*, p. 49

A LFRED, HOWEVER, DID have a plan. Reeling from the immediate shock of his overthrow, he first needed to find safety, a place
where he could compose his thoughts and consider his options. So he
headed west, away from the more troublesome shires, away from
Chippenham and Wiltshire, into Somerset where he believed a
warmer reception awaited him. It was then an untamed land, its
Levels still undrained, and, for the boy who had grown up hunting in
this near-impenetrable wasteland, there was physical safety in this
winter wilderness.

Although Asser had never dared to explicitly breathe a word of the
coup, the language he now uses to describe his lord and his predicament is not what we might expect for a reigning king.

At the same time King Alfred, with his small band of nobles and also
with certain soldiers and thegns, was leading a restless life in great
distress amid the woody and marshy places of Somerset. He had
nothing to live on except what he could forage by frequent raids,
either secretly or even openly, from the Vikings as well as from the
Christians who had submitted to the Vikings' authority.

Here is a man reduced to raiding his own people, although Asser
clearly believed that he could be excused this as they had capitulated to

the new regime. Alfred by contrast must have been aware that they really had no choice and that plundering his own subjects in mid-winter, when their food stocks were at their lowest ebb, was unlikely to rally them behind him. What his fleeting appearances from out of the mists could do, however, was demonstrate to the people of Wessex that, although he might be in hiding, he was alive. For some at least, this put a brake on their willingness to submit to the coup. For the Viking plan to succeed, Alfred would have to have abandoned the country, so he was doing the only thing still in his power: proving that he had not.

The presence of this almost ghostly Alfred worried Guthrum, who was far more used to the role of the raider. Indeed, he must have cursed himself for letting an enemy escape who, though weak, enjoyed a wraithlike existence that made him nearly impossible to fight.

And there lies the heart of Alfred's genius in this, his darkest moment. As he had fled through the gates at Chippenham, history provided two possible choices for a man in his position. He could save his life as Burgred had done, abandoning his country and his people, and hence failing in his primary duty as a Saxon king: to defend his country. Equally he could take on the role of martyr like Edmund and throw himself at Guthrum's superior forces in a suicidal attack that, one way or another, would end in death. The end result for his people, however, would be just the same: he would be cast as the justly deposed king who had gone against the will of his people, either by abandoning them or fighting to retain a throne that was no longer his. Like King Sigeberht in 757, Alfred would become just another deposed king of Wessex over whom the chroniclers had few tears to shed.

As Alfred disappeared into the hunting grounds of his youth he chose a third path. If Guthrum's puppet intended to play the part of a Saxon king in Chippenham, so Alfred would play the Viking, refusing to abide by the rules of open warfare, operating in a guerrilla band to harry and terrorize Wessex's new masters, just as he had been terrorized by them. Everywhere that the Vikings tried to assert their control he would spring up, disrupting their progress but, far more importantly, reminding those West Saxons who might help him, or who had despaired of his return, that he was still alive – that he was not simply their former, but also their future king.

For Guthrum it was essential that this annoying reminder of 'Old Wessex' was found and dispatched once and for all. There was no room in Wessex for two kings and Guthrum was determined that it would be his. But there was no immediate need for concern. As Alfred and the remnants of his retinue were fleeing west from Chippenham, they were also rushing towards a trap.

Earlier that winter another Viking force had been operating on the British mainland, persecuting the people of the kingdom of Dyfed in South Wales. Their presence there was not in itself remarkable as the Irish Vikings had been regularly preying on the Welsh coast for years, but what was noteworthy was that, at the same time that Guthrum moved south from Gloucester, this warband seems to have weighed anchor and sailed for Devon. The West was Alfred's heartland; it was the direction in which he had fled and the place where he expected the most support. Alfred does not seem to have been strong in the East, certainly not in Kent, nor even in Wiltshire, which was the territory of Wulfhere – now probably Guthrum's creature. The West would take more persuading of the new order. This made it a suitable place for a secondary Viking attack to nip any nascent pro-Alfredian resistance in the bud. With any luck it might now crush Alfred as well.

The arrival at this time of a Viking army in Devon, on Wessex's exposed west flank, could of course be pure coincidence or perhaps simply opportunism on the part of pirates who had heard that Alfred was busy elsewhere. Guthrum's previous record of mounting two-pronged attacks, however, suggests that the effort may have been concerted and planned, as does the identity of the leader of this new force. He was Ubba, brother of Ivarr and Halfdan. The Sons of Ragnar had returned.

If Guthrum knew that the rump of Alfred's household was fleeing towards a Son of Ragnar, it must have delighted him. Ubba, like his brothers, was a man around whom many legends had been built. It was said by the later St Neot's annalist that he carried with him the traditional raven banner that Vikings took into battle. The raven was an iconic bird to the Vikings and a powerful symbol of war. Pagan legends said that Odin owned two ravens called Thought and Memory, and that when ravens descended on a battlefield and began picking at the bodies of the slain, it represented their god's acceptance of the blood sacrifice that he had been offered. Indeed, so powerful was the image of the raven that it can be seen on the Bayeux tapestry, carried into battle in 1066 by the Norman descendants of the Viking Hralf the Walker, during their invasion of England. But Ubba's raven banner was different. Woven by his three sisters, it was a magical talisman that would flutter before victories but hang limp in advance of defeat.

Crossing the Bristol Channel that winter it must have fluttered vigorously in the stiff sea breeze, inspiring every warrior in the twenty-three ships of Ubba's fleet. That same baleful pennant must equally have struck fear into the hearts of Ealdorman Odda and the men of his Devon fyrd as they saw it scything towards them from their vantage point on the still-unfinished fortifications at Cynuit (probably Countisbury Hill on the Exmoor coast). Whether or not Odda knew of events in Wiltshire, he remained loyal to Alfred and he had no interest whatsoever in anything that these Vikings had to tell him about the new West Saxon realpolitik.

By the time the Vikings had drawn up their ships on the beach, the Devon fyrd had dug in as best it could, having thrown up an earth rampart around the site, and prepared for the onslaught. But Ubba was in no particular hurry. Countisbury is a precipitous hill, popular today with the more adventurous amongst hang-glider pilots, and its slopes rise high over sheer sea cliffs, making it almost impregnable. But the landscape that formed a barrier against Ubba also served to pen in Odda. The Viking assumed that it was simply a matter of time before the West Saxons surrendered. As Ubba pitched camp outside the fort, it seemed to him that he had only to wait to starve out its defenders whilst in the meantime Odda and his fyrd could do no more than gaze out at his fluttering raven banner.

But now, once again, the normal series of events was turned on its head. It was traditionally the Vikings who found themselves holed up in defended sites, surrounded by Anglo-Saxon besiegers. Shrewdly, it was their tactics in such situations that Odda now borrowed. Realizing that to remain in the fort was merely an invitation to a slow death, the men of the Devon fyrd did what Guthrum had done at Reading: they suddenly burst out and attacked. Ubba's Vikings were taken completely by surprise and in the ensuing carnage somewhere between 800 and 1,200 of his men were cut to pieces. Worse still, Ubba himself, one of the supposedly invincible Sons of Ragnar, was hacked down and his magical raven banner captured.

The complete rout of Ubba's force was a stunning reversal for Guthrum. In an era of omens, such a loss heartened those who still looked to Alfred for a way out of their current predicament whilst the capture of the raven banner sent a chill through the ranks of Guthrum's own men. Indeed, so important does this banner seem to have been, at least in Anglo-Saxon minds, that its capture is specifically mentioned in nearly all the surviving accounts of the period, making it, along with the arm-ring of Thor, one of only two uniquely Viking artefacts recorded anywhere by the chroniclers.

When the news reached Alfred, which, judging from the speed of events later in the year, it must quickly have done, he must have felt that the tide was beginning to turn. As winter slowly melted into spring, his thoughts turned to taking up more permanent headquarters from which to conduct his guerrilla war and in which to plan his bid to retake the throne. He needed a safe base, where his friends could find him but his enemies could not. It may have been the arrival of one of those friends with a detailed knowledge of the local terrain that spurred his next move. The arrival was that of his faithful Somerset ealdorman Æthelnoth and his supporters. They had either escaped from Chippenham or had gone into hiding shortly afterwards, as the chronicler Æthelweard tells us that previously he 'abode with a small band in a certain wood'. Together they made their way to the place that has ever since been associated with Alfred's name.

The site that Alfred chose for his guerrilla base was a dank and dreary spot lost somewhere between the royal estates of Wedmore and Aller, on a small islet of dry land amid the trackless wastes and waters of the Somerset Levels. The name of this place – Athelney, which means 'Isle of Princes' – suggests that this densely wooded hillock may already have been known to Alfred and the Wessex court, perhaps from hunting expeditions into the rich and dangerous marshlands of the Levels, where deer and waterfowl were to be had. Roger of Wendover describes the place as 'Girded in with fen on every side and not to be come at save by boat. Thereon is all dense alder-brake, full of stags and goats and such creatures, and in the midst one bit of open ground, scarce two acres.' It was a damp, dangerous half-world of land and water, almost impossible to find – and hence perfect. As later rebels such as Hereward the Wake would find, a knowledge of the fens, as well as the sinuous paths and waterways through their bogs and quicksands, made for a surer protection than any shield or sword. On this tiny patch of dry land, hidden in the wilderness, Alfred was not only safe from attack but free to harass both the Vikings and their collaborators with impunity.

So it was to Athelney that the king, Æthelnoth and their few remaining retainers came, shortly after the Easter of 878. As the island covers little more than 9,500 square yards there cannot have been many in the party. Few as they were, this meagre band went about building what Asser bravely calls a 'fortress' but might perhaps more accurately be called a camp, defended no doubt by ditch and bank, and perhaps woven hurdles cut from the alder at the water's edge. It was a very small kingdom indeed for the man who sat on the still-frozen fringes of Athelney at the end of that cold spring, surveying the hastily built shelters that were now his towns and vills, his forts and minsters, all rolled into one. As he looked out across his little kingdom perhaps the comforting words of the eighth-century poet Deor came to him. Deor had himself been usurped by another man and lamented the fortunes of the fallen whilst repeating the refrain: 'That passed away, this also may.'

The situation was a safe but not a happy one. The very idea of mounting a successful challenge to a Viking army from a tiny islet in a forgotten bog, using a handful of half-starved men who were reduced to living off the land, was, to say the least, fanciful. So unlikely was any form of comeback from this terrible low that in later years a whole host of stories grew up around this moment to try to explain the apparently inexplicable. The forlorn Alfred standing on Athelney that misty March was now a man on the edge of history, about to enter the world of the saints and monsters that haunted the lost places of England. As he stepped into the Levels, he had briefly left reality behind and entered legend.

The stories of Alfred's tribulations in exile have such a powerful hold, even on the modern imagination, that they have simply overwhelmed the historical evidence from this time. Alfred is still 'the man who burned the cakes', even though this is the one episode in his extraordinary life that almost certainly never happened. The nagging question that remains is: why then has this story survived?

There are numerous tales about Alfred, both fact and fable, which would seem to tell us more about the man. He has meetings with saints (which should have appealed to mediaeval chroniclers); he has battles with pagans (which should have appealed to secular story-tellers); and yet he is still, over 1,100 years after his death, remembered for burning the cakes. And it is a peculiarly unsatisfying story – of a man who gets lost in his thoughts and is brought up short by an irate peasant whose bread he has allowed to burn. If this is an allegory, what does it mean? The answer may lie back at Chippenham on Twelfth Night 878. From here we can then pick our way through the smoke and discover the real Alfred beyond.

The story of Alfred and the cakes is first recorded in an anonymous *Life of St Neot*, written probably about a hundred years after the events it describes, possibly to coincide with the translation of the saint's relics from their original resting place in Cornwall to the Cambridgeshire priory at Eynesbury, which was shortly after renamed St Neot's. The story goes that Alfred was wandering alone through the wilderness, heavy of heart and at his lowest ebb, when he came across a peasant's hut. Knocking on the door, he asked whether he might seek refuge there with the herdsman (usually called a swineherd) and his wife, whose home this was. So low indeed had Alfred sunk that his hosts did not even recognize their king but they welcomed in the down-at-heel stranger anyway, as good Christian West Saxons should. It was here that Alfred fell to dreaming, whilst the herdsman's wife busied herself cleaning the little house. But so lost in thought did the king become that he failed to notice that the bread that she was preparing for them (or cakes in some versions) was burning in the oven. When she smelt the smoke, she dashed from her work and rescued the bread from the fire, turning on the oblivious Alfred and saying: 'Look here, man, you hesitate to turn the loaves which you see to be burning, yet you're quite happy to eat them when they come warm from the oven.' Alfred, for all his former regality, simply bowed his head and accepted the scolding, vowing to take better care from then on.

That, then, in its simplest form, is the entirety of the story – a tale of a humbled king who accepts a rebuke from one of his lowliest subjects. It might be taken as no more than a reminder of Alcuin's old dictum, 'God chastiseth every son whom he receiveth.' Indeed, this has often been taken to be the entire purpose of the tale. According to the *Life of St Neot*, the saint, whilst still alive, had been something of a mentor for Alfred, having warned the young king against intemperance and prophesied that trouble would follow. After Neot died, the prophecy came true. Alfred had merely to humbly bear the punishment of God (and housewives), and pray for both forgiveness and victory. Not long after the cake incident, the story continued, the saint appeared in a dream to Alfred and promised him triumph over his enemies.

This fable was extremely popular in the mediaeval period and several retellings of it occur in which the king is variously cast either as a philosopher too intent on contemplating scripture to attend to the cakes, or as a warrior overly absorbed in fletching arrows whilst the culinary nightmare unfolds. At times he is portrayed as the unhappy worrier, forgetful of his duties; at others as the busy monarch with no time for dealing with peasant concerns. Likewise the wife is variously cast as an instrument of God, justly scolding the king, or, in one version, even as 'the evil wife' who has the temerity to stop the mighty king's daydreaming. And this is where a hint of confusion emerges. All these various versions of the tale suggest the same thing: that the reteller is unsure as to its true meaning. Is it about patience being rewarded, or kings remembering to be humble? Is it about listening to saints or learning to cook? It is somewhat elaborate and yet it has no clear motive in its telling or, if it does, that motive has been lost.

But if the legend has a connection with Alfred's ousting at Chippenham an alternative reading can be found. Whilst the tale of the burning of the cakes cannot be proved to be contemporary with Alfred, it was certainly in existence just a hundred years after his death. We might therefore expect an oral tradition to take it back nearer to his own era. If we can bring the story this close, to events as remembered by those who stood witness at Chippenham, we can see in it not simply a moralizing injunction on patience, but an allegory on kingship itself.

The purpose of the story of the cakes is not to encourage kings to be humble, or even to promote mediaeval saints' cults, but to portray the dangers of failing to tend to the needs of the kingdom. In the four years leading up to 878, Alfred had been given the opportunity to prepare better defences for Wessex and to secure his position, but he had wasted this. His inattention had led to growing dissatisfaction at home and danger from abroad; this too he had failed even to notice. Politically, his cakes were burning, and only a severe scolding by his people would awaken him to the impending disaster. That scolding had occurred at Chippenham, but Alfred had listened, he had bowed his head and accepted his people's rebuke, and now he would fight back.

If this was the original meaning of the legend it was quickly lost, as indeed Alfred would have wanted it, leaving only the faintest of folk memories of the wilderness days of a deposed king. The tale also quickly gained new purposes, bound up with the success of saintly cults. For St Neot is not the only holy man credited with turning around the history of England at this point. The writer of the chronicle traditionally attributed to Simeon of Durham, not surprisingly perhaps, credits Cuthbert (who was by then buried in Durham) with a divine intervention, as does the *Book of Hyde*, written at the abbey that would become Alfred's last resting place.

The story goes that Alfred was alone on Athelney one day while his men were out hunting and fishing, when a pilgrim appeared before him, begging alms in the name of God. Alfred was himself nearly out of supplies but he called for what he had to be brought out – some wine and a loaf – and he freely gave half to the pilgrim. The mysterious man then thanked the king and 'leaving no foot-print in the mire, vanisheth away'. If the king was in any doubt that he had been visited by some supernatural traveller, it was dispelled by the discovery that the bread and wine had miraculously reappeared again in the stores and his provisions were fully replenished. Further proof came when the foraging party returned with an unexpectedly large catch of fish. That night, as the king slept, a vision came to him of a man in bishop's clothes who said: 'O Alfred, Christ who hath beheld the uprightness of thine heart endeth even now thy troubles. For tomorrow there shall come to thee strong helpers, by whose aid thou shalt overthrow thine enemies.' When Alfred asked the apparition who he was, he replied: 'I am Cuthbert. I am that pilgrim who was yesterday here, to whom thou gavest bread. Thee and thine take I beneath my care. Remember this when it shall be well with thee.'

This is much more the sort of tale about Alfred that we might expect to have survived and its purpose is quite clear. The reason why these saints were gathering round Alfred at this difficult time has as much to do with later Saxon politics as it does with divine intervention. Neither Asser nor the Anglo-Saxon chronicler mentions the appearance of either saint at this moment, preferring to attribute events to human causes, but for later chroniclers the opportunity of placing their patron saint at this pivotal moment was simply too good to resist. In the case of the Cuthbert story, its inclusion in *The History of St Cuthbert* served to make a link in tenth-century minds between the descendants of Alfred, who by then also ruled Northumbria, and that kingdom's greatest saint. It also served as a reminder to Alfred's successors that they should continue to endow the Church at Durham if they wished to have the support of Cuthbert in return – 'Remember this when it shall be well with thee.' In the case of St Neot, the story again served to show ancient links between a kingdom, in this case Cornwall – the saint's original home, and Wessex at a time when that area too was coming under the control of the House of Ecgberht. It also of course provided a familiar story for the monks of the new St Neot's in Huntingdonshire to tell about their recently arrived Cornish relics, about which they knew practically nothing. In both cases what is particularly interesting is not what these saints could do for Alfred, but what Alfred's legend could, by association, do for the saints. No doubt the king spent much of this sorry spell praying for better days but the saints who are said later to have answered his prayers gained easily as much from their association with his legend as he did from theirs.

One other great tale survives from Alfred's time in the wilderness. It has nothing to do with saints and visions, but it helped explain in the popular imagination how Alfred made his extraordinary comeback. The story is recorded in the eleventh-century *Chronicle of St Neot's* and in the twelfth-century chronicle by William of Malmesbury. It describes the practical steps taken by Alfred to gain the upper hand against Guthrum. The story, as William of Malmesbury tells it, narrates how Alfred,

> accompanied only by one of his most faithful adherents, entered the tent of the Danish king under the disguise of a minstrel; and being admitted, as a professor of the mimic art, to the banqueting room, there was no object of secrecy that he did not minutely attend to both with eyes and ears. Remaining there several days, till he had satisfied his mind on every matter which he wished to know, he returned to Athelney.

The story as it stands is simply a flight of fancy. Guthrum and Alfred had met before so the king dared not risk being recognized and captured in person. The suggestion of the use of spies and espionage does, however, ring true in the light of the events that began to unfold some seven weeks after Alfred first came to Athelney. We know from Asser that those seven weeks in the wilderness were spent engaging in guerrilla warfare, raiding Viking foraging parties and reminding the people of Somerset that all was not yet lost. But this was really just for show. Behind the scenes something more extraordinary was also going on. Although the site of Athelney was secluded and isolated, it was close to a number of trackways, both Roman and later, traversed not only by spies but by messengers, criss-crossing the kingdom of Wessex. They brought news of Alfred's survival, as well as his plan of attack to those ealdormen and thegns who had not fled abroad and who had not yet thrown in their lot with the enemy.

That such an extensive network of contacts could be maintained from an anonymous marshy islet shows that communication in ninth-century Wessex was far from primitive. The sophisticated system that kept the king in touch with his nobles on his normal tours around his kingdom must have continued to function even whilst he was in hiding in the Somerset Levels. It also suggests that Guthrum's puppet's hold on Wessex, or at least the greater kingdom beyond the part of Wiltshire immediately around Chippenham, was not as strong as the chroniclers would have us believe.

The news that Alfred's messengers carried away from Athelney during those seven supernatural weeks of vision and visitation was that the king was alive and that he was summoning a great host, made up of every shire fyrd he could muster. They were to meet him at a secret place on a specific day and then, together, they would march against Chippenham and free the kingdom of Wessex once and for all.

That the message got out without being intercepted by Guthrum or the pro-Viking ealdormen is miraculous enough, but what is more impressive is that it received an answer. This may at one level simply reflect the failure of the Viking nominees' influence to penetrate much outside northern Wiltshire but it is also a testament to the power that Alfred still wielded over the people of Wessex. By comparison, however, when Burgred was in a situation far better than this, neither in hiding nor defeated in battle, the rapid melting away of his own support in the face of a witan in revolt, with a Viking army behind them, led to his abandoning his country without a fight. Alfred was clearly not going to follow his example. In sending out the call to arms he not only mastered the doubts that must have plagued Burgred as to how many of his own ealdormen would bother to answer his call but he also had the nerve to hear their response.

The place that Alfred chose for the first meeting of his army – his first chance to gauge what sort of a resistance he could put up – was the now lost site of 'Egbert's Stone'. Asser tells us that this place was in the eastern part of the great forest of Selwood, which then stretched from mid-Dorset to the southern edge of Salisbury Plain. It probably lay somewhere on the route between Athelney and Warminster, perhaps at Penselwood on the borders of Wiltshire and Somerset. Near by the eighteenth-century banker and eccentric Henry Hoare II built 'Alfred's Tower' as a monument to this meeting. Although we can never be sure of it, from this folly there is a good chance that we might be looking down on the place where Alfred emerged from legend, back into history.

It was to be a moment of high drama as Alfred, Æthelnoth and the survivors of Athelney emerged from the forbidding forest around 4 May 878 and saw gathered at that now long-forgotten place the ealdormen and fyrds of Hampshire, Somerset and Wiltshire. Asser can barely conceal the emotion of the moment when he writes: 'When they saw the king, receiving him (not surprisingly) as if one restored to life after suffering such great tribulations, they were filled with an immense joy.' Alfred too must have been elated as he turned the last corner on the forest path and saw on the grasslands ahead three whole fyrds rise to their feet. The main Wessex armies had all answered the call. Devon was absent, but after their battle with Ubba, and no doubt in fear of further attacks on their flank, their absence was easily excused. To the people cheering Alfred's approach, he was their once and future king. They came for the ruler he once was and they would fight for the ruler he would be again. Cuthbert's dream had come true: here were the 'strong helpers' that the saint had promised. His greatest gamble – that his own people would back him – had paid off. Now, for one night, they would rest here before marching out north, back towards the people who had betrayed him, back to Guthrum, out of the wilderness and back to the battlefield.

The Silent Army

> Think of all the times we boasted
> at the mead-bench, heroes in the hall
> predicting our own bravery in battle.
> Now we shall see who meant what he said.
> *The Battle of Maldon*, quoted in K. Crossley-
> Holland, *The Anglo-Saxon World*, p. 14

WORD MUST HAVE been filtering back to the new regime at Chippenham for some time that something was wrong in the countryside, that people were disappearing. The army that Alfred was mustering was not a professional body housed in barracks and awaiting a call to arms. It was largely made up of local farmers and boys who owed allegiance through a complex web of kinship and obligation to their lord and, through him, to the king. When not fighting they were spread out across the countryside in their farms and fields, a threat, but an intangible one, just the ghost of an army waiting to form up into something more real and more dangerous. This was the force that coalesced into reality at Egbert's Stone: the peasant levies of three counties, amounting to perhaps 4,000 men, who had melted away from their villages and fields in answer to the call to battle.

Four thousand men is not much by the standards of modern armies but in the sparsely populated shires of Wessex the absence of these men at an important time in the agricultural calendar would have been noticed, both by Guthrum's men and by those Saxons who had backed the coup. It must have been a nervous time for these two groups. With farmers drifting away from the fields and into the forest it was clear, even to a casual observer, that the fyrd was being summoned, but it was almost impossible to know either the scale of the call or the level of the response. Somewhere, at a location still unknown to Guthrum, he knew an army was forming, made of seasoned (if not professional) soldiers, many of whom would have been present at previous Viking battles, some of which they had won. These men would not be easily overawed by the raven banner.

For Alfred there was still the real danger that his messengers or fyrdmen might be intercepted on their way to the muster and have the location prised out of them, but he had planned for this. Beyond being told of their initial meeting place, his men had no need to know their final destination, so the safest thing was simply not to tell them. That was the point of meeting at Egbert's Stone just two days before he intended to join battle. When Alfred knew that he had an army, he could tell them their objective at the very last minute. Even if there were spies in the camp, it would already be too late to have much influence on the outcome. If Viking informers did gallop through the night from that muster back towards Chippenham, only a few hours behind them, on the ancient army path known as the 'Hardway', was the fyrd itself.

The morning after his triumphant emergence from the forest at Egbert's Stone, Alfred gave the order to move once more, north–east towards Iglea or 'Iley Oak'. The most likely candidate for this lost location is Eastleigh Wood in Sutton Veny, just outside Warminster, in what was then dense forest. This site was still the meeting place for the courts of the Hundreds of Heytesbury and Warminster well into the fifteenth century, and was also a gathering place for the (then illegal) Wiltshire nonconformists in the seventeenth century. It is therefore not only an area with very ancient connections but was clearly a place where people could gather without drawing undue attention to themselves. It was also just six and a half miles from where battle would be joined the following day, Alfred's last chance to organize and inspire the 4,000 men and boys in whose hands the fate of Wessex and England lay.

But as Alfred's men settled down that night they were no longer the only army in the field. Keeping secret the movements of 4,000 fyrdmen was an impossibility and at some point over the previous two days news had reached Chippenham that the shires had been summoned in such numbers that the new regime, or rather Guthrum, would be forced to act. The alternatives before him were invidious.

He could either sit tight in his fortified position at Chippenham, a favoured tactic for a traditional raiding Viking army, or he could move out to ground of his choosing, between Alfred's army and his own base, and force a pitched battle. All-out battle was certainly not an attractive option for Vikings, as numbers could weigh against them. They had always preferred a hit-and-run approach, operating in guerrilla units, keeping the fyrd in the field but never, if at all possible, bringing them to open battle. But this was different. Although Guthrum was supporting a coup, regardless of which puppet he nominated, it left him in real charge. Hence he needed to cast himself and his Viking warband as the legitimate protectors of Wessex, and Alfred's army as the marauding rebels. This was not, however, what they were, nor was it what they were good at.

Guthrum was finding himself more and more in a cleft stick. It is not known to what degree the pro-Viking witan at Chippenham was still operating but, judging from the size of the army that answered Alfred, its success had been far below expectations and it can have held little sway outside a small part of Wiltshire. Unlike Burgred, Alfred had not abandoned his people, so his people had not abandoned him. Those such as Ealdorman Wulfhere, who had supported the coup, were looking increasingly isolated. They may even by this point have given up the pretence of rule altogether. This left Guthrum with no choice but to give up the pretence of 'support for a legitimate regime' and, casting aside his role as kingmaker, make a bid for the role of king. To do this would simply mean throwing all his forces against his enemy and hoping for an all-out victory. No more sieges, no more truces, no more oaths – simply one final pitched battle. For both leaders it was the last cast of the dice.

So, against his better judgment, Guthrum made the decision, not of a pirate, but of a king, marching his men out of their camp and into the field. On the evening before battle they were just over the horizon from the shire fyrds, high above their forest meeting place, within the ancient ramparts of Bratton Camp. In choosing Bratton as the base for his army, Guthrum was clearly stating his intentions.

This ancient Iron Age hill fort, cut into the chalk at the western edge of the Salisbury Plain escarpment, had not seen military action for some eight hundred years. It had no defences, save for the ditches and banks thrown up in previous centuries, and no internal water supply. Even today Bratton remains a bleak and isolated place, its huge prehistoric ramparts only providing shelter for a handful of bedraggled sheep and a platform from which the more adventurous kite flyers launch their craft. Then it was bleaker still with no metalled road to bring visitors up the precipitous slope from the plain to the north. Instead it was a gruelling climb, rewarded with a blast of bitter wind but the same matchless view that encouraged Iron Age pioneers to fortify the site. That view took in the little village of Edington far below them from which the forthcoming battle would take its name. More importantly, it encompassed the ancient roads and trackways that crossed Salisbury Plain to the south and west – the direction in which Alfred would be coming. Guthrum had chosen this forbidding place because of its geography. With Alfred's army marching on Chippenham, he knew they would be forced to pass this way. When they did, he would block their path and whoever emerged victor from that engagement would be king of Wessex.

The following morning brought news to both camps of the disposition of their enemy. For Guthrum the plan was simple. Placing scouts along the top of the surrounding hills to report when Alfred's army came into view, he rested his men behind the ancient ramparts of Bratton and waited. Alfred would have to make the first move.

Breaking camp at Iley Oak at dawn, the fyrd climbed high on to the spine of chalk hills on which Bratton Camp stands. Marching north-east, they first took the heights of Battlesbury Hill and then marched the four miles along the broken ground of the ridge until Bratton itself came into view. By the time the men at the head of Alfred's army first saw the distinctive ring of ditches around the Iron Age hill fort, Guthrum's scouts, at least those who had escaped the vanguard of the fyrd, must have galloped back to warn Guthrum to form up. In response another line of defences was now also to be seen around the camp. In front of the grass-green ditches and banks, a darker line was now drawn – the shield wall of the Vikings.

At this point the Wessex fyrd also temporarily halted to take up its distinctive battle formation. With shields locked, swords drawn and ash spears at the ready, Alfred's army then advanced.

Marching into even 800-year-old defences was not a manoeuvre to be lightly undertaken but the chronicle writer known as Simeon of

Durham, somewhat overcome by the occasion, tells us that the West Saxons had their own 'rampart' for protection:

> With the first bright rays of the rising sun did the King alike and all the flower of his folk beclothe themselves in their war-gear, with the three-fold breastplate, to wit, of Faith, and of Hope, and of the Love of God. Arising thereafter from the ground, boldly did they challenge the combat, trusting full surely in the Mercy and Lovingkindness of the Creator, and safeguarded, as with a rampart, by the presence of their King, whose face shone even then with light, as it had been the face of an angel.

Whilst the description is perhaps a little florid, Alfred was indeed going into battle that day, as he believed, protected by his God as well as himself protecting the men of the shires as their lord. It was symbolic time of year – Whitsun – a celebration of the time when, fifty days after the Resurrection, the Holy Ghost had descended on the apostles to prove that Christ had arisen from the dead and that he was with them again. Ever since then, it had been a time of rebirth in the calendar, whose name itself derived from the white garments worn by Christian converts who were traditionally baptized during this festival. But there was another uncanny parallel. It had also been fifty days since Alfred went into hiding at Athelney. Now, here by the village of Edington, he was back, restored to his people – a promise fulfilled. It was the end of Passiontide, the end of Easter and the end of Alfred's time in the wilderness.

Asser begins his description of the events that day, as the two armies met one final time, with unusual modesty and brevity: 'he [Alfred] moved his forces and came to a place called Edington, and fighting fiercely with a compact shield-wall against the entire Viking army, he persevered resolutely for a long time; at length he gained the victory through God's will.' This rather abbreviated description of one of the most important battles ever to take place on British soil hides what must have been a brutal episode of pushing, stabbing and parrying, as the two shield walls struggled to hold their line around the broken ground of the camp. Towards evening, however, the West Saxons made a breakthrough and the Viking forces began to retreat. It was a crucial moment. As the Saxons began to take more and more ground, so Guthrum had to make one final decision. Should he stay and fight to the death as a king, or should he return to his old self – the raider – and make a dash for the relative safety of his Chippenham base? In the end, under increasing pressure, the old Viking came to the fore. Guthrum abandoned the field and, in the process, his claim to the throne of Wessex. Retreat rapidly turned to rout and Asser now uses more forceful language to describe the scene: 'He [Alfred] destroyed the Vikings with great slaughter, and pursued those who fled as far as the stronghold, hacking them down.'

Guthrum and at least some of his men did indeed reach the relative safety of Chippenham, where they managed to barricade themselves in. But if Guthrum thought he could simply revert to the old Viking way, expecting forgiveness and generous terms, he was sorely mistaken. Alfred had learnt one valuable lesson from recent events: mistrust. He had heard the oaths. He had walked heavy-hearted through the slaughtered remains of his hostages, yet seen how easily Guthrum bore the slaughter of his own. He had watched, impotently, as Guthrum had promised to leave his kingdom, only to take up position again near by; and he had stood helpless as that Viking army had driven divisions in the Wessex witan and precipitated a coup against him. For all his Christian forgiveness, this king would not allow the Vikings to slip away again. This time it would have to be to the finish.

As Alfred's men drew up outside the Chippenham fortress, they decided to take no chances. Everything left by the retreating Vikings was seized, everything that might be of use to foraging parties was removed, and every Viking who failed to make it back to the safety of the camp was caught and killed. Alfred then ordered his fyrd to set up camp, not just near by but actually against the gates – and wait.

Guthrum must quickly have realized that the situation was hopeless but there was very little he could do. The victorious fyrd at his gates was strangling him, and clearly this time there were enough of them to make even foraging parties, let alone a breakout, impossible. No doubt negotiations were rapidly opened under these circumstances, but Alfred was no longer so willing to take Guthrum at his word, whether sworn on a Bible, an arm-ring or anything else. Guthrum may have tried to bargain with the lives of any coup plotters who were still holed up with him, assuming that they had not already fled, but Alfred was not interested. His deposition had been politically humiliating and would eventually have to be written out of the records but the West Saxon conspirators were not his chief concern. In terms of rebuilding Wessex, rapprochement was what would be needed with his own people, not revenge. And besides, Alfred knew that the real power behind the bid for his throne was Guthrum, and that in dealing with Guthrum he would be dealing with the true threat. It was time to realign this struggle as Wessex versus the Vikings, not as one part of Wessex against another. In seeing the paltry reach of the coup, he could afford to be magnanimous; indeed, he would have to if he was to rebuild his witan. The way to do that was to place all the West Saxons on one side of the argument and all the Vikings on the other.

Guthrum was trapped and he knew it, while Alfred was happy for once to watch him squirm. He had negotiated terms before when he should have dictated them. Now he had time on his side, so he waited until desperation reduced both the Vikings' ability to escape and their will to bargain. After two weeks Asser reports: 'the Vikings, thoroughly terrified by hunger, cold and fear, and in the end by despair, sought peace on this condition: the king should take as many hostages as he wanted from them and give none to them; never indeed had they made peace with anyone on such terms.' It must have been a particularly bitter mid-May for these northern warriors to have been 'terrified by cold', but allowing for a little exaggeration on Asser's part it was certainly the case that they were in no position to fight. The fervent oaths that they were wont to use in such situations were no longer believed. They had made extraordinary peace terms before, whatever Asser says – as they had when they agreed to swear on their holy ring for Alfred – but with no hostages and no Danegeld for themselves in this bargain, it was clear that these were terms not simply of peace but of surrender.

The change in fortune for either leader could hardly have been more startling. Just two weeks earlier, Guthrum was effectively in command of Wessex whilst Alfred was merely a troublesome bandit. Now the roles were reversed, but it was Alfred rather than Guthrum who faced an immediate dilemma.

As a Christian king he could not do what his Viking counterparts might have done in this situation and murder his enemy's leader, as this would simply rouse resentment and allow another leader to emerge from the pack. Even a few disaffected Vikings roaming the

Wessex borders could create difficulties. Killing the entire Viking host was impractical, considering the numbers, and it was certainly unchristian in the eyes of a devout man who valued forgiveness above all else. The only option left was to extract promises of good behaviour but everyone knew that you could not trust a pagan to keep to an oath of peace that was sworn in the name of a God in which they did not believe. And the fact was that, without the ultimate sanction of God hanging over agreements, there was little that the state could do to enforce terms. There were no security officers to police the truce, no border guards to patrol its perimeter and no nationwide court system to bring offenders to justice. Vikings had said one thing and done another in England and continental Europe for years – it was perhaps their unique advantage in their dealings with Christian kingdoms – so what was to stop them doing exactly the same now?

The answer, at least in Alfred's mind, was simple: make Guthrum a Christian and then conclude a Christian peace with him. When Alfred first suggested this to his ealdormen, there must have been several raised eyebrows. It was surely a plan of unique naivety. Neither Alfred nor his men can have been unaware of the Viking record on conversions; it was an occupational hazard for Vikings to have to occasionally undergo baptism when cornered. They could then apostatize at leisure, and frequently did. But Alfred may have remembered that there were a few notable exceptions. Whilst we can never know whether the troublesome Weland would have kept his new faith in Charles the Bald's court, as he was cut down there by his own men, other Viking petitioners at the Frankish court had been baptized and had stayed that way.

As far back as 826, Charles the Bald's father had witnessed at Ingelheim the baptism of the exiled Danish king Harald Klak and some four hundred of his followers, who were said by Thegan in his *Life of Louis the Pious* to have been 'drenched in the wave of Holy baptism'. Harald had come to the court of Louis to seek help in regaining the throne of Denmark. One of the conditions for Frankish support was the Danish king's conversion. After that conversion, so confident (or so pious) was Louis that he attached an evangelizing monk to Harald's party for their return to Denmark to spread the word of God. The adventures of this man, Anskar, known as 'the apostle of the North', were later recorded in a *Life* by his disciple

Rimbert and it is from this that we get an idea of what happened at Louis' court. Rimbert tells us:

> While the emperor kept him at his court he urged him, by personal persuasion and through the instrumentality of others, to accept the Christian faith, because there would then be a more intimate friendship between them, and a Christian people would more readily come to his aid and to the aid of his friends if both peoples were worshippers of the same God. At length, by the assistance of divine grace, he brought about his conversion, and when he had been sprinkled with the holy water of baptism he himself received him from the sacred font and adopted him as his son.

In this short description lay the key to how Alfred was going to tame Guthrum. No one could have doubted that the great oaths made by the Viking at the moment of his surrender were worthless or that he took the prospect of Christian baptism very lightly. These were apparently easy terms for a cornered man. There were of course the hostages. Asser tells us that they were chosen by Alfred and therefore probably represented men whom Guthrum would prefer not to lose and in numbers that might hurt him if he did lose them. However, Vikings had troubled themselves very little about the fate of their hostage countrymen in the past and there was little reason to think that Guthrum would start now.

Alfred, however, was not simply going to have Guthrum baptized; he was going to enmesh him in the ancient Anglo-Saxon web of obligations that bound everyone in his society, from kings to slaves. In many ways Guthrum would get what he wanted, but on Saxon terms and in a Saxon fashion, and it would be this that would ensure the peace more than swords, oaths or gods. Just as Louis had promised Harald that baptism would bring 'a more intimate friendship between them', so Alfred used Guthrum's conversion not to enforce Christian oaths, but to turn his enemy from a Viking raider into a Saxon prince who had everything to gain from Alfred's friendship and everything to lose from his enmity. More even than that, Alfred held out the prospect of Guthrum becoming a Saxon king, supported by the greatest of Saxon kings. As he was part of this system, Guthrum's power would be protected but it would be power with responsibility – a chance to be a king in return for giving up the role of kingmaker. As kings with realms to protect, Alfred and Guthrum would hence be in the same situation and on the same side.

Whether or not Alfred had before him the example of Harald Klak, it was a brilliant piece of diplomacy for the ninth or perhaps any century. After three weeks of what must have been a very fragile peace, Guthrum could be found threading his way through the hidden paths of the Somerset Levels, this time in the company of Alfred, who was leading him, and his most senior men, to a small island of dry ground at Aller just a stone's throw from Athelney. This was the church nearest to Alfred's old refuge and he must often have passed it in his fugitive days. Now he was bringing his enemy to the very stage from which he had mounted his comeback.

There is still a church at Aller today, surrounded not by marsh and wetland but by tended farmland. From the perfectly flat fields of the Levels it is still possible to see that the grove of trees in which the church stands is raised very slightly above the plain and was thus, in Alfred's day, an fenland isle like Athelney. The church that he knew is long gone, however, and a Norman replacement stands on its former site, but it is still a quiet and secluded place, a world apart even from the rest of the Levels. It was into this sacred silence that the king brought Guthrum and his men.

They must have made for an odd sight – thirty Viking warriors dressed in the white robes of Christian neophytes, waiting outside this little wooden chapel for the profound mystery of baptism to begin. The ceremony itself was infused with symbolism, marking not just Guthrum's new relationship with God but also his new place in Anglo-Saxon society. Before entering the church, each catechumen was met in the doorway by the priest who blew into his face to exorcize the evil spirits that had formerly inhabited him. Inside the church, each was then required first to renounce their former errors, in this case a very public renunciation of the worship of Odin and the Norse gods, before being signed with the cross on brow, ears, eyes, nostrils, mouth, breast and between the shoulders. After this the priest placed salt in their mouths, representing the food of divine wisdom, before leading each in turn to the font. The church at Aller still possesses a font, which was once tentatively associated with this extraordinary scene, having been found in a nearby well where it was probably thrown during the Reformation. It is Norman in date, however, and so is, at best, the successor to Guthrum's font. In fact Guthrum and his men may have been completely immersed in water as was still often the case at this time – a ritual cleansing of the whole man.

Only now, following their triple renunciation of Satan, could the most important part of the ceremony take place. Holy chrism was placed on the chest and between the shoulders, and the catechumen then formally asked for baptism. The priest solemnly replied by administering the threefold ablution, making the sign of the cross three times on the head of each Viking as he was immersed in the holy water. During this most highly charged moment, Guthrum might just have felt on his shoulder the hand of his new godfather, Alfred, who was required to touch his godson at the moment of his entry into the Christian Church. For Asser this is a key moment and he is at pains to record how 'King Alfred raised him [Guthrum] from the Holy font of baptism.'

Cleansed of his former error, Guthrum was now anointed on the crown of his head with holy chrism and the place where it touched him was bound with a white linen cloth that he would wear for the next eight days. The Viking warlord, who had walked into Aller church as Guthrum, had emerged as a Christian Saxon prince, complete with a new baptismal name – Æthelstan.

The ceremony that day had great religious significance for Alfred as well as for the members of his witan who were present, but it is debatable what exactly Guthrum and his men took away in terms of their 'rebirth' into a new religion. But amid the arcane rituals of baptism other changes had taken place, which they must have understood. First, it was not Guthrum alone who had converted but, at the West Saxons' insistence, his leading men had also done so. Many years earlier in pagan Francia, their king Clovis had warned the bishop of Rheims, 'I gladly hear you, most holy father; but there remains one thing: the people who follow me cannot endure to abandon their gods.' This concern must also have faced Guthrum, who knew that, if he converted alone, it would be easy for his men to disown him and choose another pagan leader. Instead Alfred had ensured that all the leading Vikings in the army were baptized, thus preventing the troops from simply disassociating themselves from Guthrum and his peace, and continuing as before.

Then there was the matter of kinship. Alfred, in standing as Guthrum's godfather, had created a link between the House of Ecgberht and the Viking leader, an alliance that folded the former pagan into the Saxon web of duty and reward that bound the West Saxon state together. As godfather, Alfred had clearly made a public claim to precedence over his godson but he had equally bound himself to protect his new charge. If Guthrum remained loyal to Alfred in the manner of previous Saxon kings under their bretwalda, he might expect political and perhaps even military support, as well as a share in the lavish gifts that high-ranking kings were expected to distribute amongst their subjects. This could never have been the case if Guthrum had continued to rule through puppets. To drive the point home, Alfred determined to demonstrate exactly what this new relationship might offer.

Just as important as the mystical rites at Aller was the ceremony eight days later of the chrism-loosening, which was performed at the nearby royal vill of Wedmore. Here the mood was celebratory as the white linen band was removed that had bound the anointed heads of the newly baptized Vikings, marking their full entry into the Christian world. Whilst this was another religious ceremony it was, more importantly, a chance for Guthrum and his men to witness the operation of the West Saxon state and the benefits that could derive from working with it rather than against it. At Wedmore the former enemies enjoyed twelve days of feasting and gift-giving, in which Asser tells us: 'the king freely bestowed many excellent treasures on him [Guthrum] and all his men.' This was a ceremony that they all could understand, Saxons and Vikings alike, with echoes in the Christian and pagan folk tales of both cultures. To his own people, Alfred was a Biblical character, the father to Guthrum's prodigal son. To Guthrum, Alfred was Hrothgar, the king from *Beowulf*, Master of Heorot – his benefactor and overlord. The other Vikings at Wedmore no doubt also received their share of these peculiar 'spoils of defeat' just as Beowulf's companions had shared in his victory:

> Furthermore, the guardian of warriors gave
> a treasure, an heirloom at the mead-bench,
> to each of those men who had crossed the sea
> with Beowulf.

And the presence, according to Æthelweard, of Alfred's loyal friend Æthelnoth at Wedmore suggest that further ties of obligations were made between the ealdormen of Wessex and the Viking leaders, tying Alfred's firmest supporters into the deal.

All that remained now was for the Viking army to remove itself from Wessex. Strangely, their withdrawal from Chippenham was not immediate, perhaps because it took time to persuade the heathen army of the new political order or to allow Guthrum and his men time to plan their next move. Around October 878, however, the Viking army finally left the soil of Wessex and returned over the border into their client kingdom of Mercia, where they made camp at Cirencester. Wessex could breathe a sigh of relief, at least for the moment, although the darkened skies of a solar eclipse at the end of that month can hardly have been seen as a good omen for the future.

The question for Guthrum and Alfred now was where should the Viking leader make his home? Mercia was a real possibility as half of this country was still under direct Viking control and the other half was controlled by the puppet Ceolwulf II. But times and fortunes had changed, where once Alfred had been glad to see his former enemy retire across that border, he was less keen to have Viking settlers so close at hand. It was time to let the old regime play itself out and consider how to create a new one. The first stage in this would be to see what would happen on the death of Ceolwulf, who may already have been ill by this time and who died in 879 or early 880. The situation was delicate. Alfred had maintained a strong relationship with Ceolwulf but another Viking puppet from the 'C' dynasty was obviously not in his interests. For all the love he bore his new godson, the idea of Vikings ruling lands along his entire northern border from East Anglia to the Welsh marches was intolerable. If there had ever been a time when he was strong enough to dictate Viking policy in Mercia, it was now as the 'C' dynasty drew to a close and the new Mercian order began to emerge.

Then there was the kingdom of East Anglia to consider, something that became a more pressing issue in 879 when a new Viking fleet appeared on the Thames and camped at Fulham, just outside London. These Northmen were probably the rump of the army that had recently been defeated on the Loire by Louis the Stammerer's sons, Carloman and Louis III, and who had decided to try their luck on the other side of the Channel. If these Vikings thought of themselves as reinforcements for Guthrum's invasion of Wessex, they had come too late. However, they could still destabilize the fragile peace or even threaten the possessions of the one-time pagan warlord who was now calling himself Æthelstan. The presence of this fleet in the east finally goaded Guthrum into making the first move and he marched with his army out of Mercia and into East Anglia in 880. The Fulham fleet did not wait to see what sort of a reception it would get from either Guthrum or Alfred, but sailed back to Ghent to begin a thirteen-year campaign of continental raiding.

East Anglia is where Guthrum finally decided to stay. The *Anglo-Saxon Chronicle*, which had made no mention of how the kingdom had been ruled since the death of St Edmund, states that they 'settled there and shared out the land'. It was also in East Anglia that Guthrum realized one of the other benefits of the events of Aller and Wedmore. The cult of St Edmund, East Anglia's martyr-king, had grown up swiftly following his death at the hands of Ivarr the Boneless. In contrast with the dynastic saint celebrated at Mercian Repton, his seems to have been a popular rather than a royal movement. Barely a decade after his death, he was already credited with numerous miracles, and the weaving of what appear to be ancient folk legends into his story clearly implies that his veneration was a grass-roots phenomenon. Such a popular royal and Christian cult would obviously present a problem for a pagan king attempting to impose his will on the East Anglians but, as the newly baptized Æthelstan, Guthrum could use his Christianity to promote his rule. In the next decade he would go so far as to institute a coinage in his baptismal name, sharing mints and moneyers with Alfred, and indicating another conversion on his part – from pirate to trader. By the mid 890s, East Anglia was even producing a St Edmund memorial coinage, issued by the very men whose fathers had been responsible for the saint's death.

Back in Wessex, Alfred could reflect with some satisfaction on the apparent transformation of Guthrum, his own fortunes, and the new peace that these things had brought. Wessex had survived the Viking onslaught – indeed, it had been the only Anglo-Saxon nation to survive – and he could survey once more a kingdom that was truly his.

But that kingdom was a sad sight. Wessex was a wreck, her monasteries burnt and plundered, her farmers exhausted from fighting, her fields untended. Trade had been all but halted by the wars and the payment of Danegeld had emptied the royal coffers. Law was barely existent, literacy was effectively dead and Alfred was king of a wasteland. He had not triumphed, he had survived; now he must desperately make up for lost time and unite his nation. He could not know how many years he had to turn his country around before new and yet more deadly enemies came calling. He could not afford to let his cakes burn again.

I2

A New England

> You know of course that no one can make known any skill, nor
> direct and guide any authority, without tools and resources . . .
> In the case of the king, the resources and tools with which to rule
> are that he have his land fully manned: he must have praying
> men, fighting men and working men.
>
> Alfred the Great's translation of Boethius' *Consolation of
> Philosophy*, XVII, quoted in Keynes and Lapidge
> (trans.), *Alfred the Great: Asser's Life of King Alfred
> and Other Contemporary Sources*, p. 132

ALFRED'S REBUILDING OF Wessex planted the seed that, under his
descendants, would grow into the kingdom of England and it
represents the most extraordinary piece of statecraft by any ruler at any
time in these islands. Alfred was entering a period of unrivalled
creativity in which he would turn his practical mind to all the
problems of the state as it had stood before the war with Guthrum.
Never again would there be a moment's inattention.

It must have begun shortly after the celebrations at Wedmore with
the reorganization of Alfred's witan. The old council, which had at
least in part turned on him, had been largely made up of men from
another era. These were the Wulfheres and Ælfstans of his brother
Æthelred's court, and men like the thegn Milred who had been
recorded in his father's household before Alfred was even born. They
had since demonstrated admirably that their loyalty was not to Alfred
but, at best, to older members of the House of Ecgberht and, at
worst, simply to themselves. As such they were removed from office.
Of the twelve ealdormen who regularly attested charters before 878,
seven disappear after this date. In their place come eight new
ealdormen, men Alfred could trust. The old guard had made Alfred

king and they had believed that they could also unmake him. These new men were made *by* the king and without him they were nothing. They had everything to gain from loyalty and nothing from betrayal.

Amongst the bishops only one change occurs at this time with Bishop Tunberht of Winchester being replaced by Denewulf. Later mediaeval tradition had it that Denewulf had been the swineherd in the cottage where Alfred burnt the cakes, which hints that he had been a key supporter of the king's during his time in the wilderness. His elevation to the see of Winchester shortly afterwards might therefore have been a reward for such loyalty, and perhaps punishment for Tunberht for his lack of it. The story also provides a nice counterpoint to the earlier tale of another deposed West Saxon king, Sigeberht. He too had met a swineherd in the wilderness, but that particular peasant had not helped him back to the throne but had killed him in a blood feud. Swineherds, it seems, were the avenging angels of the West Saxon peasantry.

The other element of essential housekeeping for Alfred was defining and controlling the influence of other members of his family, around whom discord and rebellion might well up again. He had seen the dangers of a court where any number of princes had equal claim on the throne and he had also seen how the Vikings had exploited this. The line of descent for the throne had to be clear, without alternatives, without pretenders, and Alfred knew that that line had to be his. To ensure this, at sometime in the mid 880s he summoned his witan to a council at Langdene. We know of this meeting thanks to Alfred's will and it would form an essential part of preparing the way for that document.

Alfred says that the council was needed as there was still discontent over his inheritance, something that must have brought him a sense of grave foreboding. But this time he would not sit back and let tensions fester. Instead he gathered his council and ordered his father's will to be read to them. This reminded them of how King Æthelwulf had left everything to each of his sons in turn, leaving the last surviving son to pass on the full inheritance to whomsoever he wished. Or that at least, combined with the private agreement that Alfred had made with his brother Æthelred some years before, was how he intended it to be interpreted. Of course the witan still had the right to decide whether that interpretation was right. Alfred tells us: 'I begged them all for the love of me – and offered them my pledge that I would never bear any of them a grudge because they declared what was right – that none of them would hesitate either for love or fear of me to pronounce the common law. Lest any man should say that I wronged my young kinsfolk, the older or the younger.'

It was not, of course, a free vote, whatever Alfred said. He was forcing them to decide on their champion now, aloud and in the open, not behind closed doors and in the hushed tones of conspiracy. Every man was being required to publicly take a side and, not surprisingly, they all chose his. He reports in his will that they said: 'Now that everything in it [Æthelwulf's will] has come into your possession, bequeath it and give it into the hands of kinsman or stranger, whichever you prefer.'

What else could they have said? And to ensure that they remembered their decision, he had it written up and their names appended to the document. Next to each name would have been a cross and, as each ealdorman was called forward, he would have been required to touch the cross and make his oath – as close to a signature as most of them could manage. Alfred would soon focus his mind on that problem too.

It is a remarkable turnaround. Although neither Alfred's nor Æthelwulf's will dealt directly with the succession (this was still strictly speaking in the hands of the witan), he had persuaded his nobles to agree in public that he could distribute his entire estate however he wished. As that estate provided the money and power needed to be king, in effect the first step had been taken on the road to a truly hereditary monarchy. Alfred's children would be king after him and it had been demonstrated to the other princes of the blood, who must also have been at Langdene, that any future claim would be hopeless. There was nothing they could do – yet.

Alfred also needed to regularize relations with his former enemy. Sometime after Wedmore an official peace treaty was drawn up with Guthrum, the terms for which, at least in their original form, we no longer have. We can guess, however, from a slightly later document, often confusingly called 'The Treaty of Wedmore', that this initial draft dealt with carving out the relative spheres of influence of Guthrum and Alfred. It also provided some mechanism for how they might deal in the future with each other, and each other's people, without resorting to violence.

The time had finally come to take care of the situation in Mercia and, with it, most of England. The Viking puppet Ceolwulf II was by this time dead and his reign was to be the swansong not just of the 'C' dynasty but of an independent Mercia as a whole. Whatever the circumstances surrounding his demise, Ceolwulf was not replaced by another 'C' dynast; indeed, he was not replaced by a king at all. The man who now stepped up to rule western Mercia was an ealdorman called Æthelred who, as history would later show, had connections just as strong to the Wessex court as to the old Mercian dynasties. Sometime in the early 880s, Æthelred, ruling just as 'ealdorman', officially acknowledged Alfred as overlord. That may have been the quid pro quo for Alfred's acceptance of Æthelred's nominal rule over 'English' Mercia. The links between the two men may well have run deeper and there is a distinct possibility that this Æthelred was a relation of Æthelred Mucel, Alfred's father-in-law. A surviving Mercian charter hints that Alfred's mother-in-law, Eadburh, had connections to Mercian royalty, and certainly Asser claims that she was 'from the royal stock of the king of the Mercians'. This family would therefore have a good claim in Mercian and West Saxon eyes to that throne.

The witan that Æthelred inherited from Ceolwulf remained largely unchanged as did the ecclesiastical appointments, suggesting that the Mercians had no difficulty with the idea of being ruled by this man, but it is very noticeable that the more junior thegns who had previously signed Ceolwulf's charters disappear from the record along with Ceolwulf himself. Æthelred clearly had no need of 'C' dynasty placemen and Alfred would not allow dynastic feuding to build up again in what was now his buffer state.

Thus western Mercia fell effectively under Alfred's control, granting him what must have been his major requirement from any peace. The eastern half of Mercia, however, which the Vikings had kept for themselves since the autumn of 877, remained in Guthrum's hands. West and south of a line that could be drawn roughly down the old Roman road of Watling Street was Anglo-Saxon England, whilst to the east and north lay the Danelaw, an area that would from then on be uniquely influenced by its Scandinavian settlers. Watling Street today is still a major arterial road heading north out of London, past St

Albans and into the Midlands. It is hard to imagine how merely crossing a street could have carried a ninth-century traveller between such different worlds.

The settlement in Mercia also gave Alfred a hand in the affairs of other neighbours – the ancient kingdoms of Wales. Mercia had been trying to extend her influence over Wales for centuries and the Welsh had just as actively resisted. At times Welsh power had been so strong that a Mercian king as feared and brutal as the bretwalda Offa had been forced to construct a defended border, which we know today as Offa's (and Wat's) Dyke. This huge earthwork stretching from sea to sea consisted of a six-foot-deep ditch to the west and a twenty-four-foot rampart to the east. In total it was longer than both Hadrian's Wall and the Antonine Wall put together, making it the largest archaeological monument in Britain. This alone stands testament to the ferocity with which this border was disputed.

During the 850s power had swung back in Mercia's favour but since then another famous Welsh leader had arisen – Rhodri Mawr, or 'Rhodri the Great' – the only other man of the time to have the title 'Great' applied to him. His rule in Wales had begun in 844 on the death of his father when he inherited the relatively modest principality of Gwynedd, but he had expanded his control quickly. On his uncle's death he had inherited Powys, and his marriage to Angharad, the sister of Gwgon, ruler of Ceredigion, brought him in sight of that throne too. When his brother-in-law fortuitously died in a drowning accident in 872, Ceredigion also fell into his hands.

Rhodri was now in effect the first king of Wales but for all his success he found himself increasingly pressured on two fronts. The Mercians to the east were as always looking to exert their influence in Welsh affairs, whilst to the west, across the Irish Sea, the Dublin Vikings were also taking a very direct interest in the wealthy and ancient monasteries on his coast. In the end it had been a combination of the two that had brought about Rhodri's downfall. Having been driven out of Wales by the Danish Vikings, whom the Welsh annals refer to as 'the dark foreigners', he had returned in 877 to reclaim his lands, only to fall foul of a Mercian army and die at their hands, along with his son Gwriad.

But Rhodri had other sons and they were bent on vengeance. In 881, with Ealdorman Æthelred now in command in Mercia, those sons had brought the Mercian army to battle at Conwy and had decisively defeated it. The Welsh chronicle, known as the *Annales Cambriae*, without even feeling the need to actually mention the outcome, succinctly records: 'The battle of Conwy. Vengeance for Rhodri at God's hands.'

Now Rhodri's sons triumphantly went about extending their hegemony in the kingdoms of the southern Welsh, sending the usually proudly independent kings of Dyfed and Brycheiniog hurrying to the court of the most powerful man in England, Alfred, for protection. Of course in doing so they were playing into Alfred's hands, forcing previously independent lords to throw in their lot with him and hence extending his influence further still. Soon the kings of Glywysing and Gwent also appeared as supplicants at his court, encouraged to seek his protection, not from the sons of Rhodri, but from Æthelred of Mercia. Provided Alfred could keep the sons of Rhodri Mawr in check – or at least at arm's length, another huge territory was hence under his sway.

Across in the Danelaw, England was also changing. Place-name evidence suggests that Guthrum's Scandinavian followers were extensively settling the land, intertwining their language and culture into that of the native Anglo-Saxon population. The exact fate of those Christian Anglo-Saxons who found themselves on the 'wrong' side of Alfred's settlement is not clear. In East Anglia life for many probably continued as before, as the people were at least nominally under a Christian Viking ruler, although Guthrum's first priority must have been to portion out the best lands and titles amongst his own Danish army, leaving many locals dispossessed. Further north in the kingdom of Northumbria, centred on the Viking trading port of Jorvik, the situation is still less clear. We do know that, despite years of pagan rule, Christianity and its supporters had not been entirely driven out. The ever-practical Viking traders who rapidly moved into the city of Jorvik itself seem to have been perfectly at home with both belief systems, even issuing a coinage bearing both the Christian cross and the hammer of Thor.

For the monasteries, times had been harder. Many of them had been sacked, some repeatedly, and their inhabitants reduced to a life of wandering. Most poignant of all is the tale of the community of St Cuthbert from Lindisfarne, the first monastery to experience the Viking firestorm in 793. After years of being raided the brothers here had finally decided in 875 to heed the words of Cuthbert, who had said: 'if necessity compels you to choose between one of two evils, I would much rather you take my bones from their tomb and carry them away with you to whatever place of rest God may decree, rather than consent to iniquity and put your necks under the yokes of schismatics.' Cuthbert could not have known that it was not schismatics but outright pagans who would threaten his community; nevertheless the advice was just as relevant. Packing up the relics of Cuthbert and their famous Lindisfarne Gospels, the monks crossed the tidal causeway to the mainland for one last time and went in search of that 'place of rest' that Cuthbert had hoped they would find. It would be 120 years before the community would finally find it in Durham.

But despite this landless wandering the brothers still clearly played a role in the new Viking society of Northumbria. Our knowledge of this is preserved in an anonymous *History of St Cuthbert*, written sometime around 1050, which recounts the extraordinary and largely fabulous tale of the early conversion of a Northumbrian Viking king, but which, regardless of its details, implies that the old Christian Saxon population were at the very least surviving. The story as it has come down to us, with all its miraculous embellishments, tells how the ghost of St Cuthbert appeared to the abbot of Carlisle one night, sometime after the death of Halfdan. In the ensuing interregnum Cuthbert tells the abbot:

> Go across the Tyne to the army of the Danes, and say to them that, if they will obey me, they are to point out to you a certain boy, Guthfrith, Hardacnut's son, by name, a purchased slave of a certain widow, and you and the whole army are to give in the early morning the price for him to the widow; and give the aforesaid price at the third hour and at the sixth hour lead him before the whole multitude, that they may elect him king.

This extraordinary scene smacks of Cuthbert's other appearances in the historical events of the ninth century – always arriving just in time to save the day and collect the credit, and clearly prepared to deal with Saxons and Vikings alike. Of course Guthfrith would not get the saint's support for nothing. In return the newly elected king was also to give the community of St Cuthbert all the land between the Tyne and the Wear in gratitude. The details are certainly not to be casually believed, but the story does hint that, soon after Halfdan's death in 877, Northumbria had a Christian Viking ruler, just as East Anglia did, but elected without bloodshed and clearly under the influence of the still-powerful leaders of Cuthbert's community.

With such quiescent Vikings to his north and east, Alfred might have been forgiven for thinking that his troubles were over and that the prophecy of Jeremiah had run its course. Fortunately he was not that naive. If he needed to know what the future held in terms of the Viking threat, he had now only to look across the Channel at events unfolding in Francia. In the Carolingian dominions there was no respite from Viking attacks; indeed, the sudden outbreak of peace in England seems to have persuaded many a Viking to try his luck on the continent instead. In particular the recently crowned Holy Roman Emperor Charles the Fat, a grandson of Louis the Pious, found himself hard pressed by the Viking warlord Godafrid, who had dug himself in at Asselt on the Meuse.

Charles had inherited various of the fragmented Carolingian thrones since 879 and would two years later briefly restore the Carolingian Empire in its entirety (with the exception of Burgundy), following the death of Carloman, the king of western Francia, who was gored to death by a boar. As a result there were high hopes that his will-power and resources would enable him to stand up to the invaders and drive them back to Scandinavia. Buoyed up himself Charles had summoned a huge army to invest Godafrid's base and should have been in a position as strong as Alfred's after Edington, but subsequent events show how easily such a position could be lost. The outcome also highlights the differences in character between the weak-willed Charles and the newly invigorated Alfred.

At Asselt, despite the eventual surrender of the Viking garrison after twelve days, besieged by what the *Annals of Fulda* called an army 'to be feared by any enemy', Charles seems to have agreed to negotiate a withdrawal rather than demand terms. This may have been due to treachery in his ranks or perhaps the fear of disease in his own camp, although Hincmar of Rheims finds a simpler solution when he says that 'his courage failed him'. But even a negotiated settlement should have left Charles in charge. On the surface these terms seem very similar to those accepted by Guthrum at Chippenham – Godafrid agreed to be baptized and in return was given various lands as 'gifts' from his nominal new overlord, Charles. But closer examination reveals what a hollow victory this was. First, Charles, though victor, had to provide hostages during peace negotiations. While these continued, he also had to withdraw six miles from Asselt, hence giving Godafrid plenty of breathing space. Alfred would have known that giving a Viking an inch is as good as giving him a mile. He then granted the Vikings a bounty of gold and silver, territory in present-day Holland, as well as the right to keep the booty and the 200 (presumably Christian) slaves they had gathered so far on their campaign. This was enough to force one of the writers of the *Annals of Fulda* to complain that Charles

> did not blush to pay tribute to a man from whom he ought to have taken hostages and extracted tribute, doing this on the advice of evil men and against the customs of his ancestors the Kings of the Franks. He took away the churches' treasure, which had been hidden for fear of the enemy, and to his own shame and that of all the army which followed him, gave to those same enemies 2,412 pounds of purest gold and silver.

But worse was to come. When a group of Frankish nobles entered the camp under the terms of the treaty, they were seized by Godafrid and held to ransom. Those for whom money could not be extracted were murdered. Charles was being mocked. That the emperor could be so weak in his negotiations compared to Alfred may attest to Charles's own troubles. Modern medical commentators have suggested that his lethargy and erratic behaviour (or, as Hincmar thought, his incompetence) may have been due to bouts of epilepsy, a condition then unrecognized and untreated. But whether due to illness or ineptitude, it also points by way of contrast to the strength of the bonds that Alfred had forged between himself and a Viking host that had until recently been bent on his own death and destruction.

Nor was Charles's year about to get any better. Shortly after Asselt the Viking leaders Gorm and Sigfrid were paid off with a Danegeld that is nebulously recorded as 'several thousand pounds of silver and gold', which the emperor apparently seized largely from the treasury of St Stephen's at Metz. Nor did Metz simply lose its money. When its bishop, Wala, personally took up arms against the Vikings and was killed fighting, all he gained was a rather scathing obituary in the *Annals of Fulda*, which berate him for selling his life cheaply, having come against the enemy 'rashly with a small army'. Considering the results of Charles the Fat's coming against them with a large army, it is difficult to know what else he could have done. Later that year the turmoil reached as far as Prüm in Lorraine where the monk Regino records a sudden pagan attack on Twelfth Night, identical to Guthrum's tactic at Chippenham, in which an enemy, more beast than man, cut down the celebrating peasants without mercy and sacked the monastery.

At Rheims, the bishop Hincmar, who in calmer days had anointed Æthelwulf's child bride Judith as queen of the West Saxons, was again complaining bitterly in the *Annals of St Bertin*: 'the Northmen came as far as the neighbourhood of the fortress of Laon, and ravaged and burned all the fortresses in the surrounding area. They planned to move to Rheims and from there to come back by way of Soissons and Noyon and storm the fortress mentioned above and bring the king- dom under their control.' If there was any thought here that the St Bertin annalist was overreacting and exaggerating the danger posed by the heathens, it is rapidly dispelled by the next few lines of the annals (which he writes in the third person):

> Bishop Hincmar found out for certain that this was their plan: since the fighting men in the command of the see of Rheims were away with Carloman, he only just managed to escape by night, taking with him the body of Remegius and the treasures of the church of Rheims. His physical weakness meant that he had to be carried in a portable chair. Whilst the canons, monks and nuns scattered in every direction, he fled across the Marne and only just managed to reach a villa called Épernay.

It was quite a comedown for the prelate who had intoned the coronation *ordo* of the great Charles the Bald. He was running in fear of his life, with the holy relics of the apostle of the Franks, St Remegius, stuffed under his seat and the *Annals of St Bertin* in his hand. Those annals, like Hincmar's life, were now drawing towards a close. Just nine sentences later he put down his pen for good and left other chroniclers to document the chaos spreading through his homeland. He would never see Rheims again. Within the year he was dead.

Some of Hincmar's last words, however, were a warning to

Wessex, although neither he nor Wessex then knew it. Just before he stopped writing, he mentioned in passing a Viking called Hæsten who, he says, with his accomplices had finally left the Loire (paid off by Louis III) and moved to the coast between Frisia and the Seine. Here Hæsten could have met the remnants of the Viking army that had encamped at Fulham in 879 and might have heard of the riches to be had in Alfred's Wessex. But if this planted a seed in his mind, it would grow but slowly. In the aftermath of Guthrum's defeat, the time was not yet ripe for further probing English defences. There was still money to be made in the crumbling Francia of Charles the Fat and only when that was exhausted would Hæsten's thoughts turn to Wessex. But turn they would.

If the main theatre for Viking warfare had moved to Francia, that does not mean that Wessex was left in peace. Whilst some of the major Viking warbands undoubtedly worked in unison (such as those gathering on the French coast with Hæsten), there were many smaller independent raiding parties who buzzed around the British coast, damaging local trade and endlessly testing the delicate truce with Guthrum. They were in many ways no more than an annoyance and the Anglo-Saxon chronicler finds it hard to tear his attention away from the large-scale battles in Francia to take note of them. But since the chronicle for the 880s is being written retrospectively, the writer might be forgiven for concentrating on the foreign developments that form the prelude to the last shattering decade of Alfred's life.

Yet hidden in the few local events that are chronicled are the clues to those measures that Alfred now started to put in place to secure his kingdom, both from the ravages of the Vikings and from the dynastic squabbling that had again given them a foothold in Francia, which he was desperate to prevent reappearing at home.

During the late Victorian era, at a time that combined a high point in British imperial ambition with the millennial anniversaries of the events of Alfred's life, it was popular to claim Alfred as the founder of that force on which the later British Empire had been built – the Royal Navy. This was probably going a little too far, as imperial powers tend to do, but the mention of naval activity in the records of the 880s suggests that Alfred was systematically organizing the first coastal defensive fleet to have sailed English waters since the late Roman period. As with so much of Alfred's work in rebuilding his

Above: From this commanding position among the ramparts of the Iron Age hill fort of Bratton Camp, Guthrum lay in wait for Alfred's army. The ensuing battle would decide who would be king of Wessex

Right: This Victorian stained-glass window in the church at Wedmore depicts Alfred in the swineherd's cottage (*above*) and, *below*, the chrism-loosening ceremony that took place here in 878 when Alfred welcomed Guthrum fully into the Anglo-Saxon Christian world

Left: The ghost of Alfred survives in the *burhs* he laid out, many of which, like Cricklade, are still thriving towns today. Although no buildings from his time remain in the town, its street plan is still much as he intended

Below left: Having seen Wareham fall to a Viking army in the 870s, Alfred ensured that the remodelled *burh* had sufficient defences and resources to withstand another attack. Today the bank that encircled this settlement still stands and was actually repaired in the Second World War to help defend the town

Below: As part of the burghal scheme, some much older sites were pressed back into use. Portchester, a Roman fort and naval base designed to deflect invading Saxons, was turned into a *burh* to ward off Vikings

Tidal mudflats such as these at Bosham in West Sussex were a favourite hunting ground o
Viking pirates, ideal for their shallow-draughted ships. Alfred's larger craft nearly came to
grief when they grounded whilst attacking a Viking naval squadron in similar conditions

The monastery of Clonmacnoise was home to the Irish Scholar Suibne, whose death w
reported to Alfred by the pilgrims Dubslaine, Macbethath and Maelinmuin who, after a
perilous sea voyage from Ireland, found themselves cast up at his court

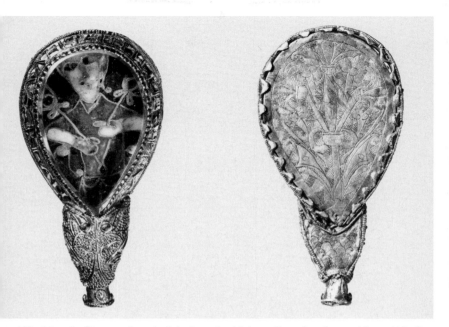

The Alfred Jewel offers a unique insight into the high quality of craftsmanship at Alfred's court. Possibly originally a bookmarker for one of his translations, it bears the inscription: 'AELFRED MEC HEHT GEWYRCAN' – 'Alfred had me made'

The Fuller Brooch, which may well have come from Alfred's court workshop, is the earliest known depiction of the five senses. Clockwise from top left: Taste, with his hand in his mouth; Smell, who stands between two large plants; Touch, rubbing his hands together; and Hearing with a hand to one ear. In the centre is Sight, representing not simply vision but gaining wisdom through the 'mind's eye', an idea close to Alfred's heart

Left: Up to 892 the
Parker manuscript of th[e]
Anglo-Saxon Chronicle
was compiled by a sing[le]
individual probably
working to the direct
orders of Alfred. This
page shows his last ent[ry]
finishing with the year
891. He then wrote th[e]
year 892 in the margin
and stopped. That year
the Vikings returned

Below: A London
monogram penny.
To celebrate his
re-foundation of
London, Alfred issued a
particularly fine coinag[e]
bearing the monogram
of the city. Trade and
commerce were the
life-blood of his plan f[or]
the defence of Wessex,
which regularly minte[d]
high-quality coinage
played a vital part

Right: Following archaeological excavations of the foundations of the Old Minster at Winchester, the ground plan was laid out in brick and can now be seen from the roof of the Norman cathedral

Below: This engraving of 1783 shows the post-Dissolution remains of Hyde Abbey, where Alfred's tomb was moved after the construction of the Norman cathedral at Winchester

This stone in the middle of Kingston in Surrey is said to be the Coronation Stone on which Alfred's son Edward and his successors were crowned

This iconic Victorian statue looks down on a greater monument to Alfred – the City of Winchester itself. From green fields or half-abandoned ruins, he turned this city and many like it into a network of defended commercial towns, crucial to England's survival nation, the genius in this lay not in sudden inspirational ideas but in a careful examination of the problems and solutions of the past, followed by an honest attempt to adapt those old solutions to the needs of the present time.

It was clear to anyone who had come across the Vikings that the key to their success was naval mobility. The ships of the day – even the most fearsome of Viking *drakkars* – were not warships in the sense of being armed or having any offensive capability themselves. They were simply highly manoeuvrable vessels with a large capacity to hold armed soldiers and a shallow draught that allowed those troops to be moved quickly and quietly to wherever they were needed. It was the Vikings' ability to strike swiftly and unexpectedly far upstream, and then melt away back to sea before any countering force could be summoned, that gave their fleet its unique advantage. It was obvious to Alfred that combating Viking naval power was the key to maintaining the peace.

In this Alfred was learning from the experience of both the Carolingians and the West Saxons. Charlemagne had ordered the creation of a coastguard service as well as a Channel fleet to watch out for and counter the arrival of Viking forces during his coronation year of 800. That system was no longer proving effective but under a strong king it might be possible to revive it. As to creating a fleet to do the fighting, there was again a precedent. Ships had plied the waterways between England and continental Europe for centuries, so there could have been no shortage of boat-building and sailing skills available on either coast. Obviously the requirements for a naval patrol vessel were somewhat different from a trading ship but again the West Saxons did have some previous experience. Æthelstan, Alfred's eldest brother, had, in the last year of his life, taken part in a naval engagement off Sandwich in Kent during which he and his ealdorman Ealhhere had defeated a small Viking force. What we do not know is whether this early battle was fought with specialist ships or simply with requisitioned trading vessels.

In the absence of evidence for battering rams or any of the more sophisticated naval weaponry in use in the Mediterranean at this date, these engagements were probably little more than land battles fought on ships. After an exchange of arrowshot or spears, the ships would have manoeuvred in the hope of forcing each other aground before being grappled together. After that their crews would have to fight between the shipped oars and stowed spars until one side was either annihilated or surrendered. If you could find a ship to fight on, you might claim to have a navy.

Asser, when writing of later naval engagements, however, refers very specifically to 'Alfred's fleet', implying that the rather haphazard arrangements of those earlier years were being replaced by a small but professionally organized coastal force. It was clearly something in which the king also took a personal rather than just a political interest, as we hear as far back as 875 that 'that summer King Alfred went out to sea with a naval force, and fought against the crews of seven ships, and captured one ship, and put the rest of flight.' It was one thing for a Saxon king to lead his men into battle; indeed, that was expected of a ruler. But the fact that he personally got involved in highly risky naval actions against a foe who had made that type of warfare their speciality shows an almost reckless desire to understand how to defeat Vikings on their own terms. All-out fighting on ships where there was nowhere to run was, after all, undoubtedly one of the more dangerous activities in a profoundly dangerous century. Nor was this action a lone occurence. Not long after the peace with Guthrum, the chronicle again records Alfred at sea (in 882), capturing two ships and killing their crews before the other two vessels surrendered to him. Just three years later the king is reported sending what was in effect a 'punishment fleet' from Kent to East Anglia to harry Viking shipping (in true Viking style) in retaliation for an alleged breach of the peace.

When Alfred took these first tentative steps towards defending the Wessex coast, it may not have been with the explicit intention of founding a navy. Alfred had nothing like the nineteenth-century imperial navy in mind when he organized it, but his personal involvement in, and systematic study of, naval forces makes him the first English leader since the late Roman Count of the Saxon Shore (who ironically was defending the coast *against* Saxons) to create an organized and professional naval defence force. He might therefore, in his own modest way, still be credited with having founded the Royal Navy. Certainly he was one of the first British rulers to realize that the key to ruling the country was its waterways, its rivers and the seas that surrounded it, as much as the land that lay between them. The success of his strategy, at least on a small scale, might then be judged from the relative absence of recorded small raids (by one or two Viking ships) in the *Anglo-Saxon Chronicle*.

It was not simply the sea defences of Wessex that needed strengthening, however. Long experience of war had also shown Alfred how a highly mobile land force, put in the field by a naval contingent and, if possible, equipped with horses, could literally run rings around the defenders of the Saxon kingdoms. Vikings had taken the lessons of naval mobility on to the land and, rarely able to match their enemy in sheer numbers, they beat them down with surprise, speed and confusion. A Viking army appeared quickly, often in the heart of a shire, having swept past whatever defences were mounted along its edge, and worked quickly to wring as much plunder and food as possible out of an area before rapidly evacuating, only to reappear sometime later at another surprise location. Even when Vikings were pinned down in defended settlements, they used night-time breakouts, feints, deceit and any other stratagem they could think of to give them back the advantage of mobility rather than take on a straight contest.

Whilst this was going on, the defenders – ealdormen and king – had to prepare their own household for battle and summon the fyrd from the fields. This huge logistical nightmare took precious time, and it was often the case that by the time the fyrd marched to face their enemy, the Vikings had moved on again. The defenders were left in a ravaged and plundered area, stripped of its food and wealth, and with no one to fight.

Of course, this traditional method of defence also required the wholehearted support of the ealdormen of the shires, those men whose call could guarantee a response from the thegns and peasants below them, down to village level. Whilst there may have been penalties for failing to obey the summons to join the fyrd, in the face of an advancing enemy there can have been little time to check that a full complement of troops had indeed arrived. The summoning of the army was therefore a cross between a lottery and a popularity contest – a call for help that would be answered on an unknown scale – and the king who called it could only hope that whatever size army arrived would be enough. If for any reason the county fyrd of one shire was not sufficient, the king was faced with the even greater problem of calling on outside fyrds, who would be reluctant to leave their own shire untended and undefended to go and fight elsewhere.

The solution that Alfred devised for this apparently intractable predicament was nothing short of a revolution and that revolution began now in the early 880s. If the Vikings could attack anywhere at any time, then the West Saxons had to be able to defend everywhere all the time. To make this possible Alfred ordered the construction of a network of defended centres across his kingdom, some built on refortified Roman and Iron Age sites, some built completely from scratch. These *burhs* were to be distributed so that no West Saxon was more than twenty or so miles – a day's march – from one of them. But building fortresses was not, of course, in itself a complete answer. Hincmar, after all, records numerous Frankish 'fortresses' (although we cannot be quite sure what he meant by the word), which seem to have done little to hinder Viking progress through his land. Defending a country required building more than just military camps. A fortress needed troops to man it, scouts and lookouts to warn it, and animals, food and fodder to provide for them all. After the predations of the 870s, and probably even without them, Wessex was not such a modern state that it could centrally fund such a huge full-time 'home guard'. It was in finding a solution to this that Alfred's real genius shone through.

The *burhs* that Alfred ordered built were not to be simply fortresses; many were to be communities – fortified towns – placed at the junctions of the trade routes, which were also of course the routes that armies travelled. If each *burh* could be a little market town on a trade route, the trade that was attracted there would help pay for its own defence, and the people drawn there by that trade would provide the manpower (and have the motivation) to defend it. It was a self-supporting protection system that provided everybody with a local refuge – their own Athelney, which generated its own finances and manpower for defence, controlled the important nodal points in Wessex's communication lines and promoted trade.

Not only was this a revolution in funding defence, it was actually a revolution in the whole English way of life. Before Alfred, urban living in Anglo-Saxon England barely existed. The Roman cities of centuries before were still in many cases empty ruins, untouched, unloved and probably feared by the Anglo-Saxon rural population. Town living was a faint memory, and those who could be said to live 'in towns' in reality simply lived within the ruined walls of places that had once been towns or, in a few exceptional cases, in small trading settlements on the coast. For those now willing to brave the ghosts of the old Roman ruins or the hardships of building a new town from scratch, there were also new benefits to be had. The duties that came with defending your *burh* also brought with them fresh incentives. Whilst the ownership of land and the right to apportion properties within a *burh* probably still lay largely with the shire ealdormen and the bishops, a new breed of individual – the burgher – was in the making. From this seed would grow a new 'middle' class of citizen, whose independent wealth created through trade not only provided for their own defence but would, over subsequent centuries, slowly lead to their exemption from more and more of the onerous duties that most rural workers owed their lords. It was the beginning of a new power base, separate from the ealdormen, where allegiances were to the *burh* and the king alone, effectively reducing the ability of rebellious noblemen to rouse their county in revolt against their ruler. These were the king's places and, if successful, they would also supply defended locations for storing the king's food rents with which he fed his household and fyrd on campaign. They might eventually even provide a source of taxation for funding more centralized schemes.

This 'defence in depth' solution also had the additional benefit of making it almost impossible for an invader to know where to attack first. Vikings, or indeed any potential invader, had traditionally attempted a quick, decisive, knock-out blow, targeting the ruler or the power centre of a kingdom. With a whole network of defended sites across the country, there was no single strategic place to attack and any attack on one area could quickly be compensated for by the others. The key to the success of the kingdom did not lie in one particular place. If one fell, then others filled the void. If you wanted to defeat a *burh*, you would have to defeat *every burh*.

It was a bold and brilliant scheme, responsible for the foundation (or refoundation) of many of the market towns and cities of southern England that still thrive today. The list includes Winchester, Wallingford, Chichester, Cricklade, Malmesbury, Worcester, Bath, Shaftesbury, Hastings, Southampton and even London. Under Alfred's successors the scheme would be taken north as well, into Mercia and Northumbria, marking out much of the pattern of urban settlement that we still live with today. Of course, persuading the population to undertake the programme, as well as organizing it to ensure some sort of uniformity of approach, was in itself an administrative problem of a scale never before attempted amongst the Saxon kingdoms of England. Miraculously, however, in English archives is preserved a document that explains exactly how this was done.

The Burghal Hidage gives a list of the sites of *burhs* and an estimation of the number of 'hides' that belong to each. In a society without maps or surveying tools, the hide was both a rough estimate of land area and an estimate of value based on the output potential of that land. Originally a hide had been a quantity of land deemed sufficient to support one family, so it might vary in size from area to area, but with the passing of time, the numbers of families living on each hide increased. Eventually this rather nebulous measure was fixed at generally 120 acres, although on more productive land the area might have been less. Each hide was required to send one man for the *burh*'s defence, so the number of hides associated with each *burh* directly corresponded to the number of men designated to defend it. In an appendix to the original document, a formula is given for calculating precisely how many men will be needed to defend a given length of *burh* wall and how much land will be needed to provide for them: 'If every hide is represented by one man, then every pole [16.5 feet] can be manned by four men. Then for the maintenance of twenty poles of wall eighty hides are required.' This provided an almost instant reckoning of the resources necessary to defend a site and, by working backwards from the figures given in the document, we can estimate the size of each settlement mentioned. Hence Winchester's 2,400 hides (at one hide per man and four men per pole of wall) would amount to 600 poles of wall length, or 9,900 feet. Winchester was actually rebuilt within the old Roman wall circuit, and that measures 9,954 feet, making the Alfredian calculation almost exact.

None of the versions of the document that survive today can be directly related back to Alfred's reign, the oldest having been destroyed in the Otho press along with Asser's biography during the great Cotton Library fire. All we now have of it is a sixteenth-century transcript of that eleventh-century manuscript, which itself must have been a copy. Internal evidence based on those *burhs* that are mentioned (as well as those that are not) suggests that its prototype probably dated from the early years of the reign of

Alfred's son, Edward the Elder, which in turn was based on Alfred's lost original.

But regardless of the problems in dating the surviving burghal list, there is no doubt that the burghal plan was Alfred's idea. Asser himself asks: 'And what of the cities and towns to be rebuilt and of others to be constructed where previously there were none?'

It was, indeed, an enormous undertaking. In the first place it required the refurbishment and renovation of numerous ancient fortifications. These included long-decayed Roman walled towns such as Winchester and even the great 'Saxon shore fort' at Portchester, built during the late Roman period, probably as a naval base to protect Roman Britain from Saxon pirates. In all these cases, walls that had been neglected for over four hundred years had to be put back into good repair and settlements laid out within them, either incorporating or replacing whatever ruins remained above ground. In other cases, even older fortifications were used, with Iron Age hill forts being pressed into use despite the fact that nothing remained of them beyond a series of earth banks and ditches. These had not seen military action since the first days of the Roman invasion at the latest, and sometimes many centuries before that.

Second, it also required the planting of new towns on greenfield sites, after which a population would have to be persuaded to go and live there, or at least near by. To help standardize this process Alfred took the first steps in town planning since the Roman era and many of the surviving *burhs* from his reign still show the ghost of his hand at work. Whilst no remains from those early settlements survive intact (with the exception of some lengths of rampart), the modern layout of streets on a carefully measured grid plan at *burhs* such as Wallingford show a remarkable uniformity. This can be traced back to Alfred's original plan to maximize the accessibility of the walls for defence whilst providing suitable living and trading plots for the new town's inhabitants. Although many centuries of cobble and tarmac have since been laid over these roads, and many generations of building have risen and fallen on each plot, the layout of these towns is still essentially that planned by Alfred over 1,100 years ago. Walking down the roads of *burhs* like these today past the evenly spaced shop frontages on either side, we are still walking through a town laid out by Alfred.

The closest one can get today to this scheme is at Wareham in

Dorset. There must have been some form of defended settlement on the banks of the river Frome at the time that Guthrum was besieged at Wareham prior to the Swanage disaster, but this was later replaced with a formal *burh*. Today, coming to the town from the water meadows to the North, you still approach a site looking much as it would have done then. All that can be seen across the meadows is a steep river bank and above that the massive earthen rampart first thrown up in Alfred's reign; the town hides somewhere behind. As you pass through the gap in the bank that marks the north gate, the town is revealed. Immediately to your left is a reminder of Anglo-Saxon times in the form of the beautiful little church of St Martin's, which is itself a thousand years old and which may lie on the site of an earlier chapel from Alfred's era. But it is not the buildings of Wareham that stand tribute to Alfred's plan, but the plan and defences of the town itself. If you turn right just inside the gate, it is still possible to walk along the massive earthen walls, which, thanks to generations of maintenance and rebuilding, have survived largely intact. These form three sides of a rectangle (the fourth side being made up by the river Frome). Just inside this circuit still runs the intramural road that once allowed defenders free movement along these ramparts, although today it is tarmacked, lit by street lamps, and with cars parked where Anglo-Saxon defenders once ran. Criss-crossing the rectangular space enclosed by these walls is the outline of the old *burh*, the grid of modern roads faithfully following the lines of those laid out in the ninth century, except in the south-west corner where the placement of a mediaeval castle wilfully ignored the old Anglo-Saxon pattern. But the siting of a Norman castle here is testament in itself to the success of Alfred's plan. Wareham became and remained a thriving and secure port, neatly and successfully organized within its original street plan, and as such was a prize worth having.

Getting such schemes off the ground in upwards of thirty locations required a huge amount of consensus. An appendix to one of the post-Conquest copies of the *Burghal Hidage* claims that the total cumulative hidage for the list is 27,000 hides. As we know that there was one man to a hide, we can calculate that some 27,000 men – perhaps a tenth of the adult population – were required to work for the new scheme. Persuading this number of people to radically alter their lives and their method of defending themselves, after a decade of war that had left them impoverished and exhausted, was an extraordinary challenge. The land grants that founded these towns might have offered the lure of *bookland* – inheritable land – to those willing to take up town life, but those grants came with three serious strings attached. These were the 'common burdens' of bridge-work, fortress-work and military service. Although they dated back over a century, with the exception of military service they had rarely been very demanding. In the light of recent Viking attacks, however, these duties took on new and onerous proportions; there is evidence that not all would-be townsfolk took kindly to them. Asser cannot help but comment on the lack of enthusiasm with which his master's ideas were sometimes taken up:

> the commands were not fulfilled because of the people's laziness, or else (having been begun too late in a time of necessity) were not finished in time to be of use to those working on them (I am speaking of the fortifications commanded by the king which have not yet been begun, or else, having been begun late in the day, have not been brought to completion).

As well as a general sense of exasperation there is a hint in Asser's tone of real foreboding, perhaps reflecting the fears communicated to him by Alfred as he watched the painfully slow progress of his people in building his new England. Nor was this simply impatience. Alfred knew that he had every reason to get the burghal scheme operating as fast as possible.

13

A Tale of Two Cities

> He gazed on his treasure – silver, precious stones,
> jewellery and wealth, all that he owned –
> and on this bright city in the broad kingdom.
> *The Ruin*, quoted in K. Crossley-
> Holland, *The Anglo-Saxon World*, p. 56

ROCHESTER, STANDING NEAR the mouth of the river Medway in Kent, today presents the image of a perfect old English city, complete with Norman castle, mediaeval cathedral and the rows of rambling, timber-framed buildings that provided a fictionalized backdrop to many of Charles Dickens' novels. But long before the city attracted tourists, it attracted trade and it has been a major strategic port since the earliest days of the Roman occupation. In the ninth century, however, it was no longer the heaving metropolis that it had either once been or would one day become. The old Roman walls then shielded a much smaller population, allowing room for fields and gardens where once Roman homes and shops had stood. Such 'garden cities' were not unusual for the period. Indeed, even Alfred's nominal 'capital' of Winchester had large areas within its walls that could no longer be called urban. The buildings there belonged to clerics and nobles rather than to the shopkeepers and tradesmen that populate true towns. Elsewhere there were trading centres, such as the soon-to-be-abandoned Hamwic near the site of modern Southampton, but that was an open town, not protected by ancient walls and without ecclesiastical or noble connections.

Rochester, however, combined elements of both types of place. As well as being a excellent seaport, it was the seat of a bishopric and home to the second church founded by St Augustine during his conversion of the Anglo-Saxons. As such it was an ecclesiastical and trading centre of some considerable wealth and importance by the standards of the day. It may even have been the place chosen by Alfred as home port for his growing fleet, as within a decade it would become the place where seized Viking warships were sent. As a port it was also, of course, well known to travellers, both friendly and otherwise. In 885 it was a group of the latter who mustered on the Frankish coast across the Channel, awaiting a favourable wind to take them over the water to the city.

The soldiers of fortune waiting to embark for Kent were a formidable force. Since they were part of the great Viking army that had been marauding through Francia for over five years, their progress had transfixed the chroniclers of the day. According to the *Anglo-Saxon Chronicle*, these were the men who had left Fulham in 879 after Guthrum's defeat and sailed back to Francia, ravaging Ghent and raiding up the river Scheldt as far as the nunnery at Condé, then along the Somme to Amiens. After spending a year at Amiens, the warband had split, one half heading east and the other moving back to the Channel with a view to raiding Alfred's coast.

The Fulham veterans in this warband could, of course, have told their commanders what awaited them in Wessex – the operation of the fyrd, the poor defences around religious sites and the topography that ideally suited the hit-and-run tactics that they favoured. Rochester was hence an obvious target for them, as it had been before as far back as 842, when both it and London were attacked with 'a great slaughter'. It had ecclesiastical wealth but a relatively small population huddled inside ancient and largely ineffectual defences. As it was near the sea, raiders could attack and pillage, yet be away again long before Alfred's fyrd arrived. A successful raid might even perhaps encourage some of the settled East Anglian Vikings out of retirement and back into the field to provide some support.

These were all reasonable expectations for the Vikings sailing across the Channel in that year, but the England in which they were about to land was not the country they had left in 879. As they came ashore, the Viking army immediately discovered that the city's defences were not as permeable as they had perhaps hoped. To their surprise the citizens of Rochester put up a staunch resistance, repelling their initial assault. To do this the city walls must have been put back into serviceable order and some provision made for a defence force – perhaps the first evidence of the successful operation of one of the new *burhs*. This put the Vikings in the unusual position of having to dig their own defences outside the city limits and besiege the townsfolk. It was not a comfortable situation for them to be in, as it took away their greatest advantage: mobility. Undeterred, however, those in command of the besieging force calculated that, despite this setback, Rochester would almost certainly fall to them before any form of relieving force could be mustered by Alfred. The history of Wessex campaigns in the 870s supported this assessment. It must have come as a great shock, therefore, when their scouts rode back into camp with the news that Alfred's force was already in the field and heading their way.

Alfred's plans for the defence of Wessex had not been limited to the building of *burhs* or the construction of a small navy. The army was also being radically reorganized and it was this that was now coming to Rochester's rescue. The problems of raising the fyrd and keeping it in the field for prolonged campaigns must have exercised Alfred during the wars with Guthrum. His solution seems to have been an integral part of the defence of his realm that he began in the early 880s. It is not until 893 that the *Anglo-Saxon Chronicle* tells us of his plan: 'The King had divided his army into two, so that always half its men were at home, half on service, apart from the men who guarded the *burhs*.' Alfred's rapid response to the Rochester raid suggests, however, that in some form this scheme was already in operation in the mid 880s. The plan to rotate service with the army was simple but brilliant. Because they were allocated a set period of service in the army, the farmers and labourers who made up the vast majority of the force were able to plan for their time away and ensure that the land they returned to at the end of their service was still productive. With a set tour of duty, every man also knew how long he was expected to serve. This reduced dissension and desertion amongst the agricultural levies, whose loyalty to the king might otherwise come a poor second to a farmer's need to take in his harvest.

The men at home were also serving, in their way, by providing the food and wealth that the kingdom needed to continue fighting and ensuring that the countryside was policed. War had traditionally been a time of opportunity for thieves and bandits, as with the entire adult male population of an area away on service for an unknown period, anarchy could reign at home. Laws had been enacted to increase the penalties for domestic crimes committed during these times but a better solution was undoubtedly to leave some men of each social rank in every area. These could then guard against sudden Viking raids, as well as protect the landholdings of themselves and their friends from less scrupulous neighbours.

Requesting such a huge commitment from the people of Wessex was not something to be asked lightly, however, and keeping a large permanent army in the field was only a realistic possibility in the face of a very present threat. In the relatively peaceful 880s it seems unlikely that the plan in its full form, with half the entire eligible male population serving at any one time, was in effect. But a smaller precursor of it now enabled Alfred to turn on the Rochester raiders with such rapidity. Arriving on the outskirts of the city, Alfred immediately attacked the Viking camp, apparently with such ferocity that this battle-hardened force simply fled. Asser tells us:

> the Vikings, abandoning their fortress and leaving behind in it all the horses they had brought with them from Francia – not to mention the greater part of their prisoners – fled quickly to their ships at the King's sudden arrival. The English immediately seized the prisoners and horses left behind by the Vikings. For their part the Vikings were forced by this unavoidable turn of events to return that same summer once again to Francia.

These Vikings may only have been a raiding party as opposed to a full invasion army but the swiftness and completeness of their defeat speaks volumes as to how Wessex was changing. In the first place a mobile Viking army, who had arrived by ship with horses (and who hence clearly intended to wage a fast-paced, raiding campaign), had been forced by the resolute citizens of Rochester to dig in. This was in marked contrast to the performance of the inhabitants of Winchester who only twenty-five years earlier had folded under a similar attack from Weland. The city's defence had bought Rochester time and that time had been well used by Alfred to get a fast-reaction force – perhaps even a mounted force – to the city to relieve its inhabitants. The speed with which that army could be mustered and dispatched must have been greatly improved by the development of *burhs*, sited a day's march apart, where the army could be fed, housed and protected each night. Often these *burhs* also helpfully stood at nodal points in the road network connecting the local *herepaths* or 'army paths' that Alfred was commissioning for the very purpose of getting his troops more quickly to where they were needed.

Of course, no event in Alfred's eventful life was as clear-cut as Asser would have us believe and the immediate aftermath of the Rochester raid was a time of some confusion. Whilst both Asser and the *Anglo-Saxon Chronicle* say no more about the incident, Æthelweard, writing just under a century later, records, in his own excitable and confusing way, incidents that are missing from the other accounts that have come down to us. He says: 'they [the Vikings] fall back to their stronghold; some fly over sea. In this year they renew the peace, giving sureties to the English, and twice in the year divide they the spoil gotten by fraud, in the densely wooded parts hard by the southern bank of the river Thames.'

Æthelweard apparently had access to some lost version of events that makes it clear that not all the Rochester Vikings immediately left England after Alfred's sudden arrival. Some made peace; indeed, they made peace twice, and both times broke their word to go raiding south of the Thames. It seems uncharacteristic of Alfred have fallen for such an old Viking ruse. The fact that his old enemies were allowed to get away with breaking their word twice suggests that Alfred was not yet in such a position that he could punish raiders with impunity. What Æthelweard also knew was that this renegade band was receiving outside help. 'The filthy crew, then holding under sway the East Angles, find them food, and suddenly do they break out towards Benfleet.' The 'filthy crew' are of course the East Anglian Vikings who had settled in that kingdom under Guthrum. The Rochester raid may in itself have been abortive but the return of Vikings to the coast of Wessex had rekindled the desire amongst some of Guthrum's men to cast aside their ploughshares and go a-Viking again.

The return of the East Anglian Vikings to the warpath was of much greater concern to Alfred than the activities of coastal pirates, but a fortunate turn of events at Benfleet gave him the opportunity to use the other new string to his bow – his navy – to some effect. It is not clear who was at Benfleet to meet the Rochester Vikings, but it seems unlikely that Guthrum himself would have risked a return to all-out war with Wessex. In any case the Rochester and East Anglian contingents that met there were not destined to go plundering after all. Æthelweard reports that the two forces fell out arguing and disbanded before ever taking the field. The East Anglians simply returned home whilst the Rochester crews finally decided to take ship and join the rest of their party back in Francia. Invading England would need some more time, and a lot more thought.

But if the East Anglians thought that they could simply drift back across the border into Guthrum's territory and return to their old lives, they were in for another surprise. Alfred, well aware of the danger that his Danish neighbours still presented, was quick to send a forceful message to Guthrum. He must either rein in his ambitions or control those of his subjects who still might look enviously across the border at Wessex. He did this not with words, but in a manner every Viking would understand: he sent a naval raiding party to ravage the East Anglian coast.

To mount a naval raid on Viking territory shows an extraordinary level of confidence on Alfred's part. He was taking a form of warfare that had arguably been invented by his enemy into their own kingdom and using it against them. Indeed, it showed perhaps a little too much confidence. Initially the plan went well and Asser eagerly explains how events unfolded after Alfred's fleet sailed round the coast from Kent: 'When they arrived at the mouth of the Stour, thirteen [actually sixteen] Viking ships rigged for battle immediately advanced to meet them. A sea-battle was joined: there was savage fighting everywhere. All the Vikings were killed and all their ships (together with all their booty) were captured.'

Whilst this was admittedly not a huge victory, for Alfred's navy to even be able to confront sixteen Viking warships marks a considerable escalation in the scale of naval action that he could undertake. To do it deep in 'enemy' territory further shows that he considered he could not only defeat any fleet brought against him but could return safely home as well. In fact, that was where he had made a miscalculation. Asser is a little more matter-of-fact in describing what happened next: 'As the victorious royal fleet was about to go home, the Vikings who lived in East Anglia assembled ships from everywhere and met in the mouth of the same river; there was a naval encounter and the Vikings had the victory.'

Whilst Asser chooses to call this simply an 'encounter' as opposed to the victorious 'sea–battle' that he had previously described, the result was still a defeat for Alfred's fleet. Although neither he nor the Anglo-Saxon chronicler mentions it, it is fair to assume that the plunder, as well as the ships that the West Saxons had taken, were restored to their former owners and that Alfred's men were lucky to escape in their own ships and with their lives.

None of the chroniclers chose to dwell on the immediate after-effects of this defeat, their gaze instead drawn inexorably back to the continent and the Viking maelstrom still brewing there. But around this time Alfred elected to make one further strategic move, possibly to directly counter this deterioration of relations with Guthrum. It would have a profound effect on later history.

The political situation of the port of London had been anomalous for some time. Traditionally London had been a Mercian city but since the Mercian state had been effectively divided between Guthrum in the east and Alfred's client Æthelred in the west, it was unclear who 'owned' the place. As it was an important trading centre near the border between the two powers, there is a reasonable chance that its status immediately after Guthrum's conversion was 'open', making it more or less a free port. This situation created certain difficulties for Alfred, however. London was not only a valuable strategic centre; it also stood on the banks of the major artery running through southern England – the Thames. With continental Vikings now encouraging more warlike elements in East Anglia to return to arms, it was becoming vital to resolve London's position one way or the other.

What Alfred or, indeed, anyone else would have meant by 'London', or rather 'Lundenwic', in the 880s bears very little resemblance to the city of today. In the early 880s the old Roman city of Londinium still lay derelict and abandoned, its walls crumbling, its imperial buildings in ruins. Inside the walls there was virtually no Saxon habitation, except perhaps a religious community based around the first St Paul's church founded on Ludgate Hill by King Æthelberht of Kent in the early seventh century (allegedly on the site of a pagan temple). There is also some documentary evidence that there may have been a Mercian royal palace, which utilized the standing remains of the Roman fort, at Cripplegate. Other than those two sites, however, the city must have appeared much as described by the Saxon writer of the poem *The Ruin*:

> Wondrous is this stone-wall, wrecked by fate;
> the city-buildings crumble, the works of the giants decay.
> Roofs have caved in, towers collapsed,
> barred gates are broken, hoar frost clings to mortar,
> houses are gaping, tottering and fallen,
> undermined by age. The earth's embrace,
> its fierce grip, holds the mighty craftsmen;
> they are perished and gone. A hundred generations
> have passed away since then. This wall, grey with lichen
> and red of hue, outlives kingdom after kingdom,
> withstands tempests; its tall gate succumbed.
> The city still moulders, gashed by storms.

The writer of *The Ruin* may actually have been portraying the Roman city of Bath but his words would have applied equally to Roman London. But if Londinium still lay in ruins, where was the bustling Lundenwic that Bede had described 150 years earlier as 'a trading centre for many nations who visit it by land and sea'?

Lundenwic was, in fact, not within the Roman city at all but next to it, to the west. The settlement stretched out along the bank of a then much wider Thames in an area that still bears its Saxon name to this day – Aldwych, or the old *wic* or settlement. The ships that brought trade to the city could be pulled up on the muddy beach that is today still called The Strand. This bustling town stretched from the edge of the Roman walls in the west, round the bank of the Thames to the outskirts of the little village of Westminster to the south-west, and then as far north as what is now Oxford Street. At its heart, around the area later known as Covent Garden, it was a mercantile centre so densely populated that it had already suffered two recorded disastrous fires in 798 and 801, with probably many more besides. But if it was a fire risk, it was a profitable one. This area produced a range of specialist goods for sale, including jewellery and ironmongery, and it also provided a market for such exotic imports as Frankish pottery and German black lavastone querns for grinding flour.

It is not known why the people of Lundenwic chose not to build within the surviving Roman defences. It may be that the site was reserved for royal and ecclesiastical use or, equally likely, the decaying and dangerous ruins were considered ill starred and unlucky by a Saxon population suspicious of the wrecked Roman cities scattered across their land. However, the choice of a site outside the Roman city had necessitated the building of some new defences, including a huge earth bank and ditch, although such defences had notably failed to keep out the Vikings in 842 (when they had also attacked Rochester), as well as in 851 and 871. Now, in 886 those defences were about to be tested again – this time by Alfred.

This may not have been Alfred's first attempt to take London, as one version of the *Anglo-Saxon Chronicle* for 883 states that Alfred sent alms to Rome in response to a promise he had made that year, 'when the English were encamped against the enemy army at London'. It seems that Alfred had prayed for success in taking the city and had pledged in exchange a promise of alms to be sent annually from then on to the threshold of the apostles. In return Pope Marinus had sent Alfred a piece of the true cross and, according to the chronicler, 'their prayers were well answered after that promise.'

This passage nevertheless presents a number of problems. First, it suggests that Alfred's prayers were answered, with the implication that he did take London in 883, although if so we have no other evidence of it. If, indeed, he did take London, he cannot have held it for long as he was besieging it again three years later. An ancient copier of the chronicle for 883 may have accidentally included material taken from the later 886 entry, but this only adds to the confusion, as the mention of Pope Marinus (who died on 15 May 884 and was recorded as such in the chronicle for 885) means that he could not have sent a piece of the true cross in response to Alfred's promise if it had been made in 886.

If that was not confused enough, there is also the question as to who it was that Alfred was besieging in 886. The population of London was largely made up of foreign traders and native Mercians, neither of which were Alfred's 'enemy' and all of whom he could simply have overawed if necessary rather than besieged. Moneyers in the city had minted coins on his behalf in the 870s and 880s, suggesting that he already had a strong influence there. This begs the question: why was the city barricaded against him?

Of course, if London really was an open city, it may well have housed a strong Viking contingent – perhaps a growing one – as

Vikings were as enthusiastic about trading as they were about raiding, and it was perhaps this element that Alfred wanted to remove. Alternatively the 883 entry may represent the only mention in the chronicles of a Viking occupation of the city in that year, which Alfred defeated. Perhaps his return three years later was therefore not to conquer London again but simply to put into action a plan that would at long last put an end to the city's vulnerability. Finally there is the possibility that some of the Rochester raiders from Benfleet had not meekly packed up and returned to Francia but had headed for a nearer and equally lucrative target, this poorly defended city.

But regardless of the force used and against whom, the *Anglo-Saxon Chronicle* makes it very clear that in 886, 'Alfred occupied London; and all the English people that were not under subjection to the Danes submitted to him.' If Viking influence had been creeping back into London, Alfred's taking of the city put a definitive end to it. When he rode across the ditch into Lundenwic the city returned firmly into English hands. What he did next ensured that it remained in English hands from that day onwards until the present time.

Alfred was not a man to shy away from large-scale social engineering. His solution to the 'problem' of defending London and that part of the Thames immediately around it was carried out on the grandest scale, with typical vision and passion. Lundenwic was to be closed and, within decades, where streets, houses and markets had stood there would be arable fields once again. In the place of this settlement, Alfred decreed that the old Roman defences of Londinium were to be restored and a new city, 'Lundenburh', was to be constructed inside them. Whatever misgivings the population of the old town might have had about returning to the ruins of the Roman city, they were overruled and work seems to have begun almost immediately. Using Alfred's favoured grid pattern, a city was laid out inside the walls, stretching 1,100 yards from east to west and 330 yards from north to south. His plan is still reflected in the city's layout to this day. Even some of the original names survive, the Anglo-Saxon word for market (*ceap*) persisting in the names Eastcheap and Cheapside.

Lundenburh was designed to protect the people of what was very much now Alfred's city, as well as to prevent future Viking invaders from skulking in the Roman ruins (as they had done in the past). But the *burh* alone could do little to protect the wide expanse of the

Thames from Viking incursions. Still fresh in every mind must have been the arrival of the Viking army at Fulham in 879, at a critical moment when Alfred was securing his peace with Guthrum. That force must have sailed past Lundenwic unmolested and Alfred was keen to ensure that this never happened again. To achieve this, Alfred looked to Francia once more and the defensive schemes of the late Charles the Bald.

Charles had realized early on that the way to protect inland Francia was to prevent the Vikings from making free use of her rivers. Beginning at Pont de-l'Arch, he had begun to develop a series of fortified bridges over the main rivers from which he could control river access, either thwarting Viking attempts to penetrate inland or blocking their escape back to the sea. Alfred now took this idea a step further and, just to the south of the ruins of the old Roman bridge, ordered work to begin on a second *burh*, which was to be known as the Suddringa Geworc – the fortress of the men of Surrey – or Southwark as we know it today. With two defended sites on opposite banks of the river, access up and down the Thames could now be tightly controlled. It was shortly after this that the first efforts were made to increase this stranglehold by rebuilding the original London bridge, which had collapsed sometime during the sub-Roman period.

Of course, Alfred knew that the success of his defensive scheme for London depended on the financial success of the *burhs* he was building. So it is not surprising that the earliest surviving charters from his new city refer to the parcelling out of river frontages for building commercial wharves at Queenhithe, which was then known as Æthelredes hyd. That these early parcels of valuable land should have been first given to Æthelred is hardly a surprise as the ruler of Mercia was key to Alfred's long-term plans for the city. London had been a Mercian city; its people may even have still considered themselves to be Mercian; and at least nominally the king had no intention of changing that. Asser could proudly boast that 'Alfred, king of the Anglo-Saxons, restored the city of London splendidly – after so many towns had been burnt and so many people slaughtered – and made it habitable again.' However, Alfred did not intend to rule London in his own name. With his plan under way, he handed control of London to Æthelred and hence back into Mercian hands. It was an act that displayed a great deal of political sensitivity. It may also have been a generous wedding present.

In Alfred's eyes it was now time to cement his relationship with Æthelred through a traditional Mercian/West Saxon marriage alliance. Æthelred was therefore betrothed to Alfred's eldest daughter Æthelflæd. A royal daughter of Wessex married a Mercian ealdorman, just as a royal son of Wessex, Alfred, had married the daughter of a Mercian ealdorman eighteen years before. With London as a dowry and Alfred as a father-in-law, this placed Æthelred in a strong position but also made it abundantly clear who was ultimately in charge. Alfred loved to hear tales of his kingly forebears and it must have brought a smile to his lips to remember the story of how the former West Saxon king Beorhtric had been controlled by his strident Mercian wife Eadburh. Now *he* had a Saxon princess, his daughter, looking over a Mercian royal shoulder.

Alfred also needed to normalize relations with his other new relative, his godson. Around this time he decided to redraft his treaty with Guthrum to take into account the new arrangements in London. Miraculously the terms of this treaty, which in itself may have been based on a treaty first agreed at Wedmore after Guthrum's baptism, survive. They give us a window into the division of England between Viking and Anglo-Saxon lords, which Alfred hoped would now be permanent.

The treaty begins: 'This is the peace which King Alfred and King Guthrum and the councillors of all the English race and all the people who are in East Anglia have all agreed and confirmed with oaths, for themselves and for their subjects, both for the living and for the unborn, who care to have God's favour or ours.' It is a typical piece of Alfredian wording, avoiding charges of autocracy by its inclusiveness, but making it equally clear that Alfred spoke for all those of 'the English race'. In contrast, Guthrum's people were markedly not even given title to their land but referred to simply 'the people who are in East Anglia'. The treaty goes on to briefly define the boundary between their kingdoms, 'up the Thames, and then up the Lea, and along the Lea to its source, then in a straight line to Bedford, then up the Ouse to Watling Street'. This line probably did not stay fixed for long, although it placed London firmly on Alfred's side, ending that particular source of friction.

What was more important perhaps were the other clauses, which defined how Danes and Saxon would from now on treat each other, wherever the boundary between their kingdoms might be drawn. These put the wergild (the blood money payable to the family of a killed man) at the very high figure of eight half-marks of gold, roughly 1,280 shillings. This was higher than the rate in previous Saxon law codes for the highest social rank and must represent the wergild of a fairly important person. The treaty goes on to add that even a lowly ceorl who owned no land was to be granted the relatively high price of 200 shillings, usually the blood-price of his landowning counterpart. Clearly these huge figures were designed to make fights between Saxons and Danes along the borders too expensive to countenance.

The last clauses set rules for trade across the boundary, showing that contact was certainly not forbidden and was probably to be encouraged. Here, however, a note of caution enters the wording and we can almost feel Alfred's hand holding back the scribe drafting the document. Firstly no one is to move permanently across the border without express permission. Alfred did not want his own people tempted away to Viking territory or his own shires slowly filling with Vikings. For those who simply wanted to trade, 'it is to be permitted on this condition, that hostages shall be given as a pledge of peace and as evidence whereby it is known that no fraud is intended'. The idea of presenting hostages for every minor transaction across the border was clearly impractical. Alfred's concern, however, was not the sort of fraud carried out by rogue traders but the possibility of Danes filtering across and settling on his land or, worse still, carrying on their former piratical careers there under the guise of trading. The Rochester raid had shown how fragile the peace with Guthrum had become. Having secured London, Alfred felt that it was time to draw a new line in the sand.

But as well as being a time for caution this was, after all, a time for Alfred to celebrate his achievements to date. It was time to make his new position explicit: to his own people, to his allies, to the nations that looked to him for protection and to any who would dare consider themselves his enemy. To this end he arranged a new form of ceremony – a great oath-taking in which his own ealdormen, and the rulers of his neighbouring kingdoms, all paid homage to him as their overlord.

Hints of Alfred's new position now also start appearing in contemporary documents. Some Anglo-Saxon charters (as well as Asser) begin to refer to him as 'King of the Angles and of the Saxons' or 'King of the Anglo-Saxons'. This implied a degree of rule across England that was in fact still some way off, as half the country was under Viking control It did, however, demonstrate a unity of leadership for the South and West of England and it also established a pecking order amongst the rulers of Wessex, Mercia and Wales. At the top – of course – was Alfred. Perhaps the word bretwalda was now whispered around court but, if it was, the speaker was missing the point. Alfred had begun a process that would make his descendants more than simply *primus inter pares*. Æthelred of Mercia was not a king who acknowledged Alfred's overlordship; he was merely an ealdorman who ruled *for* Alfred. Asser sums up the situation just after having described the new plan for London when he says: 'All the Angles and Saxons – those who had formerly been scattered everywhere and were not in captivity with the Vikings – turned willingly to king Alfred and submitted themselves to his lordship.'

Alfred was taking Wessex on a new road, not to the bretwaldaship that his grandfather had dreamt of but towards the unification of the kingdom that would become England. It was a project that would require more than just the rebuilding of towns and forts, more than just the restarting of the economy, more than fleets and armies and wars. It required a revolution in thinking. In Alfred's mind, through all the tribulations of the past years, the Vikings themselves were not the problem but merely a symptom of the problem, and all the work that he done to date was simply to treat those symptoms. Now he would turn to that problem itself and prescribe a radical cure.

14

The Summoning of the Muse

Therefore I beseech you to do as I believe you are willing to do:
as often as you can, free yourself from worldly affairs so that you
may apply that wisdom which God gave you wherever you can.
Remember what punishments befell us in this world when we
ourselves did not cherish learning nor transmit it to other men.

Alfred the Great's translation of Gregory's
Pastoral Care, prose preface, quoted in Keynes
and Lapidge (trans.), *Alfred the Great: Asser's Life
of Alfred and Other Contemporary Sources*, p. 125

THERE WAS NO such thing as bad luck in ninth-century England.
Alfred knew it and his people knew it too. Whereas today a
sudden wave of terrifying attacks, like those that the Vikings inflicted
on western Europe, might be put down to misfortune – an unexpected and unpredictable catastrophe – for Alfred that simply was
not the case. It is true that he and his predecessors on the various
English thrones had not asked for these invasions, but that does not
mean that they did not believe they had warranted them. By the mid
880s Alfred was beginning to get a grip on practical ways of controlling these incursions, but he knew in his heart that this was not
enough to prevent them from happening altogether. *Burhs*, reformed
armies and navies were all weapons in his arsenal, but no amount of
homeland defence could protect the king and his people from what he
knew was the source of the blight: God.

To understand the role of God as an ever-present and very active
player in the politics of Alfred's reign, we have to try to imagine the
world view of the Anglo-Saxon and of Alfred himself. His was a world
where God did not wait for the Last Judgment, but was intimately
involved, even on the smallest scale, in the fate of individuals and

nations on a daily basis. Alfred had grown up at a court where saints still walked and where miracles were a matter of simple reporting, not superstitious gossip. It was a world that he knew had been created by God and was watched over by God, which behaved in a way that seemed consistent with what was written in the Bible over whose compiling God had, no doubt, presided. To the ninth-century mind the Christian explanation of all things seemed altogether satisfactory, offering reasons for the existence of the world and some guide to how it was intended to work. Most of all, it offered some hope for the future, both in the present life and whatever might come next. If this was a world into which pagan Vikings could suddenly burst forth, then it must be with God's knowledge, and the suffering that they had caused amongst the people of England must have occurred with his blessing.

It may seem odd today to think of Viking warbands as instruments of the Almighty, but to Alfred that was the only explanation for their presence in his realm. God had set him and the House of Ecgberht over his people to guide them and show them the Christian path, and both he and his people had failed. In response God had shown compassion in not waiting until the last trumpet before judging them but had instead sent the Vikings to scourge them and return them to the true path.

This is not to say that Alfred thought that his fate was unalterable. He knew it was still his duty to fight the Vikings and to try to find all the practical means at his disposal to protect his land, but those measures could never be the solution on their own. What was required was a way of pleasing God so that he might put aside the Viking whip. The tribulations of the last decades were a lesson. Personally he had been shown how his own inattention could lead to the loss (albeit temporary) of his kingdom, which God had taken from him and forced him to earn all over again. Beyond that he had let his people fall into ignorance and in doing so they had strayed from him and from God. So the answer to his and his people's problems was not weaponry but wisdom. He needed nothing less than a renaissance in learning. This alone would put an end to the Viking menace.

It is certainly true that, as Alfred surveyed his realm in the mid 880s, before him lay a country where, if knowledge was not dead, it was at least resting. It was this painful and recurring thought that first prompted him to write: 'very often it has come to my mind what men of learning there were formerly throughout England . . . and how there were happy times then.' Exactly what age he was referring to is not clear but perhaps he looked back fondly to a period some 150 years earlier, when Bede had written his *History of the English Church and People*. In this the venerable monk had documented the conversion of the English to Christianity, describing how in that process they had moved from what he considered a barbarous and terrible past into an enlightened present. Alfred also undoubtedly harked back to more recent times, perhaps even his grandfather's reign, before the Vikings first arrived and, as he wearily put it, 'before everything was ransacked and burned'. Certainly the Vikings had done the burning but in Alfred's eyes they were not strictly to blame. Rather it was the English who had lost their love of books, their love of learning, and the destruction wrought on them by the heathens was simply the logical conclusion of that. It was this saddening thought that came to him when, perhaps sometime in the late 880s, he cast his mind back over the immediate past and wrote:

> Learning had declined so thoroughly in England that there were very few men on this side of the Humber who could understand their divine services in English, or even translate a single letter from Latin into English . . . There were so few of them that I cannot recollect even a single one south of the Thames when I succeeded to the kingdom.

This comprehensively damning indictment of his own father's reign cannot be simply taken at face value. There had been men of letters in his father's Wessex, men such as his father's Frankish secretary Felix and St Swithun. His stepmother Judith must also have brought with her to Wessex some of the highly literate glamour of the Carolingian court and Alfred himself must have had misty memories of the old poems read to him as a little child by his half-remembered mother, Osburh.

Alfred was simply making a point. It was certainly the case that literacy had greatly declined and outside the court it may have been almost entirely in abeyance. An example of the extent of this decline can be seen in a diploma from Canterbury of 873. This document was produced by the scriptorium attached to what should have been the most illustrious monastery in the land – the home turf of the archbishop, England's senior prelate. Yet it is almost entirely incomprehensible, a confused and garbled collection of Latin phrases and witness lists, cobbled together from old documents that the writer clearly either could not trouble himself to read or, more likely, was quite unable to read. And so it was to remedy this, to cure his country of the source of its problems, ignorance, that Alfred turned his energetic mind.

His solution was typically direct and practical. In the first instance, learning at court, as well as his own education, had to be improved. To achieve this he set out on a campaign of headhunting. The people he had in his sights were a new type of army – the best scholars he could find, at home and abroad, who had to be persuaded to come to his court and help him to turn it into a centre of learning. The identity of those who answered that call, and when, is, as with so much in this period, a matter of academic dispute, but from the mid 880s a number of names begin to appear in the records that are intimately linked to this Alfredian renaissance.

The king's first port of call in his search was Mercia where Wærferth, the bishop of Worcester, answered the summons. Wærferth had been a witness to the demise of the old Mercian state, having received grants from Ceolwulf II, but he had maintained his position in the transition to Ealdorman Æthelred's rule. He would now become a wholehearted supporter of all the facets of Alfred's scheme, actively involving himself in arranging the new defences of his home town of Worcester and contributing to Alfred's library his own enthusiastic (if rather shaky) translation of Gregory's *Dialogues*. In return he would receive grants from Æthelred in Mercia and valuable commercial property on the waterfront of Alfred's new London.

With him came Plegmund, who one (probably legendary) source claims was originally a Cheshire hermit from Plemstall or 'Plegmund's stow' near Chester. It was said that his piety had first attracted Alfred's attention, but his skills as a scholar and, perhaps more importantly, his abilities as an organizer also must have played a part. Those skills came to the fore in 890 when Alfred appointed him archbishop of Canterbury in succession to Æthelred who, either through great diplomacy or perhaps simply out of necessity, was forgiven his associations with the Chippenham coup, and who died, still in office, in 888. However, it is interesting to note that, after Æthelred, Alfred chose a foreigner, a Mercian with no local ties, to replace him.

Plegmund eagerly set about reversing the damage that years of neglect had wrought. His surviving charters, whilst not perhaps works of great literature, had qualities that, to Alfred, were far more important: they were readable and readily understandable. In this he worked closely with Beornhelm, the abbot of St Augustine's monastery, Canterbury, and together they began to erase the stain of the notorious, illiterate diploma of 873. Beornhelm himself seems also to have been favoured by Alfred; at the time of Plegmund's appointment he was dispatched to Rome with apologies for having sent no alms the previous year and a promise henceforth to send money annually. This was the origin of the English papal tax of 'Peter's pence'. The offer of it must have gone a long way to ensuring that Alfred would not experience the same friction with the papacy and with the see of Canterbury that he had suffered under Pope John VIII and Archbishop Æthelred.

In fact the timing was perfect for re-establishing friendly relations with the papacy as in 891, Formosus, an old political enemy of John VIII (who had once been threatened with excommunication by him), became pope. Formosus now wrote to the bishops of England, reminding them of their duty to their archbishop, Plegmund, and, by implication, to Alfred's government. He begins in an uncompromising tone: 'Having heard that the abominable rites of the pagans have sprouted up again in your parts and that you kept silent "like dogs unable to bark" we have considered thrusting you from the body of the Church of God with the sword of separation.' Here is a very different pope from John VIII. The allusion to the rites of the pagans 'sprouting up again in your parts' looks like a thinly veiled reference to those who sided with the Viking-backed coup (and hence against Alfred) after Chippenham. Formosus, a former missionary, was certainly not willing to condone pacts with heathens and was now explicitly threatening any English ecclesiastics who might consider the idea in the future. Putting his weight firmly behind Alfred and the new order, he signs off by warning any doubters: 'If, however, any man attempt to contend against this at any time, and to diminish it, let him know that without doubt he will be punished with a heavy anathema, and be separated for ever from the body of the Holy

Church which he tries to disturb, unless he comes to his senses.' Not since the days of Leo IV had Alfred had such a good friend in the Holy See, even if that friendship was based on little more than a shared antipathy towards a previous pope.

For Formosus at least that antipathy would have lasting consequences. Even after he died in 896 he could not escape his old enemy John VIII and his successor had his body exhumed. In an extraordinarily macabre scene, it was propped on a throne to stand trial for the charges that John had originally brought against him. The dead pope was, not surprisingly, found guilty. After he was declared unfit to have been pope, his papal vestments were torn away and the three fingers of his right hand (which he had used in consecrations) were hacked off. Finally his body was dumped in the Tiber.

Back in a less vengeful Wessex two other Mercians were summoned to court at around the same time as Plegmund and Wærferth – Æthelstan and Werwulf – whom Asser describes plainly as 'priests and chaplains'. All four Mercians were first put to work in the court itself, instructing the king in the same manner he had been instructed as a child. Asser describes how 'By day or night, whenever he had any opportunity, he used to tell them to read aloud from books in his presence – indeed he could never tolerate being without one or other of them.'

But Alfred also had ambitions to employ foreign scholars and, in casting about for them, Asser himself first came to his attention. Asser describes to us in his own words how the king went about persuading him to come to court. This clearly was not simply a matter of issuing a royal summons but required a degree of patience and diplomacy on the part of a king who was prepared to put his royal dignity aside in the pursuit of knowledge: 'When I had been warmly welcomed by him, and we were engaged in discussion, he asked me earnestly to commit myself to his service and to become a member of his household . . . He promised to pay me greater compensation for it (which indeed he was to do).'

Asser was a Welshman by birth and had grown up in the independent kingdom of Dyfed. He tells us that he had become a monk at the great monastery of St David's and had been ordained a priest there, perhaps even rising to become bishop. However, none of this would normally have brought him into the sphere of a West Saxon king for, as Asser admits, St David's was an out-of-the-way place in the 'remote, western-most part of Wales'.

He may have come to the king's attention during the negotiations with King Hyfaidd of Dyfed, who had offered submission to Alfred in return for protection from the sons of Rhodri Mawr. Hyfaidd had not been a good friend of St David's, frequently interfering in her affairs, attacking the monastery and even occasionally expelling her bishops, including a kinsman of Asser's. But in the face of the sons of Rhodri, both Hyfaidd and St David's needed protection, which may well have driven king and monks together in their approach to Alfred.

Asser and Alfred first actually met at Dean in Sussex, probably in 885 – the year of the Rochester raid – and the king immediately asked him to become a permanent member of the Wessex court. The Welshman, apparently rather taken aback by this, replied that he would have to consult with the community of St David's; this was something that he would certainly have had to do if he was their bishop. Only four days later he left the king's presence, but not before Alfred had extracted a promise from him to return in six months' time and at least consider dividing his time henceforth between Wales and Wessex. Clearly Alfred desperately wanted this man at court and if it could not be full time, part time would have to do.

Asser did not return in six months, however, but remained in Caerwent, apparently struck down with an unidentified illness. When the six months were up, anxious letters must have begun arriving from Alfred. It was in fact a whole year before Asser was well enough to make the journey once more. He found the king staying at the unidentified site of 'Leonaford' and here he passed on the news that his brethren were agreeable to the division of his time between St David's and Alfred's court. In return Alfred immediately began to reward him in the way Anglo-Saxon kings knew best: with worldly goods. Asser would be his tutor and in return Alfred would be his ring-giver, granting him lands and luxuries, which, for all his protestations to the contrary, clearly impressed Asser. Alfred kept Asser by him for eight, not six months as previously agreed, but Asser's frequent petitions for leave to return to Wales forced Alfred finally to relent. It was Christmas Eve, and the king made him a few small gifts to ensure his speedy return:

he presented me with two documents in which there was a lengthy list of everything which was in the two monasteries named Congresbury and Banwell in English. On that same day he granted those two monasteries to me, with all the things which were in them, as well as an extremely valuable silk cloak and a quantity of incense weighing as much as a stout man. He added that the giving of these trifles would not prevent him from giving me greater gifts at a future time.

It was Alfred's way of saying 'come back soon'. Asser complied, and everyone seemed happy with the exchange. Asser now possessed personal wealth in Wessex and enough incense to suffocate the brethren of St David's. More valuable still, St David's also now had the restraining hand of Alfred on his vassal Hyfaidd's shoulder, should that king again decide to interfere in the monastery's affairs.

That first long visit probably took place from May to December 886, at the time Alfred was restoring London and taking formal oaths of allegiance from the rulers of non-Viking Britain. It was the beginning of a new era and, with the finest minds Alfred could find in England now at his court, he looked abroad for more exotic imports. It cannot have been far from the king's mind that the great Charlemagne had created his court school, and begun his cultural renaissance, aided by an imported scholar and an Englishman at that – Alcuin. Now it was time for Francia to return the favour. He sent emissaries to Fulco, archbishop of Rheims, to ask for the services of his scholar and monk, Grimbald of St Bertin.

We know some of the details of the king's negotiations to procure this Frankish scholar as Fulco's reply to the request survives. In it he thanks Alfred for the gift of hunting dogs (a traditional British export since Roman times), which the king sent him as protection against the wolves that still roamed Francia. By way of return he promises to send his own more spiritual 'hunting dog' to drive away the 'wolves' that plagued Alfred, quoting the king's favourite Psalm: 'The tongue of thy dogs may be red with the same [blood] of thy enemies.' In the specific choice of Grimbald, the archbishop makes heavy weather of the trouble it will put him to and of the honours that he requires Alfred to place at Grimbald's door in return. The archbishop being a man never to use one word where ten will do, he couches his letter in terms of extreme condescension, but finally he agrees:

it is not without immense grief – as we might say – that we suffer him [Grimbald] to be torn from us, and to be separated from our sight by such a distance of land and sea. But, on the other hand, because love counts no cost, nor faith any loss, and no distance between lands separates those whom the chain of true love binds, we have most willingly granted the request of you, to whom we can deny nothing.

Fulco's letter does, however, add a number of caveats, explaining at some length that he had intended to appoint Grimbald to a bishopric himself at his earliest convenience and therefore, if he were to lose him, he should instead be granted the rank of bishop in England. In fact, although the wording is (perhaps deliberately) obscure, Fulco seems to suggest that his man should be made archbishop of Canterbury and that any mission sent to take him back to Alfred should invest him in that role forthwith.

It would have been very useful for Fulco to have his candidate on the archbishop's throne in Canterbury but it seems that Grimbald himself, a more modest monk and priest, had different ambitions. He refused the office, preferring a life in a much smaller monastery in Winchester and the post of Alfred's personal Mass-priest. After some delay this led to Plegmund being offered and accepting the Canterbury throne, leaving Alfred to explain to Fulco why the latter's plan had not come to fruition. That Fulco was eventually reconciled to the new order, however, seems clear from two other of his letters. In the first, to Alfred, he congratulates the king on appointing 'a man so good and devout and suitable . . . in the city of Canterbury'. Then, in a later letter to Plegmund himself, he congratulates the new prelate on the good work he is doing 'to cut off and extirpate the incestuous heats of lasciviousness'. This, from Fulco, was a compliment. He might not have got his man into the top position, but he had a close friend at the heart of the government of Wessex, with the ear of the king, so he was hardly going to complain.

At about the same time that Grimbald crossed the Channel, Alfred's other scholarly import arrived in England. Much less is known about the origins of John the Old Saxon, save that he probably came from a monastery in the eastern Frankish kingdom (now Germany) and thus was termed an 'Old Saxon' (to differentiate him from an Anglo-Saxon). Although his role, like that of all Alfred's scholars, was primarily to be at the king's side, John was also appointed abbot of his new monastery at Athelney. The post of running this new foundation, created in thanks for Alfred's deliverance from the wilderness, was an important one. Alfred founded only two monastic houses during his reign – here and at Shaftesbury – in part at least because it was proving extremely hard to fill vacancies in existing monasteries. Asser, in moralizing vein, attributes the abandonment of monastic life in ninth-century England to the levels of luxury in which people lived, which had tempted them away from the harsher regimes of religious houses. In truth, half a century of plunder and murder by the Vikings must have impoverished or destroyed many such houses, and made those that remained uncomfortable and potentially dangerous places to be. Despite what the hagiographies say, not every religious wanted a martyr's crown. At Athelney, however, John would come close to receiving one, not at the hands of the Vikings but at those of his own monks.

The monastery at Athelney seems to have suffered particularly from the shortage of English recruits. Alfred had therefore filled the vacancies with foreign monks and priests. To ensure that they would have successors we are told that, rather extraordinarily, he 'acquired a number of people of Gallic origin [and] ordered that certain of their children be educated in the monastery and at a later time be raised to the monastic order'. The families that he 'acquired' were probably refugees from Viking attacks in Francia during the 880s; indeed, the *Annals of St Vaast* for the period talk of people being sold 'across the sea', perhaps to be redeemed (in more ways than one) by Alfred. This unusual mix of monks, amongst whom, according to Asser, was a boy of Viking origin, does not seem to have coalesced into a happy house, however. Perhaps they did not take kindly to the regime imposed by John, for Asser at this point cuts off his narrative to recount a very strange story.

He tells us that after his brethren had gone to bed, John was in the habit of silently returning to the church at Athelney to quietly pray. This practice had come to the notice of two disaffected monks who had bribed two Gallic slaves to arm themselves and hide in the church, there to lie in wait for their abbot. The plan was that when John arrived they would murder him and dump his body outside the door of a local prostitute where, it would be claimed, he had died 'in the course of whoring'. Fortunately for John, but not for the conspirators, the abbot was apparently not only a man of God but quite capable of physically 'fighting the good fight' as well. Despite being wounded he held off his attackers long enough for help to arrive. The fleeing conspirators were eventually tracked down and brought to justice. Asser does not record what, if anything, Alfred had to say to these wretches who had not only defiled his foundation but had tried to remove one of his precious teachers, but he does add that they 'underwent a terrible death through various tortures'.

That Alfred should be so enraged as to order a death worse than that reserved for any Viking is not surprising. Learned men were hard to find and Alfred needed them for a particular project he had in mind, which he hoped would mark the beginning of the end of the Viking curse. By gathering together Asser, Grimbald, Wærferth, Werwulf, Æthelstan and Plegmund, by begging and buying time from clerics, by humbling himself before foreign prelates, by acting more like a supplicant than a king, he had mustered his new type of army. Their mission, as he saw it, would be to restore Wessex to God's favour, and to return Alfred's people to the light of wisdom and Christian truth. Wisdom was the medicine that he believed would 'cure' his country of heathen attack and he expressed his attitude towards it with great simplicity: 'I can not find anything better in man than that he know, and nothing worse than that he be ignorant.'

The plan was, like all of Alfred's ideas, uncomplicated at its heart but he had thought it out carefully and would put it into practice with the unique energy of a man who had often been knocked down but had always climbed back to his feet. Beginning in his own court, he set up a school in which the children of the nobility attending on him could be educated alongside his own. This may in itself seem unexceptional but in the context of the day it was a revolution. Alfred knew from his academic friends that Charlemagne had set up a court school to promote the learning of Latin, then the essential language of holy orders, and that Alcuin had been employed to teach his successors the value of a literate kingship. But Alfred did not merely copy this plan; instead he adapted it to the unique needs of his own land and the practicalities of administering his own kingdom. As he put it, with typical clarity: 'all the free-born young men now in England who have the means to apply themselves to it, may be set to learning (as long as they are not useful for some other employment) until such time that they can read English writings properly. Thereafter one may instruct in Latin those whom one wishes to advance to holy orders.'

Alfred's first concern was for literacy in the language of his people – English. His aim was not just to educate the sons of nobility in Latin so that they could enter the exclusive club of the Church, for which that was the essential entry requirement. He had practical need of practical people, speaking, writing and reading the language in which life in his kingdom was lived. That, combined with his love of the language of the poetry of his childhood, drove him make literacy in English the main aim of his reign.

No schools survive today from this great Alfredian plan. Outside the royal household and some monasteries it is hard to find evidence that many ever existed. At a national level the hope of a 'general literacy' was still a distant dream but amongst those over whom he had direct control Alfred could and did exert his will with some force.

His desire that his court and the nobles of Wessex should be able to read and write in English was not, of course, rooted in a simple love of literature. Alfred was still very much an Anglo-Saxon king, who believed that gift-giving and war-making were as much a part of statecraft as the dispensing of justice or the encouragement of the arts. His wish that the children at court, and his own children, become literate had to fit in with the requirements that they learn the other essential aspects of royal Anglo-Saxon life. Asser is at pains to tell us that the king's eldest son and heir, Edward, had been raised in the company of tutors and was rarely without a book. However, beyond learning to read and write satisfactorily, he was more likely to have spent his childhood, particularly in the days before there were scholars at court, in the 'manly' pursuits of a future king. What exactly that involved can be glimpsed in Asser's description of Alfred's own activities as king in the days before he was fully literate. As well as fighting the Vikings, we are told that Alfred

> did not refrain from directing the government of the kingdom; pursuing all manner of hunting; giving instruction to all his goldsmiths and craftsmen as well as to his falconers, hawk-trainers and dog-keepers; making to his own design wonderful and precious new treasures which far surpassed any tradition of his predecessors; reading aloud from books in English and above all learning English poems by heart.

It fell to Alfred's youngest son, Æthelweard, to feel the full force of the Alfredian renaissance, being brought up in the court school where he was expected to learn to read and write English and Latin. Even he, however, on reaching a suitable age (and size) would have been required to put down his books, at least temporarily, and learn how to hunt and fight like a man.

For Alfred's daughters two possible fates awaited and, similarly, they would have been prepared for those. The eldest, Æthelflæd, was obviously the most politically useful. In later life, following her marriage to Alfred's major ally Æthelred of Mercia, she would achieve fame as the 'Lady of the Mercians'. Her formidable reputation as a military leader and tactician, and her active role in administering that kingdom, which she continued to rule long after her husband's death, suggest that as a child she received an education at least as good as her brother Edward's. Judging from the very practical nature of her later career, however, this could have been gleaned as much from observing the operation of her father's court as through formal education.

Æthelgifu, the middle daughter, was, as Asser put it, 'Devoted to God through her holy virginity' and hence prepared for the Church. She would therefore have been taught to read and write as a child before being made abbess of her father's new nunnery at Shaftesbury, although Asser does not specifically mention this.

Ælfthryth, the youngest, was educated by tutors along with Edward and was clearly 'cultured' enough to be a suitable bride for a Carolingian. That Carolingian, or rather 'half Carolingian', would be Baldwin II of Flanders, whose mother was, of course, the extraordinary Judith, daughter of Charles the Bald. Fortunately at the time that Asser was writing, this marriage had not yet taken place as he would undoubtedly have had trouble finding something positive to say about Ælfthryth marrying the son of a woman who was both Alfred's stepmother and sister-in-law. Alfred saw matters more practically and whatever his opinion of Judith and her marriages to his brother and father, he knew that Baldwin II was a powerful man and a worthy son-in-law.

The move towards literacy was not a move away from the old, physical values of Anglo-Saxon government, but an attempt to add to them new and useful skills. These would become vital if Alfred was to successfully govern the huge areas over which he now held either direct power or some political influence. Alfred's dilemma was simple. As the power of the state grew, it needed greater numbers of officials to maintain it. People were required to administer justice, to carry embassies, to collect taxation and customs duties, to oversee building and defence and to negotiate political settlements. Traditionally the king had personally undertaken as much of this as possible, during ceaseless tours around the country, but this was becoming increasingly impractical as Alfred simply could not be everywhere at once.

In this plain fact lay the problem. As more and more of the duties and prerogatives of kingship were delegated to local officials, the potential for corruption and incompetence multiplied. Alfred was eager that his representatives be answerable for their actions, that their work be recorded, and that they carry out their duties fairly and competently. If they were to be seen acting on his behalf, he wanted to know that they were acting well.

He was also eager that they obey him. As it was not possible for him to instruct every one of them, all of the time, in person, the word of the king had to begin to travel by writ, via written and sealed documents bearing the will and the authority of the king. If Alfred was to be able to rule by such writs, he desperately needed people who could read and respond to them. Latin was an academic and ecclesiastical luxury. What he needed was individuals who spoke and wrote the language of his government: English.

To achieve this end Alfred was prepared to offer powerful incentives. Whilst the training of the children of nobles at court could be directly controlled by him, ensuring a future generation of able administrators, those already more advanced in years (and backward in habit) proved harder to persuade. Alfred's answer was to offer them a stark choice. When illiterate judges were brought before him, he was reported as saying:

> I am astonished at this arrogance of yours, since through God's authority and my own you have enjoyed the office and status of wise men, yet you have neglected the study and application of wisdom. For that reason, I command you either to relinquish immediately the offices of worldly power that you possess, or else apply yourself much more attentively to the pursuit of wisdom.

Faced with the threat of being stripped of rank and rights, many a middle-aged noble must have returned to his alphabet with renewed urgency.

To complement the education of his administration, Alfred also reformed his court, both to provide more equally for his people and to ensure that the burdens of government that he now laid upon them were practical and bearable. He went about this as he had his army reforms, by attempting to divide his resources, both human and financial, using a shift system.

First, so Asser tells us, he began by dividing his revenues. Alfred's income came from a variety of sources, including food-rents paid yearly by tenants on all his folkland (which might by this stage have been, at least in part, commuted to a cash payment), the profits of his own estates, the proceeds of the sale of estates, the profits of justice (for which even quite heinous crimes often attracted only a fine), customs tolls and income from minting coins, as well as tribute paid by kings who had sworn loyalty to him. All this produced a substantial sum, which Alfred decided to split in two.

One half was earmarked for secular affairs and was itself divided into three portions. The first of these was used to pay his 'fighting men' and the nobles at court who helped him to govern the country. Whilst allocating their share, he also took time to rationalize their workload. These men had their own estates to run and could not always be in attendance on the king, so to make their burden easier, they were divided into three shifts. Each shift was required to spend a month with the king, after which they could return to their own estates to manage them for the next two months, while the next shift took over.

The next third of his secular funds Alfred dedicated to sponsoring the arts. It may seem peculiar to modern eyes that Alfred should spend as much on craftsmen as on his own administration but this is not philanthropy pure and simple. In Alfred's love of the arts we see, not the modern aesthete, but the old Anglo-Saxon warlord. The skills that the king encouraged at court produced the valuable goods that Alfred needed to distribute in his role as 'ring-giver'. These encompassed a wide range of crafts, including the actual production of rings that sometimes named the giver, such as those from Alfred's father Æthelwulf and his sister Æthelswith, which still survive. They also produced elaborately fitted weapons such as the Abingdon sword with its inlaid pommel, decorative clothes fittings like the Fuller Brooch, as well as lavish book bindings, gem settings, drinking vessels and religious plate.

The third part of these funds he distributed amongst 'foreigners' visiting the court. Asser charitably puts this down to his king's willingness to take up the exhortation in Corinthians: 'God loveth a cheerful giver.' For Alfred, of course, it was also an essential piece of international diplomacy, which not only demonstrated his wealth and generosity but also encouraged the flow of information into his court as well as the flow of good reports of it into the outside world. As his sphere of influence and interest expanded beyond the narrow confines of Wessex, this was money well spent.

The tales that these travellers brought have often been incorporated into the literary works of his court, indicating the value he placed on them. So in 891 the *Anglo-Saxon Chronicle* records how three Irish monks came to Alfred 'in a boat without any oars from Ireland, whence they had stolen away because they wished to go on pilgrimage for love of God, they cared not where.' These three, named as Dubslaine, Macbethath and Maelinmuin, had set sail in a currach (a boat made from hides stretched across a frame) apparently with only enough food and water for seven days. Fortunately before those supplies ran out they were washed up in Cornwall from where they had hastened to Alfred's court. Such peculiar journeys were not, in fact, that unusual at the time. It had become popular amongst devout Irish monks to cast themselves upon the sea in small coracles with few or no provisions and see where God took them. Some he no doubt took straight to the bottom but others had achieved great reputations from these acts of blind faith. St Piran, the patron saint of Cornwall, was an early voyager. A later legend grew up that he had made the journey from Ireland on a millstone, which angry pagans had tied round his neck when they threw him in the sea. This promptly bobbed to the surface and carried the saint to Cornwall. St Ia (after whom the town of St Ives is named) was said to have made the same journey on a leaf.

Whilst such fabulous tales obviously had a place in the heart of anyone who loved a story as much as Alfred, these castaway pilgrims were also useful to the king. Dicuil, an Irish monk writing in Francia in 825, noted in his *Book of the Measurement of the Earth* that such Irish travellers had been casting themselves away since around 700, founding hermitages on any uninhabited piece of land on which they were washed up. They gradually formed a community of far-flung travellers who might bring news, perhaps even Viking news, from the outer reaches of Alfred's world. It was Dicuil himself who showed the value of such connections in his great book of geography, in which he gives the first ever descriptions of Iceland and the Faeroes. Of the Faeroes, he says: 'On these islands hermits who have sailed out from Scotia [Ireland] have lived for roughly a hundred years.' When such lands were settled by Vikings, however, the hermits quickly fled. The Vikings of Iceland (in the works of Ari Thorgilsson) claim that the anchorites did not even stop to collect their bells, books and crosiers in their eagerness to escape.

Dubslaine, Macbethath and Maelinmuin had no such news for Alfred on this occasion, however, and he had to be content with the information that the great Irish scholar Suibne had died, a fact he considered important enough to have entered in the *Anglo-Saxon Chronicle*. Then, having been fed and watered by the king and no doubt with some money in their pockets, these travellers were off again, first, they said, to Rome and then perhaps even to Jerusalem.

Sailors as well as saints brought news to Alfred's court and their stories also found a place in the writings of the period. In the translation of Orosius's fifth-century *Seven Books of Histories Against the Pagans*, prepared during Alfred's reign, there is a peculiar addition that transports us to one of those meetings between travellers and king.

The arrivals at court of the traders Ohthere and Wulfstan were important occasions for Alfred, displaying another side to his character as well as that of the Vikings he spent much of his life fighting. Both these visitors brought news to the king of life in the far North, that dangerous place whence his enemy had come. Information on the nature and habits of the people there might prove useful. Judging by what was recorded of their conversations, the geography of the land was of equal interest. But their tales also speak of another side to Viking society. These men who travelled freely amongst the Scandinavians – Ohthere, in fact, was Norwegian – were not Alfred's enemy. They were traders who travelled to the North because the North produced goods wanted by the peoples of Europe, particularly the wealthy elites in countries like Wessex. These goods included fine furs – indeed, it was said that the farther north one travelled, the better the furs became – and exotic materials such as walrus ivory for reliquaries, crosiers and even chess pieces. Wisely, Ohthere begins his visit to Alfred by presenting him with some walrus ivory before telling of his great adventure. The account begins:

> Ohthere told his lord, King Alfred, that he lived the furthest north of all Norwegians . . . He told how he once wished to find out how far the land extended due north or whether anyone lived to the North of the unpopulated area. He went due north along the coast, keeping the uninhabited land to starboard and the open sea to port continuously for three days. He was then as far north as the whale hunters go at their furthest.

The court by this point must have been transfixed. The journey he then described combined everything that interested the king: intelligence on the people of the Arctic Circle, commercial information on the goods to be had there, ethnographic curiosities, fabulous facts and promises of riches, all bound up in an epic sea voyage that could have come straight from the pages of an Anglo-Saxon poem.

Wulfstan's voyage from Hedeby in Denmark to Truso in Poland was no less interesting to the king. In the way in which both tales are recounted, we also get an idea of how Alfred must have questioned the travellers. We are told that Ohthere measured his wealth not in land, cattle, pigs or sheep, as a West Saxon might, but in terms of the numbers of wild reindeer in his herd. We are told that the best rope for ships (the navy being a particular interest of the king's) is made from walrus skin; that amongst the Ests only the poor drink mead (a common Anglo-Saxon beverage); and that there is only a very little land in Norway suitable for agriculture.

All of these facts made not just for an entertaining evening but also informed the king about the people who had tried to take his land: what they lacked, what they valued, what superior skills or technologies they possessed. In exchange for this, spending a third of his secular budget on foreign travellers no longer seems so wasteful.

The second half of his yearly income, we are told, was given over to religious uses. Again this was more than simple charity. The Church provided much of the literate portion of his government; it held vast estates (and hence great power); and its reach stretched from St Augustine's throne in Canterbury down to each and every village and villager. Furthermore, religion and politics were inseparable in Alfred's mind at a much more abstract level. For him major political issues like the defeat of the Vikings were bound up with the proper execution of his religious duties in bringing his people to God. God was watching and he knew it.

This portion of his wealth was divided into four parts, the first of which was to be given as alms to the poor of every race who petitioned him, in proportion to their need. The second portion went to fund his two monastic institutions at Athelney and Shaftesbury, very sizeable gifts that make it all the more surprising that he had such trouble in finding new recruits to join them. The third portion went to his newly founded school, which Asser insists already included 'boys not of noble birth'. Again this substantial sum of money must have gone towards more than simply the 'school', whatever was actually meant by that term. Much must have been spent on the general maintenance of education at court, the retaining of tutors for the royal children, and the provision of access to them for the children of the nobility, as well as perhaps some particularly talented children of lower birth who had come to the king's attention.

The final part was to be distributed in the form of grants to other monasteries in Wessex and Mercia, and to other religious houses farther afield in Wales, Cornwall, Gaul, Brittany, Northumbria and even Ireland. These grants were not the same as the long-term funding for Athelney or Shaftesbury, but seem to have been made on a case-by-case basis, again using the king's money to exert influence over the institution of the Church where its political weight would be of most use to him. It also, of course, had the added benefit of pleasing God and saving Alfred's soul, both of which considerations were as real to him as the need to keep key religious institutions well disposed.

Having reorganized his court with an active educational programme to provide able administrators to help him, Alfred had probably done enough. He had set his country on a path that was pleasing to God, as well as also being healthy and wealthy enough to defend itself from the scourges he might send to test them. But Alfred, uniquely amongst kings of this date, and almost uniquely in English history, wanted to go further. It was not sufficient that his people could read and understand the everyday documents of an emerging bureaucracy or even the Latin nuances of the Vulgate Bible. This was for Alfred only the beginning. Now he wanted to gather the knowledge of the ancient world, in particular the works of the early fathers of the Church, and make them available to everyone. His people would not simply be able to read; they would be able to read great things, and in coming to a better understanding of both God and the world they would put the problem posed by the Vikings far behind them. To do this Alfred proposed to gather together the greatest Latin texts then surviving and translate them into the everyday language of his people – English. He would do the work personally if necessary. First, of course, he would need to learn Latin himself.

I 5

The Great Work

I desired to live worthily as long as I lived, and to leave after my
life, to those that should come after me, the memory of me in
good works.

Alfred the Great's translation of Boethius' *The
Consolation of Philosophy*, Ch. XVII, quoted in Keynes
and Lapidge (trans.), *Alfred the Great: Asser's Life of
King Alfred and Other Contemporary sources*, p. 133

O N ST MARTIN'S Day in 887 – the year after Alfred had
refounded London – Asser tells us that a very curious event
took place at court. It is another of those occasions, like the story of
Osburh's book competition, where the year-by-year narrative is
interrupted by a vignette of court life, a misty glimpse into Alfred's
personal world, where elements of legend and memory are mingled in
the retelling of a unique moment.

Asser states rather boldly that on that day, Saturday, 11 November,
'Alfred, King of the Anglo-Saxons, first began through divine inspiration to read [Latin] and to translate at the same time, all on one
and the same day.' This extraordinary claim has often been taken as
proof that the events being described never really happened but were
simply part of a sycophantic tale designed either to flatter the king or
perhaps raise him to sainthood. But if we allow Asser a little literary
licence and the reader reads on past this paragraph, we enter a much
more believable scene in which lie the origins of Alfred's greatest
scheme.

Asser goes on to explain that he was sitting with Alfred in the royal
chamber, reading aloud to him as the king so often requested. At one
point, on hearing a particularly good passage, Alfred suddenly ordered
Asser to stop. He then produced a little book in which he asked that

the passage be written down. This was Alfred's famous *handboc* or 'enchiridion' as Asser claims he rather grandly called it. The *handboc* was simply a commonplace book – a notebook, containing the lists of religious services for the day, some psalms and prayers, plus various other quotations and bons mots that Alfred had heard in the course of an eventful life and wanted to remember. Alfred may have carried it with him since his childhood. By 887, when Asser first saw it, it was full, so the Welshman hurried off to prepare a new quire of parchment on which to write the requested passage. Soon that new quire was also filling up with other quotations and Asser, delighted by this unexpected love of knowledge in a Saxon king, compares his master to 'the busy bee, wandering far and wide over the marshes in his quest, eagerly and relentlessly assembling many various flowers of Holy Scripture'. Perhaps the simile appealed to the king for he would later call one of his own translations of selected works his *Blostman* or 'blooms'.

However, Alfred was not satisfied merely to have quotations written in the book for him. Asser tells us that he immediately wanted to read them for himself and translate them into the language of his people – English. That he achieved all this on one day is certainly fanciful. He must already have been able to understand spoken Latin as how otherwise did he communicate with his European scholars? But on that St Martin's Day lie the beginnings of an extraordinary literary career. Through the passages collected in his enchiridion, Alfred began to learn Latin and, with the help of his scholars, to translate them into English. This was what he wanted to do above all else. Now he could begin his great work: of choosing the most important books in the world and translating them into a language that made them available not just to clerics and scholars but to all his people. These books would show his nobles how to govern; remind his bishops of their duties to their flock; and inspire his people with knowledge and wisdom that would bring them closer to God and hence farther from the reaches of their Viking enemies.

It was an astonishing plan for its day. The knowledge contained in books was written in Latin for a reason: to ensure that it was only available to the select few who had a familiarity with this already-dead language. By controlling who could and who could not learn Latin, access to vital religious works – works that explained 'everything' to the mediaeval mind – was limited. This granted clerics huge power over their congregations, and it also granted bishops and kings powerful rights of patronage over them. Secular documents in Latin, such as legal notices, further fettered an illiterate society, by requiring specialist intermediaries to interpret them. Now Alfred wanted to begin to open up this world of knowledge, first to the court and then beyond. Admittedly the peasants in the fields of Wessex would not be able either to read or write in English, but they could be read *to*, just as Alfred was, and if the language used was English they would not just hear but also understand. Amongst the higher echelons of society, whom Alfred was *forcing* to become literate, his choice of works would also further extend his influence and improve the perception of his administration, by providing what were essentially 'handbooks for government' – manuals for how to behave when the king could not be there to hand down orders in person. Written orders that could be understood by everyone could take the will of the king anywhere and, unlike the words of messengers or the memories of nobles, could not, as one grant from the reign of Alfred's son puts it, 'be brought to naught by the assault of misty oblivion'.

This was the beginning of a revolution in English life and it was in many ways centuries ahead of its time. When John Wycliffe translated the Bible into English in the late fourteenth century (some five hundred years later), so infuriated did the pope become that, after Wycliffe's death, he ordered his body to be dug up and his bones crushed and scattered in the river. Wycliffe's follower, Jan Hus, was burnt at the stake. Alfred had clearly never suggested translating the whole Bible into English. However what he did begin was the process of translating the language of law and kingship, and that of religion, out of an arcane tongue that was *meant* to be incomprehensible to most people and making it available in a way they all understood. This was to have ramifications down the centuries, involving the people of England much more intimately in the formation of England, something that was then of course no more than an idea to Alfred. It lead to a greater involvement in law, a higher degree of literacy and a closer involvement with documents (whether or not they could be read by the individual or had to be read by someone else) even amongst the lowest echelons of mediaeval society. In short, it began to take the process of the government of England out of the realm of folk memory and the monopoly of a Latin-speaking elite, and put it into the hands of the people.

This is not to say that Alfred wanted a classless society. He lived in a world that still tolerated slavery. A memorandum from his own estate at Hurstbourne Priors in Hampshire, drawn up towards the end of his reign, gives some idea of what he expected even from his own peasants:

> First from every hide they must render 40 pence at the autumnal equinox, and six church 'mittan' of ale and 3 sesters of wheat for bread, and they must plough 3 acres in their own time, and sow them with their own seed, and mow half an acre of meadow as rent in their own time, and make it into a rick, and supply 4 fothers of split wood as rent likewise in their own time, and at Easter they shall give 2 ewes with 2 lambs – and we reckon 2 young sheep to a full-grown sheep – and they must wash the sheep and shear them in their own time, and work as they are bidden every week except three.

This was not the work of a king who wanted to tear down the class system, far from it; Alfred owed his position to an intricate, kin-based social structure. He simply wanted his rule to be communicated clearly and for his people to be allowed to develop a more active role in what he hoped they would come to see as *their* and not merely *his* kingdom. Just as a *burh* was co-operative, so was the kingdom.

So the question that must have most exercised Alfred and his court in those early days was what needed writing or translating. Probably the first work of this new era was Alfred's law code, which may have been compiled as early as the year the king first began to learn Latin, 887.

Anglo-Saxon law operated very differently from modern systems of justice. In an unpoliced society, where there were only two options for dealing with criminals: allow them to live or kill them, different ways of judging guilt and meting out punishment were devised. Trial, where guilt was not obvious, could involve oath-helping, where individuals swore to the good character of a defendant (although it is not clear whether this meant swearing that they had behaved well in a particular incident or simply swearing that they were usually a 'good sort'). Without juries to weigh up the arguments of supporters and opponents in a case, oaths, which held the prospect of divine retribution for those who took them in vain, were seen as one of the few ways of ensuring that parties were telling the truth.

In doubtful or very serious cases, the entire process could be left in God's hands to decide through a trial by ordeal. Four types of ordeal were used in Anglo-Saxon England. First, there was trial by hot water, in which the accused was required to retrieve a stone from a pot of boiling water with his or her bare hand. The ensuing scalds were then bandaged and left for three days. After that time the hand was inspected and, if it was healing, the accused was considered innocent. If it was festering, however, God had clearly shown his displeasure and the accused was guilty. A similar process took place in trial by fire, in which the accused had to carry a red-hot iron bar a prescribed distance. Their burnt and bleeding hand would be bandaged to await the same assessment as before. In trial by cold water, the accused was lowered into a large water butt. If they sank to a specific depth, they were innocent; if they did not they were guilty. Either way they were removed from the butt before they drowned. The final method, used for the clergy, was trial by food, in which the accused was given very dry food to eat – a piece of consecrated bread and some goat's cheese. If they managed to swallow this without water and without choking, they were innocent.

It was to settle the question of how to proceed when guilt had been established that Alfred wrote his laws. He begins with quotations from the Old Testament as he muses on the laws of Moses and then considers how Jewish law was adapted to Christian use in later centuries. He goes on to reaffirm the Golden Rule, stating: 'A man can think on this one sentence alone, that he judges each one rightly; he has need of no other law-books. Let him bethink him that he judge to no man what he would not that he judged to him, if he were giving the judgement on him.' Only now does he come to his most important point. Having stated that, in general, all 'first offences' can be dealt with by fines, as was Anglo-Saxon custom, he says that there is one crime that can have no second chance. That of course, is the crime of treachery against a man's lord. It was a crime of which Alfred had had bitter personal experience. Even now that he is back in the ascendancy with the days of Chippenham far behind him, he cannot proceed further without reminding his witan that this is the one thing he will never tolerate. The wound was still too deep.

Now Alfred can lay down his own laws, which he says he decided upon, in his own practical manner. He had studied all the existing laws and had weighed up the good and the bad, only adding new things where they were necessary. We can imagine the court scene as Asser and his fellow scholars read Biblical injunctions and the old Saxon law codes of Ine and Offa, one after the other, discussing each with the king before he decided whether they had a place in his new society.

Most important of all to Alfred is that 'each man keep carefully his oath and pledge'. Again it is a law born out of cruel experience. In fact, in this little phrase we may also see Alfred trying to exert a whole new level of legal control on his people. Under later kings it was required of all free people of adult age (usually considered in this period to be twelve years old) to swear an oath of loyalty to the king, which included a promise that they would not engage in crime. Any crime that was later committed by them could be considered to be a breaking of the oath of loyalty made to the monarch – in short, treason. In these eight words of Alfred we can see the genesis of this idea and the first reference to a universal loyalty oath, which would not only help to ensure that Alfred was never betrayed again but which would grant him and his government special sanctions against those who sought to undermine his society. Having said this, he then makes it abundantly clear what the penalty for breaking such an oath would be: death.

Alfred goes on to tackle all the usual crimes of Saxon life. He considers what to do in cases of murder and theft, dealing in nearly every case with the appropriate 'blood money' compensation that was the usual fine paid to the victim of a crime (or their family) by its perpetrator. This was not an age of long-term imprisonment as the state structure did not exist to support it, but neither was it an age of arbitrary capital punishment, which was only reserved for the most serious of crimes. Instead, fines were the tools with which he attempted to govern his fledgling nation. Even in cases of theft from a church, where the punishment usually involved the cutting off of the hand with which the crime was committed, that hand could be saved, or 'redeemed' as he puts it, by paying that proportion of its owner's wergild – his blood money. Not only did every person have a financial value, but every part of them did too, right down to their fingers and toes.

There were, of course, exceptions, which speak volumes of the king's own concerns and betray a very real fear that must still have lodged in his heart. Witchcraft, which he might reasonably have thought had a role in his long-term illness, was punishable by death. If anyone drew his weapon in the king's hall, the king alone was to decide whether he lived or died. People wishing to trade in Wessex were required to come before the king's reeve with the men they intended to take with them, to prevent Viking raiding parties from pillaging the country in the guise of traders. To ensure the smooth operation of the new army, anyone caught breaking and entering whilst the fyrd was summoned had to pay double compensation (Alfred did not want his soldiers worrying about their homes and livelihoods whilst out on campaign).

Alfred needed his law codes for two very important reasons. First, they were a signal to the people of England that he was a major figure, a lawmaker, like Ine and Offa before him. With many of the other rulers of England and Wales now effectively his clients, this set a propaganda framework over them all and made a public show of his regality. Second, it was also a vital part of the king's growing administration – a handbook for the men he chose as judges when he could not be there in person. With the king's influence having expanded over such a large territory, this must have been particularly urgent as the sheer weight of litigation increased beyond that which one king and judge could carry. At the end of the day, however, the highest court in the land remained the king himself. A letter dating from his son's reign gives an insight into the legal operation of Alfred's personal court, which was clearly permanently sitting and endlessly petitioned. The letter concerns the career of the thief Helmstan, who had stolen a belt from Æthelred, an act that quickly became the pretext for a protracted series of legal claims and counter-claims over a piece of land at Fonthill in Wiltshire. At one point the suitors brought the case directly to Alfred. The letter says: 'we went in to the King and told him how we proposed to settle the matter, and the king stood and washed his hands at Wardour within the bower.' Clearly Alfred was on duty even when washing his hands in his hall, but on this and, no doubt, many other occasions, he stopped, carefully questioned the protagonists and got them to agree on a suitable way forward. It was obviously the sort of 'on the hoof' judgment that he produced time and again, every day, and the writer of the letter was keen not to have it overturned: 'if one wishes to change every judgment which King Alfred gave, when shall we have finished disputing?'

These judgments gained Alfred a reputation as a particularly just king, to such a degree, in fact, that his usefulness in legal cases survived beyond his own death. The Fonthill letter ends with Helmstan still in trouble, this time for cattle rustling, and on the run. In the end, pursued by his enemies and proclaimed an outlaw, he flees to Winchester where he seeks sanctuary at Alfred's tomb. There was clearly some legal mechanism behind this as by reaching the sanctuary of the old king's grave he gained the right to safe passage and yet another hearing from the king.

But whilst these laws demonstrate Alfred's concern for justice amongst his people, they are not of themselves very different from the Saxon laws that came before, except where they betray the king's own personal demons. The great part of Alfred's project was still to come, the translation of those books, which, he tells us, 'are the most necessary for all men to know'.

Exactly how he went about this huge task of translation can be glimpsed in his preface to his first attempt, the *Pastoral Care* of Pope Gregory. Here he says:

> I then began, amidst the multifarious afflictions of this kingdom, to translate into English the book which in Latin is called Pastoralis, in English Shepherd-book, sometimes word for word, sometimes sense for sense, as I learnt it from Plegmund my archbishop, and from Asser my bishop, and from Grimbald my mass-priest and from John my mass-priest. After I had mastered it, I translated it into English as best I understood it and as I could most meaningfully render it.

Here then we see Alfred's academic army mustered – his personally chosen scholars, gathered round to read and explain Pope Gregory's work to the king, and to take down his translations and interpretations of its meaning. The men of Alfred's renaissance.

The work he had selected to begin his project with was an excellent choice. Pope Gregory (known as St Gregory the Great) was a hero to the people of Saxon England, thanks largely to Bede. It is Bede who tells us the story that, having seen English slaves in the Roman market, he asked who they were and was told they were 'Angles'. He famously replied that to him they were not 'Angles' but 'angels', and he set about planning a mission to convert the people of this distant land. The man he sent was St Augustine, the founder of the cathedral of Canterbury and the first archbishop in what was then pagan southern England.

As such Gregory was a familiar character, perhaps even viewed as a saviour by the English. But Gregory was no plaster saint. He had been a very real and very active pope from 590 to 604 and his *Pastoral Care* was a highly effective manual designed to inform the clergy of their duties and responsibilities towards their flock. It was just the sort of book Alfred was looking for, born out of the same desire to regularize the work of clerics, and he hoped it would prove to be the inspiration for a renaissance in Church life. More than this, the practical guidance it contained applied just as much to those in positions of power outside holy orders as in them, hence fulfilling his requirement that these books should be most useful for *all* men to know.

Alfred was not about to simply translate this or any other book, however. In his preface to it, he is at pains to point out that he sometimes translated word for word, but also sometimes sense for sense. This little statement hides what is to us today the most important element of his books. Where Alfred translates sense for sense, he often in fact completely diverges from his text, giving us his own thoughts on power, friendship, love and fate. These asides are a unique insight into the mind of an Anglo-Saxon king, an opportunity for a man who could reasonably claim to be the founder of what would one day become England to speak to us directly across eleven centuries. He is one of only a handful of rulers in English, British or even world history whose authentic voice we can still hear, and in his case it is far from the usual self-serving pomposity. Instead we hear the words of a man well aware of the youthful failings that nearly lost him the kingdom, which he now hopes to redeem through his writings:

> Very often a man is responsive to the lessons of adversity, even though he previously refused to respond to his instructor's morals and precepts. But even though afflictions teach and instruct him, if he acquire the kingdom, he immediately becomes perverted with pride at the people's reverence for him, and becomes accustomed to flattering praise.

The project begun with Gregory's *Pastoral Care* would continue for the rest of Alfred's life and would include translations by the king himself as well as others at his court.

His next personal work (although the order is sometimes disputed) was probably a translation of Boethius' *The Consolation of Philosophy*. This remarkable book was, at first reading, a more unusual choice. Boethius was a late fifth-century Roman who had risen to prominence at the court of the Ostrogothic ruler, Theoderic the Great, but he had fallen from favour, having allegedly conspired with the Byzantine Empire to overthrow his master. As he languished in prison awaiting a terrible death by torture, he wrote *The Consolation of Philosophy*, in which he imagines himself visited by Lady Philosophy. She helps him to understand the irrelevance of power and fame, and reconciles him to his impending and violent death. As originally written, this profound philosophical work makes no mention of a Christian God, but instead frequently quotes Plato, implying that Boethius was probably a neo-Platonist. Early Christian writers, however, saw in Lady Philosophy's calm words a Christian message, adding overt Christian references and, in the process, transforming it into one of the most popular books of the whole Middle Ages. It was in this form, as a Christian meditation on earthly vanity, that it came down to Alfred. He could immediately identify with the troubled author languishing in prison, awaiting the turn of the wheel of fate just as he himself had done when hiding in the Somerset Levels. It was perhaps in remembering this time, when Ealdorman Æthelnoth of Somerset came to his side after so many others had abandoned him, that he diverged from Boethius' text and wrote:

> Then I say that true friends are the most precious of all this world's blessings . . . For in this world a man desires everything else because he may thereby acquire either power or worldly pleasure, except a faithful friend. One loves a friend sometimes out of affection, sometimes out of trust, even though no other return is expected from him . . . But in this world's fortunes and its present wealth one makes enemies more often than friends.

In his next book Alfred strayed yet further from word-for-word translation, finishing with something more akin to his *handboc* – an anthology of his own thoughts, quotations from the classics and translations. This work was based on St Augustine of Hippo's *Soliloquies*, in which the saint has a dialogue with 'Reason' whilst awaiting his baptism in 387. In it Reason asks him what it is he wants to know and Augustine replies rather sweepingly, 'God and the soul.' It is a large subject and Alfred clearly has his own thoughts to add to St Augustine's. He begins his translation faithfully enough, although adding his own thoughts where he thinks it appropriate, but just after halfway through the second book he begins to diverge, including other materials by St Augustine, St Gregory, St Jerome, Boethius and others, along with his own contemplations.

For some time it was argued that this book, which only survives in one very mutilated manuscript, *was* his *handboc*, a book that anyone who has gone in search of Alfred would dearly love to see. In truth this is not the book Asser describes but in its pages lies the ghost of Alfred's notebook. We can imagine Alfred, working through the *Soliloquies*, suddenly reminded of another quote or idea, and turning to the little book where he had written down those things he had heard that had struck him as interesting or useful. Perhaps most interesting of all is his own preface to the work in which, in a metaphor very much of his day, he describes how he had spent his life gathering knowledge – how he had put together his *handboc* – and how he wished others now to follow:

> I then gathered for myself poles and posts and beams, and handles for all those tools that I knew how to work with, and house-lumber and building-lumber, and the most beautiful trees for each of those buildings that I knew how to make. Whatever amount I could manage, that I bore away. Nor did I ever come home with any load without wishing that I could bring home the whole forest, if I could carry all of it. On every tree I saw something that I needed at home. Therefore I instruct everyone who is capable and has many a wagon that he make his way to that same wood where I cut down these posts. Let him fetch more there for himself and heap his wagons with beautiful sticks so that he might weave many a fair wall and erect many a splendid house and build a beauteous manor and there always, and there might pleasantly and peacefully dwell therewith both in winter and summer, as I now have not yet done!

In his final work Alfred turned to an act of personal devotion and a translation in which he does not, due to its nature, stray far from the original material. This is his translation of the Psalms, which he had known from childhood and selections of which he had heard most days of his life. To him these were more than religious, more than beautiful; they were personal. It was believed at the time that these songs were written by King David, who ruled Israel around 1000 BC and with whom Alfred could easily identify. David too had suffered terrible adversity and, in an introductory note to the second psalm, Alfred makes the parallel clear: 'The text of the following psalm is called "psalmus Dauid", that is "David's Psalm" in English. It is so called because David in this psalm lamented and complained to the Lord about his enemies, both native and foreign, and about all his troubles. And everyone who sings this psalm does likewise with respect to his own enemies.' Alfred had spent a lifetime fighting foreign foes, as well as doubters at home, and so he must often have sung this psalm. He perhaps took heart in the Biblical tale of how, as King Saul tried ever more devious ways to kill David, so David prospered. Also it cannot but have reminded him of his time in the wilderness, abandoned by much of his witan, when David sings: 'And why do the kings of the earth rise up, and noblemen come together against God, and against him whom He chose as lord and anointed?' In the Anglo-Saxon, Alfred even uses the term 'ealdormen' for 'noblemen', reminding everyone of his own betrayal. But, like David, he had overcome his native enemies, and his triumphant reappearance at Egbert's Stone had led on to a great victory against his foreign foes. At Edington, Alfred had met his own Philistine army and his own Goliath of Gath in the form of the Viking warband and its leader Guthrum. And he had won.

Of the other books in Alfred's great scheme we know of several that probably come from his circle but over which there is still argument as to what role, if any, Alfred himself had in their compilation. In the choice of each of them, however, we can see the mind of the king at work.

Foremost amongst these works must be Asser's *Life of Alfred* although it does not seem to have become a popular or widely read book in the Anglo-Saxon period. This fact, together with the very haphazard construction of the text itself and its abrupt end, all suggest that the book may never even have been finished and was not intended for 'publication' as part of Alfred's literacy scheme at all. Instead this most unique of all Anglo-Saxon documents probably has a place later in Alfred's story.

Pope Gregory's *Dialogues* certainly was intended as part of the scheme, however; indeed, it may have been the first translation, and it was the work of Alfred's Mercian bishop Wærferth. Although Wærferth's name appears nowhere in the text, the distinctive dialect of the work hints at a Mercian author. Further evidence for that authorship also comes from the insistence by Asser that it was Wærferth whom the king ordered to produce the work, and from the presence of a preface by the king himself at its beginning. Alfred tells us in that preface that he had the book written so that 'I may, amid the troubles of this world sometimes think on the things of heaven.' So Alfred's purpose in having this book translated was purely for comfort. It is not a major philosophical work like Boethius', nor does it provide useful instruction like the *Pastoral Care*. Instead it is a collection of tales of the lives and miracles of the saints, showing how the intercession of holy men and women had a direct effect on everyday life. This appealed to Alfred at two levels.

First, it was a wonderful anthology of fabulous stories, not only of the usual 'curing of sickness' and 'raising from the dead' variety but including incidents of magical marvels. In its pages are tales of metal billhooks lost in rivers that are miraculously reattached to their handles (following a suitable prayer); of fantastical fires that look real but do not burn; of unbreakable glass cruets; and of empty barrels that magically overflow with oil. In short, it is filled with just the sorts of tales of enchantment and wonder that had been the bread and butter of the Anglo-Saxon poets of centuries past whose work Alfred so loved.

Second, this was not mere fantasy dished up for the king. Gregory's purpose in writing the book was to demonstrate the effectiveness of prayer in almost every situation. It gave examples, many of which Gregory insisted he had on first-hand authority, of how the saints' prayers brought people back from the dead and helped them walk across water. It even demonstrated the efficacy of prayer in the more mundane problems of everyday life such as lifting heavy weights and mending broken pots. To a modern audience it can look like nothing more than superstitious wishfulfilment; indeed, the Alfredian scholar Charles Plummer once referred to it as 'a mere sort of lucky bag or wishing cap for the obtaining of anything that is wanted'. But in the ninth century these examples provided comfort and some form of spiritual armour. Alfred had little need of praying for broken pots to mend themselves, of course, but the belief that the prayers of good men could alter any situation was fundamental to him. In an apparently cruel and random world, the knowledge that God was listening and that his help could be sought in all matters was essential. The God who answered a peasant's prayer to restore a broken cooking pot was the same God who had answered Alfred in the wilderness and restored his throne. A book of prayers for all occasions was therefore as useful to his project as a book of laws for all occasions.

The final two great works of translation from this time are Orosius's *Seven Books of History Against the Pagans* and Bede's *History of the English Church and People*.

Orosius was a friend and pupil of St Augustine of Hippo who had written his *Seven Books of History Against the Pagans* at the saint's instigation. The book is an attempt to tell the history of the world from the Fall to the late fourth century (when he was writing) as a history of how God had guided humanity. Its purpose was mainly to shore up Christian (and particularly Augustine's) doctrine in the face of two late fourth-century dangers: heresy, particularly that of the British monk Pelagius, and apostasy. For many living at the time, the rise of Christianity in the Roman Empire had not had the renewing and revitalizing effect that was hoped for from an omnipotent Christian God. By AD 410, Rome itself had been sacked by the Visigoths under Alaric and it must have looked to many like the pagan days of the earlier empire had been, frankly, better. Even amongst those who held on to their faith, there were now divisive arguments about why the condition of man had apparently deteriorated and what this implied about the failings of the Church's teachings. In the face of this, Orosius set out to prove that in fact life had not grown harder since the introduction of Christianity but, on the contrary, people had simply forgotten how miserable pagan times had been.

This message – that Christian days were always preferable to pagan ones – must must had struck a chord with Alfred, particularly when he looked back at how his own people had flirted with the idea of rule by a pagan warlord rather than continued war and pillage under their own Christian king. They too had, in his eyes, been duped into thinking that such a life might be easier but his victory at Edington had proved beyond doubt that Christianity always triumphed in the end, and that the new England he was now building was a far happier place than Wessex could ever have been under Guthrum or his puppets.

As is so often the case with Alfred's choice of book, however, Orosius had another use. Whilst it was not a particularly well-written work and it was certainly not historically very accurate, it did provide examples of military strategy. In putting together his history Orosius drew on many sources that were probably not available to Alfred, including Junianus Justinus' work on the rise of the Macedonian monarchy, Julius Caesar on the conquest of Gaul, Tacitus on the military career of his father-in-law Agricola, and Florus' history of Rome to 25 BC. This gave Alfred access to some of the finest military minds of the ancient world and it may well have been from these works that he first hit on the idea of splitting his army into two sections, one in the field and one guarding at home, as the Amazons are said to have done.

The other translation was an obvious choice. Bede's *History of the English Church and People* was the first great chronicle of the English. It granted them a foundation myth, telling a rousing tale of the heroism of the early evangelists and demonstrating how the conversion of Anglo-Saxon peoples to Christianity had ushered in an age of peace and happiness. As Alfred read it, he must have longed for the apparent calm and harmony that Bede describes when he writes, around 730, that 'peace and prosperity prevail in these days, many of the Northumbrians, both noble and simple, together with their children, have laid aside their weapons, preferring to receive the tonsure and take monastic vows rather than study the arts of war.' It was a model – if an idealized one – of the state that Alfred hoped to create, but it offered more than mere wishful thinking. Orosius had penned a history of the world; Bede had narrowed the focus to deal with the origins of the Anglo-Saxon people and Alfred's own ancestors (or those he claimed as ancestors). These two books placed Alfred's own reign in historical context, as part of the dramatic, universal sweep of history. But Bede was simply a prologue to the other work that Alfred commissioned, probably in the late 880s. Apart from Asser's biography of Alfred, this was the only other new work, the only volume generated from scratch, although it did draw on many earlier sources. It would be the final stroke in establishing Alfred and the House of Ecgberht as the rightful rulers of a Wessex that was fast growing into an England. This was the *Anglo-Saxon Chronicle*.

Although so few documents from the ninth century persist in even one copy, the *Anglo-Saxon Chronicle* survives today in nine manuscripts, eight entirely in English and one in a mix of Latin and English. The presentation of so many versions implies that this was one of the major undertakings of Alfred's state and also that it was intended for wide distribution around his kingdom. The *Anglo-Saxon Chronicle* purports to be a year-by-year account of life in the kingdoms of England, which in its earliest form covers the period from 60 BC to around AD 892. That final date, during Alfred's reign, as well as the presence of a genealogy of the Wessex kings in the 'A' manuscript, which goes as far as Alfred but no further, clearly suggest that the origins of the document lie with him and his court.

But the *Anglo-Saxon Chronicle* is not in fact the year-on-year annal of events that it first appears to be. It is rather a selection of events, often little more than a list of accessions and deaths interspersed with fabulous tales, recorded with varying degrees of accuracy in chronological form but written up long after most of them occurred. By the beginning of the ninth century, however, the information becomes more solid and the gaze of the chronicler focuses firmly on Wessex. Up to this point the entries had been no more than a combination of available data from other sources and events that Alfred, or those around him, considered important in leading the reader towards the 'main event' – the rise of the House of Ecgberht and the rule of Alfred. By the time the *Chronicle* enters Alfred's own reign, it gains not only greater detail but a new urgency as the writer tracks the movement of Viking armies around England and coldly records the fate of those who opposed Alfred. At times one can almost hear Alfred at the writer's shoulder, remembering events, calling to mind the battles and the betrayals, the foes and the fallen friends. But by the time Alfred began his literacy programme, the *Chronicle* has again taken a different turn. The records for the 880s, with the exception of the events at Rochester and London, largely involve actions far away, across the Channel in Francia. It is as though the writer has suddenly been distracted and has almost forgotten Wessex, the very reason behind the book's existence.

There are two possible explanations for this. It was around this time that Alfred began employing his foreign scholars and we may be seeing the hand of Grimbald at work, directing the writing away from the relative peace of England to the Viking storm in his homeland. Alfred was always eager for news from abroad so the information brought by foreigners such as Grimbald could easily have made its way into his *Chronicle*, thus demonstrating the cosmopolitan world view of his new court.

It is also possible that even by the end of the 880s the *Anglo-Saxon Chronicle* was still not being written yearly but was actually compiled retrospectively from a vantage point in the early 990s. Certainly in the oldest surviving version – the Parker Manuscript in Corpus Christi College, Cambridge – the entry is written for 891, '892' is inscribed in the margin, and then there is nothing. Such a writer in the last years of Alfred's life would have every reason to concentrate on the violent events of Francia in the previous decade, for the horrors of yesterday's Francia would be visited on tomorrow's Wessex. Alfred and his new nation were about to be put to one final, terrible test.

16

The Testing Time

And the same year after Easter at the Rogation Days or before, there appeared the star which is called in Latin 'cometa'.

> *Anglo-Saxon Chronicle* for 891, quoted
> in D. Whitelock (ed.), *English Historical*
> *Documents*, vol. I, no. 1, p. 184

THE LAST DECADE of the ninth century began well for Alfred, or at least so it seemed. Around 890 his old enemy Guthrum died, finally drawing a line under the most turbulent episode in Alfred's life. Although he had not been a true enemy of the West Saxons for the previous twelve years, the chroniclers could not resist one final dig at the man who had caused their hero such trouble. Æthelweard in particular, who was a descendant of Alfred's brother, cannot leave the matter with a simple record of his death but feels compelled to add: 'He breathed out his soul to Orcus.' The choice of this name was very deliberate. The Roman God Orcus was the pagan god of the underworld and, most appositely, the punisher of oath-breakers. Æthelweard had no doubt of what awaited Guthrum in the next life, baptism or no baptism.

At home Alfred's plans for a new Wessex (and, indeed, the prototype for England) were also beginning to bear fruit. With Plegmund's election to the see of Canterbury in 890, ending the two-year interregnum since the death of Archbishop Æthelred, the situation amongst Alfred's academics was settled and the work of producing those books 'most necessary for all men to know' was well under way. There was good news personally for Asser as well. He learnt around 891–2 that his monastery's old enemy, Hyfaidd of Dyfed, had died, leaving his flock free at last from that turbulent king's predations. And if the latest news from his native Francia had reached him, Grimbald, too, had reason for some good cheer.

Wessex and Francia's fortunes had diverged in recent years. As Wessex had begun to organize under Alfred, so Francia had continued to fragment. It was this decay in the once-great Carolingian state that had attracted Vikings back to feast on the remains. The last years of the reign of Charles the Fat had not been happy ones. After the humiliation of Asselt, a number of Viking warbands continued to extort huge payments of Danegeld from the Frankish authorities, and those authorities continued to pay. In 884, 12,000 pounds of gold and silver were paid over in return for peace. Then, showing their supreme confidence and absolute disdain for their enemy, the Viking warband coolly killed their hostages and continued plundering the region – for who was to stop them? By 886 one of these warbands was besieging Paris where its count, Odo, scrambled to put up whatever defence he could. Abbo of Fleury, in recording the events, tells us: 'The Northmen came to Paris with 700 sailing ships, not counting those of smaller size which are commonly called barques. At one stretch the Seine was lined with the vessels for more than two leagues, so that one might ask in astonishment in what cavern the river had been swallowed up, since it was not to be seen.' The number of ships is certainly an exaggeration but their effect is not. The Seine was physically blocked with Viking vessels, preventing any use of one of France's major rivers.

Abbo goes on to describe Odo's defence of the city in a siege that lasted for over a year and in which he displayed a personal courage and cunning that would have far-reaching consequences for the French monarchy as a whole. Not only is Odo recorded as stealthily slipping through Viking lines to maintain communication with the outside world but, whilst he was in the city, his resourcefulness kept his people and their hopes alive. It seems he even resorted to chemical warfare with something approaching the 'Greek Fire' that the Vikings of the Mediterranean expedition had encountered in their actions against Arab fleets:

> the redoubtable Odo . . . never experienced defeat and . . . continu-
> ally revived the spirits of the worn-out defenders. He ran along the
> ramparts and hurled back the enemy. On those who were secreting
> themselves so as to undermine the tower he poured oil, wax, and pitch,

which, being mixed and heated, burned the Danes and tore off their scalps. Some of them died; others threw themselves into the river to escape the awful substance.

Despite these successes, eventually the siege began to take its toll on the Parisians, not least due to an outbreak of disease, in which bodies were piled up within the city walls with no room to bury them. In desperation Odo petitioned Charles the Fat for help. Charles, who was in Metz (always being more interested in his German and Italian lands), finally tore himself away and marched with an army to the outskirts of Paris. As usual, however, he did not attack but decided to negotiate, offering the Vikings 700 pounds of silver and a free hand to devastate the country around Sens (that is, Burgundy) at will, if they agreed to withdraw. The Vikings responded as practically as ever, taking the money and running. A fee was always better than a fight. The people of Burgundy were abandoned to this warband and to their fate. Charles, for his part, claimed that they had never been very loyal to him in the first place, so they deserved the horrors now headed their way.

None of this cast Charles in a very good light. The contrast between his unsuccessful and expensive policy of appeasement and the heroic physical actions of men like Count Odo of Paris made such differences all the more stark. Nor did it help that, in an age when rulers were meant also to be fighters, Charles was often ill, possibly with epilepsy, whilst Odo was strong and vigorous. Charles paid the price for his failures the following year when on 11 November 887 he was deposed by Arnulf of Carinthia, the illegitimate son of his brother Carloman. Whilst Arnulf took the eastern Frankish kingdoms, the people of west Francia made their break with the Carolingians, choosing their own king: who else but Odo of Paris.

The fortunes of the Viking warbands in Francia now began to change. In 889, Odo paid off a host threatening Paris, which then moved on Brittany, but they met with ferocious resistance from the Bretons. The survivors moved on again, this time to Noyon, and from there eventually to the area around Leuven in modern-day Belgium where they dug in. Here they came to the attention of Arnulf who, unlike his uncle, was a fighter, not a negotiator. On 1 November 891, Arnulf brought this Viking force to battle near the city on the banks of the river Dijle and won a crushing victory over them, which resonated through the chronicles of the day. It was said at the time that the river was entirely blocked with the bodies of the Viking dead and the city of Leuven still claims that the red–white–red stripes of their city flag represent the blood-soaked banks of the Dijle after the carnage.

Another warband meanwhile was being tracked across Francia, this time by Odo of Paris. These Vikings were led by a man who would go on to become a legend amongst the Normans, the man whom Hincmar had mentioned in the dying paragraphs of his own chronicle – Hæsten. Hæsten's career up to that point had already been spectacular. He was the Viking credited with leading an expedition into the Mediterranean and on his return he had taken to raiding Francia. The year 890 saw him on the frontier with Lorraine where he entered into typical Viking negotiations, with Rodulph, abbot of St Vaast. Under the illusion that he had bought off these Vikings with an agreement to allow them to travel unhindered through St Vaast's territory, the naive Rodulph was taken aback to find that Hæsten attacked and sacked the monastery anyway before travelling (unhindered) on his way.

It was whilst this warband was camped in Amiens that news of the defeat on the Dijle must have come to Hæsten. Around the same time, Odo also attacked him and might have gained as significant a victory as Arnulf's, had his camp guards not been foolishly taken by surprise, forcing his army to retreat. But if not a victory for Odo, this was another clear warning that the new leaders of Francia were less likely to pay and more likely to fight – something that Vikings avoided if at all possible. When a widespread famine and blight followed close behind these reverses, Viking warbands must reasonably have taken to reconsidering their position.

The improving fortunes of the Frankish kings against the Vikings, combined with the progress being made at home, must have lightened the hearts of everyone at Alfred's court. But this stream of good news also contained warnings within it, which Alfred would ignore at his peril. In 1066 a comet – a well-known harbinger of doom to Anglo-Saxons – would presage their defeat at the hands of the Normans. Similarly, at Rogationtide in 891, a comet was also seen in the sky. Few can have doubted that trouble would follow and, surely enough, it did.

The death of Guthrum might have put an end to one dangerous

Viking's career, but Alfred at least had reason to mourn his passing. For all the oath-breaking, and all the fighting, for every occasion on which some East Anglian Vikings had joined other raiders in violation of the peace treaty, East Anglia under Guthrum had been generally peaceful. Here was a warlord whom Alfred really could do business with, someone who saw the advantages of ruling peacefully using an Anglo-Saxon model. Guthrum had minted coins that were exchangeable in Wessex; he had even used his baptismal name of Æthelstan; and after Edington he never again invaded Wessex. He was, in many ways, Alfred's greatest success. Of course we can never know whether Guthrum really did believe the Christian vows that he made at Aller but he certainly believed in their value in establishing him as a legitimate ruler, and this belief must have extended to those directly around him. Now that he was gone, an old devil might be dead, but which new devil would step into his shoes?

Then there was the situation in Francia. Despite the rejoicing over the victory on the Dijle, Alfred knew well that what was good for Francia was often very bad for England. Vikings who were finding life difficult there might look elsewhere for easier spoils and, sure enough, the same thought had occurred to the survivors of the Leuven and Amiens warbands now gathering on the Flanders coast. They were packing to leave, loading everything – their families, their animals and their treasure – on to line after line of ships for the short crossing to England. Here then may well lie the reason for the first writer of the *Anglo-Saxon Chronicle* getting no further than writing the date for the year 892. In 892 there would be little time for writing.

The first sign of trouble on Alfred's coast came in the autumn of that year. Aided by the Franks who willingly provided ships to speed their departure, the now-starving survivors of the Viking army that had been defeated by Arnulf finished their preparations and sailed en masse for England. The sight of their arrival in the Rother estuary must have sent a knot into the stomach of every Anglo-Saxon. This was not another raiding party, a mere handful of pirates looking for easy loot. Two hundred and fifty ships clouded the horizon, and in their holds lay an army intent on conquest and settlement.

Their arrival was sudden and unexpected. Landing some four miles up the Rother, they immediately came across Alfred's defence mechanism, a *burh* known as Eorpeburnan at an unidentified site (possibly Castle Toll near Newenden). But this was not a well-defended fort, ready to repel invaders. Asser complained bitterly in his *Life* that people would not take seriously enough Alfred's injunctions about *burh*-building, that amid peace they saw no reason to prepare for war. Alfred, of course, knew better and at Eorpeburnan the *burh* workers would pay a heavy price for their tardy progress.

The site was unfinished and unprotected. Only a handful of workmen were there that day when a force of well over 2,000 Viking warriors approached. Those in the Viking army who had heard of the dangers of Alfred's new defences from the survivors of the Rochester raid must have thought them a laughable exaggeration. If this was a *burh*, there was little to fear in England. The site was quickly overrun and the workmen slaughtered. Disdaining these poor attempts at defence, the victorious pagans did not trouble themselves to reuse the site for their own camp, preferring to build one from scratch to their specifications at Appledore on the edge of the Romney Marsh in Kent. Here they awaited the next step.

That step happened almost immediately. As news was reaching Alfred of the destruction of Eorpeburnan, so another Viking fleet of eighty ships was gliding into the Thames estuary, and at their head was Hæsten. His army disembarked and dug in at Milton Regis just across the river Swale from the Isle of Sheppey. This immediately presented Alfred with a major dilemma. He now faced a classic two-pronged Viking attack, from two highly mobile and probably mounted armies who clearly intended to stay. If he attacked one, the other would be free to range across his kingdom, creating havoc. More dangerous still, with the controlling hand of Guthrum gone, if the East Anglian or even the Northumbrian Vikings heard of the invasion, he might also face further attack along the entire north-east frontier of Wessex and Mercia.

Thanks to his army reforms, Alfred was at least able to put the fyrd in the field and move it relatively quickly to the front line where he took up a position directly between the two Viking camps. Here he could monitor the two forces and try to disrupt any communication between them, if indeed they were working together. But this was clearly not going to be a simple set-piece battle like Edington, as he was unlikely to force two armies as slippery as these into the field at the same time and place. Any move he made against one would be exploited by the other, as the Vikings themselves may have planned before leaving Francia. The only option was to attempt to negotiate away one threat to leave time to deal with the other.

The easiest, cheapest and quickest group to deal with first was Hæsten's. He only had eighty ships with him, giving him a fighting force of at least 800 men, perhaps more, but it was still a relatively small number compared to the Saxon fyrd. So it was to Milton Regis that Alfred's emissaries went initially. What actually happened next can only be reconstructed through later hints in the sources, as no Wessex chronicler in Alfred's pay was likely to report at first-hand on the failure that followed.

It seems that the king approached Hæsten with an offer similar to the one he had made Guthrum – take up Christianity, take the gifts of your new Saxon overlord and go in peace. Hæsten accepted, for which he had his own reasons. He himself may already have been baptized at this point, perhaps having had to go through this inconvenient rite out of expediency during a previous reversal on the continent. It was therefore agreed that his two sons would be baptized, probably in Alfred's refounded London, with Alfred and the Mercian leader Æthelred standing as their godfathers. The ceremony was followed by the traditional gift-giving such as Guthrum had experienced at Wedmore. It also provided a suitable cover for what was, in effect, a payment of Danegeld by Alfred in return for Hæsten's withdrawal from his kingdom.

It must have seemed a reasonable pact to Alfred and it was a tactic that had worked before, but there were key differences. It was Hæsten's small sons, not the man himself, who had been enmeshed in the Saxon web of mutual obligation and there was not necessarily much in the deal for their father. Furthermore, Hæsten had no kingdom to retire to, as had Guthrum, so he had nowhere obvious to exercise his 'Anglo-Saxon'-style rule, had he been so inclined. Finally, the gifts following the baptisms were not, at least in his eyes, the beginning of a mutually beneficial agreement with his new overlord, but appeared to be simply a traditional bribe to remove him. Hæsten was used to taking these bribes and, as we know from St Vaast, he did not consider that they placed him or his army under any obligation whatsoever. Alfred would come to bitterly regret this failure to understand the difference between his old enemy and his new one.

But if the negotiations with Hæsten did not buy peace, they did at least buy a little time. The Vikings withdrew a small distance to a new base at Benfleet in Essex, perhaps at the suggestion of veterans of the Rochester raid who had camped there before when they sought the help of the East Anglians. This move gave Alfred breathing space to turn his attentions to the Appledore Vikings, but it also highlighted another problem. With Hæsten now on the edge of the East Anglian kingdom, there was every likelihood that he would petition the Vikings there for help in fighting Wessex. With Guthrum dead, there was also every chance that they would agree. In an attempt to nip this in the bud, Alfred immediately sent out messengers to both the East Anglian and Northumbrian Vikings, reminding them of the oaths they had given him and looking for some sort of surety for their good behaviour. In the case of the East Anglians, who must have presented in his mind the clearest and most present danger, seven 'preliminary hostages' (as the *Anglo-Saxon Chronicle* calls them) were even selected. Seeking hostages from one enemy and paying off the other must have seemed, even to Alfred, like a retrograde step. He well knew where such policies had led in the past but, faced with these large incursions – larger than any of the armies from his earlier Viking wars, there was little else at present he could do.

By now it was the spring of 893 and just after Easter a raiding party of the Appledore Vikings struck out, using the dense cover of the then heavily wooded Andredesweald (now known as the Weald of Kent) to move west, ravaging areas of Hampshire and Berkshire. But these counties were no longer the easy raiding grounds they had once been. As the warband moved back through Surrey, they were confronted at Farnham by a West Saxon fyrd under the command of Alfred's son, Edward the Elder. This was not a Saxon army exhausted by months in the field, criss-crossing the length and breadth of Wessex in pursuit of an elusive and highly mobile enemy, but a mobile force in itself, supported by local *burh* garrisons. They had the provisions, shelter and transport links to ensure that the fyrd travelled quickly and freely. The result was a Viking rout in which the Norsemen were forced to abandon the booty taken in their recent raids and flee, crossing the Thames, according to the *Anglo-Saxon Chronicle*, at a place that did not even have a ford. In some disarray they moved north up the river

Colne into Buckinghamshire, eventually making camp near Iver on an island then known as Thorney.

For a while this looked like a Viking defeat. Holded up in Thorney, they were unable to move out owing to a serious injury that their leader had sustained at Farnham while Edward the Elder and his fyrd closed in on them. Alfred too was now on his way to relieve his son and, with the arrival of his army, the war, at least on this front, would surely be over. But now the West Saxons had to pay for the mistakes they had made earlier in the campaign.

Timing was crucial as Edward the Elder began his siege of Thorney. His men were coming to the end of their period of service and must have been anxious to return home. Although Alfred was bringing reinforcements, if he did not arrive soon there was a very real danger that his son's men would melt away back to their homes, leaving the Vikings free to break out. This outside possibility became hard fact when tidings reached Wessex of a new threat. The Northumbrian and East Anglian Vikings showed once again that their oaths stood for nothing and, under the command of a Northumbrian pirate called Sigeferth, they had launched a fleet of 140 ships to attack Alfred at the other end of his kingdom, in the West. Alfred now learned that Exeter was besieged by this fleet whilst another squadron ravaged the north coast of Devon. He was caught. Having detached a small force to march to London, he had no choice but to turn his main army back and head west to meet this new challenge. His son at Thorney would have to survive as best he could.

With Edward's army running out of provisions and time, the whole dynamic of the situation at Thorney was changing. Even when Ealdorman Æthelred of Mercia arrived from London, together with the contingent that Alfred had sent there to warn him of the Viking threat, the moment for outright victory had passed and the time for negotiation had come. The result was that, with the usual profuse oaths and promises, and having handed over the usual hostages, the Thorney Vikings were allowed to leave their camp and quit Wessex. But they did not go far. By this point, if not earlier, Hæsten was in control of both warbands and the Vikings from Thorney marched, not back to Appledore, but to Benfleet where he had prepared new fortifications. Those camp followers left at Appledore also now weighed anchor and sailed to Hæsten's side.

Fortunately experience had taught Æthelred not to trust Viking oaths. His London contingent shadowed their enemy to Benfleet where they waited for an opportunity to lance this festering sore. By this time Hæsten had comfortably settled into his usual practice of raiding the locality from the safety of his fortified base. It was whilst he was out on one of these expeditions that Æthelred of Mercia struck.

We can only assume that the raiding party out with Hæsten was substantial as Æthelred and his men were able to easily storm the Benfleet base in their absence and completely overwhelm it. The Anglo-Saxon chronicler is delighted: 'Then the English . . . stormed the fortress and captured all that was within, both goods, and women and also children, and brought all to London; and they either broke up or burnt all the ships, or brought them to London or Rochester.'

The description of what they found in the Viking camp, and what they did with it, is interesting. The presence of women and children shows that Hæsten's army was not simply made up of raiders but of would-be conquerors, who had brought their families with them to claim and settle the land if they could. It also shows that Æthelred, working closely with his father-in-law Alfred, had a new appreciation of the threat presented by their ships and chose to destroy all those that the West Saxons could not use, splitting the rest between Æthelred's city of London and Alfred's port of Rochester. These were not the actions of an army keen for their enemy to leave, but those of one spoiling for a fight.

Another, more valuable treasure also fell to Æthelred at Benfleet. Amongst the captured families were Hæsten's own wife and his two sons – the boys who had only recently been baptized as part of their supposed truce. These three were immediately dispatched to Alfred with what must have been the clear hope that such important hostages would bring Hæsten to heel forthwith.

But Alfred had another surprise in store for anyone expecting to see Hæsten's family ransomed in return for his departure. When they arrived at court, he immediately released them and sent them back to Hæsten, along with further financial 'gifts'. It is a move that seems baffling to a modern reader – to have so powerful a bargaining tool and then to simply give it away – but there was method in the king's madness. The *Anglo-Saxon Chronicle* gives the official reason: one of the children was his godson, and the other was the godson of

Ealdorman Æthelred, so it was his duty to return them to their father. At one level, as a devout Christian, Alfred certainly believed that this was the morally correct thing to do. Perhaps he even vainly believed that such a magnanimous act, combined with other gifts, might persuade Hæsten of the value of having Alfred as an ally and not an enemy. But at a more practical level, he also knew the reality of dealing with a man like Hæsten. Returning his family made it appear that Alfred had no need of them, that he was confident of victory even without them. It also sent out the message that he was giving the Viking another chance, that a deal was still on the table if he wished to take it. In truth, in his heart he also knew that women and children, whoever they were, were useless in such circumstances, as in all his experience he had never known a Viking to shed a tear over the death of a hostage. There was no reason to believe that Hæsten was any different. Threatening his family would have little effect on him.

What undoubtedly did concern Hæsten was the destruction of his Benfleet base. He quickly withdrew to Shoebury where he regrouped and where he was soon joined by major new East Anglian and Northumbrian contingents. Shoebury was not to be a fighting base, however, but merely a refuge for those non-combatants with his army and their goods. From here they could quickly escape into Viking East Anglia if attacked again, whilst Hæsten and his men made an audacious dash across the country. From the survivors of the Thorney siege and the Benfleet raid, he had learnt that attacking the heart of the shires and the well-organized armies of Æthelred and Edward the Elder was simply too costly. He may have had some success in harrying the areas immediately around his bases but these could not provide food and booty for ever and they were clearly too heavily defended to allow him to carve a kingdom from them. Western Mercia might prove different, however, and by skirting the burghal defences of Wessex and approaching at speed, while Alfred was otherwise engaged in Devon, he might just establish himself in Mercia before Alfred was able to take action.

With this in mind Hæsten's army moved out west and cut across the country along the Thames and then up the Severn to Buttington near Offa's old boundary with Wales. If Hæsten had hoped for support from old Welsh allies, however, he was in for a shock. After the wars of the sons of Rhodri Mawr, the Welsh princes had decided that their future lay with Alfred's protection; indeed, even one of the sons of Rhodri, Anarawd, king of Gwynedd, had submitted to him. Nor were the people of western Mercia any more welcoming. Alfred may have been too busy dealing with the Devon Vikings to counter a threat here but he had delegated the defence of this area to some of his most trustworthy ealdormen. The *Anglo-Saxon Chronicle* proudly tells us: 'The Ealdorman Æthelred and Ealdorman Æthelhelm and Ealdorman Æthelnoth and the king's thegns who were then at home at the fortress assembled from every borough east of the Parrett, and both west and east of Selwood, and also north of the Thames and west of the Severn, and also some portion of the Welsh people.' Here then was proof of Alfred's administrative hold on his new greater Wessex. Æthelred of Mercia had not allowed Hæsten to outrun him but had crossed the country in hot pursuit. When he arrived he found that Æthelhelm, the ealdorman of Wiltshire, was ready with his troops, along with Alfred's most loyal lieutenant, Æthelnoth of Somerset, and his fyrd. Furthermore, the king had managed to call on the oaths of allegiance that the Welsh kings had given to him to demand service from their people as well. This large and cosmopolitan army then besieged the Vikings at their Buttington camp and waited.

The soldiers now lining up to take on Hæsten and his men were not alone. Asser tells us indirectly that he wrote his biography of his king in this year, as he tells us that Alfred was forty-three at the time of writing. Clues within his text also indicate that he was writing for a readership who for the first time came to support Alfred – his own people, the Welsh. Throughout the book he is at pains to give the Welsh equivalent of English place names, something that may have been necessary for his readers' understanding as, despite the two nations' proximity and regular contact, the Welsh and Anglo-Saxon languages rarely borrowed words from each other. Occasional exceptions include the Welsh use of the Anglo-Saxon term for 'hawk' and the Anglo-Saxon adoption of the Celtic *brocc* for badger. In explaining the geography of his work, he also uses a unique Welsh idiom. Whereas today we orientate ourselves north (with north at the top of a map), the Welsh looked east and orientated themselves around that compass point. Hence when describing events in the North Asser uses the term 'on the left hand', and 'on the right hand' to mean 'to the south'. So in 893, Asser was also actively involved in the war, not with a sword but a pen, writing a work of history and propaganda that would explain to his own people why they had made the correct choice in submitting to the West Saxon king and why they should now support him in his battle with the Vikings. This would also explain the peculiarly haphazard nature of the work – half chronicle, half policy statement – and the contradictory portraits of Alfred himself as sometime Christian saint, sometime sickly scholar and sometime powerful warrior. It also provides an explanation of the sudden end to the work, which does not so much summarize as simply stop.

The work that we call Asser's *Life of King Alfred* may be just a collection of notes and stories, still only half finished, never properly collated or written up, but gathered together in great haste in that dangerous year of 893 as Asser's own personal contribution to the war, his own attempt to get his people on board. If this was the case, the presence of Welsh forces at Buttington might reasonably demonstrate its success. It also, purely by coincidence, provides us today with the first biography of a king in Anglo-Saxon and British history.

Whether or not Asser's Welsh compatriots ever got to read his work, they and many others answered the call of the king he so admired. This army soon held Buttington in a stranglehold. It took several weeks but eventually the Vikings began to fall prey to their only truly implacable enemy: famine. Unable to raid the locality or even escape for long enough to forage for food, they eventually resorted to eating their horses. For an army whose survival depended on quick movement, it was a desperate measure.

There is little now in the pretty Border village of Buttington to suggest what this Viking horde once suffered there, although the ramparts of the fort they built were reported as still being visible as late as 1874. Although they are now gone, it is still clear from a standpoint in the churchyard that overlies where these last grim meals were once taken that these Vikings were well and truly hemmed in. Directly to the west lay the river Severn but without ships this was more of a barrier than an escape route. To the west ran Offa's Dyke, behind which rose the steep and unwelcoming slopes of the Long Mountain. Only the relatively flat floodplains to the north and south offered any hope of escape, and they were controlled by Alfred's men.

The besiegers, however, had no such handicaps and Alfred's

burghal system was able to keep them supplied in the field for longer than it would take the Vikings to starve. In the end desperation forced an outcome. Hæsten and his men made one final attempt to break out. The result was a devastating defeat for the pagans and a victory for the West Saxons, which, Æthelweard tells us, was still boasted of in his day, a century later. In 1838, some 300 skulls and portions of skeletons were discovered in a series of circular pits in the south-east corner of the churchyard. Local tradition maintains that these must be the Viking victims of the siege and the escape bid.

For the Vikings who did survive and find freedom, there followed another dash back across England, back to Essex where their families and goods were quickly dispatched farther north to the relative safety of East Anglia. They were now hunted men and a winter at Shoebury was obviously not an option. Together with more fresh North-umbrian and East Anglian reinforcements, they instead marched north, farther from the *burhs* of Wessex, farther from the reorganized fyrd, skirting the lands where Alfred held sway until they came to a deserted Roman city in the Wirral called Chester. It was a strange place for a winter camp, but the crumbling Roman walls, unused for some 450 years, at least provided a degree of defence. Hæsten and his men must have hoped that this might provide a strong base for a recovery, closer to the safety of friendly Northumbria and far from the king of Wessex.

But this would not prove to be the Viking Promised Land either. Whereas previously any Anglo-Saxon king might have been grateful to an enemy who withdrew so far from his heartland, Alfred was not. The West Saxon fyrd pursued the Vikings from Essex all the way to Chester. Although they did not arrive in time to prevent them making their camp in the ruins, they satisfied themselves with seizing all the crops and animals in the immediate vicinity and killing any stragglers found outside the walls. Then after just two days, with the area entirely denuded of all resources, they raised their siege and left a bitter winter to do their work for them.

By the early spring of 894, hunger forced the Vikings to leave the city but they did not dare seek food or booty in the dangerous lands of Mercia. Instead they chose to raid in North Wales, in the kingdom of their former Viking ally, Anarawd ap Rhodri. For Anarawd it was a lesson in the dangers of turning on the pagans, but insufficient to persuade him to renounce his new ally, Alfred. Asser clearly thought it no more than natural justice for a king who had once made a pact with these devils, from which, as he curtly puts it, 'he had got no benefit, only a good deal of misfortune'. Subsequently they carefully made their way back south, taking a circuitous route through Viking-held Northumbria and East Anglia, so that, as the *Anglo-Saxon Chronicle* says, 'the English army could not reach them.'

Back in Essex they set up camp on the island of Mersea where they were joined by the remnants of the fleet that had been giving Alfred such trouble in Exeter. The *Chronicle* mentions no spectacular battles in Devon during this period and, in contrast to Buttington, it seems likely that Alfred pursued a policy of containment, using his newly reorganized defences to prevent the Viking host from breaking out and ravaging the county on any scale. With this army curbed, he could afford to allow the resources of his kingdom to be directed against the more dangerous Hæsten. In the end, again around the spring of 894, the Northumbrian and East Anglian fleets in Devon tired of trying to gain a foothold there and withdrew. Unlike Hæsten's men, they already had a homeland and their main interest, other than in promoting further Viking conquests, was in harvesting plunder. This they had failed to do and, as any Viking leader knew, failing to provide loot for your crews was not a recipe for staying in command. The two fleets therefore each went their separate ways and sailed for home. En route, however, the East Anglians could not resist stopping off at Chichester for one final attempt to profit from the expedition. Here they rashly attacked another well-defended and well-organized *burh* and were driven back, losing some of their ships and hundreds of men in the process. The south coast was no longer a happy hunting ground for pirates. The remaining ships returned home with little to show for their adventure.

According to Æthelweard, the other contingent, led by the Northumbrian Sigeferth, sailed round Land's End and into the Irish Sea where he attacked Sigtryggr Ivarrson, then the king of Viking Dublin. It seems that fighting a fellow Viking, and a son of Ivarr the Boneless at that, was now preferable and more profitable than fighting Saxons.

17

The Last Battle

This is not dawn from the east, no dragon
flies here, the gables of the hall are not burning,
but men are making an attack. Birds of battle screech,
the grey wolf howls, spears rattle,
shield answers shaft.

The Finnesburh Fragment, quoted in
K. Crossley-Holland, *The Anglo-Saxon World*, p. 6

WITH THE RAISING of the siege of Exeter and the removal of Sigeferth to a new theatre of war in Ireland, Alfred could now at last march back east towards London and the remnants of the main Viking army holed up at Mersea. It was now the late autumn of 894 and the situation there was changing quickly and dramatically. Without the support of a Viking fleet, there was nothing to distract the full force of the Saxon fyrd from bearing down upon the Northmen and they began to look cornered. All their mobility had gone, either through the destruction of large numbers of their ships at Thorney and Benfleet, or because of their having eaten many of their horses at Buttington and Chester. Now they also appeared to be leaderless.

After 893, Hæsten disappears from the *Anglo-Saxon Chronicle*, which is strange, considering how carefully chroniclers had followed his career. His fate remains a mystery. Perhaps after Alfred returned his family to him, he did agree to quit the realm and withdraw to Francia (by that time he must certainly have been looking back fondly on the easy pickings he had enjoyed there before the famine). It is also possible that he was killed in one of the main actions, although it seems inconceivable that the chroniclers would have failed to celebrate the fact. Equally he may have died from wounds or even simply old age. He had been campaigning since at least 859 and reference to him as a leader, even at that early date, suggests that he already had some years of experience behind him. Alfred was at the time still only ten years old, making the Viking a decade or more his senior. By 894, Hæsten must have been weary after thirty-five or more years of fight and flight, in his fifties at least – an old, old man in an age when the average male life expectancy was around thirty-eight. Whatever happened to him, he is not mentioned at all during the last actions of the war, and since he had played so prominent a part earlier on, that can only imply his absence. He had slipped back into those cold North Sea mists from which the Vikings had first emerged almost exactly a century before.

Whoever was in charge at Mersea – and there may now have been more than one leader of the straggling warbands assembled there – the *Anglo-Saxon Chronicle* does not grant him the dignity of a name. Clearly, whoever he was, he was neither so forceful nor so important a character that he required identifying. However, he was capable of decisive action as Alfred approached London. Once again the Viking families and baggage were shipped off to the safety of East Anglia as the remaining warships were launched for one final campaign. This time they rowed up the Thames as far as the river Lea, then up the Lea following the precise boundary marked out in the treaty between Guthrum and Alfred. Somewhere in the vicinity of Hertford, roughly twenty miles north of London, they camped, building themselves a fortress in which to overwinter.

It was both a bold and a profoundly circumspect move. In this new position they posed a clear and present threat to Alfred's and Æthelred's new *burh* of London. From here they might either launch a direct attack on the city or simply control and consume the resources of the Hertfordshire hinterland that helped to keep London alive. Yet this was hardly in the same league as Guthrum's daring raids into the Wessex heartlands and his attempt to overthrow the crown itself. These Vikings were making their threat from the relative security of the border with the Danelaw, on which they were actually camped, and they can hardly have hoped to penetrate much farther into Wessex. That they were an annoyance, as they intended to be, was certain and they would have to be crushed, but their original grand dream of settling in southern England must by this point have been dead. They were not settlers but blackmailers, hoping to create enough trouble to be paid to leave.

If that was their hope, it was misplaced. Neither the Londoners nor Alfred were in the mood for payment this time. Instead, the following summer, an expeditionary force set out from the city to confront the warband. The progress of the war, and the difference between how this and the last one had been prosecuted, must have buoyed up the London garrison as it marched north towards Hertford. However, their initial confidence displayed a lack of understanding of how the tide in the earlier campaigns had actually been turned. Arriving at the strongly fortified and well dug in Viking position, they immediately and rashly attacked, but were driven off in a savage battle that left four of the king's thegns dead. It was a serious reverse and it should have been avoided. Alfred's success in the previous war with the Vikings had not come from fielding one huge, devastating army, however much that idea appealed to the Anglo-Saxon warrior mentality. He was winning by attrition – never letting the enemy get a foothold, never letting them rest, always making them fight for food, never, ever leaving them alone but never forcing a fight where there was no need. This was an unnecessary fight and the London garrison paid the price.

Alfred had to react quickly. Autumn was approaching and, with the London garrison bloodied and humbled, London's harvest was vulnerable. Not only could the Vikings on the Lea feed themselves but they could easily lay waste the surrounding area, destroying what they could not use and leaving Alfred's prize new *burh* to starve. It would be an immense humiliation and worth a great deal of Danegeld. This tactic had worked for the Anglo-Saxons at Chester and there was no reason to think that the Viking survivors of that terrible, starving winter were not prepared to inflict a similar misery on the people of London.

Reaching London, Alfred immediately set off north up the Lea to inspect the enemy position. Setting up camp between the city and the Viking fortress, he posted pickets throughout the countryside to guard the peasants as they brought in the harvest and thus neutralized the immediate threat. But this was only a stopgap solution. The base on the Lea could not be allowed to remain but equally it had proved highly resistant to direct attack. It was the sort of quandary that had baffled earlier kings, leading many to reach for Danegeld to provide at least temporary relief, but for Alfred the solution now seemed simple.

Instead of driving them out, he would hem them in. Their defences would become their own prison and, as was always the case with Vikings, in the end they would either sue for peace or run.

Surveying the river environs south of the enemy camp, he began looking for a suitable bottleneck where the river was relatively narrow and the surrounding landscape constricted around it. Having found just such a place, he moved his camp there and immediately set about building two fortresses, one on each side of the river. As soon as the Vikings became aware that Alfred was preparing to choke off their escape route, they fled. These were men who had been at Buttington and Chester, and they had tasted enough horseflesh and famine for one lifetime. Leaving their precious ships behind, they galloped west on horses, some of which they must have brought from Mersea, no doubt augmented by others taken from the Hertfordshire countryside after their defeat of the London garrison. The *Anglo-Saxon Chronicle* tells us, 'Then the English army rode after the enemy,' giving its first clear indication that at least part of the fyrd – a rapid reaction force – was definitely mounted by this time. This Viking warband could not therefore simply drift away into the countryside but was forced to undertake a 125-mile dash west across Mercia with the fyrd in close pursuit. Eventually they reached the settlement of Bridgnorth on a bend in the river Severn in Shropshire, where they found they had just enough of a lead to fortify a position and dig in.

It was now the winter of 895–6. Shortly after the Vikings had made camp, Alfred and his army arrived in the area. What happened next is a source of much contention, not least because the *Anglo-Saxon Chronicle* tells us that nothing did. Back on the Lea the people of London had seized the abandoned camp and commandered the ships they could use, breaking up those that they could not, ensuring once again that the Vikings were left with no seaborne transport. Nor were the East Anglian or the Northumbrian fleets at sea either to provide a necessary diversion or to aid an evacuation. Indeed, the friendly assistance provided by the northern Vikings to the warband may have ended altogether by this point as in the previous year the ever-faithful ealdorman Æthelnoth of Somerset had made a special journey to York. Æthelweard says that this was a military operation but it seems more likely to have been a diplomatic mission to neutralize the Northumbrian support for the invaders. If so, it was a wise and timely move on Alfred's part. By then

King Guthfrith of York was either ill or dead (sources differ as to exactly when he died) and York was involved in its own war with its Scandinavian neighbours over the ownership of Rutland. In 895 that great survivor Archbishop Wulfhere of York also died. The time was therefore ripe to remind the Northumbrians of their peace oath and to remove them from the military equation.

With the Vikings having so few remaining allies, it seems surprising that Alfred did not force one final battle at Bridgnorth, a decisive crushing blow to bring an Edington-like conclusion to this war. But the chronicles are silent. Instead we are merely told that the following summer 'the Danish army divided, one force going into East Anglia, and one into Northumbria; those that were moneyless got themselves ships and went south across the sea to the Seine.'

What happened at Bridgnorth in that winter of 895 will forever remain a mystery. Both sides now had reason to come to terms and such a practical but inglorious end to four years of war might explain the silence from a chronicle written for Alfred and designed to exalt his military achievements. But whether or not Alfred agreed that winter to pay one final Danegeld to ensure his enemy's departure, as some modern commentators maintain, or whether the Vikings simply sued for a peaceful exit from a long and bitter war, the result was undoubtedly a victory for Alfred.

Four years earlier, two Viking armies had landed in 330 ships laden with all their families and goods, having every intention not of raiding but of conquering Wessex for themselves. What they found, however, was a land whose king had found a way to neutralize the tactics that had made them the scourge of Europe. Wessex and Mercia were now organized and defended in depth, able to respond to attacks on any front and unwilling to be drawn into the cat-and-mouse stratagems of the previous war. Alfred had learnt that speed was the key to Viking success – their ability to draw defenders to one area and then slip away to another, to strike where they were least expected and disappear again before battle lines could be drawn. In response, he had defended his whole country with an adaptive network of strong points that allowed him to dictate the pace of war.

He had also gained a vital insight into the true nature of Viking raiding. Behind the tales of horror recorded by contemporary annalists, Viking armies were not great battle winners, but rather terrorists, attacking the weak and unsuspecting and sowing fear in their wake. Given the chance, a Viking army would not fight but would either swear peace (and then break it) or flee. When they found themselves in a kingdom that was defended throughout, where every place expected an attack and every place could be defended, they were out of their depth. Any single *burh* could be taken, but they could not all be taken, and those surrounding the one under threat had the men and resources to come to its aid.

Nor was Alfred himself playing the game they expected. Anglo-Saxon warrior kings (and Carolingians for that matter) found glory in open battle at the head of their armies. Alfred, however, did not. Instead of forming up a single cumbersome fyrd that could easily be sidestepped, he harried his enemy, never giving them time to settle, never giving them freedom to forage for food and never giving them freedom of movement. It made for an exhausting war for everyone concerned but the difference was that Wessex was prepared for it. Each *burh* was a source of refuge and of provisions for Alfred's armies, but it was off-limits to the raiders. Alfred's army was at home everywhere, whilst his enemy was at home nowhere.

Eventually, after twisting and turning for four years, those raiders had nowhere left to run. Wessex and Mercia were not for the taking, and those who wished to find new homes in England would either have to settle in the already Scandinavian territories of Northumbria and East Anglia, or return across the Channel to Francia and again try their luck there. It is not known how many made the Danelaw their choice but by this point the Viking force had clearly dwindled to a shadow of its former self. The host that had arrived in 330 ships – an army larger than Ivarr's or Guthrum's – set out across the Channel to Francia in just five. In short, their invasion had completely failed.

By the summer of 896, when Alfred watched the remnants of that Viking army sail away, he was an old man of forty-seven. He could not have guessed that they would be the last army he would ever face. As they vanished over the horizon, he returned once more to improving both the mental and physical defences of his country. He could never know it, but he finally had peace and he would have just three short years left in which to enjoy it.

The *Anglo-Saxon Chronicle*'s comment on the end of the war is curious, but it speaks volumes as to how Alfred had changed his kingdom. Instead of revelling in the dispersal of the enemy army, it takes a peculiarly downbeat, perhaps even a peculiarly 'English', line, saying: 'By the grace of God, the army had not on the whole afflicted the English people very greatly; but they were much more seriously afflicted in those years by the mortality of cattle and men.' Noting that disease was a greater enemy than the Vikings might have been true at one level but claiming that Hæsten's men had not troubled the English *very greatly* is disingenuous as best. What it does, of course, hint at is a certain pride in the manner with which the threat had been dissipated. It was awkward for the chronicler that the war had not ended with a classic set-piece battle in which his hero the king could lead out the men of the fyrd to total victory like a latter-day Beowulf. It was also awkward that the king had not been present at all the major engagements. Times, however, had changed and so his language had to change with it. Alfred was not simply a warlord, he was the administrator of a nascent kingdom, which operated very differently from the old pagan Anglo-Saxon kingdoms of centuries past. Alfred could not be everywhere at once so he delegated; he could not win wars like this through personal bravery, so he did not try to, and hence he could not be made to fit the model of the heroes from the old stories he so loved.

The chronicler was faced instead with an astute and careful king who had prepared his country well, who had analysed his enemy and used his resources – the bundles of wood of his metaphor – as best he could to bring a return to lasting peace as quickly as possible. So, when asked the question, 'How did they defeat such a terrible enemy?' the chronicler becomes perhaps the first Englishman to simply wave a nonchalant hand and casually say, 'Oh, it was nothing really.'

For all the *Anglo-Saxon Chronicle*'s sanguine indifference, the end of the land war did not bring a complete end to hostilities. Whilst Hæsten's men were no longer a threat, he had stirred up the East Anglians and Northumbrians and they proved harder to settle. In 896, Wessex was not confronted by all-out warfare but a return to endemic raiding by bands who were probably not under the direct control of their respective kings but who had regained a taste for piracy and were reluctant to give it up. After Bridgnorth, Alfred immediately turned his mind to the next step in safeguarding his country – securing his coast – as well as to dealing with these pirates in particular. The

Chronicle gives a detailed account of how he went about this, which shows the king continuing his energetic policies whilst also giving an insight into how sometimes even Alfred could be proved wrong.

We are told that the pirates worrying the coast were not equipped with the latest technology but were largely using 'the warships which they had built many years before'. These were presumably the craft left over from Ivarr and Guthrum's wars, which had gained a new lease of life in the recent conflict. The fact that they were old-fashioned vessels also suggests how effective Alfred and his men had been at destroying or confiscating the ships brought over by Hæsten. Faced with this enemy, Alfred typically set his mind to finding his own fresh solution and he believed he had found this in the ships themselves. If the Vikings were forced to use old ships, he would gain the upper hand by building new ones.

The vessels he had seen on his coast were either of the Scandinavian type suitable for pirate raiders or the Frisian-type ships that undertook much of the cross-Channel trade. The king decided that as neither was suitable to his needs, he would have to design his own 'as it seemed to him to be most useful'. The configuration he hit upon was considerably larger than that of previous vessels, being twice as long as some and manned by sixty or more oars. This may have simply been due to the fact that Alfred could muster fighting men more easily than he could find shipbuilders and sailors. If he could not have a great many ships, he would have a few large ships carrying a bigger crew. This gave an advantage in the traditional naval battles of the day where an attacking ship would be lashed to its victim and the crew would jump aboard for hand-to-hand combat. Larger ships would be more stable during such attacks and could hold more men for the actual fighting than those of the enemy.

If these were Alfred's main considerations, however, he had made a mistake. Large ships were all well and good out to sea, but Viking naval actions were more likely to occur close in to shore, where Alfred's patrols might come across raiders in the creeks and estuaries of southern England. This created difficulties for the king's new ships, of which the *Anglo-Saxon Chronicle* gives a timely example.

During 896 six Viking vessels began raiding the Isle of Wight and the Dorset shore using their usual hit-and-run tactics to loot coastal settlements. The effects were severe enough to be brought to the attention of the king. He ordered a squadron of nine of his new ships to intercept and destroy them. Patrolling down the coast, they found the Vikings in an estuary on the south coast. Three of the enemy ships were drawn up on land whilst their crews raided inland. The other three were still afloat, however, and when they saw the English take up a position blocking their escape route out of the estuary, they attacked. Initially the battle went very well for Alfred's fleet, with the first two enemy ships being boarded and their crews killed. Whilst attacking the third vessel, however, the heavier English ships, with their deeper draught, ran aground, leaving a remaining skeleton crew of just five men on the third Viking vessel to escape with their ship.

It was at this moment that the three other pirate crews began returning to their boats. The English suddenly found themselves in a precarious position. Three of their vessels were stuck fast on the same side of the estuary as the Vikings, whilst the other six had grounded on the far bank and were unable to help. As the tide fell the Vikings saw their opportunity. If they had to fight, they were not going to wait until the other six English ships could join in, so they waded through the thick mud towards the three stricken English vessels. First they would pick off these three crews, then wait and see what time and tide brought to them. For the English trapped on board, there was nothing for it but to fight, and nothing for their compatriots on the other bank to do but watch.

The battle on the riverbank was fierce and bloody, with one of Alfred's officials and a member of his household losing their lives. Along with them died a number of Frisians and their specific mention in the *Anglo-Saxon Chronicle* can be taken to imply that such a loss was worth noting. The peoples of Frisia and England had a lot in common. Their languages and even their cultures were very similar; they were both Christian, both victims of the Vikings and hence allies. Unlike the English, however, the Frisians were formidable sailors. The great traders of the ninth century, they pried the waters of the Channel and the North Sea, creating their own communities in English trading towns such as York. Because their seamanship was so well known in England, Alfred had wanted to harness it. They were therefore as valuable as his boats, so their deaths were recorded with real sadness.

In total, sixty-two English sailors lost their lives in the fight, compared to 120 Vikings, but by the time the English had the upper hand the tide had risen far enough to refloat the lighter Viking ships. Their crews used the opportunity to escape while Alfred's boats were still stuck fast. We can only imagine the jibes shouted across the water as the pirates slipped away although any triumphalism on their part would prove premature. With severely depleted and injured crews, two of the vessels foundered on the Sussex coast and were washed ashore where their occupants were captured. Only one of the raiders limped safely home to East Anglia.

This first encounter was hardly a great success for Alfred's new design of ship. He had failed to take into account the lessons he had learnt so well on land – that speed and manoeuvrability were every-thing – and had hence lost the initiative. His boats were too large and cumbersome for coastal engagement, drawing too much water and changing direction with difficulty. But even this was only a partial failure. Considering the scale of almost unopposed raiding that had plagued his coast for much of his reign, the mere fact of having a fleet was a success in itself and although the losses had been heavy they were nothing compared to those of the enemy. Of the six Viking ships that had been terrorizing the Isle of Wight and Dorset, two had been captured and their crews killed, two more had been driven ashore and their crews captured, one had escaped with only five men left on board, and just one other had returned home intact, although even its crew was described as 'greatly wounded'. Nor would the captured crews live to fight another day. Brought before Alfred at Winchester, they were about to see another side to this famously forgiving man. No bargains would be struck with these men, no oaths made, no payments offered to leave. Instead he ordered them all to be hanged. They were pirates and they deserved a pirate's death.

No doubt such raiders remained an annoyance for the rest of Alfred's life, but they were no more than a slight affront to his royal dignity. The tactics and the nautical ability of his new fleet must have improved with time and the reports that came back to East Anglia with those Vikings who survived even that first incompetent attack must have discouraged others. For the remaining years of Alfred's life, the *Anglo-Saxon Chronicle* records no major attacks, no enemy incur-sions, no sacking of cities or even any pirate raids. It was the most peaceful time that Alfred had ever known, a time when he could return to what he considered the real work of defence, of creating a safe land filled with what he hoped would be intelligent, well-read and pious subjects. A time to return to that forest from which he had taken the timber to build a nation where perhaps he might now 'pleasantly and peacefully dwell therewith both in winter and summer – as I have not yet done!'

18

Great

I watched four fair creatures
travelling together; they left black tracks
behind them. The support of the bird
moved swiftly; it flew in the sky,
dived under the waves. The struggling warrior continuously
    toiled, pointing out the paths
to all four over the fine gold.

      Anglo-Saxon Riddle, quoted in K. Crossley-
      Holland, *The Anglo-Saxon World*, p. 222

A LFRED'S LAST YEARS saw his great scheme to restock the libraries
of his kingdom finally bear fruit. His translation programme
actually continued throughout the dislocations of the previous war,
further proof of how well the new state of greater Wessex had
weathered this last storm. His first personal contribution, the translation of Pope Gregory's *Pastoral Care*, was probably finished during the
war and copies sent to each of the bishoprics in the kingdom. It was his
proudest moment, in which we may well get as physically close as we
ever can to the king.

Before sending out this, the first fruits of his own labours, Alfred
tells us that he ordered an 'æstel worth 50 mancuses' to be placed in
each copy. What an *æstel* was remains open to interpretation although
the term probably comes from the Latin *hastula*, meaning a small spear
or splinter. Later mediaeval sources suggest that the term was used for a
bookmarker or book pointer, either to mark a place or to help a reader
follow each line as they read. Such an item would be ideal to
accompany Alfred's book. It would also give the king an opportunity
to fulfil his old Anglo-Saxon duty as a ring-giver by presenting his
bishops with a precious jewel to accompany his precious book. And it

would speak to all who saw it of the wealth and sophistication of his court, where, Asser tells us, he employed 'his craftsmen, who were skilled in every earthly craft and whom he had assembled and commissioned in almost countless quantity from many races'.

Remarkably there is even a chance that one of these *æstels* survives. In 1693 an object was discovered in a cart rut at North Petherton, near Athelney in Somerset. It was a jewel from the late ninth century, consisting of a gold frame holding in place a block of transparent rock crystal over a cloisonné enamel picture of a seated figure. Three things immediately aroused interest in this strange object, beyond its obvious value, and in 1718 it was given to the University of Oxford where it could be studied more closely. The first noteworthy point about the jewel was the figure. Decorated in vivid blue and green enamel, it depicts a seated man holding two 'stalks' with what appear to be flowers or decorations at one end. This figure has been variously identified as a king holding the sceptres of his regalia, a saint, the pope or even Alexander the Great. Perhaps more likely is that the figure is Christ, holding two floral-headed sceptres and representing 'the wisdom of God incarnate'. More recently it has even been suggested that the figure may be a personification of Sight as it bears some resemblance to the near-contemporary Fuller Brooch in the British Museum on which are depicted the five senses.

The second interesting thing about the jewel is the shape. The gold frame, and the rock crystal cover, both taper at one end and the frame becomes the head of a ferocious mythical beast holding something in its mouth. The nature of that something remains a mystery as all that has survived is the empty socket and the pin that once held whatever it was in place. Nevertheless, there is every possibility that it was the wooden or even ivory pointer of an *æstel*.

But it is the final point of interest that brings us closest to Alfred and to the great literacy scheme that he began. Around the frame of the jewel an inscription is cut in fine gold openwork, which reads: +AELFRED MEC HEHT GEWYRCAN — 'Alfred Had Me Made'. Here is our clearest direct contact with the king himself, in a simple statement that says everything about the man and his times. If this is indeed one of those valuable markers sent out by the king with his books, then here we might have a rare piece of physical evidence for Alfred's world – an object he once proudly held and a symbol of everything he hoped for. Certainly it was a precious jewel, perhaps the finest piece of Anglo-Saxon craftsmanship since the creation of the Sutton Hoo treasure 250 years earlier. Like that treasure, it also carried a message over and above its sheer bullion value. It showed the king's wealth and generosity, but it also carried a message about his great project, in the figure of Christ (or Sight) as the personification of wisdom. This, Alfred believed, could only be had through the reading of books.

More books now followed in quick succession. The translation of Orosius's *Seven Books of History Against the Pagans* was in circulation by the early 890s. By 893, with the Vikings still at large in England, Wærferth of Worcester finished his translation of Pope Gregory's *Dialogues*. Alfred himself moved on to his Boethius, and then St Augustine's *Soliloquies*, whilst unknown hands worked on Bede's great *History* and the urgent new entries in the *Anglo-Saxon Chronicle*, which, during the last war, gain an immediacy that almost suggests Alfred's personal recounting of events.

But with the end of the war, and without further comment from Asser, our personal connection with Alfred loosens. The king's final years are an enigma, not because there was anything to hide but because the need for a dramatic narrative of his reign had gone, fled with the Vikings back into the Danelaw and back over the sea to Francia. What we do know is that he continued his work, both in building the physical structure of his nation and in providing it with the spiritual tools that he believed it needed.

In 898 or perhaps slightly later, Alfred and his witan met at Chelsea to discuss further the restoration and rebuilding of London. This incident provides our last glimpse of the living Alfred in the records. Here the king confirmed the land grant that he had previously made to Bishop Wærferth, together with a new grant next door to Archbishop Plegmund, allowing both men to moor boats on the wharves alongside their plots. Foremost in his mind was still the need to make his *burhs* commercial successes, not simply military forts, and in granting prime lands to his most faithful servants he hoped to stimulate the trade that would make his city flourish. And it did. Those wharves would form the seed around which a new port of London would slowly grow until, by the end of the seventeenth century, London had become the largest, busiest and wealthiest city on earth.

There was also time for a final personal project. All his life Alfred had carried with him his *handboc*, his commonplace book, adding new texts and prayers to the lists of religious services and the Psalter (the collection of Psalms) that had formed its core. Indeed, his whole plan to promote literacy amongst his people might be said to have formed around that kernel. And now he returned to those Psalms, those 150 songs and laments from an ancient world so alien to his but in whose thoughts and passions were reflected his own. Asser tells us that Alfred had a particular fondness for the Psalter, so translating it was not solely a valuable exercise in turning into English one of the most important texts of the Middle Ages, but a labour of love. At the time the Psalter was divided into three books of fifty psalms each; indeed, in Ireland at the time it was known as 'the three fifties', but of these we only now have Alfred's translation of the first third. That he should leave unfinished what he must have considered his greatest of works seems impossible in so devout and dedicated a man. If logic and the later chronicler William of Malmesbury are to be believed, the reason for this is that the king simply ran out of time.

Alfred died six nights before All Hallows Day, on Friday, 26 October 899. He was either fifty or fifty-one years old. Naturally, his passing is marked in the *Anglo-Saxon Chronicle* but its entry for so momentous an event is surprisingly downbeat. This document had been created to prepare the way for the House of Ecgberht – to show the world that the destiny of Alfred and his heirs was to rule the country he had raised from the ashes. And yet when it comes to that founding father's death, it simply states: 'He was king over the whole English people, except for that part which was under Danish rule, and he had held the kingdom for one and a half years less than thirty; and then his son Edward succeeded to the kingdom.'

There is in fact little emotion expressed in the *Anglo-Saxon Chronicle* at this date over any death so perhaps this matter-of-fact notice is only to be expected. The great encomia for dead kings would have to wait for later writers and Alfred's heirs. But for all its terse nature, the *Chronicle* does declare that Alfred was 'king over the whole English people' before somewhat bashfully qualifying that with 'except for that part which was under Danish rule'. It is a great statement, modestly put. There had been bretwaldas before, men as great as Offa who for all their threats and bluster had seen their dynastic plans collapse within a generation. There had been heroes and saints arrayed against the pagans but the martyr's crowns that they gained had always been at the expense of their earthly ones. And then there had been Alfred.

Alfred was the only true survivor of the Viking attacks of the ninth century. The Anglo-Saxon royal House of Mercia had gone for ever along with those of East Anglia and Northumbria. Across the water Charlemagne's Frankish empire lay shattered in a thousand warring pieces, still picked over by the Viking ravens. Alfred alone had survived and the way that he had found to do it began a revolution. The integration of the *burhs* into the defensive system of Wessex gave its people a vested interest in providing for their defence and, for the first time, gave them some say in their destiny. Once a hunted man, driven into a lonely wilderness, Alfred had brought together his people with a vision that left far behind the vested and fractious interests of the wealthy elites, and that led to the provision of opportunity and access, if not for all, then for many more. Alfred found a way to make the survival of Wessex, his Wessex, everyone's concern and everyone's business by granting them each their own refuge, their own Athelney. In doing so he cut across the dynastic fault lines that regularly tore apart Anglo-Saxon states, by distributing the country's wealth, power and self-determination far beyond the confined ranks of his nobles. He then set about creating a government in which he personally did not have to act in all things but could, through literacy, ensure that the king's justice was meted out fairly and uniformly across his kingdom. Furthermore, in demanding literacy amongst those charged with dispensing that justice, he ensured that his officers obeyed his writ and remained accountable for their actions.

Alfred wanted a kingdom where the people of each market town would want to defend their property and their king because their prosperity *was* the state's prosperity and therefore they had something to gain from its protection. If England is a nation of shopkeepers, as Napoleon once jibed, it was Alfred's doing and it is perhaps his and the country's greatest achievement. It was still a long way from universal suffrage and a welfare state but it marked the beginnings of aspiration in English society – being given the opportunity and having the belief that it was possible to die in a different financial or social condition than the one you had been born into. As such, even in the ninth century, it held within it the seeds of the Industrial Revolution and hence the origins of the modern world. The brainchild of one who had known what it was to be an outsider, it was the single unifying thought of the age and under his descendants it became the template for the building of the nation of England.

The man who took up that challenge was Alfred's eldest son Edward. He had already proved himself as a warrior at Farnham and his father had made careful provision for him in his will, granting him extensive lands across the kingdom to ensure his succession. This was the man who stood in the autumnal gloom of the Old Minster at Winchester, made even darker than usual by the towering presence of the New Minster already rising up next to it, as his father's body was laid to rest. But with him that day, along with the ghosts of his father and St Swithun, was another more unwelcome spectre from Alfred's past – the ghost of Chippenham.

The transition from Alfred's reign to that of Edward the Elder's was not as smooth as the old king would have hoped. He had worked hard to clear the way for Edward and, if a charter from Rochester dated 898 is to be trusted, had even made him his co-ruler by that date. But in the same will that gave his son the money and lands with which he needed to secure the kingdom lay the clues to another betrayal. Many years before at Langdene, the other princes of the blood – the children of Alfred's older brothers – had been forced to remain bystanders as Alfred laid the groundwork for his will. At that meeting all the witan had agreed that Alfred had the right to leave what he wanted to whom he wanted and, as they well knew, that meant leaving everything to his own children.

At the time no one dared gainsay so powerful a ruler, but now, with Alfred gone, one of those kinsmen felt wronged and took steps to betray the dead king's wishes one final time. Æthelwold, the son of Alfred's older brother Æthelred, was not happy to see the throne pass to Edward and he immediately moved to seize the old family sites of Wimborne, where his father was buried, and Twinham (now Christchurch, Hampshire). Æthelwold hoped that these family power centres, like Burgred's at Repton, would hold the keys to the kingdom and from here he intended to fight for the throne. Barricaded behind the walls of Wimborne, he announced that he 'would either live there or die there' – a bold if rather vainglorious call for the witan to choose between the children of Æthelred and the children of Alfred. But the ealdormen of Wessex did not reply.

Edward, however, replied in forceful manner. Three miles to the north-west of Wimborne stands Badbury Rings, another of those Iron Age forts that had gained a new lease of life in the troubled years of the ninth century. It stands now much as it did then, a formidable battery of grassy ditches and banks cut around a hill in ages long past and for reasons that were already long forgotten in Edward's day. But this was where he now brought and camped the fyrd, not for the protection offered by its concentric rings of ramparts but for its vantage point over Wimborne away in the distance. It was a tactic designed to intimidate and it worked. With Edward's loyal fyrd darkening the skyline, the rebellious Æthelwold chose neither to live nor die at his Wimborne stronghold, but instead ran away.

If Æthelwold had hoped for support from others in the witan as he staked his claim in Wimborne, he was mistaken. The traitorous Ealdorman Wulfhere had been closely associated with his father and he may have hoped that he could inspire a similar opposition movement in others. But Wulfhere was gone – certainly disinherited and possibly dead – and no other ealdorman seems to have answered his call. This was not the witan that had made Æthelwulf or Æthelred, but a witan made *by* Alfred. Æthelwold was forced north to a greater betrayal, back to the people who had provided the force behind the original Chippenham coup, back to the Vikings.

In Northumbria, Æthelwold seems to have been accepted either as king (according to some versions of the *Anglo-Saxon Chronicle*) or at least as a rightful, or useful, claimant to the throne of Wessex. As such he was able to mobilize a fleet to sail south and take Essex, before fomenting rebellion amongst the always troublesome Vikings of East Anglia. It was becoming clear that Æthelwold would only be happy with an outcome decided on the battlefield. Events finally came to a head in 903 at Holme where Edward the Elder faced his cousin in person.

It could on one level so easily have been a second coup. If the witan had turned against Edward whilst Æthelwold was in Wimborne, Alfred's line might have been extinguished. Later, if he had been able to call up a sufficiently threatening Viking army to overawe the ealdormen of the eastern shires and persuade them to join him rather than fight him, Æthelwold might have come to the throne with merely the threat of violence. Even without them, he must still have hoped that, backed by the Northumbrians and East Anglians, he could at least repeat the feats of Guthrum.

But the Wessex of 903 was a different country to what it had been in 878. The ealdormen now preferred the benefits of a larger, stable kingdom, as reconstructed by Alfred and inherited by his son, to the promises of a pretender. If the men of the eastern counties were frightened by the appearance of a Viking army under Æthelwold (and Edward had to make seven appeals to the men of Kent to get them to join him), they were not, in the end, overawed, knowing who ultimately was the stronger. At rock bottom, if Æthelwold hoped to repeat the successes of Guthrum, he was living in the past. Alfred had completely overhauled the defence and administration of his realm, giving his son those vital tools with which to defeat this last claimant.

The outcome at Holme was decisive. The Viking king of East Anglia was killed, as was Brihtsige (possibly a Mercian 'B' dynast trying to make a comeback) and, finally, Æthelwold himself. Alfred had fortified his country in body and mind after his own betrayal. The success of that work was reaped by his son, who would go on to begin the conquest of the Danelaw and the creation of a single nation called England. It was a legacy worthy of the title 'Great'.

But it was not the Anglo-Saxon chronicler who granted Alfred that title, 'Great'. His concern was with promoting the living member of the House of Ecgberht and, with Alfred's death, his pen moved on 'over the fine gold' to record Edward's story. Indeed, no Anglo-Saxon dubbed Alfred great. Whilst Grimbald would soon become St Grimbald, whilst Alfred's wife would be remembered fondly as 'The true and beloved lady of the English', and his daughter would receive the title 'The Lady of the Mercians', Alfred was to them simply 'King Alfred'.

This is not to say that they were not aware of his achievements or fond of his memory. Bishop Wulfsige, in the poem he attached by way of a preface to the translation of Gregory's *Dialogues*, calls him: 'Alfred of the English, the greatest treasure-giver of all the kings he had ever heard tell of, in recent times or long ago, or of any earthly king he had previously learned of.' But to the Anglo-Saxons of a nascent England he was only a beginning. The full credit for the work that he set in train would ultimately go to those descendants who turned Alfred's idea of England into a reality.

Instead, what eventually made Alfred 'Great' was not his military victories or his administrative reforms but what he loved best – his books. Alfred's translations were well known throughout the later Anglo-Saxon period and beyond, and by the time a new generation of historians appeared after the Norman Conquest his reputation was already that of the wisest of kings. In the works of Simeon of Durham, William of Malmesbury, Henry of Huntingdon, Florence of Worcester, Geoffrey Gaimar and many others, his mediaeval reputation was nurtured and his love of learning held up as a mirror for all rulers. Tales gleaned from Asser and the *Anglo-Saxon Chronicle* were elaborated on and 'improved' with supposedly Alfredian proverbs and bons mots until he became the epitome of wisdom. It was in this role then, finally, in the sixteenth century, that historians first began to call him 'Alfred the Great'.

In the post-mediaeval era his fame continued to grow in a newly confident and increasingly imperialistic England, where he began to be held up not simply as a example of wise kingship but as the founder of a nation with a destiny to rule the world. He was seen as having planted the seed that would grow into England but which would go on to become Great Britain and expand from there across the globe. He was rapidly becoming the foundation myth of the British Empire and it is perhaps no surprise to find that the song 'Rule Britannia' first occurs in *Alfred: a Masque* produced in 1740. Not that Britain had a monopoly on the king. The fledgling United States Navy also claimed Alfred for its founder and their first flagship, brought into commission during the War of Independence to fight the British, was proudly named *Alfred*.

By this point the image of Alfred was already becoming clouded once more. The quiet wisdom that had seen the translation of those books 'most necessary for all men to know' had been superseded by an almost superhuman omnipotence. The dogged determination of Alfred's fightback from Athelney had been transformed into the first triumph of a nation of Christian soldiers with a duty to bring the benefits of Anglo-Saxon government to the whole world (whether they liked it or not). The real Alfred had disappeared again into the mists of the Somerset Levels, behind the smoke rising from the oven where the cakes still lay burning.

What had happened to the real Alfred? Even his physical remains were by this time long lost. After his initial burial in the Old Minster at Winchester in 899, his body had been moved to the New Minster next door on its consecration in 903. Here, to one side of the altar, he rested next to his wife Ealhswith for the rest of the Saxon period. In 1066, however, William the Conqueror, a descendant of Alfred's Viking contemporary Hralf the Walker, the founder of the Norman state, seized the throne of England and began sweeping away memories of the Anglo-Saxon royal past. The Old Minster was to be replaced with a Norman cathedral, and the New Minster and its monks were to be moved to Hyde Abbey, just beyond the city's walls. The bones of many of the old kings were gathered up during that building project and reside today in the boxes that stand above the choir screens in Winchester Cathedral. Here are the jumbled remains of Ecgberht and Æthelwulf but Alfred is not with them. His bones were taken up by the monks of New Minster and went with them to Hyde Abbey where he was reinterred in front of the high altar and where he remained until the Dissolution of the Monasteries.

After the Dissolution, the old king's grave fared less well. The site of Hyde Abbey was turned into a private house and the site of his burial was forgotten. Later, in 1788, it became a Bridewell – a 'house of correction' – and one of the first jobs of the prisoners was to clear the site of rubble. In the process they uncovered Alfred's tomb, which the prison warden later told an antiquarian was made from a single block of stone encased with lead. He also told him of the tomb's fate. The prisoners had stripped off the lead and sold it, emptied out the bones and fragments of clothing, then broken up the coffin and reburied it, empty. Alfred's now unidentifiable remains are probably still lying in Winchester, scattered in the topsoil somewhere between a row of Victorian houses and a car park.

But Alfred is not gone. His influence continues to resonate through the modern world like that of no other mediaeval king. His ghost is not in one part of Winchester but in all of it. The streets of the city centre are laid out to the plan he first devised, as are those of dozens of other towns across England, and their existence and prosperity owe their beginnings to him. Something of him still also resides in the laws that govern those towns and the nation beyond, and in his belief that the government of the country should be conducted, and conducted accountably, in the language of its people – English. But most of all

Alfred lives on in his books, in his own words – the words that made him 'Great'. These are the thoughts of a king from eleven hundred years ago who can still talk directly to us from the beautiful, terrible world of the ninth century and explain the events that led him to sow the seed of a nation:

> In the midst of prosperity the mind is elated, and in prosperity a man forgets himself; in hardship he is forced to reflect on himself, even though he be unwilling. In prosperity a man often destroys the good he has done; amidst difficulties he often repairs what he long since did in the way of wickedness.

Notes

Abbreviations

AB – J. Nelson (trans.), *Annals of St Bertin*, Ninth Century Histories, vol. I, Manchester University Press, 1991

AG – S. Keynes and M. Lapidge (trans.), *Alfred the Great: Asser's Life of King Alfred and Other Contemporary Sources*, Penguin Books, 1983

ASC – *Anglo-Saxon Chronicle*

AW – K. Crossley-Holland, *The Anglo-Saxon World*, The Boydell Press, 1982

EHD – D. Whitelock (ed.), *English Historical Documents*, vol. I, Eyre & Spottiswode, 1968

Prologue: Losing Alfred, pp. 7–18

9 'A proiect touching'. Petition drawn up by Robert Cotton, John Dodderidge and James Ley, Cotton MS Faustina E.V., f. 89.

10 'in ye Room above the Library'. Report of Humphrey Wanley's Commission to the House of Commons concerning the Cotton Library, Bodleian MS Add. D. 82, f. ii.

12 '23 [Oct.]. A Fire broke out'. *Gentleman's Magazine*, 1 (1731), 451.

13 'The Right Honorable the Speaker'. Report from the Committee Appointed to View the Cottonian Library . . . [signed by] W. Whiston, printed for R. Williamson and W. Bowyer, 1732.

15 'most wretched edition'. Hearne, Collections (OHS).

17 'safely relegated to the relative obscurity'. C. Plummer, *The Life and Times of Alfred the Great*, p. 8.

1: The Prophecy of Jeremiah, pp. 19–40

23 'a hunter can't afford to be timid'. *Ælfric's Colloquies*, quoted in B. Raffel and A. Olsen, *Poems and Prose from the Old English*, p. 205.

23 'eels and pike, minnows, trout'. *Ælfric's Colloquies*, op. cit., p. 206.

23 'Not I! . . . catching whales is dangerous'. *Ælfric's Colloquies*, op. cit., pp. 206–7.

24 'Is there a man'. *Ælfric's Colloquies*, op. cit., p. 209.

24 'the staff of life'. *Ælfric's Colloquies*, op. cit., p. 210.

24 'because he provides us'. *Ælfric's Colloquies*, op. cit., p. 211.

24 'No matter who or what you are.' *Ælfric's Colloquies*, op. cit., p. 212.

27 'contra paganos marinos'. S134, MSS: 1, BL Cotton Jul. D. ii, 105 v.– 106 r. (s. xiii).

27 'dire portents appeared'. ASC (D) (793), quoted in EHD, I, p. 167.

27–8 'In that same year'. *Historia Regum*, attrib. Simeon of Durham, quoted in EHD, I, p. 247.

30 'Consider carefully, brothers'. Letter of Alcuin to Ethelred, king of Northumbria (793, after 8 June), quoted in EHD, I, no. 193, p. 776.

30 'Behold, judgment has begun'. Letter of Alcuin to Ethelred, king of Northumbria (793, after 8 June), quoted in EHD, I, no. 193 p. 777.

30 'was well merited'. Letter of Alcuin to Higbald, bishop of Lindisfarne and his monks (793, after 8 June), quoted in EHD, I, no. 194, p. 778.

30 'youths taken into captivity'. Letter of Alcuin to Higbald, bishop of Lindisfarne and his monks (793, after 8 June), quoted in EHD, I, no. 194, p. 779.

31 'Out of the north'. Jeremiah 1: 14, King James Version.

31 'from east to west'. ASC (815), quoted in EHD, I, no. 1, p. 170.

33 'He was the eighth king'. ASC (D) (829), quoted in EHD, I, no. 1, p. 171.

36 'great slaughter'. ASC (836), quoted in EHD, I, no. 1, p. 172.

37 'both Cornish and Danes'. ASC (838), quoted in EHD, I, no. 1, p. 172.

38 'unjust acts'. ASC (757), quoted in EHD, I, no. 1, p. 162.

38 'For truly, as I think'. Letter of Alcuin to the Mercian ealdorman Osbert (796–7), quoted in EHD, I, no. 201, p. 787.

39 'we ourselves and our heirs'. S1438 in J. Campbell, *The Anglo-Saxons*, p. 140.

40 'The lines of blood'. *Annals of St Bertin* (839), quoted in AB, p. 43.

40 'sins of men'. *Annals of St Bertin* (839), quoted in AB, p. 43.

40 'for three days and nights'. *Annals of St Bertin* (839), quoted in AB, p. 43.

2: *Invitation from the Wolf, pp. 41–58*

42 'bishops, priests and scholars'. *Annals of Ulster* (U840.1), CELT (Corpus of Electronic Texts): a project of University College, Cork, College Road, Cork, Ireland.

43 'This was surely'. *Annals of St Bertin* (841), quoted in AB, p. 51.

43 'heathen men'. ASC (841), quoted in EHD, I, no. 1, p. 173.

44 'gold-friend'. *The Wanderer*, quoted in AW, p. 47.

44 'gift-throne'. *The Wanderer*, quoted in AW, p. 48.

44 'Accept this cup'. *Beowulf*, quoted in AW, p. 97.

44 'at the same time'. Restoration by Berhtwulf, king of Mercia, of various estates to the Church of Worcester (28 March 840), quoted in EHD, I, no. 86, p. 480.

46 'Farewell, and as soon as.' Letter of Lupus, abbot of Ferrières, to Ealdsige, abbot of York (852), quoted in EHD, I, no. 216, p. 808.

47 'I pray that my petition'. Letter of Lupus, abbot of Ferrières, to Felix, King Æthelwulf's secretary (852), quoted in EHD, I, no. 218, p. 810.

49 'On the spear side'. The will of King Alfred (873–88), quoted in EHD, I, no. 96, note 1, p. 495.

52 'Young men must always'. *The Wife's Lament*, quoted in AW, p. 53.

52 'famous butler'. Asser, *Life of King Alfred*, Ch. 2, quoted in AG, p. 68.

53 'Because of the difficulty'. William of Malmesbury, quoted in S. Crawford, *Childhood in Anglo-Saxon England*, p. 112.

54 'Alfred found learning dead'. Inscription on the statue of Alfred the Great, Wantage, Oxfordshire.

55 'remained ignorant of letters'. Asser, *Life of King Alfred*, Ch. 22, quoted in AG, p. 75.

55 'However, he was a careful listener'. Asser, *Life of King Alfred*, Ch. 22, quoted in AG, p. 75.

58 'made a great slaughter'. ASC (845), quoted in EHD, I, no. 1, p. 173.

3: *The Decimation of Æthelwulf, pp. 59–78*

61 'found Rome built of brick'. Suetonius, *Lives of the Twelve Caesars*, Ch. XXIX.

63 'At this time the lord Pope'. Asser, *Life of King Alfred*, Ch. 8, quoted in AG, p. 69.

64 'we have now graciously'. Extract from a letter of Pope Leo IV to Æthelwulf, king of Wessex (853), quoted in EHD, I, no. 219, p. 810.

68 'I, Æthelwulf, king'. Grant by Æthelwulf, king of Wessex, in connection with the tithing of his land, of land near Rochester to his thegn Dunn (855), quoted in EHD, I, no. 89, p. 484.

68 'beyond the sea to Rome'. Grant by Æthelwulf, king of Wessex, in connection with the tithing of his land, of land near Rochester to his thegn Dunn (855), (EHD, I, no. 89, p. 484) as translated in C. Plummer, *The Life and Times of Alfred the Great*, p. 74.

76 'indescribable forbearance'. Asser, *Life of King Alfred*, Ch. 13, quoted in AG, p. 71.

76 'the entire nation was'. Asser, *Life of King Alfred*, Ch. 13, quoted in AG, pp. 70–1.

77 'Yea, kings may rule'. Boethius, *Consolation of Philosophy*, Alfredian translation, Ch. XXIX, quoted in Walter John Sedgefield (trans.), *King Alfred's Version of the 'Consolations' of Boethius, Done into Modern English, with an Introduction.*

77 'In this document'. Asser, *Life of King Alfred*, Ch. 16, quoted in AG, p. 72.

78 'he enjoined on his successors'. Asser, *Life of King Alfred*, Ch. 16, quoted in AG, p. 73.

4: Legends of the North, pp. 79–94

80 'what you would really call men'. Maes Howe, chamber tomb translation, quoted in Graham-Campbell et al (eds), *A Cultural Atlas of the Viking World*, p. 142.

82 'But because their association'. *Annals of St Bertin* (859), quoted in AB, p. 89.

83 'the Vikings were cut down'. Asser, *Life of King Alfred*, Ch. 18, quoted in AG, p. 74.

87–8 'Now, make a bier for me'. Dudo of St Quentin's *Gesta Normannorum*, ed. and trans. Felice Lifshitz, II, f. 8 v. to 12 v: available online at http://www.the-orb.net/orb_done/dudo/dudintro.html.

89 'Three nights together'. 'Saga of Ragnar Lothbrok', *The Saga of the Volsungs, the Saga of Ragnar Lodbrok, together with the Lay of Kraka*, trans. Margaret Schlauch, New York: Norton, 1930; reprinted New York: The American Scandinavian Foundation, 1949, 1964; reprinted New York: AMS Press, 1976.

90 'because of the way he was'. *The Tale of the Sons of Ragnar*, P. Tunstall (trans.), 2003.

90 'Æthelbald . . . against God's'. Asser, *Life of King Alfred*, Ch. 17, quoted in AG, p. 73.

91 'But to wed one's stepmother'. Bede, *A History of the English Church and People*, trans. Leo Shirley-Price, Book I, Ch. 27, p. 74.

93 'Æthelred and I'. The will of King Alfred (873–88), quoted in EHD, I, no. 96, p. 492.

5: The Arrival of the Sons of Ragnar, pp. 95–111

96 'I asked him [Æthelred]'. The will of King Alfred (873–88), quoted in EHD, I, no. 96, p. 492.

96 'and he said that he would'. The will of King Alfred (873–88), quoted in EHD, I, no. 96, p. 492.

97 'united through the devil'. Abbo of Fleury's *Life of St Edmund, King of East Anglia before 870*, from the Anglo-Saxon version as it appears in Sweet's *Anglo-Saxon Primer*, pp. 81–7.

98 'The Northmen who had sacked'. *Annals of St Bertin* (865), quoted in AB, p. 129.

99 'with no hereditary right'. ASC (867), quoted in EHD, I, no. 1, p. 1176.

99 'The little pigs would grunt'. Saxo Grammaticus, *The Danish History*, Book IX, in Oliver Elton (trans.), *The Nine Books of the Danish History of Saxo Grammaticus*, p. 4.

103 'Ivarr, who dwelt in York'. *The Tale of the Sons of Ragnar*, P. Tunstall (trans.), personal communication.

106 'Since the pagans'. Asser, *Life of King Alfred*, Ch. 30, quoted in AG, p. 77.

109 'God chastiseth every son'. Letter of Alcuin to Higbald, bishop of Lindisfarne and his monks (793, after 8 June), quoted in EHD, I, no. 194, p. 778, quoting Hebrews 12: 6.

110 'All this Elias'. *Bald's Leechbook*, Book 2, Ch. 64, quoted in O. Cockayne, (ed.), *Leechdoms, Wortcunning and Starcraft in Early England*.

110 'inward tenderness'. *Bald's Leechbook*, Book 2, Ch. 64, quoted in O. Cockayne (ed.), *Leechdoms, Wortcunning and Starcraft in Early England*.

6: The Wild Boar of Ashdown, pp. 112–128

113 'Pippin, son of Pippin'. *Annals of St Bertin* (864), quoted in AB, p. 111.

113 'traitor to his fatherland'. *Annals of St Bertin* (864), quoted in AB, p. 119.

115 'just like a wolf'. Abbo of Fleury's *Life of St Edmund, King of East Anglia before 870*, op. cit., pp. 81–7.

115 'Ivarr, our king, bold'. Abbo of Fleury's *Life of St Edmund, King of East Anglia before 870*, op. cit., pp. 81–7.

116 'He was entirely covered'. Abbo of Fleury's *Life of St Edmund, King of East Anglia before 870*, op. cit., pp. 81–7.

116 'Where are you now, friend? . . . 'Here, here, here'. Abbo of Fleury's *Life of St. Edmund, King of East Anglia before 870*, op. cit., pp. 81–7.

118 '10 vats of honey'. The laws of Ine (70.1), quoted in EHD, I, no. 32, p. 371.

119 'great slaughter'. ASC (871), quoted in EHD, I, no. 1, p. 177.

120 'the Danes had possession'. ASC (871), quoted in EHD, I, no. 1, p. 177.

122 'declaring firmly that'. Asser, *Life of King Alfred*, Ch. 37, quoted in AG, p. 79.

122 'like a wild boar'. Asser, *Life of King Alfred*, Ch. 38, quoted in AG, p. 79.

123 'the entire Viking army was put'. Asser, *Life of King Alfred*, Ch. 39, quoted in AG, pp. 79–80.

126 'and each of us gave to the other'. The will of King Alfred (873–88), quoted in EHD, I, no. 96, p. 493.

7: The Lonely King, pp. 129–145

130 'as soon as they saw the place'. Rudolf of Fulda, *Life of Leofgyth, abbess of Tauberbischofsheim*, quoted in EHD, I, no. 159, p. 720.

131 'In the island of Britain'. Rudolf of Fulda, *Life of Leofgyth, abbess of Tauberbischofsheim*, quoted in EHD, I, no. 159, p. 719.

132 'took over the government'. Asser, *Life of King Alfred*, Ch. 42, quoted in AG, p. 80.

132 'Look . . . you know that desire'. Alfred the Great's translation of Boethius' *The Consolation of Philosophy*, XVII, quoted in AG, p. 132.

133 'victorious in virtually all battles'. Asser, *Life of King Alfred*, Ch. 42, quoted in AG, p. 81.

134 'the Saxons made peace'. Asser, *Life of King Alfred*, Ch. 43, quoted in AG, p. 81.

137 'I, Ealdorman Alfred'. 'The Presentation of the "Golden Gospels" to Christchurch', quoted in EHD, I, no. 98, p. 497.

137 'that no man be so presumptuous'. 'The Presentation of the "Golden Gospels" to Christchurch', quoted in EHD, I, no. 98, p. 497.

138 'This, however, the above-mentioned'. Lease by Wærferth, bishop of Worcester, of Nuthurst, Warwickshire, in order to obtain money to pay tribute to the Danes (872), quoted in EHD, I, no. 94, p. 490.

142 'a foolish king's thegn'. ASC (874), quoted in EHD, I, no. 1, p. 178.

142 'swore oaths to them'. ASC (874), quoted in EHD, I, no. 1, p. 178.

143 'Imhar, king of the Northmen'. *Annals of Ulster* (U873.3), CELT op. cit.

144 'women of their own kindred'. Extract of a letter of Pope John VIII to Burgred, king of Mercia (874), quoted in EHD, I, no. 220, p. 810.

8: Providence, pp. 146–156

148 'slipped past'. ASC (876), quoted in EHD, I, no. 1, p. 179.

151 'on the Holy ring'. ASC (876), quoted in EHD, I, no. 1, p. 179.

151 'off the inmost house'. *Eyrbyggja Saga*, Ch. 4, in *The Saga Library*, vol. II: *The Story of the Ere-Dwellers*, trans. William Morris and Eirikr Magnusson (London: Bernard Quaritch, 1892).

152 'after his own fashion'. *Annals of St Bertin* (858), quoted in AB, p. 86.

152 'relics'. Asser, *Life of King Alfred*, Ch. 49, quoted in AG, p. 83.

152 'And then, under cover of that'. ASC (876), quoted in EHD, I, no. 1, p. 179.

153 'one hundred and forty of their ships'. Geoffrey Gaimar, quoted in E. Conybeare, *Alfred in the Chroniclers*, p. 180.

154 'great oaths'. ASC (877), quoted in EHD, I, no. 1, p. 179.

155 'in a wretched little hut'. *Annals of St Bertin* (877), quoted in AB, p. 202.

155 'His attendants opened him up'. *Annals of St Bertin* (877), quoted in AB, p. 202.

155 'But because of the stench'. *Annals of St Bertin* (877), quoted in AB, p. 202–3.

9: Betrayal, pp. 157–170

157 'Mother's Night'. Venerable Bede, 'De Temporum Ratione' in F. Wallis (trans.), *Bede: The Reckoning of Time*, Translated Texts for Historians, 29 (Liverpool: Liverpool University Press, 1999), p. 254.

158 'two companies danced in a ring'. Quoted in J.B. Bury, 'The Ceremonial Book of Constantine VII Porphyrogennetos', *English Historical Review*, 22 (1907), 209–27, 417–39.

161 'victorious in virtually all battles'. Asser, *Life of King Alfred*, Ch. 42, quoted in AG, p. 81.

162 'He commands that you share'. Abbo of Fleury's *Life of St Edmund, King of East Anglia before 870*, op. cit., pp. 81–7.

163 'For we have been at pains'. Letter of Pope John VIII to Ethelred, archbishop of Canterbury (end of 877 or early 878), quoted in EHD, I, no. 222, p. 812.

163 'We, however, exhort and warn'. Letter of Pope John VIII to Ethelred, archbishop of Canterbury (end of 877 or early in 878), quoted in EHD, I, no. 222, p. 812.

163 'We have admonished your king'. Letter of Pope John VIII to Ethelred, archbishop of Canterbury (end of 877 or early 878), quoted in EHD, I, no. 222, p. 813.

164 'In this year in midwinter'. ASC (878), quoted in EHD, I, no. 1, p. 179.

164 'small force'. ASC (878), quoted in EHD, I, no. 1, p. 179.

166 'he deserted without permission'. Grant by King Edward the Elder of land in Wylye to Æthelwulf, with a vernacular agreement made by the latter (901), quoted in EHD, I, no. 100, p. 499.

168 'occupied the land of the West Saxons'. ASC (878), quoted in EHD, I, no. 1, p. 179.

169 'journeyed in difficulties'. ASC (878), quoted in EHD, I, no. 1, p. 179.

10: *The Once and Future King, pp. 170–182*

170 'At the same time King Alfred'. Asser, *Life of King Alfred*, Ch. 53, quoted in AG, p. 83.

174 'abode with a small band in a certain wood'. Æthelweard, 7, quoted in E. Conybeare, *Alfred in the Chroniclers*, p. 138.

174 'Girded in with fen'. Roger of Wendover, 12, quoted in E. Conybeare, *Alfred in the Chroniclers*, p. 186.

175 'fortress'. Asser, *Life of King Alfred*, Ch. 55, quoted in AG, p. 84.

175 'That passed away, this also may'. Deor, quoted in AW, p. 5.

176 'Look here, man'. Vita S. Neoti, quoted in AG, p. 198.

176 'God chastiseth every son whom he receiveth'. Letter of Alcuin to Higbald, bishop of Lindisfarne and his monks (793, after 8 June), quoted in EHD, I, no. 194, p. 778, quoting Hebrews 12: 6.

177 'the evil wife'. Homily on St Neot, quoted in AG, p. 199.

178 'leaving no foot-print in the mire'. Simeon of Durham [37], quoted in E. Conybeare, *Alfred in the Chroniclers*, p. 154.

178 'O Alfred, Christ who hath beheld'. *Liber de Hyda*, quoted in E. Conybeare, *Alfred in the Chroniclers*, p. 32.

178 'I am Cuthbert. I am that pilgrim'. *Liber de Hyda*, quoted in E. Conybeare, *Alfred in the Chroniclers*, p. 32.

179 'accompanied only by one'. William of Malmesbury, *Deeds of the English Kings* [121], quoted in E. Conybeare, *Alfred in the Chroniclers*, p. 164.

181 'When they saw the king'. Asser, *Life of King Alfred*, Ch. 55, quoted in AG, p. 84.

11: The Silent Army, pp. 183–197

187 'With the first bright rays'. Simeon of Durham [39], quoted in E. Conybeare, *Alfred in the Chroniclers*, p. 154.

187 'he [Alfred] moved his forces'. Asser, *Life of King Alfred*, Ch. 56, quoted in AG, p. 84.

188 'He [Alfred] destroyed the Vikings'. Asser, *Life of King Alfred*, Ch. 56, quoted in AG, p. 85.

189 'the Vikings, thoroughly terrified'. Asser, *Life of King Alfred*, Ch. 56, quoted in AG, p. 85.

190 'drenched in the wave of Holy baptism'. Thegan, *Life of the Emperor Louis*, in *Monumenta Germaniae Historica: Scriptores*, II, (Hanover, 1829), pp. 585–604.

191 'While the emperor kept him'. Rimbert, *Life of Anskar, the Apostle of the North, 801–865*, Ch. VII, quoted in Charles H. Robinson, *Anskar, The Apostle of the North, 801–865, translated from the Vita Anskarii by Bishop Rimbert his fellow missionary and successor* (London: SPCK, 1921).

191 'a more intimate friendship between them'. Rimbert, *Life of Anskar, the Apostle of the North, 801–865*, Ch. VII, op. cit.

193 'King Alfred raised him [Guthrum]'. Asser, *Life of King Alfred*, Ch. 56, quoted in AG, p. 85.

193 'I gladly hear you'. Gregory of Tours, *The History of the Franks*, Book II, Ch. 31, quoted in Earnest Brehaut, *Gregory of Tour's History of the Franks*, (New York: Columbia University Press, 1916).

194 'the king freely bestowed'. Asser, *Life of King Alfred*, Ch. 56, quoted in AG, p. 85.

194 'Furthermore, the guardian of warriors'. *Beowulf*, quoted in AW, p. 94.

196 'settled there and shared out the land'. ASC (880), quoted in EHD, I, no. 1, p. 181.

12: A New England, pp. 198–217

200 'I begged them all'. The will of King Alfred (873–88), quoted in EHD, I, no. 96, p. 493.

200 'Now that everything in it'. The will of King Alfred (873–88), quoted in EHD, I, no. 96, p. 493.

201 'from the royal stock of the king of the Mercians'. Asser, *Life of King Alfred*, Ch. 29, quoted in AG, p. 77.

202 'the dark foreigners'. *Annales Cambriae* (850), op. cit.

203 'The battle of Conwy. Vengeance'. *Annales Cambriae* (880), trans. James Ingram (London: Everyman Press, 1912).

204 'if necessity compels you'. Bede, *Life and Miracles of St Cuthbert*, quoted in J.A. Giles, (trans.) *Ecclesiastical History of the English Nation*, Everyman's Library, 479 (London: J.M. Dent; New York: E.P. Dutton, 1910), pp. 286–349.

204 'Go across the Tyne'. Extracts from the anonymous *History of St Cuthbert*, quoted in EHD, I, no. 6, p. 261.

205 'to be feared by any enemy'. *Annals of Fulda* (882), trans. Timothy Reuter (Manchester University Press, 1991), p. 92.

205 'his courage failed him'. *Annals of St Bertin* (882), quoted in AB, p. 224.

206 'did not blush to pay tribute'. *Annals of Fulda* (882), op. cit., p. 93.

206 'several thousand pounds of silver and gold'. *Annals of St Bertin* (882), quoted in AB, p. 225.

207 'rashly with a small army'. *Annals of Fulda* (882), op. cit., p. 91.

207 'the Northmen came as far'. *Annals of St Bertin* (882), quoted in AB, pp. 225–6.

207 'Bishop Hincmar found out'. *Annals of St Bertin* (882), quoted in AB, p. 226.

210 'that summer King Alfred went out'. ASC (875), quoted in EHD, I, no. 1, p. 179.

214 'If every hide is represented'. *The Burghal Hidage*, quoted in AG, p. 194.

215 'And what of the cities and towns'. Asser, *Life of King Alfred*, Ch. 91, quoted in AG, p. 101.

217 'the commands were not fulfilled'. Asser, *Life of King Alfred*, Ch. 91, quoted in AG, p. 102.

13: A Tale of Two Cities, pp. 218–231

219 'a great slaughter'. ASC (842), quoted in EHD, I, no. 1, p. 173.

220 'The King had divided his army'. ASC (893), quoted in EHD, I, no. 1, p. 185.

221 'the Vikings, abandoning their fortress'. Asser, *Life of King Alfred*, Ch. 66, quoted in AG, p. 87.

222 'they [the Vikings] fall back'. Æthelweard, 11, quoted in E. Conybeare, *Alfred in the Chroniclers*, p. 139.

222 'The filthy crew'. Æthelweard, 11, quoted in E. Conybeare, *Alfred in the Chroniclers*, p. 139.

223 'When they arrived at the mouth'. Asser, *Life of King Alfred*, Ch. 67, quoted in AG, p. 87.

223 'As the victorious royal fleet'. Asser, *Life of King Alfred*, Ch. 67, quoted in AG, p. 87.

225 'Wondrous is this stone-wall'. *The Ruin*, quoted in AW, pp. 55–6.

225 'a trading centre for many nations'. Bede, *A History of the English Church and People*, trans. Leo Shirley-Price, Book II, Ch. 3, p. 104.

226 'when the English were encamped'. ASC (883), quoted in EHD, I, no. 1, p. 181.

226 'their prayers were well answered'. ASC (883), quoted in EHD, I, no. 1, p. 181.

227 'Alfred occupied London'. ASC (886), quoted in EHD, I, no. 1, p. 183.

228 'Alfred, king of the Anglo-Saxons'. Asser, *Life of King Alfred*, Ch. 83, quoted in AG, pp. 97–8.

229 'This is the peace', 'The Treaty between Alfred and Guthrum', prologue, quoted in AG, p. 171.

230 'up the Thames, and then up the Lea'. 'The Treaty between Alfred and Guthrum', prologue, quoted in AG, p. 171.

230 'it is to be permitted'. 'The Treaty between Alfred and Guthrum', prologue, quoted in AG, p. 171.

231 'King of the Angles and of the Saxons'. See King Alfred's Charter for Ealdorman Æthelhelm, quoted in AG, p. 178.

231 'King of the Anglo-Saxons'. Asser, *Life of King Alfred*, Ch. 83, quoted in AG, p. 97.

231 'All the Angles and Saxons'. Asser, *Life of King Alfred*, Ch. 83, quoted in AG, p. 98.

14: The Summoning of the Muse, pp. 232–251

234 'very often it has come to my mind'. Alfred the Great's translation of Gregory's *Pastoral Care*, prose preface, quoted in AG, p. 124.

234 'before everything was ransacked and burned.' Alfred the Great's translation of Gregory's *Pastoral Care*, prose preface, quoted in AG, p. 125.

234 'Learning had declined so thoroughly'. Alfred the Great's translation of Gregory's *Pastoral Care*, prose preface, quoted in AG, p. 126.

236 'Having heard that the abominable rites'. Letter of Pope Formosus to the bishops of England, quoted in EHD, I, no. 227, p. 820.

236–7 'If, however, any man attempt'. Letter of Pope Formosus to the bishops of England, quoted in EHD, I, no. 227, p. 821.

237 'By day or night, whenever he had'. Asser, *Life of King Alfred*, Ch. 77, quoted in AG, p. 93.

237 'When I had been warmly welcomed'. Asser, *Life of King Alfred*, Ch. 79, quoted in AG, p. 93.

238 'remote, western-most part of Wales'. Asser, *Life of King Alfred*, Ch. 79, quoted in AG, p. 93.

239 'he presented me with two documents'. Asser, *Life of King Alfred*, Ch. 81, quoted in AG, p. 97.

239 'The tongue of thy dogs may be red'. Letter of Fulco, archbishop of Rheims, to King Alfred (883–c.890), quoted in EHD, I, no. 225, p. 816.

240 'it is not without immense grief'. Letter of Fulco, archbishop of Rheims, to King Alfred (883–c.890), quoted in EHD, I, no. 225, p. 816.

240 'a man so good and devout and suitable'. Abstract of a letter from Fulco, archbishop of Rheims, to King Alfred (890 or soon after), quoted in EHD, I, no. 223, p. 813.

240 'to cut off and extirpate'. Abstract of a letter from Fulco, archbishop of Rheims, to Plegmund, archbishop of Canterbury (890 or soon after), quoted in EHD, I, no. 224, p. 813.

241 'acquired a number of people'. Asser, *Life of King Alfred*, Ch. 94, quoted in AG, p. 103.

241 'across the sea'. *Annals of St Vaast* (882), quoted in J.H. Robinson (ed.) *Readings in European History*: vol. I, (Ginn & Co., 1904), p. 71.

241 'in the course of whoring'. Asser, *Life of King Alfred*, Ch. 96, quoted in AG, p. 104.

242 'underwent a terrible death through various tortures'. Asser, *Life of King Alfred*, Ch. 97, quoted in AG, p. 105.

242 'I can not find anything better'. Alfred the Great's translation of Augustine's *Soliloquies*, quoted in H.L. Hargrove (trans.), *King Alfred's Old English Version of St Augustine's Soliloquies Turned into Modern English*, (New York: Henry Holt & Co., 1904), p. 121.

242–3 'all the free-born young men now in England'. Alfred the Great's translation of Gregory's *Pastoral Care*, prose preface, quoted in AG, p. 126.

243 'did not refrain from directing the government'. Asser, *Life of King Alfred*, Ch. 76, quoted in AG, p. 91.

244 'Devoted to God through her holy virginity'. Asser, *Life of King Alfred*, Ch. 75, quoted in AG, p. 90.

245 'I am astonished at this arrogance'. Asser, *Life of King Alfred*, Ch. 106, quoted in AG, p. 110.

247 'God loveth a cheerful giver'. 2 Corinthians 9: 7, quoted by Asser, *Life of King Alfred*, Ch. 101, quoted in AG, p. 106.

247 'in a boat without any oars'. ASC [891] Ch. 102, quoted in AG, pp. 113–14.

248 'On these islands hermits who'. Diciul, *Liber de Orbis Mensura Terrae*, quoted in J. Graham-Campbell et al. (eds.), *A Cultural Atlas of the Viking World*, p. 166.

249 'Ohthere told his lord'. Ohthere's Account, in *Two Voyagers: Ohthere and Wufstan at the Court of Alfred the Great*, trans. Christine E. Fell, (York: William Session Ltd., 1984) p. 18.

250 'boys not of noble birth'. Asser, *Life of King Alfred*, Ch. 102, quoted in AG, p. 107.

15: The Great Work, pp. 252–268

252 'Alfred, King of the Anglo-Saxons'. Asser, *Life of King Alfred*, Ch. 87, quoted in AG, p. 107.

253 'the busy bee, wandering far and wide'. Asser, *Life of King Alfred*, Ch. 88, quoted in AG, p. 100.

254 'be brought to nought by the assault of misty oblivion'. Grant by King Edward the Elder of land at Wylye to Æthelwulf, with a vernacular agreement made by the latter (901), quoted in EHD, I, no. 100, p. 499.

255 'First from every hide'. Statement in Anglo-Saxon of services rendered at Hurstborne Priors, Hampshire, quoted in D. Douglas and G. Greenway (eds.) EHD, I.

256 'A man can think on this one sentence alone'. The laws of Alfred (871–99), Int. 49.6, quoted in EHD, I, no. 33, p. 373.

257 'each man keep carefully his oath and pledge'. The laws of Alfred the Great (871–99) [I]2, quoted in EHD, I, no. 33, p. 373.

258 'we went in to the King'. Old English letter to King Edward the Elder, explaining the history of an estate at Fonthill, Wiltshire (899–924, probably early in the reign), (EHD, I, no. 102, p. 502), as translated in C. Plummer, *The Life and Times of Alfred the Great*, p. 125.

259 'if one wishes to change every judgment'. Old English letter to King Edward the Elder, explaining the history of an estate at Fonthill, Wiltshire (899–924, probably early in the reign), quoted in EHD, I, no. 102, p. 502.

259 'are the most necessary for all men to know'. Alfred the Great's translation of Gregory's *Pastoral Care*, prose preface, quoted in AG, p. 126.

259 'I then began, amidst the multifarious'. Alfred the Great's translation of Gregory's *Pastoral Care*, prose preface, quoted in AG, p. 126.

260 'Very often a man is responsive'. Alfred the Great's translation of Gregory's *Pastoral Care*, Ch. 3, quoted in AG, p. 128.

261 'Then I say that true friends'. Alfred the Great's translation of Boethius' *The Consolation of Philosophy*, XXIV, quoted in AG, p. 133.

262 'God and the soul'. Alfred the Great's translation of St Augustine of Hippo's *Soliloquies*, Book I, Ch. 7, quoted in Thomas A. Carnicelli (ed.) *King Alfred's Version of St Augustine's 'Soliloquies'*.

262 'I then gathered for myself'. King Alfred, preface to his translation of St Augustine of Hippo's *Soliloquies*, in AG, p. 138.

263 'The text of the following psalm'. King Alfred, from the prose translation of the Psalter, Psalm II, quoted in AG, p. 153.

263 'And why do the kings of the earth'. King Alfred, from the prose translation of the Psalter, Psalm II.2, quoted in AG, pp. 153–4.

264 'I may, amid the troubles of this world'. Alfred's preface to Werferth's transation of Gregory's *Dialogues*, quoted in C. Plummer, *The Life and Times of Alfred the Great*, p. 142.

264 'a mere sort of lucky bag'. C. Plummer, *The Life and Times of Alfred the Great*, p. 143.

266 'peace and prosperity prevail in these days'. Bede, *A History of the English Church and People*, trans. Leo Shirley-Price, Book V, Ch. 23, p. 332.

16: The Testing Time, pp. 269–283

269 'He breathed out his soul to Orcus'. Æthelweard, 16, quoted in E. Conybeare, *Alfred in the Chroniclers*, p. 140.

269 'most necessary for all men to know'. Alfred the Great's translation of Gregory's *Pastoral Care*, prose preface, quoted in AG, p. 126.

270 'The Northmen came to Paris'. Abbo of Fleury, *Wars of Count Odo with the Northmen in the Reign of Charles the Fat*, quoted in Bouquet, *Recueil des Historiens des Gaules et de la France*, vol. VIII, pp. 4–26, translation in James H. Robinson, *Readings in European History* (Boston: Ginn & Co., 1904), vol. I, pp. 164–8.

270–1 'the redoubtable Odo'. Abbo of Fleury, *Wars of Count Odo with the Northmen in the Reign of Charles the Fat*. op. cit., pp. 164–8.

278 'Then the English . . . stormed the fortress'. ASC (893), quoted in EHD, I, no. 1, p. 186.

280 'The Ealdorman Æthelred and Ealdorman Æthelhelm'. ASC (893), quoted in EHD, I, no. 1, p. 187.

283 'he had got no benefit, only a good deal of misfortune'. Asser, *Life of King Alfred*, Ch. 80, quoted in AG, p. 96.

283 'the English army could not reach them'. ASC (894), quoted in EHD, I, no. I, p. 187.

17: The Last Battle, pp. 284–294

287 'Then the English army rode after the enemy'. ASC (895), quoted in EHD, I, no. 1, p. 188.

288 'the Danish army divided'. ASC (896), quoted in EHD, I, no. 1, p. 188.

290 'By the grace of God, the army'. ASC (896), quoted in EHD, I, no. 1, p. 188.

291 'the warships which they had built many years before'. ASC (896), quoted in EHD, I, no. 1, p. 189.

291 'as it seemed to him to be most useful'. ASC (896), quoted in EHD, I, no. 1, p. 189.

293 'greatly wounded'. ASC (896), quoted in EHD, I, no. 1, p. 189.

294 'pleasantly and peacefully dwell therewith'. King Alfred, preface to his translation of St Augustine of Hippo's *Soliloquies*, quoted in AG, p. 138.

18: Great, pp. 295–305

295 'æstel worth 50 mancuses'. Alfred the Great's translation of Gregory's *Pastoral Care*, prose preface, quoted in AG, p. 126.

296 'his craftsmen, who were skilled'. Asser, *Life of King Alfred*, Ch. 101, quoted in AG, p. 106.

298 'He was king over the whole English people'. ASC (900), quoted in EHD, I, no. 1, p. 190.

300 'would either live there or die there'. ASC (900), quoted in EHD, I, no. 1, p. 190.

302 'The true and beloved lady of the English'. 'The Metrical Calendar of Hampson', quoted in *Analecta Bollandiana*, 104 (1986), 79–125.

302 'The Lady of the Mercians'. Mercian Register (912), quoted in EHD, I, no. 1, p. 194.

302 'Alfred of the English'. Bishop Wulfsige's preface to the translation of Gregory's *Dialogues*, quoted in AG, p. 186.

305 'In the midst of prosperity'. Alfred the Great's translation of Gregory's *Pastoral Care*, Ch. 3, quoted in AG, p. 128.

A Note on Sources

BEARING IN MIND the sheer volume of material written on Anglo-Saxon England in general and Alfred in particular, it would be impossible to provide a comprehensive list of sources without doubling the length of the book. Fortunately this is made unnecessary by the magnificent bibliography compiled (and constantly revised) by Professor Simon Keynes at Trinity College, Cambridge, details of which can be found on his website at http://www.trin.cam.ac.uk/sdk13/sdk13home.html.

This note provides some pointers to the source materials on which this book is based.

The best place to begin any exploration of Alfred's life is with Keynes and Lapidge's *Alfred the Great: Asser's Life of King Alfred and Other Contemporary Sources* (Penguin Books, 1983). This not only provides masterful translations of many of the main original sources for the period but adds a comprehensive introduction and extensive notes. The other major source for original written materials is *English Historical Documents*, vol. I, edited by Dorothy Whitelock (Eyre & Spottiswode, 1968), which provides translations of a huge range of contemporary sources, including the main versions of the *Anglo-Saxon Chronicle*, Alfred's laws and some of his charters, as well as letters to and from Alfred and his court.

Of the original continental sources, the *Ninth Century Histories* series from Manchester University Press provides excellent translations of the *Annals of St Bertin* (by Janet Nelson) and *The Annals of Fulda* (by Timothy Reuter). A part of the *Annals of Xanten* is available in translation in *Readings in European History*, vol. I, edited by James Harvey Robinson (Ginn & Co., 1904), together with sections from the *Annals of St Vaast*. The English entries in the *Liber Vitae of Brescia* are discussed by Keynes in 'Anglo-Saxon Entries in the Liber Vitae of

Brescia', which appears in *Alfred the Wise: Studies in Honour of Janet Bately*, edited by J. Roberts and J.L. Nelson (D.S. Brewer, 1997). Rimbert's *Life of St Anskar* is translated by Charles H. Robinson in *Anskar: The Apostle of the North, 801–865, translated from the Vita Anskarii by Bishop Rimbert his fellow missionary and successor* (SPCK, 1921).

Of the Welsh and Irish sources for the period, the Corpus of Electronic Texts project (http://www.ucc.ie/celt/publishd.html) at the University of Cork now provides a translation of the *Annals of Ulster*, whilst the *Annales Cambriae* appear in James Ingram's *The Anglo-Saxon Chronicle* (Everyman Press, 1912).

For the later mediaeval sources a selection of chroniclers' entries on Alfred's reign can be found in Conybeare's *Alfred in the Chroniclers* (Elliot Stock, 1900), whilst Sweet's *Anglo-Saxon Primer* (OUP, 1961) has a translation of Abbo of Fleury's description of the death of St Edmund.

There are numerous publications by Kevin Crossley-Holland translating Anglo-Saxon literature and a very good selection of these are printed in his *The Anglo-Saxon World* (The Boydell Press, 1982). Alternative translations can also be found in Raffel and Olsen's *Poems and Prose from the Old English* (Yale University Press, 1998).

The Authenticity of Asser

Finally, I should say something on the question of the authorship of Asser's *Life of King Alfred*.

There are a number of books and papers that deal fairly exhaustively with this question. The first to query the authenticity of Asser was Thomas Wright in 1842; his theories have since been roundly refuted by both Plummer in 1901 and Stevenson (1959). However, the argument has continued to rage. In 1949 V.H. Galbraith nailed his colours to the mast of the doubters in the chapter titled 'Who Wrote Asser's Life of Alfred?' in his book *An Introduction to the Study of History* (C.A. Watts & Co., 1964). This was, in turn, elegantly refuted by Dorothy Whitelock in the chapter titled 'The Genuine Asser' in her book *From Bede to Alfred* (Variorum, 1980).

The issue was not dead, however, but merely resting. In 1995

Alfred Smyth in his scholarly and polemic tome *Alfred the Great* (Oxford University Press) declared that the work we attribute to Asser was actually compiled in Ramsey at the turn of the tenth century by a monk called Brytferth. An excellent counter-argument to this, as well as a complete discussion of earlier views, is put forward by Richard Abels in an appendix to his *Alfred the Great: War, Kingship and Culture in Anglo-Saxon England* (Addison, Wesley Longman, 1998). No doubt the controversy will continue.

Select Bibliography

Ab Ithel, J.W. (ed.), *Annales Cambriae*, Rolls Series, 1860

Abbo of Fleury, *Life of St. Edmund King of East Anglia before 870*, in Sweet's *Anglo-Saxon Primer*, trans. K. Cutler, 9th edn, OUP, 1961

Abels, Richard, *Lordship and Military Obligation in Anglo-Saxon England*, University of California Press, 1988

Abels, Richard, 'King Alfred's peace-making strategies with the Vikings', *Haskins Society Journal*, 3, 1991

Abels, Richard, *Alfred the Great: War, Kingship and Culture in Anglo-Saxon England*, Addison, Wesley Longman, 1998

Alexander, Michael (trans.), *Beowulf*, Penguin Books 1973

Bartlett, R., *Trial by Fire and Water: The Medieval Judicial Ordeal*, OUP, 1986

Bately, J., *The Literary Prose of Alfred's Reign: Translation or Transformation*, King's College, London, 1980

Bately, J. (ed.), *The Old English Orosius*, Early English Texts Society, supplementary series no. 6, 1980

Bede, *A History of the English Church and People*, trans. L. Sherley-Price, Penguin Books, 1955

Biddle, M. and Hill, D., 'Late Saxon planned towns', *Antiquaries Journal*, 51, 1971

Biddle, M. and Kjølbye-Biddle, B., 'Repton and the Vikings', *Antiquity*, 66, 1992

Blackburn, M.A.S. and Dumvill, D.N. (eds.), *Kings, Currency and Alliances: History and Coinage of Southern England in the Ninth Century*, The Boydell Press, 1998

Blair, John, *The Anglo-Saxon Age: A Very Short Introduction* (Very Short Introductions series), Oxford Paperbacks, 2000

Bowker, Alfred (ed.), *Alfred the Great, Containing Chapters on his Life and Times*, Adam & Charles Black, 1899

Bright, J.W. and Ramsay, R.L. (eds.), *Liber Psalmorum: The West-Saxon Psalms*, D.C. Heath, 1907

Brooks, N., 'England in the ninth century: the crucible of defeat', *Transactions of the Royal Historical Society*, 29, 1979

Brooks, N., *Early History of the Church of Canterbury: Christchurch from 597 to 1066*, Continuum International Publishing, 1984

Bussby, Frederick, *Saint Swithun, Patron Saint of Winchester*, Friends of Winchester Cathedral, 1997

Byock, Jesse L., *Viking Age Iceland*, Penguin Books, 2001

Campbell, A. (ed.), *The Chronicle of Æthelweard*, Nelson Mediaeval Texts, 1922

Campbell, James (ed.), *The Anglo-Saxons*, Phaidon Press Ltd, 1982

Carnicelli, T.A. (ed.), *King Alfred's Version of St Augustine's Soliloquies*, iUniverse, 1999

Chaplais, P., 'The Anglo-Saxon chancery: from the diploma to the writ', *Journal of the Society of Archivists*, 3, 1965–9

Clemoes, P. and Hughes, K. (eds.), *England Before the Norman Conquest: Studies in Primary Sources Presented to Dorothy Whitelock*, CUP, 1971

Cockayne, O. (ed.), *Leechdoms, Wortcunning, and Starcraft in Early England*, 3 vols., Rolls Series 35, 1864–6

Conybeare, Edward, *Alfred in the Chroniclers*, Elliot Stock, 1900

Craig, G., 'Alfred the Great: a diagnosis', *Journal of the Royal Society of Medicine*, 84, 1991

Cramp, Rosemary, *Studies in Anglo-Saxon Sculpture*, Pindar Press, 1999

Crawford, Sally, *Childhood in Anglo-Saxon England*, Sutton Publishing, 1999

Crossley-Holland, Kevin, *The Anglo-Saxon World*, The Boydell Press, 1982

Crossley-Holland, Kevin (trans.), *The Exeter Riddle Book*, The Folio Society, 1978

Cubitt, Catherine, 'Sites and sanctity: revisiting the cult of murdered and martyred Anglo-Saxon royal saints' in Cubitt, Catherine (coordinating ed.), *Early Medieval Europe*, vol. IX, no. 1, Blackwell, 2000

Davis, R.H.C., 'Alfred the Great: propaganda and truth', *History*, 56, 1971

Davis, R.H.C., 'Alfred and Guthrum's frontier', *English Historical Review*, 97, 1982

Denford, Geoff, *Wintanceaster, Saxon and Medieval Winchester*, Winchester Museums Service, 2001

Doble, C.E. (ed.), *Remarks and Collections of Thomas Hearne*, Vol. I, Oxford Historical Society, 1884

Dolley, R.H.M., 'The Chronology of the Coins of Alfred the Great' in Dolley, R.H.M. (ed.), *Anglo-Saxon Coins: Studies Presented to F.M. Stenton*, Methuen, 1961

Douglas, David C. and Greenaway, George W. (eds.), *English Historical Documents*, vol. II, 1042–1189, Eyre Methuen, 1981

Dumville, D.N., *Wessex and England from Alfred to Edgar: Six Essays on Political, Cultural, and Ecclesiastical Revival*, The Boydell Press, 1992

Dyson, T., 'King Alfred and the restoration of London', *London Journal*, 15, 2, 1990

Edwards, Ben, *Vikings in North West England*, Lancaster University, 1998

Fleming, R., 'Monastic lands and England's defence in the Viking age', *English Historical Review*, 100, 1985

Frantzen, A.J., *King Alfred*, Twayne's English Authors, ser. 425, G.K. Hall, 1986

Galbraith, V.H., 'Who Wrote Asser's Life of Alfred?' in Galbraith, V.H., *An Introduction to the Study of History*, C.A. Watts & Co., 1949, repr. 1964

Gibson, M.T. and Nelson, Janet (eds.), *Charles the Bald, Court and Kingdom*, BAR international series 101, 2nd edn., 1990

Graham-Campbell, James et al (eds.), *A Cultural Atlas of the Viking World*, Andromeda Oxford Ltd, 1994

Graham-Campbell, James et al. (eds.), *Vikings and the Danelaw: Papers from the Proceedings of the Thirteenth Viking Congress, Nottingham and York, 21st–30th August 1997*, Oxbow Books, 2001

Grammaticus, Saxo, *The Danish History*, Book II, in Oliver Elton (trans.), *The Nine Books of the Danish History of Saxo Grammaticus*, Norroena Society, New York, 1905

Grierson, P., 'Grimbald of St Bertin's', *English Historical Review*, 55, 1940

Grundy, G.B., 'The ancient highways and tracks of Wiltshire, Berkshire and Hampshire and the Saxon battlefields of Wiltshire', *Archaeological Journal*, 75, 1918

Hall, Richard, *The Viking Dig*, Bodley Head, 1984

Hall, Richard, *English Heritage Book of Viking York* (English Heritage), B.T. Batsford, 1994

Hall, Richard, *English Heritage: York (English Heritage)*, B.T. Batsford, 1996

Hallam, Elizabeth (ed.), trans. A. Savage, *Anglo-Saxon Chronicles*, Papermac, 1988

Hamerow, Helena and MacGregor, Arthur (eds.), *Image and Power in the Archaeology of Early Medieval Britain: Essays in Honour of Rosemary Cramp*, Oxbow Books, 2001

Härke, Heinrich, *Archaeology, Ideology, and Society: The German Experience*, Peter Lang Publications, 2002

Harvey Robinson, James (ed.), *Readings in European History*, vol. I, Ginn & Co., 1904

Haslam, J. (ed.), *Anglo-Saxon Towns in Southern England*, Phillimore, 1984

Hill, David, *An Atlas of Anglo-Saxon England*, Blackwell, 1984

Hills, Catherine, *Blood of the British: From Ice Age to Norman Conquest*, George Phillip, 1986

Hills, Catherine, *The Origins of the English* (Duckworth Debates in Archaeology), Gerald Duckworth & Co. Ltd, 2002

Hines, John (ed.), *The Anglo-Saxons from the Migration Period to the Eighth Century: An Ethnographic Perspective* (Studies in the History of Archaeoethnology), The Boydell Press, 1997

Hines, John, *The Scandinavian Character of Anglian England in the Pre-Viking Period* (*British Archaeological Reports*), British Archaeological Reports, 1984

Hinton, D., *Alfred's Kingdom: Wessex and the South 800–1500*, J.M. Dent, 1977

Hobley, B., 'Lundenwic and Lundenburh: Two Cities Rediscovered', in Hodges, R. and Hobley, B., *The Rebirth of Towns in the West AD 700–1050*, Council for British Archaeology Research, report 68, 1988

Hunter Blair, P., *An Introduction to Anglo-Saxon England*, CUP, 1956

Ingram, James, *The Anglo-Saxon Chronicle*, Everyman Press, 1912

Keynes, S., 'A tale of two kings: Alfred the Great and Æthelred the Unready', *Transactions of the Royal Historical Society*, 5th ser., 36, 1986

Keynes, S., 'The control of Kent in the ninth century', *Early Mediaeval Europe*, 2, 1993

Keynes, S., 'The west Saxon charters of King Æthelwulf and his sons', *English Historical Review*, 109, 1994

Keynes, Simon and Lapidge, Michael (trans.), *Alfred the Great: Asser's Life of King Alfred and Other Contemporary Sources*, Penguin Books, 1983

Keynes, S., 'King Alfred and the Mercians' in Blackburn, M.A.S. and Dumville, D.N. (eds.), *Kings, Currency and Alliances: History and Coinage in Southern England in the Ninth Century*, Boydell Press, 1998

Kirby, D.P., 'Northumbria in the reign of Alfred the Great', *Transactions of the Architectural & Archaeological Society of Durham and Northumberland*, 11, 1965

Kirby, D.P., 'Asser and the life of King Alfred', *Studia Celtica*, 6, 1971

Kirby, D.P., *The Earliest English Kings*, Macmillan, 1991

Krautheimer, R., *Rome: Profile of a City, 312–1308*, Princeton University Press, 1980

Lapidge, M., Blair, J., Keynes, S., and Scragg, D. (eds), *The Blackwell Encyclopaedia of Anglo-Saxon England*, Blackwell Publishing, 1999

Lavelle, Ryan, *Fortifications in Wessex c. 800–1066*, Osprey Publishing, 2003

Loyn, H.R., *The Governance of Anglo-Saxon England 500–1087*, Stanford University Press, 1984

Loyn, H.R., *The Making of the English Nation: From the Anglo-Saxons to Edward I*, Thames & Hudson, 1991

Lucy, S., *Early Anglo-Saxon Cemeteries of East Yorkshire (British Archaeological Reports)*, British Archaeological Reports, 1998

Lucy, S. and Reynolds, A. (eds.), *Burial in Early Medieval England and Wales*, Society for Mediaeval Archaeology, monograph 17, 2002

Lund, Niels (ed.), trans. Christine Fell, *Two Voyagers at the Court of King Alfred: The Ventures of Ohthere and Wulfstan together with the Description of Northern Europe from the Old English Orosius*, William Sessions, 1984

Nelson, Janet L., ' "A king across the sea": Alfred in continental perspective', *Transactions of the Royal Historical Society*, 5th ser., 36, 1986

Nelson, Janet L. (trans.), *The Annals of St-Bertin*, Ninth-Century Histories, vol. I (Manchester Medieval Sources Series), Manchester University Press, 1991

Nelson, Janet L., 'Reconstructing a Royal Family: Reflections on Alfred, from Asser, Chapter 2' in Wood, N. and Lund, N. (eds.), *People and Places in Northern Europe 500–1600: Studies Presented to Peter Sawyer*, Boydell Press, 1991

Nelson, Janet L., 'The Political Ideas of Alfred of Wessex' in Duggan, A.J. (ed.), *Kings and Kingship in Medieval Europe*, King's College, London, Mediaeval Studies, 10, 1993

Nelson, Janet L., 'Anglo-Saxon England c. 500–1066' in Saul, N. (ed.), *The Oxford Illustrated History of Medieval England*, OUP, 1997

O'Sullivan, Deirdre and Young, Robert, *English Heritage Book of Lindisfarne* (English Heritage), 1995

Owen, Olwyn, *The Making of Scotland: The Sea Road: A Voyage through Viking Scotland* (The Making of Scotland), Birlinn Ltd, 1999

Page, R.I., *Chronicles of the Vikings: Records, Memorials and Myths*, University of Toronto Press, 1995

Peddie, John, *Alfred the Good Soldier: His Life and Campaigns*, Millstream Books, 1989

Peddie, John, *Alfred: Warrior King*, Sutton Publishing, 2001

Percy, Stephen, *Tales of the Kings of England: Stories of Camps and Battlefields, Wars and Victories, from the Old Historians*, Charles Tilt, 1840

Plummer, Charles, *The Life and Times of Alfred the Great, being the Ford lectures for 1901*, Haskell House, 1970

Pollard, J.D., *Seven Ages of Britain*, Hodder & Stoughton, 2003

Preston, Eileen, *Curious England* (Shire Album 22), Shire Publications, 1977

Pulsiano, Philip and Treharne, Elaine (eds.), *A Companion to Anglo-Saxon*

Literature and Culture (Blackwell Companions to Literature and Culture), Blackwell Publishers, 2001

Raffel, Burton and Olsen, Alexandra H. (trans. and eds.), *Poems and Prose from the Old English*, Yale University Press, 1998

Reuter, Timothy (trans.), *The Annals of Fulda, Ninth-Century Histories*, vol. II (Manchester Medieval Sources Series), Manchester University Press, 1993

Reynolds, Andrew, *Life and Landscape in Later Anglo-Saxon England*, Tempus Publishing, 1999

Reynolds, Andrew, *Later Anglo-Saxon England*, Tempus Publishing, 2002

Richards, Julian D., *English Heritage Book of Viking Age England* (English Heritage), B.T. Batsford, 1991

Richards, Julian D., *Viking Age England*, Tempus Publishing, 2000

Richards, Julian D., *Blood of the Vikings*, Hodder & Stoughton, 2002

Roberts, J. and Nelson, Janet (eds.), *Alfred the Wise: Studies in Honour of Janet Bately*, D.S. Brewer, 1997

Robinson, Charles H. (trans.), *Anskar: The Apostle of the North, 801–865, translated from the Vita Anskarii by Bishop Rimbert his fellow missionary and successor*, SPCK, 1921

Savage, Anne (trans.), *The Anglo-Saxon Chronicles: The Authentic Voices of England, from the time of Julius Caesar to the Coronation of Henry II*, Phoebe Phillips Editions, 1982

Sawyer, P.H., *From Roman Britain to Norman England*, Routledge, 1998

Sawyer, P.H., *The Oxford Illustrated History of the Vikings*, OUP, 1998

Sedgefield, W.J. (ed.), *King Alfred's Old English Version of Boethius De Consolatione Philosophiae*, OUP, 1899

Sedgefield, W.J. (ed.), *King Alfred's Version of the 'Consolations' of Boethius, Done into Modern English, with an Introduction*, OUP, 1900

Shipley Duckett, Eleanor, *Alfred the Great: The King and His England*, University of Chicago Press, 1956

Shipley Duckett, Eleanor, *Death and Life in the Tenth Century*, University of Michigan Press, 1988

Smyth, Alfred P., *Scandinavian York and Dublin*, Irish Academic Press, 1987

Smyth, Alfred P., *King Alfred the Great*, OUP, 1995

Stafford, P., 'The king's wife in Wessex', *Past and Present*, 91, 1981

Stenton D.M. (ed.), *Preparatory to Anglo-Saxon England, being the Collected Papers of Frank Merry Stenton*, OUP, 1970

Stenton, F.M., 'The Danes at Thorney Island', *English Historical Records*, 27, 1912

Stenton, F.M., *Anglo-Saxon England*, OUP, 1943

Stevenson, William Henry, *Asser's Life of King Alfred, together with the Annals of Saint Neots erroneously ascribed to Asser*, OUP, 1959

Stuckey, Douglas, *Alfred the Great, 849–899* (The Wessex Series), Wessex Books, 2000

Sturdy, D., *Alfred the Great*, Oxbow Books, 1995

Sweet, H. *Anglo–Saxon Primer*, Oxford University Press, 1953

Sweet, H. (ed.), King Alfred's West-Saxon version of Gregory's pastoral care', *Early English Texts Society*, 45 and 50, London, 1871

Treharne, Elaine M. (ed.), *Old and Middle English: An Anthology* (Blackwell Anthologies), Blackwell Publishers, 2000

Vince, A., *Saxon London: An Archaeological Investigation*, B.A. Seaby, 1990

Wainwright, F.T., 'Æthelflæd, Lady of the Mercians' in Finberg, H.P.R. (ed.), *Scandinavian England*, Phillimore, 1975

Wallace-Hadrill, J.M., *Early Germanic Kingship in England and on the Continent*, OUP, 1971

Weigall, Arthur, *Wanderings in Anglo-Saxon England*, Hodder & Stoughton,

Whitelock, Dorothy, 'The Prose of Alfred's Reign' in Stanley, E., *Continuations and Beginnings: Studies in Old English Literature*, Nelson, 1966

Whitelock, Dorothy (ed.), *English Historical Documents, vol. I, c. 500–1042*, Eyre & Spottiswode, 1968

Whitelock, Dorothy, 'The Genuine Asser' in Whitelock, Dorothy, *From Bede to Alfred: Studies in Early Anglo-Saxon Literature and History*, Variorum, 1980

Wilson, D.M. (ed.), *The Archaeology of Anglo-Saxon England*, CUP, 1976

Winchester National Pageant: The Book of the Words and Music, Warren & Son, 1908

Winterbottom, Michael (ed. and trans.), *Gildas: The Ruin of Britain and Other Works* (History from the Sources), Phillimore & Co. Ltd, 1978

Wood, Michael, *In Search of England: Journeys into the English Past*, Penguin Books, 2000

Index

Place names have been indexed selectively and are generally identified by their modern-day county.

Dynastic references e.g. 'B' dynasty' will be found under the *The Anglo-Saxon Chronicles*.